Sensory Warfare in the Global Cold War

Perspectives on Sensory History

Books in the Perspectives on Sensory History series maintain a historical basis for work on the senses, examining how the experiences of seeing, hearing, smelling, tasting, and touching have shaped the ways in which people have understood their worlds.

Mark M. Smith, General Editor
University of South Carolina, USA

EDITORIAL BOARD
Camille Bégin
University of Toronto, Canada

Martin A. Berger
Art Institute of Chicago, USA

Karin Bijsterveld
University of Maastricht, Netherlands

Constance Classen
Concordia University, Canada

Kelvin E. Y. Low
National University of Singapore, Singapore

Bodo Mrozek
Leibniz Institute for Contemporary History, Germany

Alex Purves
University of California, Los Angeles, USA

Richard Cullen Rath
University of Hawai'i, USA

Sensory Warfare in the Global Cold War

Partition, Propaganda, Covert Operations

Edited by Bodo Mrozek

The Pennsylvania State University Press
University Park, Pennsylvania

In cooperation with

Library of Congress Cataloging-in-Publication Data

Names: Mrozek, Bodo, 1968– editor.
Title: Sensory warfare in the global Cold War : partition, propaganda,
  covert operations / edited by Bodo Mrozek.
Other titles: Perspectives on sensory history.
Description: University Park, Pennsylvania : The Pennsylvania State University Press, [2024] |
  Series: Perspectives on sensory history | Includes bibliographical references and index.
Summary: "Examines how the Cold War used and changed human sensoria in different stages
  of the conflict from partition to propaganda and secret warfare, and contributes to a better
  understanding of sensory aspects in ongoing and future conflicts"—Provided by publisher.
Identifiers: LCCN 2024022707 | ISBN 9780271097404 (hardback)
Subjects: LCSH: Cold War—Social aspects. | Cold War—Psychological
  aspects. | Senses and sensation—History—20th century.
Classification: LCC D842 .S448 2024 | DDC 909.82/5—dc23/eng/20240520
LC record available at https://lccn.loc.gov/2024022707

Copyright © 2024 The Pennsylvania State University
All rights reserved
Printed in the United States of America
Published by The Pennsylvania State University Press,
University Park, PA 16802–1003

The Pennsylvania State University Press is a member of the Association of University Presses.

It is the policy of The Pennsylvania State University Press to use acid-free paper. Publications on uncoated stock satisfy the minimum requirements of American National Standard for Information Sciences—Permanence of Paper for Printed Library Material, ANSI Z39.48–1992.

Cover credits: (*center*) Hoover Institution Library & Archives, Washington, DC, Radio Free Europe / Radio Liberty corporate records, box 2427, © Radio Free Europe / Radio Liberty, Inc.; (*inner ring*) Courtesy of National Archives, Photographs of American Military Activities, ca. 1918–ca. 1981, no. 11-1-NA 111-SC-634782-001; (*outer ring*) Courtesy of Bundesarchiv/SELKE, Germany, B 206-1915 BND.

Contents

List of Illustrations [vii]

Acknowledgments [viii]

List of Abbreviations [ix]

INTRODUCTION: Sensory Warfare in the Global Cold War [1]
Bodo Mrozek

PART I: SEDUCTION, MANIPULATION, OTHERING

1. Chocolate Paratroopers and Eisenhower Packages for Eastern Europe: Nourishing Partition Through Colors and Taste [21]
Victoria Phillips

2. Between Soir de Paris and Red Moscow: Olfactory Front Lines in Polish Perfumery [41]
Stephanie Weismann

3. Beyond the Bamboo Curtain: Sensing the Chinese Cultural Revolution [58]
Cyril Cordoba

4. Sensual Sirens: Gendering Berlin's Cold War Telephony [73]
Mark Fenemore

PART II: PARTITION, PROPAGANDA, SENSORY BORDERS

5. Breaking the Aquatic Sound Barrier: Hearing Yourself and Your Enemy Across the Taiwan Strait [93]
Dayton Lekner

6. Listening to the Voices of Exile: Radio
   Free Europe in Romania   [112]
   Andreea Deciu Ritivoi

7. Hearing Korea, Seeing Cuba: NO-DO as Sonic and
   Visual Propaganda in Francoist Spain   [131]
   José Manuel López Torán

8. The Smell of the Berlin Wall: Olfactory Border
   Management at the Inner-European Frontier   [147]
   Bodo Mrozek

PART III: MIND CONTROL, COVERT OPERATIONS, OVERT WARFARE

9. Hallucinated Sensations: Brainwashing and Mind
   Control in Psychochemical CIA Experiments   [167]
   Walter E. Grunden

10. To Inform and Deceive: Sensory Approaches in the
    Military Propaganda of Cold War Germany   [184]
    Carsten Richter

11. Sniffing the Enemy: Chemical Detection
    During the Vietnam War   [203]
    Christy Spackman

12. Heroes at the Hindu Kush: Seeing the Afghan
    War Through the Soviet Lens   [220]
    Markus Mirschel

List of Contributors   [239]
Index   [243]

Illustrations

1.1. CARE package   [31]
2.1. French perfume Soir de Paris   [48]
2.2. Polish perfume Pani Walewska   [48]
3.1. Tourist's photo taken at Tiananmen Square on April 8, 1976   [61]
4.1. Photo excerpt of *Fräulein vom Amt* (1954) from "Illustrierte Film-Bühne"   [75]
5.1. Beishan broadcasting tower, Guningtou, Taiwan, 2020   [96]
6.1. 1965 Crusade for Freedom campaign of Radio Free Europe / Radio Liberty   [120]
7.1. Film still from Spanish NO-DO newsreel on the Korean War, December 10, 1951   [139]
7.2. Film still from Spanish NO-DO newsreel on the Cuban Missile Crisis, November 5, 1962   [143]
8.1. Olfactory map of the south of West Berlin, November 15–December 4, 1974   [153]
8.2. West German intelligence photo of the inner-German border, May 9, 1969   [156]
10.1. Military propaganda magazine *Rührt Euch*, 1972   [193]
10.2. *Volksarmee*, 1964   [196]
11.1. E63 Manpack Personnel Detector, 1966   [209]
12.1. Soviet photo of an Afghan soldier escorting six "counterrevolutionaries," spring 1980   [224]
12.2. Soviet photo of a Soviet battalion crossing the "Bridge of Friendship," February 15, 1988   [234]

Acknowledgments

The work on this collection is a truly international collaboration. The editor of this book would like to thank first of all the contributors for their cooperation and their patience in the process of editing this book. The book would not have been possible without the help of a number of institutions and individuals. An initial workshop and the work on the manuscript was funded with the generous support of two Berlin-based foundations. We would like to thank all board members and especially Marion Werwoll and Matthias von Bismarck-Osten at the Stiftung Luftbrückendank and Michael Bienert at the Ernst-Reuter-Archiv. Further cooperation partners of the workshop are the Berlin Center for Cold War Studies of the Leibniz Institute for Contemporary History and the Centre for Contemporary and Digital History of the Université du Luxembourg. We would like to acknowledge Magnus Brechtken, Agnes Bresselau von Bressensdorf, Elke Seefried, Martina Steber, and Andreas Wirsching (Leibniz Institute for Contemporary History) as well as Andreas Fickers (Luxembourg Centre for Contemporary and Digital History). Furthermore, we are indebted to a number of distinguished experts who commented on some of the individual contributions: Viktoria von Hoffmann, Robert Jütte, Daniel Morat, Éricka Wicky, and †Jan Plamper (d. November 30, 2023), who sadly cannot witness the publication of this volume that owes him so much. Raphaëlle Auclert, Anastasia Chirkova, Kaete O'Connell, Philipp Nielsen, Joshua Simon, Marcel Streng, and Pavel Vasilyev made substantial contributions to our discussions. Furthermore, we received detailed and profound advice from two anonymous reviewers to whom we owe our gratitude. Adam Blauhut did a terrific job in copyediting the individual chapters and in translating one chapter into English. At The Pennsylvania State University Press, the manuscript was carefully supported by Archna Patel, Josie DiNovo, and Alex Ramos and accurately edited by Stephanie M. Scott. Nils Bergmann and Jonas Jung issued the index. Jula Skomski helped with fact checking. Jula Skomski helped with fact checking. Last but not least, the editor and the authors would like to express their gratitude to Mark M. Smith, who opened his distinguished book series Perspectives on Sensory History to this manuscript.

BODO MROZEK, JUNE 2024

Abbreviations

BArch	Bundesarchiv (German Federal Archives)
BStU	Der Bundesbeauftragte für die Unterlagen des Staatssicherheitsdienstes der ehemaligen Deutschen Demokratischen Republik (Stasi Records Agency, now within the BArch)
BV	Bibliothèque de la Ville de La Chaux-de-Fonds
CWIHP	Cold War International History Project (of the Wilson Center)
DPRK	Democratic People's Republic of North Korea
DTIC	Defense Technical Information Center
FRG	Federal Republic of Germany
GDR	German Democratic Republic
GRU	Glawnoje Raswedywatelnoje Uprawlenije (Main Directorate of the General Staff of the Armed Forces of the Russian Federation)
HU OSA	Vera and Donald Blinken Open Society Archives at Central European University, Budapest, Hungary
KMT	Kuomintang (Chinese Nationalist Party)
LAB	Landesarchiv Berlin (Berlin State Archive)
MfS	Ministerium für Staatssicherheit (Ministry for State Security) of the GDR
NO-DO	Noticiario y Documentales (News and Documentaries, Spain)
NVA	Nationale Volksarmee (National People's Army) of the GDR
OKSVA	Ograničennyj kontingent sovetskich vojsk v Afganistane (Limited Contingent of Soviet Troops in Afghanistan)
PHJ	Fonds Madeleine et Paul-Henri Jeanneret
POW	prisoner(s) of war
PRC	People's Republic of China

PSB	Psychological Strategy Board
PSK	Psychologische Kampfführung (Psychological Warfare Division) of the FRG
RFE	Radio Free Europe
RIAS	Radio in the American Sector (of West Berlin)
SED	Sozialistische Einheitspartei (Socialist Unity Party) of the GDR
SIS	Secret Intelligence Service of the UK
Stasi	Staatssicherheit (State Security Agency) of the GDR
TASS	Telegráfnoe agéntstvo Sovétskogo Sojúza (Soviet News Agency)

Introduction

Sensory Warfare in the Global Cold War

Bodo Mrozek

The cases addressed in a recent research report are most unusual. One night in 2016, an individual assigned to the US Embassy in Havana, Cuba, was awakened by a "severe pain and a sensation of intense pressure in the face, a loud piercing sound in one ear with directional features, and acute disequilibrium and nausea. Symptoms of vestibular and cognitive dysfunction ensued." As the report notes, the source of this intersensory confusion was "mysterious." The individual was not the only embassy employee to display enigmatic symptoms. Other Havana staff suffered pain, and similar complaints were heard from diplomats attached to the embassies in Moscow and Guangzhou (and in 2021 in Hanoi).[1]

According to the report, which was published in 2020, several of the affected individuals developed long-term symptoms such as "tinnitus, visual problems, vertigo, and cognitive difficulties." Although the report admits that the causes of the symptoms had not been determined, far-reaching theories were offered in the report's aftermath. There was speculation that infrasound, ultrasound, or microwaves had been transmitted by an unknown device that could pierce walls, take out human targets without killing them, and leave not a single trace of its existence—in other words, a weapon that many Cold Warriors had dreamed about throughout a conflict that had been fought partially through clandestine channels. Had this weapon become a reality in the early twenty-first century?

The Scottish sound studies scholar and DJ Steve Goodman (a.k.a. kode9), who coined the term "sonic warfare" in his study on sound conflicts,[2] devoted the audio paper "Dossier 37" to the report. In this paper he describes the document as "drenched in uncertainty and disinformation."[3] For Goodman, the alleged sensory attacks were in fact rooted in the efforts of Donald J. Trump's administration "to retreat from closer ties with Cuba." They occurred in an environment of fake news and propaganda spread by Trump's press team, an "unsound nexus" of "AI [artificial intelligence]-intensified deep audio-visual fakery . . . entangled in a meme complex which is still ongoing." In April 2024, investigative journalists from three media outlets reopened the case, now linking it to activities of the notorious Russian GRU unit 29155, based on internal documents and GPS motion patterns.[4] In a first reaction, officials from US Intelligence Agencies did not confirm the results of this investigation. But even if the entire episode should remain in the shadow realm between covert actions and propaganda warfare, the broader political question remains: Is a new Cold War being fought with secret weapons, or did the old Cold War in fact never end?

With the Russian attacks on Ukraine in 2014 and 2018 and, most recently, the economic, political, and cultural bans against Russia as a result of its war of intensified aggression against Ukraine after February 24, 2022, there seems to be a return not only to a Cold War but also to a hot war on European soil. However, a series of events in the recent past indicates that secret warfare was never really abandoned. These include the radioactive contamination of former Russian agents in London, the poisoning of Russian opposition leader Alexei Navalny (renewing a notorious KGB tradition from the 1950s to the 1970s, when "rare poison" was already the weapon of choice),[5] and numerous fake-news and hacking attacks on elections and government networks.

However, to answer this question in full, we must initially turn to the various forms of sensory warfare within the Cold War, which is the focus of the present book. *Sensory Warfare in the Global Cold War* is the first work to draw on a broad range of case studies to analyze how this conflict affected the senses and how sensory methods in turn shaped the conflict. Extending Steve Goodman's concept of sonic warfare to include sensory warfare, the authors examine other sensoria beyond hearing.[6]

Their efforts tie in with current trends in cultural history and conflict studies. With scholars in both disciplines finally "coming to their senses," sensory aspects of domestic and international conflicts have become a topic of interest, and the methods and questions addressed by both fields have intertwined in fruitful ways.[7] Scholars of sensory history have recently investigated individual aspects of conflicts, focusing not only on sight and sound but increasingly on other sensoria as well. Recent research has undertaken a broad analysis of nonmilitary forms of conflict such as slavery and racism, and historiographical approaches target a range of military campaigns, from the American Civil War and the Russian Revolution to the two world wars of the twentieth century.[8] These studies examine how war as the most extreme form of conflict has been perceived and how it in turn has changed contemporary perception.

War on the Senses

In a groundbreaking book, Mark M. Smith investigates the American Civil War through the eyes, ears, noses, tongues, and stomachs of those who lived through it. According to him, war affects all senses not only in "hot" conflicts but also in their aftermaths: "War is hell on [the senses]; the violence of it engraves sensory memory in ways other experiences cannot approach, memory so powerful it can be relived, over and over again. Indeed, as far as the senses are concerned, all war is total war, pushing them to their limits and beyond, dulling and then overwhelming and then dulling them again. Distinctions become muddied, nerves fray, and the sense of self shatters."[9]

Modern warfare, which was perhaps experienced for the first time in the Crimean War (1853–56) and the American Civil War (1861–65), can be seen as a decisive break in the history of warfare. Modern instruments such as binoculars, telescopes, and cameras (the last having been used for the first time in the Crimean War) "weaponized" the eye.[10] The sounds of shells from long-distance artillery brought war to civilian areas, shaping the auditory experience of soldiers and the civilian population. The ability to distinguish different projectiles by the vibrations of detonations or the sound of the trajectory proved a lifesaving skill. The death toll was unknown but ultimately so vast that it was often impossible to bury the bodies before decomposition set in. The resulting "stench of death" signaled the absence of civilization. Taste played a similar role. When hunger was used as a weapon in drawn-out sieges, it dissolved the old social hierarchies of taste, with members of different social classes literally eating from the same pot—or in some cases even from the same garbage pile. At the front, the old form of battle in open fields came to an end. Now, warfare meant digging deep into the ground, diving under water, or flying up into the sky. In the mud and dust of position warfare, colors became murky and the old bright uniforms useless. The "observant men" of military staff were forced to abandon their "Enlightenment approach to warfare" in favor of a multisensory strategy.[11]

The world wars of the twentieth century intensified these trends. Camouflage, armor, motorization, *technicalization*, and, most significantly, trench fighting all changed warfare dramatically in terms of both its intensity and extension. In the First World War, new acoustics were developed not only to allow communication via audio (and visual) signals but also to disturb the enemy's ears and eyes. These new forms of warfare directly assaulted the sensory organs. Gas attacks, which the German military staff used for the first time on the Western front, targeted the enemy's respiratory organs and became known as the "invisible death," heralding a new kind of horror.

Olfaction underwent additional significant changes in wartime. As Juliette Courmont concludes in her analysis of French and German nationals during the First World War, negative olfactory clichés about human beings emerged when former neighbors were "othered" by having unbearable stenches attributed to them, thereby renewing stereotypes from the Franco-Prussian War (1870–71).[12] These clichés vanished soon after the war ended, yet the sheer number of negative olfactory stereotypes in the press, in scientific and medical research, and in private documents, letters, and diaries raises the question whether the propaganda efforts changed contemporary perceptions to the point at which the "other" was in fact sensed as different. In addition, behind the front lines, there was another war being fought against illness and epidemics, a war that was at times just as dangerous and deadly as the one waged against a heavily armed human enemy. The weapons in this war were hygienic and medical measures; the enemies were rats, bugs, fleas, lice, microbes, and viruses; and the effects were stenches, itches, nausea, and numerous forms of pain—and death.[13]

The collective experience of modern warfare left not only the individual senses but also the entire human sensorium changed. As Michael Bull points out, "The sensory intensity of warfare led many combatants to feel a sense of alienation whilst on leave at home, for the war seemed more real than domestic peace."[14] In his view, this led to "dislocation and transformation of sensory experience."[15] War was based on new technologies, and these technologies also shaped the postwar periods. Although new forms of industrial food preservation were originally invented to feed those at the front (canned food was in fact developed for Napoleon Bonaparte's troops), they went on to industrialize civil nutrition in the decades to follow. According to media theorist Friedrich Kittler, stereophony was first invented for bomber pilots, whom it guided to targeted areas by transmitting separate audio signals to each ear through headphones.[16] Media technologies were increasingly used as propaganda tools. Speakers and sirens in militarized soundscapes became what R. Murray Schafer refers to as "signal sounds."[17] In Nazi Germany, alarm systems and safety routines created shared listening routines that sonically shaped the so-called *Volksgemeinschaft* and helped mobilize the population for war.[18] In the Second World War, the Stuka dive bombers of the German Luftwaffe were equipped with air-driven sirens to spread fear in enemy countries. The war fought with submarines, prototypes of which had been developed in the American Civil War, grew more intense and produced new sonification techniques, such as the audio signals of the fathometer. Such innovations were refined in the submarine arms race of the Cold War.[19] The new military technologies even left their mark on historiography—Marc Bloch, for example, the French *officier de renseignement* and later historian, systematically analyzed aerial photos in his studies of the agrarian history of the Middle Ages.[20] Numerous military inventions were optimized, and some went on to play a key role in the Cold War (e.g., secret reconnaissance flights and satellite photography). Such technological developments could have long-lasting effects. According to Paul Cornish, Nicholas J. Saunders, and Mark M. Smith, sensory signals "can evidently survive long after the end of the direct experience of conflict . . . even to the extent of forming an element of post-traumatic stress more than half a century later."[21] As these authors conclude, this finding applies equally to the major global conflict of the second half of the twentieth century.

However, the Cold War is still uncharted terrain for sensory history. Although it was a conflict in which military strategies and weapons of mass destruction were always on the *horizon of expectation* (Karl Mannheim), it differed from preceding conflicts in terms of its duration and methods.[22] Simmering for decades, it was marked by alternating phases of intensified conflict and détente. Using mainly nonlethal methods, it was also a war of politics, culture, and propaganda that addressed different sensoria.[23] This propaganda was one of many expressions of conflict, but in fact it went beyond this. As Nicholas J. Cull and B. Theo Mazumdar explain, propaganda "had a profound impact on the course of the Cold War: it surged in the early years; it flourished in the Third World during the middle years of the conflict; it reshaped during the period of détente and arguably played a key role in the ending of the Cold War."[24]

Consequently, the innovative and internationally emerging field of sensory history is especially well suited to studying the Cold War with an emphasis on its microstructures. The seminal work of historians in this field—among other scholars such as cultural anthropologists, cultural studies experts, and sociologists—has paved the way for a fundamentally different understanding of historical and contemporary problems.[25] Analyzing sensory warfare affords to go below the surface of reason and political thought and at the same time to focus on the historicity of the senses. Forming the core of the sensory history approach to the Cold War is the supposition that sensory warfare has deep, long-term effects that transcend politics, historical breaks, and turning points and underlie the mechanisms and cultural effects of bloc-building and the othering of people into distinguishable communities. What is often unconsciously perceived as micropolitics can lead to enduring differences that divide societies and move beyond the established concepts of traditional political history. Lasting for decades, the Cold War was a major event that "transformed the sensory world so dramatically that it seemed almost a brand-new creation," as David Howes observes in *A Cultural History of the Senses in the Modern Age*.[26] Understanding perception not primarily as a mechanistic interface between the human self and the outside world but also as a socially learned, culturally shaped, and historically specific mode of active *sensing*,[27] the authors of the present volume proceed on the assumption that human senses can be politically "governed" in a Foucauldian sense. Although they come from different academic fields and specializations such as Cold War studies, Eastern and Central European history, area studies, literature, film, and media history, they share an active and broad understanding of sensing.

Politicizing the Sensorium: Cold Warfare

Before the Cold War unfolded as a military standoff with highly weaponized and deadly borders, with covert operations and even hot wars in countries such as Korea, Vietnam, and Afghanistan, an underlying partitioning process took place. This was most obvious in Germany and especially in Berlin, where the front lines of the new military sectors cut through neighborhoods, streets, houses, and even a cemetery. But the same applies to entire continents. Not only was the Cold War a standoff between the two superpowers and their allies, but it was also a conflict closely intertwined with the "political and social development in the Third World," as Odd Arne Westad notes in a comment that emphasizes the global dimension of the conflict.[28] But even inside the political blocs that the superpowers formed with their closest allies, the conflict divided neighbors into distinct communities, split families, and turned friends into strangers, political opponents, and even enemies. Images became political icons that were used as weapons on the media front. Invisible and inaudible communication channels were developed, military methods were refined, and consumer goods were politicized.[29] Secret police developed overt and covert sensory practices, as did opposition groups and underground movements. And it was not only sensory but also sensual matters that became political in numerous espionage affairs.

How precisely did this "othering" function and how was it sensed? What were the sensory measures of the Cold War conflict—not only those incorporating vision and sound but also those that made use of the "close senses" of taste, smell, touch, and pain, whether in cultural policies, propaganda and counterpropaganda, or open warfare? How did the political partitioning of the world into (more or less) homogeneous blocs change contemporary sensescapes? How were *imagined communities* (Benedict Anderson) transformed into *sensed communities*?[30] And what were the long-term effects of this sensory alienation beyond political ruptures and historical turning points?

These are the key questions addressed by the chapters of this volume. In its examination of a wide range of sensoria, *Sensory Warfare in the Global Cold War* adopts the intersensory approach that sensory studies have lately emphasized, moving away from the older multisensorial concept.[31] Intersensory approaches focus on the interrelations between different sensoria rather than following one single sensorium. In fact, a comprehensive intersensory study of specific phenomena is probably unattainable, as neuroscientists believe there are eighteen or more human systems of perception, including the "new" senses such as equilibrium, thermos reception, and pain.[32] For this reason, some chapters are devoted to a single sensorium, but even in these chapters, the authors explore the interplay with other sensoria—colors and taste, haptics and smell, vision and sound.

Traditionally, Cold War studies often described the history of the conflict as being driven by anonymous superpowers. Monolithic blocs were compared and contrasted, geopolitical strategies were identified as agents, papers by unnamed authors at think tanks and organizations were studied, weapons were counted, and territories were measured. When it comes to human agency, the focus was often placed on the (overwhelmingly male) players at the uppermost levels of government: heads of state, general secretaries, chancellors, commanders in chief, and secret police directors. In contrast, the present book centers on the human sensorium. Such an approach makes it possible to break down the macro perspective into micro processes that unfold on an everyday level. One consequence is that women emerge alongside men as central figures—e.g., as the target audience for mass propaganda campaigns involving food deliveries or household technologies or in the politicization of perfumes. And women were key actors on the front lines of the conflict as well, developing tactics for public diplomacy in important intelligence positions (e.g., Eleanor Lansing Dulles), carrying out propaganda strategies as announcers in the sonic warfare across the "Aquatic Frontier" between the two Chinese republics (e.g., Chen Xinmei and Chen Feifei), or working the switchboards of civil and military communication systems, like the mostly female telephone operators in East Berlin (e.g., "Erika"). Not only gender but also class and race are at the basis of this book: class is a key factor in the analysis of sensory warfare addressing especially workers' needs and tastes or the bourgeois music tastes in the Romanian programming of Radio Free Europe; racism is at the ground of the olfactory detection techniques of the US Army during the Vietnam War.

Covert Action: Sensory Warfare and Emotions

Shifting the focus to human agency in politics and everyday life does not mean ignoring the general objectives of Cold War strategies, including deterrence, containment, the "balance of power," and détente.[33] Rather, it entails keeping in mind the general objectives of geopolitics, ideology, and military strategy while also examining in detail how these policies were executed in concrete tactics and how they actually affected contemporaries—or, more precisely, how they were sensed. This focus ties in with recent approaches that view public diplomacy as a crucial nonmilitary method of fighting conflicts. For example, research has examined how asymmetric conflict diplomacy employs different modes of listening, including "surreptitious listening" and "tactical listening," both of which aim to build trust or "readjust public diplomacy messages and correct misconceptions."[34] Public diplomacy often includes covert tactics such as "psychological operations" (PSYOPs), which are defined as "planned operations to convey selected information and indicators to foreign audiences to influence emotions, motives, objective reasoning, and ultimately the behavior of foreign governments, organizations, groups, and individuals."[35]

The last decade has seen the publication of the first groundbreaking histories of emotions in the Cold War.[36] One important issue, as Hélène Miard-Delacroix and Andreas Wirsching argue, is the idea of "supra-individual emotional conventions that can be understood as normative sets."[37] However, as Mark M. Smith notes in his recently published *Sensory History Manifesto*, emotions are closely interrelated with sensory experience.[38] The history of this sensory experience is microhistory, often even nanohistory, and it takes a close look at phenomena such as light rays, sound waves, and scent molecules. It puts cognitive and processes and collective *emotives* (William M. Reddy) center stage,[39] studying taste buds, sensory receptors, and nerve channels in action. Several chapters in this volume address the emotions stimulated by sensory signals: the excitement caused by Spanish propaganda newsreels, the desire expressed in the male gaze of Europeans visiting China, and the production of fear in a wide variety of forms—the fear of being caught listening to Western radio stations in Cold War Romania, and the fear of losing loved ones in the Afghanistan war, triggered by photos of planes transporting the bodies of fallen Soviet "heroes."

In the process, *Sensory Warfare in the Global Cold War* highlights the sensed and emotional experiences of eyewitnesses to history (but also those of earwitnesses and nosewitnesses), analyzing both top-down and bottom-up processes: What policies of repression, partition, and propaganda had an impact on people? And, from the inverse perspective, what behaviors, consumer needs, and protests (often in the form of a refusal to participate) trickled up from below and finally had to be taken seriously by Cold Warriors at various levels of government? In doing so, sensory histories of the Cold War pursue what is in fact a contradictory goal: to rehumanize an inhumane conflict.

Stages of Cold War Sensory Conflict

In contrast to world history, global history rarely addresses all continents at the same time. While the term *global history* may suggest worldwide coverage, as Sebastian Conrad explains, "this is not necessarily the case." To the contrary, "many topics are best displayed in smaller frames."[40] As a process, a subject matter, and a methodology, global history can result even in local histories, highlighting regional aspects of processes that are broadly understood as dominated by North-West (or East-West) connections, structures, or conflicts while at the same time keeping those power structures in mind. The authors of the individual chapters of this book come from eight countries and examine a wide range of areas. Without claiming or even attempting to be comprehensive, this book delves into examples from Afghanistan, China, Germany, Hungary, Poland, Romania, the Soviet Union, Spain, Switzerland, Taiwan, the United States, and Vietnam. Some of the chapters also touch on Albania, Austria, Cuba, Czechoslovakia, Korea, and Yugoslavia. The general temporal focus is on early postwar events and extends through four decades of conflict, looking at many aspects of what is only insufficiently covered by the generalizing term "Cold War." In fact, what underlies the local examples analyzed in this book is a much more complex global puzzle made up of overarching and undermining bilateral and multilateral conflicts (such as the East-West conflict, which is not identical with the Cold War, the Soviet-Afghan conflict, the Chinese partition, and numerous national schisms including the ones in fascist Spain and between pro-communist and anti-communist factions in "neutral" Switzerland).[41]

Nevertheless, this book is not organized by geography, chronology, or sensoria. Rather, the three parts reflect different stages of intensity in the Cold War sensory warfare. These stages did not unfold linearly and successively. They overlapped, sometimes following the cycles of heightened tension and détente, sometimes occurring erratically and locally.

The first part of the book, "Seduction, Manipulation, Othering," is devoted to the micropolitics of partition: the subtle, slow change that occurred below the surface of traditional policies and was often sensed unconsciously. Of interest here are the politically guided efforts to seduce the "other" into changing sides.

As Victoria Phillips demonstrates in her opening chapter on gastrodiplomacy,[42] directly after the Second World War, officials at the US Psychological Strategy Board launched their first operations to win not only the hearts and minds but also the stomachs, tastebuds, noses, and eyes of former enemies. Although the West's original goal in providing food to Soviet-occupied countries was to fight famine and feed former allies and enemies, the programs aimed at much more than just nutrition. American efforts to deliver certain tastes and colors through products that lacked any nutritional value (such as chewing gum and cigarettes) connected political messages to sensory experience.

Women also figure strongly in the chapter by Stephanie Weismann, who demonstrates how the "Sovietization" of the Polish perfume industry failed once women began demanding substitutes for unattainable French perfumes. Polish women's long-established collective "Western" sensory taxonomies had significant consequences for the Polish economy. Weismann studies this process using the example of the Inter-Fragrances brand, whose founder became one of the first Polish millionaires and eventually played an important role in transforming the socialist republic into a market economy.

The sensory taxonomies covered not only smell but also taste and could be created through secret and public diplomacy tactics. As Cyril Cordoba demonstrates in his study, sight and hearing also changed during the Cold War. Analyzing tapes and films made by Swiss visitors to Communist China, he reconstructs the male gaze at the exoticized "other" and shows how the sound, color, and food of the Chinese Cultural Revolution were sensed by Western sympathizers, who brought back food and tea as well as documentation of their experiences on film and tape and used this documentation in public lectures.

Mark Fenemore's exploration of early telephony in Cold War Berlin offers an initial analysis of gendered listening, focusing on the most intimate form of conflict, played out through wires. At a time when connections were controlled by telephone operators, the human factor posed a risk in secret information technology. Combining both surveillance and gender studies, Fenemore analyzes a conflict in which not only sensory but also sensual encounters were politicized.

In the second part of the book, "Partition, Propaganda, Sensory Borders," readers learn that these micropolitics were not fleeting but could have profound and long-lasting effects. Several chapters describe the drifting apart of sensory communities under the political divisions and the growing significance of media in the course of conflict.

Dayton Lekner's chapter on listening at the "aquatic sound barrier" across the Taiwan Strait shifts the focus to a battleground in Asia. From 1953 to 1992, Xiamen (China) and Jinmen (Taiwan) were engaged in a sonic war, broadcasting propaganda messages and music from speaker towers to enemies across the sea. The psychological tactics involved recording and broadcasting the voices of relatives of the enemy soldiers on the other side of the strait and deliberately arousing emotions such as fear and sadness.

This type of targeting also took place in Cold War listening. In her contribution, Andreea Deciu Ritivoi examines efforts by US-financed radio stations to target audiences in Central Eastern Europe, especially Romania. Developing an "acousmatic voice," the CIA-backed station Radio Free Europe, for example, sent messages and ideas not only through text but also through sound. As Ritivoi explains, this sound was "more cosmopolitan than local" and "eloquent in a classical, bourgeois sense." Furthermore, such Cold War broadcasts created new methods of covert private hearing as a result of the danger they posed to audiences fearful of getting caught listening. The ether war eventually had bloody consequences when the Romanian secret service conspired in the bombing of a Munich radio station.

In fascist Spain, NO-DO cinema newsreels became the most important channel for spreading a propagandistic view of the world, since television was not widespread in Spain in the 1950s and 1960s. However, as José Manuel López Torán shows, the Spanish newsreel coverage of the Korean War and the Cuban Missile Crisis did more than just provide information on current conflicts around the globe. Through the associative visual strategies employed by the NO-DO newsreels, these short films sought in an unobtrusive way to create legitimacy for the Spanish Civil War, which was fought about two decades ago.

Finally, in my own chapter on the inner-German border, I set out to demonstrate how smells were one of the factors that could accelerate political conflict. Based on ideas from actor-network-theory and a reading of archived sensory protocols, I show how environmental pollution and weed killers along the so-called death strip, as well as an alleged "smell of death," were discussed in conjunction with several political conflicts that ultimately involved the highest level of German-German diplomacy. And even the border itself smelled, odorized by "smell barriers" to prevent animals from illegally crossing the border and setting off alarms.

The third part of this book is devoted to the most extreme stage of the Cold War, marked by several hot conflicts. Titled "Mind Control, Covert Operations, Overt Warfare," it focuses on borderland shootouts, military encounters, and hot wars within the broader ideological and economic framework of a bipolar (though in fact much more complex) world order. The chapters investigate sensory measures in what are often referred to as "proxy wars" in Central and East Asia. In fact, these wars had their own specific dynamics, features, and local consequences and were thus much more than just peripheral muscle-flexing by the superpowers. By addressing various attempts to reprogram the human mind and body through the techniques of psychological warfare, psychoactive drugs, and secret experiments in the shadow realm of intelligence services, it also delves into the fringe sciences and covert operations in hot conflicts.

Examining a notorious chapter of Cold War intelligence, Walter E. Grunden tracks attempts to "brainwash" agents through sensory deprivation. In infamous experiments that failed quite dramatically, the CIA used sensory deprivation and psychoactive drugs, attempting to turn agents into willing killers, but ultimately produced brain-dead zombies, their senses dulled, some of whom never returned to a normal state.

At the same time, traditional media such as leaflets and newspapers continued to be an important means of propaganda, particularly when military personnel were the target audience. In his chapter on military propaganda in the two German states, Carsten Richter analyzes how the sensory monotony of barracks life made young East and West German draftees an easy target for (often sexualized) propagandistic visions of a better life "on the other side." To protect the recipients of the messages, propaganda departments meticulously adapted and camouflaged the brochures, making them look and haptically feel as if they were domestic media when in fact they were fabricated by the enemy and sought to convince the recipients to desert or even to turn their weapons against their own country.

Olfaction was also a factor in warfare, as Christy Spackman demonstrates. She focuses on the "people sniffer," a device developed during the Vietnam War to detect the enemy by electronically measuring smell molecules in the air. Citing military documents, Spackman reports that the device's effectiveness in the field remained uncertain. However, US Army strategists found a new use for the device in their propaganda war: they declassified the secret weapon and in presentations to the US media pretended they were in possession of superior military technology in an attempt to convince the increasingly war-weary American public to continue supporting the inglorious war.

In a final chapter on sensory warfare in a military conflict, Markus Mirschel views the 1980s Afghan War through the Soviet lens, emphasizing the changing role of military propaganda photography. While originally rooted in pictorial traditions of the Second World War, the Soviet-Afghan War produced new icons such as the "black tulip" (a metaphorical description of the Antonov planes that transported corpses back to the Soviet Union). These planes, originally idealized by military photographers as a symbol of the superior weapons of the Soviet Army, now came to represent defeat and grief and thus demilitarized what Robert Jütte calls the "armed gaze."[43]

Cold Sensory Warfare: An Ongoing History?

Global approaches to the Cold War challenge common beliefs. In the West, the Cold War has often been regarded as a closed book, perhaps the last chapter of what Eric Hobsbawm calls the "age of extremes."[44] However, it is a book that might now be reopened, after the return of hot warfare to the Middle East and even Europe.[45] In Asia, one of the "major battlefields for East–West conflict,"[46] the Cold War never ended. The military standoff between North and South Korea at the thirty-eighth parallel has continued to the present day along a border that calls to mind the iron curtains of the 1960s. Lately, the opponents returned to Cold War-style sonic and olfactory warfare when North Korea reacted on Southern activists' border-crossing balloons loaded with Western media including K-Pop music by sending back their own balloons full of manure and human waste.[47] Tensions also intensified between China and Taiwan, where a covert war is still being waged, one that involves espionage and military strikes that at times ignite and keep alive fear of another hot war in the twenty-first century. In demonstrations against China in Hong Kong, protesters have recently used umbrellas to ward off tear gas attacks by the police, turning a defensive weapon against olfactory warfare into a political icon (and thus a visual weapon). These "weapons" were ultimately criminalized and banned by the authorities. Colors have also become political weapons in several "color revolutions" around the globe, including in Ukraine's Orange Revolution of 2004.

Propaganda warfare in the form of "fake news" or manipulated photographs is more widespread today than in the twentieth century with its analog photography. Its target groups are larger, and it can be disseminated more quickly than the old Cold Warriors ever imagined. Fake news is being used in Russia's war aggression against Ukraine, and radio stations are still an important tool for undermining censorship in totalitarian regimes. Independent radio stations currently face immense difficulties in Eastern European states such as Belarus, Hungary, Russia, and intermittently also Poland, where politicians had turned to authoritarian models. Radio Free Europe, founded during the Cold War, is still on air and online in the 2020s, now taking part in the information war between Russia and Ukraine. These are just a few of the many examples that show that sensory warfare is still a common method in current conflicts.

The Cold War did not invent sensory warfare, but as the longest global militarized conflict of the twentieth century, it brought some of its measures to cruel perfection. In order to determine whether today's covert conflicts should be regarded as ongoing history or as a new Cold War, we first need to study the sensory legacy of the Cold War. This book makes sense of a senseless global conflict that was fought not only *on* but also *through* the senses.

Notes

1. Katie Bo Williams and Jeremy Herb, "US Investigating Possible Mysterious Directed Energy Attack near White House," CNN, April 29, 2021, https://edition.cnn.com/2021/04/29/politics/us-investigating-mysterious-directed-energy-attack-white-house/index.html; Graison Dangor, "'Havana Syndrome' Reportedly Held Up Kamala Harris' Vietnam Visit. What Is It?," Forbes, August 24, 2021, https://www.forbes.com/sites/graisondangor/2021/08/24/kamala-harris-vietnam-visit-reportedly-held-up-by-havana-syndrome-scare/?sh=4cd1f68464ad.
2. Goodman, *Sonic Warfare*.
3. Goodman, "Dossier 37."
4. Journalists of The Insider, 60 Minutes and Der Spiegel. See Roman Dobrokhotov, Christo Grozev, and Michael Weiss, "Unraveling Havana Syndrome: New evidence links the GRU's assassination Unit 29155 to mysterious attacks on U.S. officials and their families", in: The Insider, April 11, 2024, https://theins.ru/en/politics/270425 (April 21, 2024).
5. Jong, "Intelligence and the Cold War," 313.
6. See Mrozek, "Bewaffnete Organe."
7. See Howes, "Foreword: The Engagement of the Senses"; Smith, *Sensory History*.
8. See Smith, *Smell of Battle*; Smith, *How Race Is Made*; Plamper, "Sounds of February, Smells of October"; Leonard, "Sensorial No Man's Land"; Kettler, *Smell of Slavery*.
9. Smith, *Smell of Battle*, 6.
10. See Jütte, *History of the Senses*, 325–26; Encke, *Augenblicke der Gefahr*, 18.
11. Smith, *Smell of Battle*, 42–43.
12. See Courmont, *Odeur de l'ennemi*.
13. See Bourke, *Story of Pain*, 222–30.
14. Bull, "Sensory Media," 224.
15. Bull, "Sensory Media," 224.
16. See Kittler, "Rock Music."
17. In his classical, widely debated soundscape concept. See Schafer, "Soundscape," 101.
18. See Birdsall, *Nazi Soundscapes*, 104.
19. See Cote, *Third Battle*, 69–78.
20. See Bloch, "Plans parcellaires," 557. On this topic, see Raulff, *Ein Historiker im 20. Jahrhundert*, 92–123.
21. Cornish, Saunders, and Smith, introduction to *Modern Conflict and the Senses*, 4.
22. The term *horizon of expectation* was popularized by the German historian Reinhart Koselleck, who actually adapted it unmarked from the Hungarian sociologist Karl Mannheim. See Mrozek, "Die sogenannte Sattelzeit," 137.
23. See Gienow-Hecht, "Culture and the Cold War"; Laugesen, *Taking Books to the World*; Crowley and Pavitt, *Cold War Modern*; Mrozek, "G.I. Blues and German Schlager."
24. Cull and Mazumdar, "Propaganda and the Cold War," 323.
25. See Smith, *Sensing the Past*; Le Breton, *Sensing the World*.
26. Howes, "Introduction: 'Make it New!,'" 1.
27. See Smith, *Sensing the Past*; Le Breton, *Sensing the World*.
28. Westad, *Cold War*, 396; Latham, "Cold War in the Third World."
29. See Rosenberg, "Consumer Capitalism"; Zhuk, "Soviet Studies and Cultural Consumption"; Priestland, "Neoliberalism, Consumerism."
30. Benedict Anderson coined the term *imagined communities* in 1983. See Anderson, *Imagined Communities*, 6, passim. On the adaption of his term for sensory history, see Mrozek, "Sensed Communities."
31. See Howes, *Empire of the Senses*, 9–12.

32. See Mrozek, "Achtzehn Sinne."
33. See Gaddis, "Grand Strategies."
34. Di Martino, "Spectrum of Listening"; Cull, "Reading, Viewing."
35. Kilbane, "Dutch Boy at the Dike?"
36. See Greiner, Müller, and Walter, *Angst im Kalten Krieg*; Starck, *Between Fear and Freedom*; Biess, *German Angst*, 95–129, 298–307.
37. Miard-Delacroix and Wirsching, "Emotionen und internationale Beziehungen," 22.
38. See Smith, *Sensory History Manifesto*.
39. See Reddy, *Navigation of Feeling*, 105–109.
40. Conrad, *What Is Global History?*, 8, 12.
41. See Lüthi, "Sino-Soviet Split"; Irwin, "Decolonization and the Cold War."
42. See Rockower, "Guide to Gastrodiplomacy."
43. Jütte, *History of the Senses*, 114.
44. Hobsbawm, *Age of Extremes*, 3, passim.
45. In respect to the Gulf War, see Brands, *From Berlin to Baghdad*, 302–34.
46. Bagnato and Guderzo, introduction to *Globalization and the Cold War*, 1.
47. Shaimaa Khalil and Thomas Mackintosh, "South Korea to resume loudspeaker broadcasts over border in balloon row", BBC, June 10, 2024, https://www.bbc.com/news/articles/c1rr92dwqnyo.

Bibliography

Anderson, Benedict. *Imagined Communities: Reflections on the Origin and Spread of Nationalism*. London: Verso, 2006.

Bagnato, Bruna, and Max Guderzo. Introduction to *The Globalization of the Cold War: Diplomacy and Local Confrontation, 1975–85*, edited by Bruna Bagnato and Max Guderzo, 1–6. Cold War Series 25. New York: Routledge, 2010.

Biess, Frank. *German Angst: Fear and Democracy in the Federal Republic of Germany*. Oxford: Oxford University Press, 2020.

Birdsall, Carolyn. *Nazi Soundscapes: Sound, Technology, and Urban Space in Germany, 1933–1945*. Amsterdam: Amsterdam University Press, 2012.

Bloch, Marc. "Les plans parcellaires: L'avion au service de l'histoire agraire en Angleterre." *Annales d'histoire économique et sociale* 2, no. 8 (1930): 557–58.

Bourke, Joanna. *The Story of Pain: From Prayer to Painkillers*. Oxford: Oxford University Press, 2014.

Brands, Hal. *From Berlin to Baghdad: America's Search for Purpose in the Post-Cold War World*. Lexington: University Press of Kentucky, 2008.

Bull, Michael. "Sensory Media: Virtual Worlds and the Training of Perception." In Howes, *A Cultural History of the Senses in the Modern Age*, 219–41.

Conrad, Sebastian. *What Is Global History?* Princeton: Princeton University Press, 2016.

Cornish, Paul, Nicholas J. Saunders, and Mark M. Smith. Introduction to *Modern Conflict and the Senses*, edited by Nicholas J. Saunders and Paul Cornish, 1–10. London: Routledge, 2017.

Cote, Owen R., Jr. *The Third Battle: Innovation in the U.S. Navy's Silent Cold War Struggle with Soviet Submarines*. Newport: Naval War College Press, 2003.

Courmont, Juliette. *L'odeur de l'ennemi, 1914–1918*. Préface d'Alain Corbin. Paris: Armand Colin, 2010.

Crowley, David, and Jane Pavitt, eds. *Cold War Modern: Design, 1945–1970*. London: V&A, 2008.

Cull, Nicholas J. "Reading, Viewing, and Tuning in to the Cold War." In Leffler and Westad, *Cambridge History of the Cold War*, 2:438–59.

Cull, Nicholas J., and B. Theo Mazumdar. "Propaganda and the Cold War." In Kalinovsky and Daigle, *Routledge Handbook of the Cold War*, 323–39.

Di Martino, Luigi. "The Spectrum of Listening." In Snow and Cull, *Routledge Handbook of Public Diplomacy*, 21–29.

Encke, Julia. *Augenblicke der Gefahr: Der Krieg und die Sinne*. Munich: Wilhelm Fink, 2006.

Gaddis, John Lewis. "Grand Strategies in the Cold War." In Leffler and Westad,

Cambridge History of the Cold War, 2:1–21.

Gienow-Hecht, Jessica. "Culture and the Cold War in Europe." In Leffler and Westad, *Cambridge History of the Cold War,* 1:398–419.

Goodman, Steve. "Dossier 37: Unidentified Vibrational Objects on the Plane of Unbelief." *Contemporary Journal* 3 (2020). https://thecontemporaryjournal.org/strands/sonic-continuum/dossier-37.

———. *Sonic Warfare: Sound, Affect, and the Ecology of Fear.* Cambridge: MIT Press, 2009.

Greiner, Bernd, Christian Th. Müller, and Dierk Walter, eds. *Angst im Kalten Krieg.* Studien zum Kalten Krieg 3. Hamburg: Hamburger Edition, 2011.

Hobsbawm, Eric. *The Age of Extremes: The Short Twentieth Century, 1914–1991.* London: Abacus, 2020.

Howes, David, ed. *A Cultural History of the Senses in the Modern Age.* 2nd ed. 6 vols. London: Bloomsbury Academic, 2019.

———, ed. *Empire of the Senses: The Sensual Culture Reader.* Oxford: Bloomsbury, 2005.

———. "Foreword: The Engagement of the Senses." In *Modern Conflict and the Senses,* edited by Nicholas J. Saunders and Paul Cornish, ix–xxiii. London: Routledge, 2017.

———. "Introduction: 'Make it New!'—Reforming the Sensory World." In Howes, *A Cultural History of the Senses in the Modern Age,* 6:1–30.

Irwin, Ryan M. "Decolonization and the Cold War." In Kalinovsky and Daigle, *Routledge Handbook of the Cold War,* 91–104.

Jong, Ben D. "Intelligence and the Cold War." In Kalinovsky and Daigle, *Routledge Handbook of the Cold War,* 305–19.

Jütte, Robert. *A History of the Senses: From Antiquity to Cyberspace.* Oxford: Blackwell, 2004.

Kalinovsky, Artemy M., and Craig Daigle, eds. *The Routledge Handbook of the Cold War.* New York: Routledge, 2014.

Kettler, Andrew. *The Smell of Slavery: Olfactory Racism and the Atlantic World.* Cambridge: Cambridge University Press, 2020.

Kilbane, Mark J. "Dutch Boy at the Dike? Military PSYOP as Public Diplomacy." Paper presented at the 57th Conference of the Political Study Association, University of Bath, United Kingdom, April 11–13, 2007.

Kittler, Friedrich A. "Rock Music: A Misuse of Military Equipment." In Kittler, *Truth of the Technological World,* 152–64.

———. *The Truth of the Technological World: Essays on the Genealogy of Presence,* translated by Erik Butler. Stanford: Stanford University Press, 2013.

Latham, Michael E. "The Cold War in the Third World, 1963–1975." In Leffler and Westad, *Cambridge History of the Cold War,* 2:258–80.

Laugesen, Amanda. *Taking Books to the World: American Publishers and the Cultural Cold War.* Amherst: University of Massachusetts Press, 2017.

Le Breton, David. *Sensing the World: An Anthropology of the Senses.* London: Bloomsbury, 2017.

Leffler, Melvyn P., and Odd Arne Westad, eds. *The Cambridge History of the Cold War.* 3 vols. Cambridge: Cambridge University Press, 2010.

Leonard, Matthew. "A Sensorial No Man's Land: Corporeality and the Western Front during the First World War." *Senses and Society* 14, no. 3 (2019): 257–70.

Lüthi, Lorenz M. "The Sino-Soviet Split and its Consequences." In Kalinovsky and Daigle, *Routledge Handbook of the Cold War,* 74–88.

Miard-Delacroix, Hélène, and Andreas Wirsching, eds. *Emotionen und internationale Beziehungen im Kalten Krieg.* Schriften des Historischen Kollegs 104. Munich: De Gruyter Oldenbourg, 2020.

———. "Emotionen und internationale Beziehungen im Kalten Krieg." In Miard-Delacroix and Wirsching, *Emotionen und internationale Beziehungen im Kalten Krieg,* 1–22.

Mrozek, Bodo. "Die achtzehn Sinne." *Merkur* 74, no. 852 (2020) 5: 59–66.

———. "Bewaffnete Organe: Sensory Warfare." *Merkur* 75, no. 871 (2021) 12: 49–58.

———. "G.I. Blues and German Schlager: The Politics of Popular Music in Germany during the Cold War." In *Made in Germany: Studies in Popular Music*, edited by Oliver Seibt, Martin Ringsmut, and David-Emil Wickström, 122–31. New York: Taylor and Francis, 2021.

———. "Sensed Communities." *Merkur* 76, no. 879 (2022) 8: 43–53.

———. "Die sogenannte Sattelzeit: Reinhart Kosellecks Geschichtsmetapher im Erfahrungsraum des Krieges." *Zeitschrift für Religions- und Geistesgeschichte* 75 (2023) 2: 133–53.

Plamper, Jan. "Sounds of February, Smells of October: The Russian Revolution as Sensory Experience." *American Historical Review* 126, no. 1 (2021): 140–65.

Priestland, David. "Neoliberalism, Consumerism, and the End of the Cold War." In Kalinovsky and Daigle, *Routledge Handbook of the Cold War*, 401–15.

Raulff, Ulrich. *Ein Historiker im 20. Jahrhundert: Marc Bloch*. Frankfurt: S. Fischer, 1995.

Reddy, William M. *The Navigation of Feeling: A Framework for the History of Emotions*. Cambridge: Cambridge University Press, 2001.

Rockower, Paul. "A Guide to Gastrodiplomacy." In Snow and Cull, *Routledge Handbook of Public Diplomacy*, 205–12.

Rosenberg, Emily S. "Consumer Capitalism and the End of the Cold War." In Leffler and Westad, *Cambridge History of the Cold War*, 3:489–512.

Schafer, R. Murray. "The Soundscape." In *Sound Studies Reader*, edited by Jonathan Sterne, 95–103. London: Routledge, 2012.

Smith, Mark M. *How Race Is Made: Slavery, Segregation, and the Senses*. Chapel Hill: University of North Carolina Press, 2006.

———. *Sensing the Past: Seeing, Hearing, Smelling, and Touching in History*. Berkeley: University of California Press, 2008.

———. *Sensory History*. Oxford: Berg, 2007.

———. *A Sensory History Manifesto*. University Park: Pennsylvania State University Press, 2021.

———. *The Smell of Battle, the Taste of Siege: A Sensory History of the Civil War*. Oxford: Oxford University Press, 2015.

Snow, Nancy, and Nicholas J. Cull, eds. *The Routledge Handbook of Public Diplomacy*. New York: Routledge, 2020.

Starck, Kathleen, ed. *Between Fear and Freedom: Cultural Representations of the Cold War*. Cambridge: Cambridge Scholars, 2010.

Westad, Odd Arne. *The Cold War: A World History*. New York: Basic Books, 2017.

Zhuk, Sergei I. "Soviet Studies and Cultural Consumption." In Kalinovsky and Daigle, *Routledge Handbook of the Cold War*, 351–68.

PART I

SEDUCTION, MANIPULATION, OTHERING

CHAPTER 1

Chocolate Paratroopers and Eisenhower Packages for Eastern Europe

Nourishing Partition Through Colors and Taste

Victoria Phillips

On June 16, 1953, a mass demonstration of workers pushed forward in front of the iconic Brandenburg Gate, their flags and fists a bit blurred in the newsman's photograph.[1] They had stripped the East German flag of its emblem, which featured the workers' golden hammer and the intellectuals' compass encircled by an ear of grain representing farmers. All these elements signified German bondage to the Kremlin's Marxism. Behind the men, the women pushed forward.[2]

As wartime leftovers, the women stood in lines for food and water. They crushed the eggshells after the eggs had been devoured, feeding the powder to the children for nourishment.[3] In East Berlin, women cleared the rubble of war brick by brick, rebuilding houses with makeshift walls. The women who volunteered as construction workers got a better food allotment. Those who insisted on remaining "housewives only" were given ration cards known as "hunger cards" or a "map to the cemetery."[4]

On news broadcasts from the West, the women heard about themselves and how they were about to break under the pressure: more work, less food.[5] RIAS (Radio in the American Sector) began with a simple melody you could pluck out on a piano, with eight single chords. Then a male voice introduced rhymed phrases about freedom, and the news began.[6] Then the radio drama *Polish Tea Party*—set at the Polish Mission in Berlin—recounted a celebration directly after Joseph Stalin's death that spared no "elaborateness or expense." An announcer declared, "Everything was offered: caviar, lobster, various kinds of fried meats and fish in mayonnaise, and so on, English and American brands of whiskey, French wine." To stir the memory of tastes and induce salivation, the announcer added after a pause, "And countless cakes and tarts."[7] In the communist news reports, these same people read and heard that there was plenty of food, but they took their place in lines at dawn, and the store shelves were often bare by the time they were allowed inside. The East Germans had read that the West Germans were poor, but then a small package of something good would arrive by mail from the other side of a country that had been divided less than a decade before. So when the time came, female workers defiantly posted signs in the streets: "Wir Streiken" ("We're Striking").[8]

After the June 1953 uprising, any East German who crossed into West Berlin and showed an identity card would receive a bundle of food branded American: "Eisenhower packages," named for US president Dwight D. Eisenhower, contained pure white flour and sugar, rich brown coffee and cocoa. Under the slogan "Goodwill Is a Weapon," the United States used food, particularly its color, in psychological warfare.[9] Goodwill and humanitarianism, alongside hospitality and gifts, were used to incite, encourage, and maintain active dissent against Moscow. The project was executed by a woman in Washington, DC, Eleanor Lansing Dulles, and targeted women on the communist home front, bringing the political into the domestic sphere.

Theory: Food as a Weapon

My analysis rests on theorizations of "supple" power and the senses, alongside food, gender, and political biography.[10] Michel Foucault writes, "Power is tolerable only on condition that it mask a substantial part of itself. Its success is proportional to its ability to hide its own mechanisms." He calls this the "supple mechanisms of power."[11] In the Cold War's "total war," a term introduced into the American lexicon by Nelson A. Rockefeller, the power of propaganda and US "nation branding" derived from continued, integrated experiences that targeted the senses for "greater synergistic effect in order to build emotional bonds."[12] Food offerings acted as supple power to sell American freedom. Jacques Derrida's work on hospitality and Pierre Bourdieu's theorization of gifts shed light on the power mechanisms of food delivery in 1953.[13] East Germans were invited into the West, thus illustrating Derrida's description of power relations between host and guest.[14] Hospitality depends on the idea that there is no immediate demand for reciprocity. Although Eisenhower underscored this point in public declarations about the food program, bonds and hierarchies were in fact established.[15] Reflecting Derrida's idea of a hospitable host, Bourdieu believed that the gift-giver must conceal self-interest.[16] In addition, gifts create "social meaning" through bonds; he noted, "If brothers make gifts, then gifts make brothers."[17] In this case, German-to-German bonds were refabricated across political lines drawn by the fallout of war. As Bourdieu concludes, "Presents [gifts] intended to maintain the everyday order of social intercourse almost always consist of food."[18]

With historians "coming to their senses" and the rise of the sensory turn in history, color has been understood as a particular aspect of visual power.[19] In nineteenth-century Germany, Johann Wolfgang von Goethe noted that the experience of color and the saturation of hues brought meaning through the sensations of human warmth, excitement, peace, and inspiration.[20] By the early twentieth century, color had become a key driver of the food industry's efforts to create desire, as Ai Hisano, a historian of the senses, states.[21] Color seduced the imagination and carried connotations of smell and taste.[22] Hues and saturations denoted "richness, force, prestige, beauty, love, death, blood and fire."[23] Madison Avenue determined that, for Washington, "color was the national salesman for America."[24] Freedom brought plenty—as well as a plenitude of visual sensations.

The historiography of food studies is growing, and scholars have been delving into the Cold War. Food challenges any clear demarcation of "hard" and "soft" power: the manipulation of supply leads to a slow death; the commodity can be fashioned to create the outcomes desired by traditional "soft" power exercises. Food became one staging ground of ideology, with Soviet collectivism pitted against Western individualism. Ideological battles over modernity, and thus industrial modernization, set the stage for food as supple power; new techniques of canning, freezing, and dehydrating foods, developed during the Second World War, came to symbolize the modern kitchen, home, and spaceship.[25] In this way, food became a powerful focal point for psywar and diplomacy.

Historians tie food to the kitchen and thus to gender: as "housewives" and "homemakers," women infiltrated the grassroots level of everyday life, which became political during a Cold War that featured the 1959 Kitchen Debate. As "Republican Mothers," women fed the next generation.[26] As shoppers and family cooks, they became a primary target group, and advertisers studied how to appeal to the female eye. In the case of East Berlin and the "cemetery" ration cards for housewives, food for the home was a welcome gift that allowed women to tend to those who could not fend for themselves, including children and the elderly. Thus, even as they fulfilled a basic human need—caloric intake—the US food gifts quietly reinforced American gender norms by literally sending communist women back into the kitchen.

Food as a Cold War psychological weapon became a Dulles family affair in Washington. Although the two brothers, Allen Dulles and John Foster, have been featured in Cold War histories, psychological warfare was also engaged in by a woman in the family. During the Second World War, Allen Dulles, who later became CIA director under Eisenhower, was stationed in Switzerland as a spy for the Office of Strategic Services. Allen worked with the psychoanalyst Carl Jung, whom he recruited as "Agent 488," to understand totalitarian leaders, including Adolf Hitler, and the psychology of the crowd. During the Cold War, Jung became Allen's "senior advisor" on a weekly, if not almost daily, basis.[27] Switzerland, as a neutral center of internationalism, had become home to the Red Cross, which eventually would assist in the Berlin food program.[28] Allen's brother, John Foster, worked in diplomatic and legal circles. Their sister, Eleanor Lansing Dulles, graduated from Bryn Mawr College in 1917, having flourished in her psychology studies, and immediately went to war-torn France to serve the war effort. She engaged with the economists who set the terms of the Treaty of Versailles before receiving her PhD in international finance at Harvard University in 1927. Her specialty was the psychology of economic behavior. In the 1930s, a General Electric fellowship took her to Germany, where she met with the Nazi propaganda minister to understand his practices. Afterward, she worked for the US government under Franklin D. Roosevelt. At the end of the Second World War, she began serving in the State Department. She became head of the Berlin desk in 1952. By the time Stalin died in 1953, her brothers had joined her and the Eisenhower administration—Allen Dulles as CIA director and John Foster as secretary of state.

Unlike most of the other women who walked the halls of the State Department, by 1952 Dulles had her own office. She was a master of what I call supple power, and once noted herself that to be effective, a woman had to take "an invisible position."[29] She used her supple power in Washington, sitting in on top-secret meetings, sometimes unnoticed as a woman assumed to be a stenographer, or intercepting classified "Eyes Only Dulles" communications meant for a brother. Yet according to Moscow, Dulles worked with her brother "stirring up new gangster acts of sabotage."[30]

"Eisenhower Packages": Political Gifts of Taste

With the death of Stalin in 1953, Washington went on high alert. The "Plan for the Psychological Exploitation of Stalin's Death" detailed ideas region by region, including gift programs for all satellite states.[31] Berlin was a key location: divided into zones, the capital city, an "island of democracy" inside Soviet-controlled East Germany, provided a railway system for communists to cross into the West (or the other way round) and experience the fruits of capitalism. It also allowed them to escape as defectors or refugees. For Dulles, East Germany was primed for revolt: over the previous two years, more than half a million people had left the East for the West through Berlin.[32] In January and February 1953, the flow of refugees swelled. When Dulles arrived in Berlin in 1952 with the Psychological Strategy Board's list of possible projects for the US ambassador, including a small Disney World for the divided city, the ambassador suggested that she install a modern kitchen in Berlin, "because the best thing in America is the kitchen." She said she would "add it to our list" but did not.[33] However, understanding psychological power, Dulles considered stockpiling food in Berlin.

Having worked at the State Department in Austria, Dulles understood the power of food, particularly in divided nations: she had arrived in Europe again just after Hitler's suicide and before the end of the Second World War. In divided Vienna, she gained stature while she worked on reconstructing the country—"trading coal for cabbage [with the Soviets] as only a woman can."[34] Indeed, unknown to many, Austria had become the only European country in which the Soviets accepted Marshall Plan assistance, however minimal.[35] From this experience, Dulles had come to understand the subtle power of "goodwill" gifts. Under her watch, CARE (Cooperative for Assistance and Relief Everywhere) packages had been distributed to the population as a precursor to the Marshall Plan. CARE International relied on "loans" from the US government to provide the population with packages made up of surplus army goods: canned meat, vegetables, fruit, tins of jam, instant coffee, powdered milk, granulated sugar, cocoa, biscuits, and even a can opener. Sometimes the packages included chewing gum and a pack of nine cigarettes—both products lacking any nutritional value. The contents stimulated both the eye and the palate: ruby reds, greens, the snow white of sugar and flour, the rush caused by sugar on the tongue and the waves of sweet taste that continued while chewing gum. And the smells: coffee, chocolate, and the aroma of sweet Kentucky tobacco. Foods spoke of material plenty in their thick cans, which stood in contrast to the thin or damaged Soviet tins. Instant items demonstrated the power of American modernization. In addition, the packages were thoughtful, coming with a can opener and matches. As a not-for-profit foundation, CARE could bring relief and even joy under Dulles's watch through this apolitical gesture removed from early US-USSR geographical power struggles.

In Vienna in June 1948, Dulles watched in shock as the Soviets imposed a blockade on Berlin, preventing food and fuel from entering. This feeling was followed by a disdain that inspired action. "Operation Vittles" began under General Lucius D. Clay: military planes navigated treacherous airspace and landed in Berlin every thirty seconds, bringing eight thousand tons of supplies each day from June 26, 1948, to September 30, 1949. Chocolate bars attached to tiny parachutes were famously dropped by an American pilot for the German children below and then systematically adopted by the Air Force to replace bombs with sweets in the public mind. That year, Dulles was called back to Washington, where she added Berlin to her portfolio.[36] She wrote, "The will of the [Germans in West Berlin] to hold fast to their freedom became the salient fact [and] amply justified our determination to come to their aid." Yet humanitarian aid was only the start: "The political importance was wider, and constituted a crucial element in the resistance to communist expansion everywhere."[37]

In 1950, a crowd of four thousand joined Dulles alongside General Clay, who became known as the "Father of Berlin," for the first ringing of the American-gifted Freedom Bell, funded by the Crusade for Freedom.[38] Dulles noted that children's pennies had funded the bell, despite the fact that the moneys had been engineered by the CIA, her brother's territory. As Dulles said of her work in Berlin, "I took a possessive, psychological approach."[39]

Yet the death of Stalin in March 1953 created a "lull" in traffic over the East-West divide, frustrating Dulles and Washington's psychological strategists.[40] However, the following month brought Dulles's big break: Bulgaria. In early April, numerous female "comrades" had been left off the work roster at the tobacco depot in Plovdiv. "You should be glad to have one piece of bread," those with husbands were told. Women staged "long angry tirades" for work, and functionaries reported to Moscow on the "propaganda" that had been circulating and had led to the unrest. "People gather at the cooperatives waiting in lines for bread and milk," wrote one official. His conclusion: "Propaganda is carried out in this way." Yet propaganda for protest was lived experience.[41] On May 3, hundreds of people struck. The women were at the front. "I'll strangle you!" one cried. A party member reported to Moscow that the "absolutely desperate" strikers wanted food and "that was what led to their fury."[42]

Unrest spread from Bulgaria to Hungary, leading to economic turmoil. Dulles used her "very effective grapevine" in Europe, exchanging letters with contacts to understand the situation in Germany.[43] Dulles petitioned Washington to build large stockpiles of food in Berlin. To support her case, the High Command officially reported on food shortages in East Germany. With Eleanor having whispered in his ear, the High Commissioner recommended in a closed Washington meeting that food distribution programs be explored as psychological propaganda to bring goodwill and humiliate the Soviets.[44] Dulles noted of the food, "The specific things I did I thought of myself."[45]

President Eisenhower asked the Psychological Strategy Board (PSB) to suggest "men" who could run a food operation for all the satellite nations, including East Germany. The board concluded that food gifts would indeed feed unrest, but for the maximum "impact," the program should wait until a crisis and "people are hungry."[46] No man was appointed. When the time was right, the unmentioned Eleanor Dulles took command.

In the late spring, Dulles egged her brothers forward to build stockpiles in Berlin, and on June 1, 1953, John Foster called her into his office and announced, "I got you some money today. I got you fifty million."[47] Dulles celebrated her purchasing power by buying sugar, wheat, cocoa, cereals, flour, butter, and margarine.[48] "There isn't a time limit on spoilage," she announced upon purchasing powdered milk, canned meat, canned fish, and coffee in a nod to modern canning and packaging technology.[49] The stashes in the West's warehouses began to swell. Working to Dulles's advantage, the Communist Party newspaper reported on the admission of past mistakes, which shocked and confused many party members and the wider populace, including farmers.⁵⁰ Yet in seeming contradiction to the apology, work quotas would be raised with no corresponding rise in salary or benefits. Detractors felt their mettle. In Washington, Eleanor Dulles insisted to the PSB, "In order to have a good psychological impact we had to be quick about what we were doing."⁵¹

Psychological Warfare Through the Senses

Dulles flew to Berlin. At 9 a.m. on June 16, workers went on strike. Dulles reported from her desk, "They climbed down off the scaffolding and walked through the streets." Thousands joined from the sidewalks. Dulles observed, "They chanted in unison: 'Decrease the production quotas. Lower the prices in state-owned stores. Down with government.'" And of key import to Dulles, who planned psychological strategy: "We want butter, not an army."⁵² Later that day, the East German government announced that work quota increases would be "voluntary," but the workers now demanded indemnity for all demonstrators, free elections, and—importantly for Dulles—price cuts for food.⁵³ Of the Soviet and East German officials, Dulles said, "They were definitely in a panic."⁵⁴

From her office the next day, Dulles could hear the echoes of guns shooting, the roundup of shouting protesters, and the Soviet tanks rolling in, recalling, "It makes you almost weep to hear this thing."⁵⁵ The American men told her to stay put, but she made her way through the streets as Soviet-trained soldiers opened water hoses on protesters to drive them back, catching the women's dresses. At the Berlin Red Cross, in tents readied outside, she began assisting, offering the several thousand wounded protesters hot food.⁵⁶

The following day, the Red Cross distributed food packages made available from the stockpiles managed by Dulles. Mirroring the CARE operation in Austria, Dulles "loaned" government food to the Red Cross. Dulles knew that the Red Cross understood that the food distribution was American "psychological warfare" and expressed her doubts "that they'd do it." However, it was hard for them to refuse, she concluded.⁵⁷ With ten-pound packages, Dulles opened up the doors to plenty. The government-funded RIAS advertised available food, and Dulles used her "word of mouth" network.⁵⁸ After braving the border in Berlin and showing an East German identity card, before receiving the package each East German person had their name and address recorded by the Western officials, along with any information about their household that could be gleaned. Although this list was theoretically constructed to prevent what I call "double dipping," it also offered information for future analysis and use.[59] The "psychological" approach garnered practical results with the names and addresses of those who came West.

Momentum in the East accelerated, aided by railroad workers and telephone operators who spread the news. Across East Germany, women and men protested against work rules and shortages of bread, the staple of the home.[60] After the protests were officially quelled on June 24, Dulles flew back to Washington.[61] She recalled her arrival in Washington from Berlin for a State Department historian: "The first thing that came to my office was a message from my brother Allen saying, 'Can't we do anything for the people in East Germany?'" Allen was not known for his altruism, but both he and Eleanor understood the power of psychology from his Swiss Agent 488. "Yes, we can do something," she said. "Allen, we can get food in."[62] Indeed, she had already.[63] Accepting an official position in Washington, Eleanor Dulles became chair of the PSB committee. "Everybody agreed with the things that I put forward," she remembered, "and I decided that from then on I could go on without any committee because a committee is a time-consuming business. And within a few days we had arranged with the bureaucratic preparations and so on for what developed into the food package program."[64] The committee then officially "borrowed" from the stockpiles accumulated by Dulles to offer the Red Cross a "loan" that had already been accepted. "If the program became successful," she decided, the State Department would "take over the end of the aid program."[65] She explained, "I told these young men in the State Department, 'When you know what you're doing, you should push with energy on it.'"[66] On July 15, the third Dulles sibling, John Foster, officially joined the effort, with the State Department backing the formal distribution of fifty thousand packages that would swell to hundreds of thousands each day. Eleanor's ten-pound parcels became known as "Eisenhower packages."

The food packages hit the senses, but only when opened. The grocery-brown paper packages tied with string and stamped with an American insignia were handed from person to person, with West reaching over a table to East, offering a smile and a few words in the shared German language. The packages contained Jack Frost or Domino cane sugar, Tasty Rice, and Gold Medal flour or just "golden flour," advertised with hues of pure white and golden swirls. The taste of the food inside—corned beef, liver loaf, and Vienna sausages—was suggested by reds, pinks, and burgundies. Candy bars, coffee, cocoa, apricot preserves, and jars of honey were decorated in a European style with fleur-de-lis and other baroque-type imprints. Recipients were impressed by the modern technology of egg and milk powder: just add water. Then there was the promise of sun-yellow margarine.[67] Some offerings were wrapped in polka dot paper and tied with string, reminiscent of a birthday present.[68] US studies had shown that it was mainly color that communicated to people whether foods were fresh or stale, clean or sullied, rancid or pure.[69]

Tasting with the Eye: Food Colors as Visual Weapons

"Hidden" in plain sight, placed in knapsacks or tucked under blankets or babies in strollers, the food all crossed into the Soviet zone.[70] The packages were snuck past neighbors, and once behind closed doors, the colors of the foods inside the tins might be shocking to people who had grown used to the bare gray building walls in the East. Tins of hamburger meat patties were depicted in "warm red" to achieve a "wholesome" look.[71] The parcels with butter or margarine equated the two products with their pale yellow color, uniformity, and freshness.[72] The peas added light green to the palate. The saturated orange of peaches in sweet syrup was completely smooth; there was no hint of unripe green fruit or a worm in the middle. These peaches were remarkable: even the pits had been removed. The clean white of the flour, sugar, and milk inspired thoughts of the modern, the holy, the pure, like the clothing of angels.[73] The saturation of the even, unadulterated colors emphasized purity, freshness, and modernity when used with staples, dried foods, luxury items, and all the fruits of capitalism (see fig. 1.1).

The distinct differences between American and Soviet food caught the eye: according to US sources, Soviet cans of meat, when opened, appeared dried at the edges, even green.[74] Newspapers blamed lax workers or even saboteurs who sided with the "imperialists" and brought thin pins to work, where they pierced tiny, imperceptible holes in the cans. By 1953, 75 percent of the canned meat from Hungary, according to reports from émigrés, was "rancid, taste[d] terrible, or [was] inedible."[75] Soviet butter "was only good as soap."[76] The Soviet "proof" was not "in the pudding," whether canned or boxed. The West delivered.

In the early summer months, the propaganda worked, even if the people never brought the food home. "Many Germans, even from regions far away in the GDR [German Democratic Republic], are coming to Berlin to pick up

Fig. 1.1
Selling with colors:
CARE package. Photo:
Maik Rositzki / CARE
International.

packages," Polish intelligence reported.[77] Dulles recalled that, as the handheld packages were carried into the East, "the Russians were put in a very queer position. If they stopped people coming in to get food, it would stir the populace up still further. If the Russians let them come in [to West Berlin,] . . . each one got a sense for himself and his family that America was helping."[78] Yet rumors circulated, and RIAS reported that at the border train station, the East German government had installed kiosks where those returning from the West with packages were required to donate the "imperialist" food to "starving" West Berliners—who never saw a thing.[79]

The East Germans attempted to stop the flow of food with propaganda. Posters showed plentiful food coming from Eastern Bloc farms together with graphic depictions of hunger in the West.[80] Confusing the issue, newspapers admitted the existence of food shortages in the East but explained that they were because the Americans had "driven farmers into the concentration camps of the West," where, without a home or land, they were "condemned to wage slavery."[81] The visual propaganda included cartoons, with one featuring Eleanor Dulles as a cheap overweight prostitute dancing for margarine with her brother, Allen, standing behind her, egging her on, labeled "CIA."[82]

Growing desperate, the East Germans offered their own communist "food packages" to West Berliners, including "pensioners and the unemployed." All the West Berliners had to do was go to the East and present their identity cards. As opposed to the 260,000 packages given by the United States to the East Germans, on August 1, the East Germans had only fifty "Western" takers in the East. Most were denied packages because upon inspection of their identity cards it was determined by communist officers that the seekers were from the East themselves, double dipping, as it were.[83]

Operation Christmas East: Europeanizing the Food Program

Inspired by the operation in East Germany, and perhaps the Soviet copycat response, Eisenhower instructed Eleanor Dulles to start food package programs to Hungary, Poland, and Czechoslovakia.[84] Propaganda minister C. D. Jackson sent Allen Dulles the official "President's Proposed Plan to Institute a Food Program for the Satellite States Similar to the Current Program for East Germany." Hungary and Poland were particularly primed, experiencing shortages of "fats, sugar, eggs, rice, flour, wheats, dried fruits and vegetables, canned meats, and yeast," much of which was being sent to East Germany to quell that population's unrest, thus fueling satellite unrest.[85]

As August wore on, with workers hiding more and more food in backpacks and perambulators, East German border searches became more invasive. Tensions escalated, with "clashes" reported at crossing points in East Berlin. In Potsdam and Cottbus, police fired on mobs in railway stations. When the government suspended railcars to Berlin, workers at chemical plants near Halle attempted a mass march to the city for food packages. The capitalistic "profiteers" who sold food were placed on trial and given severe punishments, which were reported on in newspapers.[86] The United States determined that goodwill had been an excellent weapon, but if lives were endangered by the offering, the psychology of the gift and its seductive power became tainted. Dulles agreed, and by early fall 1953, the program had been officially suspended.[87]

Although fall 1953 marked the official end to the program, the food operations continued under the heading "Top Secret."[88] According to Dulles, to get packages past Communist Bloc customs officials, the Americans "changed the label on the sacks and boxes and made [them] the gift of the

Russians."[89] Despite these forged customs marks indicating the packages were Soviet-to-Soviet bloc mailings, if opened for inspection by East German officials, the colorful branded items inside betrayed their origins as 100 percent American. Yet planning continued. American agencies mailed packages to potentially hungry dissidents, "Aunt Hilda and Uncle Fritz," whose names had been gathered that summer when the dissidents had collected Eisenhower packages.[90] Dulles herself gathered "bona fide" names or even just addresses in Poland and Hungary from German friends. She noted, "This was another move of what you might call psychological warfare."[91] Accurately assessing the program, Polish officials in East Germany reported to Moscow that the food program was "a propaganda trick and a way to recruit new spies and saboteurs." It was tied to "a fascist American underground" and encompassed "a broad international network."[92]

Some in Washington's conference rooms argued that the food program could not be extended to the satellite nations if there were no shortages. Others disagreed. With winter approaching and no natural disaster in sight, solutions were sought. The coming Christmas season provided inspiration in the fight against the "atheist" Soviets. The PSB initiated "Operation Christmas East," which would deliver CARE's packaged milk, canned beef and gravy, rice, vegetable shortening, sugar, prunes, raisins, and honey from "the land of milk and honey." CARE sought private donations from Americans, and government planning became specific: employees were encouraged not to send Christmas cards to office friends and instead to donate the money they would have used on cards and stamps to CARE in boxes set out in lobbies. Indeed, the cash till was topped off by the CIA in coins and bills.[93] CARE dubbed the program "Operation Reindeer."

That spring, numerous other ideas were floated. Of the food, Dulles said, "It was a queer sort of propaganda gesture on our part," and new ideas followed.[94] With the 1954 Easter holiday not far off, Jackson proposed dropping Bibles as well as fourteen-pound CARE packages on satellite nations using balloons. Others objected: if spoiled food were found days after a drop, it could be used by the communists to demonstrate American wastefulness.[95] Dulles considered ways to encourage a one-year anniversary revolt for East Berlin in June, but with no success. Eisenhower announced Public Law 480, which allowed the export of surplus US goods, and he referred to the "Eisenhower packages" when announcing the program: "We asked no remuneration, no return, no exchange of goods. We just put it there for humanitarian purposes." But onlookers noted the propaganda effect.[96]

Summer brought a windfall: after heavy rains, the Danube flooded, causing crop damage and food shortages in Hungary, Czechoslovakia, Romania, and Yugoslavia.[97] Concerning the government response, the PSB wrote, "On the food matter, [Allen Dulles] thinks it is pretty important to set it up so it does not look like propaganda."[98] In public, Eisenhower offered assistance to all affected areas. Although Romania refused to accept help, Hungary and Czechoslovakia accepted support from CARE. After the crisis eased, the government continued to closely monitor natural disasters and potential food shortages in the satellite nations, and packages continued to be sent.[99]

1956 became a banner year for those who believed the seeds had been planted by the food propaganda. June again provided inspiration with the Poznań uprising in Poland, and the United States and CARE sent food packages in response, fueling discontent through the more porous Polish mail channels. In addition, Polish dissidents who received goods in bulk could more easily forward the enticing goods to Hungarians than the Americans. Soviet-to-Soviet nation mail flowed more easily with fewer checks. Desires were monitored and fulfilled, parcel by mailed parcel: people wanted sugar, coffee, chocolate, and "fruits from warm climates."[100] And they received them. With the sweet tastes of chocolate, sugar, and capitalist "fruits," "total Cold War" was waged with the help of Radio Free Europe's Crusade for Freedom programming and with balloon leaflet operations in tow. With the 1956 uprising in Hungary, while radio incited violence, in the aftermath CARE sent packages to refugees in Hungary and other nations including food as well as farming supplies and other goods.

Conclusion: The Supple Power of Seduction

Despite the brutal and deadly suppression of the Hungarians and the lack of immediate US support for the protesters, the CIA continued to be inspired by "the food situation in the restless bloc nations" and anticipated more "worker dissatisfaction."[101] Indeed, Albania needed potatoes, sugar, oils, and vegetables; options were studied and packages sent in.[102] Since the weather and natural disasters could not be relied on, but distribution and supply problems were endemic to the Soviet system, the US government program and CARE pressed forward with package programs through 1958. Dulles concluded, "Of course the food itself meant a lot to the families, but it was the political significance that mattered."[103]

This public-private model of food gifting was so successful that by 1958 the Soviets had created successful dummy companies "to squeeze out" the United States.[104] Agencies like Parcels to Russia, Inc., Central Parcel Service, and the Globe Travel Service collected dollars from Americans in New York and Chicago for Eastern Bloc gifts to "friends and relatives." If "imitation is the sincerest form of flattery," then the Soviet riff on the American project is "proof in the pudding" that person-to-person and seemingly apolitical gifts of food with appealing tastes and colors served as a potent Cold War weapon.

Early plans for the US pavilion in Moscow included an American kitchen stocked with Gold Medal flour and other delights.[105] Food gifts continued because "shortages will continue to plague the housewife." Once again, women were at the center of Cold War strategies. Using goodwill as a weapon, US packaging, from branding to stamps and the foods inside, would encourage dissent through supple power mechanisms and give women the "freedom" to choose the home front, thus reinforcing Western capitalistic gender norms. These packages all came from the "land of milk and honey," as Washington called the United States.[106] Featuring homes stocked with American symbols of plenty—milk and flour flowing white and pure, honey and sugar sweet and golden, and powders and thick tin cans both reliable and modern—psychological propaganda and the supple power of the seduction of the senses targeted populations judged ripe for dissent, person by person, home to home. Although overshadowed in the historiography by the 1959 Kitchen Debate in Moscow, food "operations" that relied on tropes ranging from religious crusades to balloons, mothers, and Santa Claus used color to militarize the sensorium in Cold War battles for "hearts and minds."

Notes

1. *West Germany Demonstrators*, photograph, BBC, https://www.bbc.co.uk/programmes/pooh5jrd.

2. "Germany 1953," Population Pyramids of the World from 1950 to 2100, United Nations, https://www.populationpyramid.net/germany/1953/.

3. Bardeleben, oral history with the author, November 29, 2011, New York, transcript available with permission of the author, otherwise closed, Victoria Phillips Collection, Music Division, Library of Congress, Washington, DC.

4. Treber, *Mythos Trümmerfrauen*, author's translation.

5. Feiereisen, "They 'Tried' to Divide the Sky."

6. Dietrich von Thadden, "The RIAS in Berlin: The RIAS Identification," sound recording, https://www.rundfunkschaetze.de/en/der-rias/.

7. Foreign Relations (15040), Item No. 7592/53, "Poland: *Polish Tea Party*," Source Berlin, July 22, 1953, http://hdl.handle.net/10891/osa:1ab1dcec-bc52-4054-9271-b171d4114489_l, Vera and Donald Blinken Open Society Archives, Central European

University, Budapest, Hungary (hereafter HU OSA).

8. Harmin Patil, *Uprising of 1953 in East Germany*, photograph, Alchetron, https://alchetron.com/Uprising-of-1953-in-East-Germany.
9. Ellul, *Propaganda*, 257.
10. Smith, "Producing Sense," 842.
11. Foucault, *History of Sexuality*, 1:86.
12. "First Phase-Axis Penetration," box 7, folder 59, series O, RG 4, FA350, Nelson A. Rockefeller personal papers, Rockefeller Archive Center, Tarrytown, NY; Gienow-Hecht, "Nation Branding," 755–79; Alexander and Nobbs, "Multi-Sensory Fashion Retail Experiences," 420–21.
13. Derrida, "Hostipitality," 6; Derrida, *Adieu . . . to Emmanuel Levinas*, 19; Derrida, "Hospitality," 65.
14. Derrida, "Hospitality," 82.
15. Derrida, "Hospitality," 82.
16. Bourdieu, *Outline of a Theory of Practice*, 6.
17. Heal, *Power of Gifts*, 7; Berking, *Sociology of Gifting*.
18. Bourdieu, *Outline of a Theory of Practice*, 7.
19. Jay, "In the Realm of the Senses," 315; Le Breton, *Sensing the World*, 53, 55.
20. Goethe, *Theory of Colours*.
21. Hisano, *Visualizing Taste*, 3.
22. Hisano, *Visualizing Taste*, 1.
23. Le Breton, *Sensing the World*, 53.
24. Hisano, *Visualizing Taste*, 29, 31, 242n64.
25. Moor, "Operation Hospitality," 293.
26. Tunc, "Eating in Survival Town," 182.
27. Bair, *Jung*.
28. Scaglia, *Emotions of Internationalism*.
29. Dulles, *Chances of a Lifetime*, 256.
30. "Official Correspondence and Reports, 1931–1968," clippings, box 11, folder 1953, Eleanor Lansing Dulles Papers, 1880–1984, Dwight D. Eisenhower Library, Abilene, KS; Ostermann and Byrne, *Uprising in East Germany*, 138, 163; Alison Smale, "60 Years Later, Germany Recalls Its Anti-Soviet Revolt," *New York Times*, June 18, 2013, A4; Wasserstein, *Barbarism and Civilization*, 494.
31. "Plan for the Psychological Exploitation of Stalin's Death," March 17, 1953, RDP80-01065A000300040061-4, Central Intelligence Agency (hereafter CIA).
32. Ostermann and Byrne, *Uprising in East Germany*, 158.
33. Dulles, *Chances of a Lifetime*, 258.
34. Dulles, *Chances of a Lifetime*, 258; author's interview with Joan Dulles.
35. Stourzh and Mueller, *Cold War over Austria*.
36. Dulles, *Chances of a Lifetime*, 184.
37. Dulles, *Chances of a Lifetime*, 185.
38. "City Hears Peals of Freedom Bell: The Freedom Bell Welcomed at City Hall," *New York Times*, September 9, 1950, 32.
39. Dulles, "Reminiscences of Eleanor Lansing Dulles: Oral History Interview with Eleanor Lansing Dulles," reel 14, page 564 (hereafter ELD, Reel Number:Page Number, e.g., R14.564), Dwight D. Eisenhower Library, Abilene, KS; Presidential Project, Oral History Research Office, Oral History Collection, Rare Books and Manuscript Collection, Columbia University, New York, NY.
40. ELD, R13:535–36.
41. Ostermann and Byrne, *Uprising in East Germany*, 89.
42. Ostermann and Byrne, *Uprising in East Germany*, 89; FR: Stephan Kiradzhiev, Depot at BDT Monopol—Plovdiv branch, "Report on Disturbances at the Tobacco Depot in Plovdiv, Bulgaria," May 7, 1953, Digital Archive, Wilson Center, Washington, DC, https://digitalarchive.wilsoncenter.org/document/111324.
43. ELD, R13:537.
44. "862B.03/5–1153: Telegram," The Acting Director of the Berlin Element, HICOG [High Commission for Germany] (Maynard) to the Office of the United States High Commissioner for Germany, at Bonn, Berlin, May 11, 1953, no. 707, Germany and Austria, 1952–1954, Volume VII, Part 2, Historical Documents, Foreign Relations of the United States, Office of the Historian, Department of State, Washington, DC (hereafter "862B.03/5–1153: Telegram," FRUS VII), 942–46.
45. "862B.03/5–1153: Telegram."
46. "President's Proposed Plan to Institute a Food Program for the Satellites Similar to the Current Program for East Germany," July 14, 1953, RDP80R01731R003300320004-1, CIA.
47. ELD, R14:568.
48. ELD, R14:578–79.

49. ELD, R14:578–79.
50. Ostermann and Byrne, *Uprising in East Germany*, 20.
51. ELD, R15:613.
52. ELD, R15:598.
53. Hutchinson, "History and Political Literature," 369; Ostermann and Byrne, *Uprising in East Germany*, 164.
54. ELD, R15:593.
55. ELD, R14:585. While the death toll is officially set at fifty-five, the number of protesters killed has been estimated at well over one hundred. In addition, several thousand may have been sent to penal camps. See Timothy Jones, "Berlin Commemorates 1953 Uprising in East Germany," *Deutsche Welle*, June 17, 2017, https://www.dw.com/en/berlin-commemorates-1953-uprising-in-east-germany/a-39289423. For a range of accounts, see Dale, *Popular Protest in East Germany*, 9–11; Green, *Politics of the New Germany*, ch. 2.
56. ELD, R14:585.
57. ELD, R15:624.
58. ELD, R14:564.
59. Lists der Nachzügler zur Paketaktion, B Rep 002, Nr. 1772, Landesarchiv Berlin.
60. Pritchard, *Making of the GDR*, 211.
61. Ostermann and Byrne, *Uprising in East Germany*, 170.
62. ELD, R15:625.
63. ELD, R15:619.
64. ELD, R15:619.
65. ELD, R14:571.
66. ELD, R14:566; "862B.03/5–1153: Telegram," FRUSVII.
67. Carolyn Hughes Crowley, "Aid in Small Boxes," *Smithsonian Magazine*, April 30, 2001, 35, https://www.smithsonianmag.com/history/aid-in-small-boxes-42294902/.
68. Photographs, Victoria Phillips Collection, box 23, folder 42, Music Division, Library of Congress, Washington, DC.
69. Herrick, "Food Colors Increase Attractiveness," 659, quoted in Hisano, *Visualizing Taste*, 232n10.
70. "Editorial Note," No. 735, FRUSVII, 1624.
71. Hisano, *Visualizing Taste*, 47–49.
72. Visser, *Much Depends on Dinner*.
73. Birren, *Selling with Color*, 105, 114, 125.
74. "Czechoslovakia, Standard of Living [Food]," Item 11437/53, November 18, 1953, http://hdl.handle.net/10891/osa:a0440516-8ca5-4fca-ac33-7a97b370754a_l, HU OSA.
75. "Czechoslovakia," Item 10388/55, December 23, 1952, http://hdl.handle.net/10891/osa:c307c5dc-8edf-4c2c-a6cf-53186e2c3874_l, HU OSA.
76. "Czechoslovakia, Standard of Living [Rations]," Item 15698/5, http://hdl.handle.net/10891/osa:839a342d-d855-4594-b833-30c596cceob_l, HU OSA.
77. "Report of the Polish Diplomatic Mission in Berlin for the Period 21 June–31 August 1953," September 1953, A MSZ, Dep. IV, Niemcy, NRD, sygn. 10/366/40, HPPPD, Digital Archive, Wilson Center, Washington, DC, http://digitalarchive.wilsoncenter.org/document/112607.
78. ELD, R15:612–13.
79. "East German Action Against the Western Food Program," August 4, 1953, RDP79R00890A000100070029-8, CIA; "Report of the Polish Diplomatic Mission."
80. "East German Action."
81. "Eastern Germany," Item 04397/53, April 27, 1953, http://hdl.handle.net/10891/osa:ebdcbfb5-4107-42ad-aa59-6fe96f6efae6_l, HU OSA.
82. *Windstärke 12*.
83. "East German Action."
84. ELD, R15:622.
85. "Poland, Standard of Living [Food]," Item 8998/53, September 3, 1953, http://hdl.handle.net/10891/osa:1c26f16a-39e5-46a0-b576-f498c61421c3_l, HU OSA.
86. "Poland, Standard of Living [Food]."
87. ELD, R15:618.
88. ELD, R15:618.
89. ELD, R15:615.
90. ELD, R15:615.
91. ELD, R15:619.
92. "Report of the Polish Diplomatic Mission."
93. "Exchange of Christmas Cards," October 15, 1954, RDP62S00545A000100020055-4, CIA.
94. ELD, R15:622.
95. "848.49/10–1353 Telegram," The Secretary of State to the Embassy in Poland, October 13, 1953, No. 46, FRUSVIII.
96. William Lambers, "Food for Peace: Eisenhower's Unsung Initiative Can Be

Obama's Most Powerful Tool for Peace," History News Network, September 2, 2009, The George Washington University, https://historynewsnetwork.org/article/61472.

97. "864.49/8-1354 Telegram," The Minister in Hungary (Ravndal) to the Department of State, August 13, 1954, No. 57, FRUS VIII.

98. Memorandum of a Telephone Conversation to Eisenhower, from Secretary of State and the Director of Central Intelligence (Dulles), June 29, 1956, FRUS VIII.

99. Memorandum of a Telephone Conversation to Eisenhower, from Secretary of State and the Director of Central Intelligence (Dulles), June 29, 1956, FRUS VIII.

100. "Life in Czechoslovakia," November 12, 1953, RDP80-00809A000500250161-3, CIA.

101. "The 1956/57 Food Situation in European Satellites," October 17, 1956, RDP79T00935A000400130001-6, CIA.

102. "1956/57 Food Situation."

103. ELD, R15:613.

104. "Reds Get Millions Here to Insure Food Gifts," July 11, 1957, RDP78-01634R000100110012-6, CIA.

105. "1956/57 Food Situation."

106. "1956/57 Food Situation."

Bibliography

Archival Sources

Central European University, Budapest, Hungary: Vera and Donald Blinken Open Society Archives, Records of the Radio Free Europe / Radio Liberty Research Institute, Radio Free Europe Information Items: General Records, Polish Unit.

Central Intelligence Agency, Washington, DC: Freedom of Information Act Electronic Reading Room, Foreign Relations of the United States Historical Documents, Office of the Historian, State Department.

Columbia University, New York, NY: Rare Books and Manuscript Collection.

Dwight D. Eisenhower Library, Abilene, KS: Eleanor Lansing Dulles Papers, 1880–1973; C. D. Jackson Papers, 1931–1967; Abbot Washburn Papers, 1938–2003.

George Washington University, Washington, DC: Special Collections Research Center, Eleanor Lansing Dulles Papers, 1867–1993.

Landesarchiv Berlin, Berlin, Germany: B Rep 002, Nr. 1772.

Library of Congress, Washington, DC: Music Division, Victoria Phillips Collection, oral history with Armgard von Bardeleben.

Rockefeller Archive Center, Tarrytown, NY: Nelson A. Rockefeller: Personal Papers.

Wilson Center, Washington, DC: Digital Archive, Interviews and Oral Histories, Eleanor Lansing Dulles.

Published Sources

Alexander, Bethan, and Karinna Nobbs. "Multi-Sensory Fashion Retail Experiences: The Impact of Sound, Smell, Sight and Touch on Consumer Based Brand Equity." In *Handbook of Research on Global Fashion Management and Merchandising*, edited by Alessandra Vecchi and Chitra Buckley, 420–43. Hershey: IGI Global, 2016.

Bair, Deirdre. *Jung: A Biography*. New York: Little, Brown, 2003.

Berking, Helmuth. *A Sociology of Gifting*. Translated by Patrick Camiller. London: Sage, 1999.

Birren, Faber. *Selling with Color*. New York: McGraw-Hill, 1945.

Bourdieu, Pierre. *Outline of a Theory of Practice*. Translated by Richard Nice. New York: Cambridge University Press, 1977.

Dale, Gareth. *Popular Protest in East Germany, 1945–1989*. London: Routledge, 2016.

De Grazia, Victoria. *Irresistible Empire: America's Advance Through Twentieth-Century Europe*. Cambridge: Harvard University Press, 2005.

Derrida, Jacques. *Adieu . . . to Emmanuel Levinas*. Translated by Pascale-Anne Brault and Michael Naas. Stanford: Stanford University Press, 1999.

———. "From Adieu à Emmanuel Levinas." *Research in Phenomenology* 28 (1998): 20–36.

———. "Hospitality, Justice and Responsibility." In *Questioning Ethics: Contemporary Debates in Philosophy*, edited by Richard Kearney and Mark Dooley, 65–83. London: Routledge, 1999.

———. "Hostipitality." *Journal of the Theoretical Humanities* 5, no. 3 (2000): 3–18.

Dulles, Eleanor Lansing. *Chances of a Lifetime: A Memoir*. New York: Prentice Hall, 1980.

Ellul, Jacques. *Propaganda: The Formation of Men's Attitudes*. Translated by Konrad Kellen and Jean Lerner. New York: Knopf, 1965.

Feiereisen, Florence. "They 'Tried' to Divide the Sky: Listening to Cold War Berlin." *Colloquia Germanica* 46, no. 4 (2013): 410–32.

Foucault, Michel. *The Archaeology of Knowledge*. Translated by A. M. Sheridan Smith. New York: Harper & Row, 1976.

———. *The History of Sexuality*. Vol. 1. *The Will to Knowledge*. Translated by Robert Hurley. New York: Penguin Books, 1998.

Gienow-Hecht, Jessica. "Nation Branding: A Useful Category for International History." *Diplomacy and Statecraft* 30, no. 4 (2019): 755–79.

Goethe, Johann Wolfgang von. *The Theory of Colours*. Translated by Charles Lock Eastlake (1840). London: F. Cass, 1967. Reprint, Delhi: Lector House, 2019.

Green, Simon. *The Politics of the New Germany*. London: Routledge, 2011.

Heal, Felicity. *The Power of Gifts: Gift Exchange in Early Modern England*. New York: Oxford, 2014.

Herrick, Horace T. "Food Colors Increase Attractiveness in Harmless Fashion." *Food Industries* 1, no. 14 (1929): 659–703.

Hisano, Ai. *Visualizing Taste: How Business Changed the Color of What You Eat*. Cambridge: Harvard University Press, 2019.

Howes, David, ed. *A Cultural History of the Senses in the Modern Age*. 6 vols. London: Bloomsbury, 2014.

Hutchinson, Peter. "History and Political Literature: The Interpretation of the 'Day of German Unity' in the Literature of East and West." *Modern Language Review* 76, no. 2 (1981): 367–82.

Jay, Martin. "In the Realm of the Senses: An Introduction." *American Historical Review* 116, no. 2 (2011): 307–15.

Le Breton, David. *Sensing the World: An Anthropology of the Senses*. Translated by Carmen Ruschiensky. Paris: Métailié, 2006. Reprint, London: Bloomsbury Academic, 2017.

Mohnhaupt, J. W., and Shelly Frisch. *The Zookeepers' War: An Incredible True Story from the Cold War*. New York: Simon and Schuster, 2017.

Moor, Angela. "Operation Hospitality Las Vegas and Civil Defense, 1951–1959." *Nevada Historical Society Quarterly* 51, no. 4 (2008): 292–310.

Ostermann, Christian F., and Malcom Byrne. *Uprising in East Germany, 1953: The Cold War, the German Question, and the First Major Upheaval Behind the Iron Curtain*. Washington, DC: Central European University Press, 2001.

Pritchard, Gareth. *The Making of the GDR: From Antifascism to Stalinism*. Manchester: Manchester University Press, 2000.

Scaglia, Ilaria. *The Emotions of Internationalism: Feeling International Cooperation in the Alps in the Interwar Period*. New York: Oxford University Press, 2019.

Schmacks, Yanara. "'Only Mothers Can Be True Revolutionaries': The Politization of Motherhood in 1980s West German Psychoanalysis." *Psychoanalysis and History* 23, no. 1 (2021): 49–73.

Smith, Mark M. "Producing Sense, Consuming Sense, Making Sense: Perils and Prospects for Sensory History." *Journal of Social History* 40, no. 4 (2007): 841–58.

Stourzh, Gerald, and Wolfgang Mueller. *A Cold War over Austria: The Struggle for the State Treaty, Neutrality, and the End of East-West Occupation,*

1945–1955. Cambridge: Harvard University Press, 2018.

Treber, Leonie. *Mythos Trümmerfrauen: Von der Trümmerbeseitigung in der Kriegs—und Nachkriegszeit und der Entstehung eins deutschen Erinnerungsortes*. Essen: Klartext, 2014.

Tunc, Tanfer Emin. "Eating in Survival Town: Food in 1950s Atomic America." *Cold War History* 15, no. 2 (2015): 179–200.

Visser, Margaret. *Much Depends on Dinner: The Extradentary History, Mythology, Allure and Obsessions, Perils and Taboos of an Ordinary Meal*. New York: Grove, 1986.

Wasserstein, Bernard. *Barbarism and Civilization: A History of Europe in Our Time*. New York: Oxford University Press, 2007.

Windstärke 12: Eine Auswahl neuer deutscher Karikaturen. Dresden: VEB Verlag der Kunst, 1953. https://research.calvin.edu/german-propaganda-archive/wind.htm.

CHAPTER 2

Between Soir de Paris and Red Moscow

Olfactory Front Lines in Polish Perfumery

Stephanie Weismann

Polish perfumes had an air of "domestic elegance," Soviet fragrances were considered "extremely stinky," and French scents smelled of a "more colorful life." The olfactory location of the Polish People's Republic among the Polish domestic cosmetics industry, Soviet emanations, and Western scents seems to reflect the country's conflicting, in-between position within the Eastern Bloc and Europe more broadly. Poland has always been an area of geopolitical interest for both the East and the West. During the Cold War, the battle over spheres of influence was also fought on an olfactory level. Sniffing through the perfume landscape in Communist Party–led Poland, this chapter follows olfactory notions in Cold War Europe by poking its nose into cosmetics products and their semantics. It focuses not on smells, per se, but on the meaning and perception of these smells for people in Poland.[1] Considering the role of sensations, especially olfaction, in producing sociality, identity, and culture,[2] it explores the sensory orders of Cold War Europe, looking at how olfactory denotations and connotations played a role in Poland's self-positioning: ideological front lines were in part reflected in and affirmed by cosmetics products and their respective scents. Although the olfactory notion of conflicts[3] and identity[4] have been considered in previous studies, the Eastern European realm has rarely been the focus of such sensory analyses.[5] Yet the Iron Curtain situation and the anticipatory potential of smells provide a most interesting field of research.

Sources include interviews about individual experiences of smell,[6] selected discussions from internet forums,[7] advertisements for cosmetics in women's magazines,[8] and the history of the Polish cosmetics industry. The chapter discusses encounters with smell and ideas about odor and assesses Poland's (perfumery) positioning in the 1970s and 1980s. Finally, it examines how smells are remembered, taking into account that "olfaction plays a vital role in one's active (re)construction of the past."[9] As recollections are suffused with individual and collective sensations and emotions,[10] the chapter seeks to link physiological phenomena with the social and cultural spheres.[11]

(Un)Scented Socialism?

The Eastern Bloc has hardly ever been associated with pleasant smells or refined cosmetics. Instead, the dominant image of the region was one of scarcity and totalitarianism. Many sensory recollections of Eastern Europe under state socialism mention the "totalitarian" smells of cooked cabbage or noxious disinfectants[12]—smells that stood in contrast to the seductive scents of French perfumes or the "clean" odors of German detergents. Although the regimes of smell in Cold War Europe were certainly not so fixed, impressions and ideas about odors played—and continue to play—a significant role in defining "better" and "worse" as well as notions of "we" and "others."[13] Smell functions as a (social) medium that can be employed to formulate constructions and judgments of "others" (whether based on race, class, gender, or ideology) and to establish sensory orders. These sensory orders are culturally and ideologically learned[14] and denote the normative moral and aesthetic value of a smell.

The cosmetics sector was highly influential both in the formation of Communist Party–led governments in Eastern Europe and their dissolution, albeit with differing nuances. From the turn of the nineteenth century, progress in Europe was measured by fighting malodors.[15] Since then, the level of stench or scent in a place has served as an indicator of civilization.[16] Soaps and cleaning articles thus played a crucial ideological role also in establishing a notion of the ideal human body in the new workers' states. The production of soap to maintain the hygiene and thus the health of workers was a prominent part of the Soviet Union's first five-year plan from 1928 to 1933.[17] The same can be observed in the early years of the Polish People's Republic. The nationalization of industry after the Second World War involved several production plants for cosmetics. The introduction of new hygiene standards to broad swathes of the population, especially in the countryside, was a major part of the modernization agenda of the young Communist Party–led state.[18] Bad smells, usually of the organic variety, were equated with backward housing and working conditions, which in turn were attributed to the "capitalist" or "feudalist" society of prewar Poland. For this reason, soap was the most vigorously distributed cosmetics product in the country, and its main purpose was to reduce epidemics known as "dirty hands diseases."[19] The intense public discourse about the necessity of hygiene and the battle against organic odors reflected the eager efforts of the new Polish government to establish a healthy, clean state body.

Indeed, the first generation born in the Polish People's Republic appears to have had a disinclination toward strong smells—but also toward strong aromas. In the oral interviews conducted for this chapter, narratives about personal hygiene practices and the use of cosmetics repeatedly invoked the idea of "unscented cleanliness."[20] "Just be clean, that's all; you don't have to smell of anything to be clean"—this was the prevailing attitude of the predominantly female interviewees born in the 1950s and early 1960s. One interviewee remarked, "I somehow was taught it was best to be natural. When you're clean, washed, even only with this hard soap . . . then you're clean and fragrant. You don't have to smell artificial."[21] Cleanliness was thus defined as a state of not smelling; who or what did not smell was considered clean. Initial ideas about cleanliness and body hygiene were based not on smelling pleasant but on avoiding emitting any odors. This infatuation with inodorous cleanliness clearly reflects the major hygiene interventions of early state socialism, but it also hints at the sparse assortment of cosmetic products, which attests to the generally difficult economic situation in the early decades of postwar Europe. Thus, both body odors as well as body scents provoked strong emotions.[22]

In Bad Odor

Smells have high potential to provoke judgments.[23] Yet apart from our individual attitudes toward certain smells, impressions of odors also give information about the perceived superiority or inferiority of cultures and serve as an expression of distinction:[24] the sociologist Anthony Synnott aptly stated, "We do sniff each other out, literally as well as figuratively."[25] Body odors as well as the quality and cost of fragrances do symbolize the class structure of society. However, the aforementioned noticeable emphasis on unscented cleanliness cannot be read only with regard to body odors and personal hygiene. This general mistrust toward strong smells played out ideologically as well, including in images and notions of "the West" and "the East."

People not only fought the bodily smells of "backward" hygienic conditions but also wrinkled their noses at the heavy perfumes imported from the Soviet Union. Soviet perfumes distributed in Poland had a rather bad reputation. Both in the interviews conducted for this chapter as well as in recollections exchanged on the internet, the Soviet perfumes are unanimously recalled as strong, primitive, and tasteless—and they are sometimes even referred to as "insecticides."[26] The historically grounded Polish mistrust of everything "Russian" also played out olfactorily. Soviet scents, subsumed under the Russian term *ruskie duchi* (духи), were considered obtrusive and dominant.[27] A female interviewee born in 1959 remembers, "They reeked intensely, indeed. But I think that this somehow also reflected them as Russian, these perfumes. They were absolutely stifling and very strong. Really, they were associated with stench."[28] Soviet perfumes were, like the Soviet Union, literally in bad odor. While strong organic smells were considered a health threat, the fragrance of Soviet perfumes like Red Moscow (Krasnaya Moskva) indicated that something else was "foul" in the country. The skeptical attitudes toward Soviet scents in Poland underline the symbolic meaning of odors for national or ideological ideas and stereotypes.

Interestingly, what was considered the epitome of the Soviet scent (or stink)—namely, the Red Moscow perfume—reflects a French perfumery connection from the Tsarist Empire, as recently shown in Karl Schlögel's *Der Duft der Imperien*.[29] Late imperial Russia was considered a center of global perfumery, and St. Petersburg and Moscow were home to several French cosmetics enterprises. Among the most prominent were Rallet—Russia's preeminent manufacturer of fine perfume, soap, and cosmetics and the official supplier to the Tsarist Court—and its chief competitor, Brocard. Thus, the perfumery smellscape of the golden age of Russian perfumery and cosmetics between 1821 and 1921[30] was mainly shaped by French perfumers. In 1913, Rallet's technical director, Ernest Beaux, introduced the legendary perfume

Bouquet de l'Imperatrice Catherine II in honor of the tercentenary of the Romanov dynasty. This fragrance would later serve as the basis for the most French of French perfumes, Chanel No. 5, and it may also have influenced the Soviet cult scent Red Moscow.

When Ernest Beaux left Bolshevik Russia and returned to France after the Russian Revolution, he carried in his personal baggage the recipe for his legendary Romanov fragrance, which he would later adapt to French noses. Ultimately, none other than Coco Chanel would choose the fifth sample he provided, thus giving birth to Chanel No. 5. Brocard's main perfumer, Auguste Michel, however, stayed in the Soviet Union and continued to work for his former company, now bolshevized and renamed Novaya Zarya (New Dawn). Novaya Zarya was destined to become the largest perfume and cosmetics company of the Soviet Union. Both star perfumers of French origin had been disciples of Alexandre Lemerciers, master perfumer of the Rallet company in Tsarist Russia, and they knew each other's creations well. While Beaux had created Chanel No. 5 on the basis of his Romanov perfume, Auguste Michel, with the same background as a French perfumery expert in Tsarist Russia, created the most famous of Soviet perfumes, Red Moscow, in 1925. Thus, the classics of French and Soviet perfumery have more in common than is generally assumed. Although they belong to different worlds and ideologies, they both epitomize in their own ways the end of a previous belle epoque and a revolution put into a flacon—as stated by Schlögel.[31] Transformations in the cosmetics sector and novel fragrances marking a new era can also be observed in the case of Poland.

An Air of Prosperity

French perfumes—as well as German soaps and detergents—always had a much better reputation in Poland than did domestic or Soviet cosmetic products. In the late 1960s, several strikes and riots rocked the Eastern Bloc. People in Poland protested the increases in food prices, among other austerity measures, and demanded affordable products. Edward Gierek, who was appointed first secretary after the tensions of 1968, decided to quiet the Polish people's unrest by, among other things, providing access to a larger number of consumer goods. With the help of foreign loans, he established something of a socialist welfare state, fostering newfound economic prosperity and raising living standards. After the proclamation of the "border of friendship" with East Germany in 1972, massive trader tourism and a transborder shopping culture emerged.[32] Officials were quick to realize the great value of having a secondary marketplace to provide citizens with cheaper and more available goods. The shopping trips were meaningful cultural and sensory experiences, and it was especially the smells of the scenery across the border that shaped ideas about the possibility of a different way of living.

The interviewees often described their first experiences of East Germany with language like "It was like entering a new sphere, above all another zone of smells."[33] From the Polish perspective, this specific German "smell zone," as an epitome of "well-being," applied to both East and West Germany: "Germany? Everything there smelled extraordinarily pleasant."[34] This paradise was captured in the toilets that smelled better but mainly in the scent of consumer goods—coffee, detergent, canned ham, and (Fa) brand soap. The border of friendship with East Germany provided the bodily experience and realization that, across the western boundary, things just smelled better. Pleasant smells belong to the most prominent agents of "well-being." The Gierek era introduced several pleasant new smells and a novel olfactory landscape, simulating a newfound sense of prosperity after the rather unprosperous years of Gierek's predecessor, which had been symbolized by "unscented cleanliness."

In addition to trips and experiences with other (state socialist) countries, in 1972 the newly founded Polish chain of hard currency shops named Pewex (short for "internal export company") introduced a world of foreign goods. Pewex was described as an "orgy of odors"[35] and a "place of longing."[36] One could go there not only to buy Western goods with hard currency but also to indulge in the olfactory prosperity of French perfumes, American cigarettes, Barbie Doll plastic, Swiss chocolate, and German soaps. Consumer goods "from abroad"—whether perfumes, cigarettes, soaps, or clothes— were usually considered not only more prestigious and better-quality but also phenomenologically superior, which added to their desirability. Consumerism is based not only on the function of objects but also on their physical constitution, color, material—and smell.

The expanded social policy of the early 1970s deliberately considered the consumer interests of the Polish people. The cosmetics industry figured as one of the most prominent symbols of prosperity, epitomizing lifestyle and chic. Cosmetics were more visible in the 1970s than they were before—for example, cosmetic products from Polish state enterprises were more broadly advertised in women's magazines.[37] Even with the wider variety of domestic goods, it was mostly the scents from abroad that anticipated a better life.

The promising odors of the day reached Poland via private imports, official hard currency stores, and gifted packages from the West. The gifted packages encompassed highly coveted goods such as coffee, German detergents and soaps, and French perfumes. In particular, Masumi ("the scent of luxury in the Polish People's Republic"[38]) and Blasé boomed in Poland. In contrast to their Soviet counterparts, they emitted wafts of "civilization" and "cultivation." Even today, these brands retrospectively evoke reactions like "What a smell! They smelled of the West, of freedom, of the colorfulness of life over there."[39] The experienced "other" smells generated expectations and associations with the mentioned spaces and moments of encounter with Western goods. They nourished the imagination of a better and more pluralistic life.

Polish Smell Marks

Still, the prospering Polish People's Republic was not only a sphere for influences from both East and West. In the 1970s, it also left its mark on the olfactory map of perfumery in Cold War Europe. One effect of Poland's economic rise was the expansion of the assortment of cosmetics sold by the state company Pollena.[40] Although there have always been various scented waters and eaux de cologne on the Polish market, in the 1970s two iconic perfumes were launched that today are still remembered as the embodiment of socialist luxury. Named Być może (Perhaps) and Pani Walewska (Mrs. Walewska), the perfumes marked a new national Polish self-conception within the Eastern Bloc and Europe more broadly. Released in 1972, Być może was also known as the "socialist version of Chanel No. 5."[41]

In later years, the stylization of the name "Być może" was supplemented with an ellipsis and the word "Paris." "Być może . . . Paris" brought a whiff of French chic to the streets of Poland. There followed "Być może . . . Rome" and "Być może . . . London." Interestingly, there was never an edition "Być może . . . Moscow." Być może was the subtle, affordable odor of state socialist prosperity, the dream of many young girls and women. In 1976, Pollena launched the more luxurious perfume Pani Walewska. This provoked associations that were even more obviously European but also clearly Polish. The scent of Pani Walewska was the epitome of female elegance at the time. Made from high-quality French-sourced ingredients, it was named after Napoleon Bonaparte's Polish lover, Maria Walewska. Thus, the perfume alluded to Poland's significance for and within Europe: the idea that Poland embodied the desire of Europe (emphasized by its feminine Polish name "Polska").

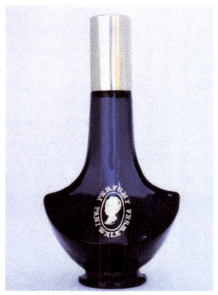

Fig. 2.1 French perfume Soir de Paris. Photo © Collection du Musée International de la Parfumerie, Grasse-France.

Fig. 2.2 Polish perfume Pani Walewska. Photo: Muzeum Mydła i Historii Brudu.

This is not only a reference to Napoleon's love life or the generally strong Polish-French relations but also to the topos of Poland as the beloved heart of Europe, which has played a major role in Poland's historical self-narrative for centuries.[42] Thanks to this perfume, a Polish woman (who in real existing socialism was usually a working mother with multiple responsibilities) could feel like a serious player in the European desirability game. Not surprisingly, the blue color of its flacon was unmistakably inspired by the French classic Soir de Paris (Evening in Paris), which was immensely popular—but hard to purchase—in the Eastern Bloc. Pani Walewska was advertised as a scent for all women "who would like to take possession of their personal Napoleon."[43] Accordingly, Pani Walewska's iconic flacon shape hinted at Napoleon's hat in an upside-down position (see figs. 2.1 and 2.2).[44]

Both Być może and Pani Walewska symbolize the peak of consumer culture and prosperity in the Gierek era. Although these perfumes were in principle affordable for everyone, they were considered prestigious because they, like many other popular items of domestic production, were rarely in stock. Their Western-oriented yet still very Polish femininity clearly emphasized Poland's affiliation with Europe but at the same time spread European elegance in the Soviet Union. In the eastern part of the Eastern Bloc, Poland was regarded as the "West of the East," and Warsaw has often been called the "Paris of the East."[45] In the Soviet Union, Polish perfumes were considered the embodiment of luxury and Western chic.[46] Poland was a major producer of cosmetics and personal care goods for the Eastern Bloc, especially for the Soviet Union.[47] Polish products, including clothes and cosmetics, enjoyed great popularity and quickly sold out in Soviet stores.[48] The two perfumes Być może and Pani Walewska were massively exported to the Soviet Union[49] and are part of the collective memory of post–Eastern Bloc societies. As mentioned above, the senses are central to the memory of past experiences.[50] This becomes especially evident with memories of perfumes: the interviews conducted for this chapter and the user comments from Fragrantica (an online encyclopedia of perfumes that appears in many languages, including Polish, Russian, Ukrainian, and German) provide insights into numerous recollections and stories about selected perfumes from the period of state socialism, including those about Polish perfumes in the Soviet Union. Thus, the assortment of soaps, shampoos, and perfumes, as well as consumer behaviors, not only sheds light on cultural practices and economic entanglements but also indicates national (self-) positioning.

Competitive Cosmetics

Regional scent marks and competitive cosmetics are of special interest when considered against the political backdrop of the Cold War. In 1976, the Polish population began smelling a new wave of opposition to the existing government with the rise of the Solidarity movement. It is no accident that the male scent Brutal was introduced in this time of political crisis and indebtedness. Brutal is modeled on the French Brut from 1964; however, the moment of its launch in 1977 is striking. While men in socialist Poland at best smelled of traditional eaux de colognes, mostly based on prewar classics such as Przemysławka, this new perfume stood out not only because of its name but also because of a rather disconcerting advertising slogan: "Female emancipation is a figment, an attempt to flee nature, a denial of male domination over the fair sex, an artificial distortion of the world."[51]

    This olfactory manifestation of a "brutal" new patriarchy putting the members of the "fair sex" in their place seems to indicate a new conservatism that was tightly linked to the upcoming (economic) political crisis.

Brutal might have been the olfactory answer of a crisis-torn paternalistic state to the elegant Pani Walewska of Poland's welfare socialism. In 1981, the Polish government introduced martial law to bring order to the situation; there was the fear of Soviet intervention. The economic situation was tense: people remember only vinegar and mustard on otherwise empty shop shelves. Basic sanitary articles like toilet paper were lacking, and the state was in urgent need of hard currency from abroad. On many levels, there was something in the air—including new odors. Indeed, cosmetics, perfumes, and artificial flavoring boomed during Poland's crisis years in the early 1980s.[52]

When the planned economy was obviously about to fail, the Polish diaspora (Polonia) was invited to invest their capital in Poland. These first ventures out into the unknown terrain of capitalist entrepreneurship banked on seemingly apolitical or even innocuous cosmetics—scented bath foam and shampoos and dynamic colorful advertisements.[53] Taking into account that odors have the most evocative qualities, these new scents and flavors clearly hit the mark in the context of the crisis and confirmed something like a Polish "lipstick effect"—meaning that, especially in times of crisis, people are eager to invest in affordable little pleasures such as cosmetics.[54]

Among the most successful businessmen of this strange era of private business and petty capitalism under state socialism was a man who traded in artificial flavors and perfumes, Ignacy Soszyński. He had turned his back on state socialist Poland in the 1960s and made a fortune with perfumes and artificial aromas, first in France and then in Morocco. After receiving an invitation from the Polish government in the late 1970s, he founded a company called Inter-Fragrances.[55] This meaningful name invoked the entangled olfactory relationship between East and West. Inter-Fragrances successfully distributed artificial flavors for cakes and lemonades, providing artificial lemon flavoring at a time when real lemons were unavailable. Similar Polonia companies introduced shampoos with the intense scent of green apples, thus eclipsing the common state socialist shampoos made with hops and nettle: "This was an absolute sensation. I remember that it was a rarity. The smell of the West. In my opinion, the first general scent associated with Western Europe was the smell of the shampoo Green Apple."[56] Olfaction is significantly associated with experiences of transition.[57] This interrelation of scents and crisis and the sensory consequences of social transformations proved especially powerful during the transformative processes in Poland in the 1980s. Indeed, Soszyński soon became one of the most influential entrepreneurs in Poland and the first millionaire in the Eastern Bloc.[58]

In the 1980s, it was clear that the cosmetics sector in Poland was a state affair and the country itself was a battleground of influences. The state economy was weak, and state companies were crumbling. Soszyński was asked to contribute hard currency to rescue one of Poland's major cosmetics plants, Pollena Miraculum, which produced the perfume Pani Walewska. In 1981, he made money available so the plant could purchase important raw materials from France, and in exchange Soszyński used Miraculum's infrastructure for the production of his own cosmetics. Consequently, he was accused of speculation, which caused a major public scandal and turned him into something of a public enemy. In 1985, the Soviet Union became involved in Pollena Miraculum, signing a contract for Polish-Soviet cooperation.[59] This agreement envisioned a direct railway connection to secure the export of Pollena-produced perfumes and cosmetics from Krakow to the Soviet Union (90 percent of Pollena Miraculum's production was exported to the Soviet market).[60] At the time, this mingling of state socialism with limited capitalism was epitomized by the common interest of private and Soviet investors in the firm. Over the course of the 1980s, the founders of today's most successful Polish cosmetics companies—Dr. Irena Eris, Inglot, and Ziaja—also began mixing their first face creams in their private kitchens.[61]

In the 1980s, these diverse olfactory landscapes and influencers were reflected in the advertisements for perfumes, shampoos, and bath foams in Polish women's magazines. In the publication *Uroda* (Beauty), for example, one could find the scents of the Soviet Sojuzchimexport alongside Polonia-distributed fragrances, Polish-made cosmetics, and products from other Eastern Bloc states such as Bulgaria.

The Polish people still turned up their noses at the advertised Soviet-made perfumes due not only to their aromatic composition but also to advertising slogans like "What do Russian forests smell like?" Polish consumers were more likely to associate Russian forests with the gulag experiences of Poles in the Siberian forests than with the smell of Russian nature. In contrast, Polish products stood for good old domestic quality. Polonia fragrances, instead, seemed sexier because of the seductive colors of their packaging and the appeal of their marketing. An ad from the Polonia company Emmanuelle Cosmetics features a flacon flanked by red high heels with black bathroom tiles visible in the background. The bottle itself contributes to this image of capitalist luxury by showing a palm tree on a beach-fringed island surrounded by the sea and the brand name "Blue Pacific." Especially in the unstable 1980s, those years that were the most formative in creating the stereotypical image of the Eastern Bloc as dull, gray, and poor, the simultaneous promotion of these manifold fragrances and cosmetics products in women's magazines reflected the crucial transformative processes that were taking place—referring both to an already past present as well as to an imminent future. Although the Polish state companies subsumed under Pollena were privatized in the 1990s, the perfume lines Być może and Pani Walewska are still being produced today. The perfumes have claimed a place and earned a reputation not only in the Polish market but also in other post–Eastern Bloc countries. Poland today is a major player in the European cosmetics market, mostly thanks to the aforementioned private cosmetics initiatives dating back to the 1980s: Dr. Irena Eris, Inglot, Ziaja, and Oceanic, which is run by Soszyński's descendants.[62]

Conclusion

Following the olfactory traces of perfumes and cosmetics in the Polish People's Republic, we can detect imaginings of Poland's place in Europe between Soviet emanations and the fragranced anticipation of "the West." Sniffing around the Polish bathroom and its cosmetics products throughout the 1970s and 1980s, we can read the entangled relationship between state socialist and capitalist markers of smell during the Cold War. Although pleasant smells generally indicate prosperity, perfumes and cosmetics proved to be highly influential, especially in times of scarcity and political instability. Only a few other economic sectors sold as many dreams and expectations as did the cosmetics sector; the promising power of scents was especially evident in the transformative times of crisis in the 1980s and 1990s. Odors, among them the scents of cosmetics, reflect socioeconomic conditions and cultural practices and function as markers of specific lifestyles. They can serve as olfactory sensors of contemporary political and economic situations and sociocultural sensitivities. During the Cold War, Poland found itself exposed to whiffs from the West as well as from the East. It also had a major local cosmetics industry, and its products shaped collective experiences of state socialism not only at home but in the Eastern Bloc and beyond. These various encounters with smells shaped Poland's self-conception and positioning within the Eastern Bloc and Europe as a whole. Although the perceptions and memories of smells are always shaped by individual experiences, recollections of certain times and realities of the past or present are grounded not only in time and place but also in taste and smell.[63] Smells, and especially the smells of cosmetics, play a crucial role in recollecting the era of the Cold War, and certain perfumes are now part of the collective memory of Cold War Europe. The study of sensory experiences and the significance of sensations makes it possible to sniff out new perspectives on Cold War atmospheres and tensions. Changes in smells highlight transformations in tastes, generations, and ideologies and their influence on geopolitical constructions and historical eras.

Notes

1. Classen, *Worlds of Sense*, 6; Smith, *Sensing the Past*.
2. Howes, *Sensual Relations*.
3. E.g., Saunders and Cornish, *Modern Conflict and the Senses*; Smith, *Smell of Battle*.
4. Low, *Scents and Scent-sibilities*; Synnott, *Body Social*; Vannini, Waskul, and Gottschalk, *Senses in Self, Society, and Culture*.
5. With a few exceptions focusing mainly on the Russian realm: Plamper, "Sounds of February, Smells of October"; Romaniello and Starks, *Russian History through the Senses*; Levinson, "Povsyiudu chem-to pakhnet" (Everywhere it smells of something).
6. Sixty narrative interviews on general experiences of smell and local smellscapes, with people born between 1950 and 1975, were conducted by the author in the Polish city of Lublin in 2019 and 2020. Subsequent citations include the initials, year of birth, and sex of each interviewee.
7. These include, for example, discussions from the online perfume encyclopedia *Fragrantica* in its Polish, Ukrainian, and Russian versions.
8. On the "male" perfumery landscape of the Polish People's Republic, see Weismann, "Es liegt was in der Luft."
9. Vannini, Waskul, and Gottschalk, *Senses*, 98; see also Engen, *Odor Sensation and Memory*.
10. Vannini, Waskul, and Gottschalk, *Senses*, 97.
11. Hamilton, "Proust Effect," 106.
12. Neidhart, *Russia's Carnival*, 89–90; Pirogovskaya, "Odour of Chlorine."
13. Classen, "Odor of the Other."
14. Herz, "I Know What I Like."
15. See Corbin, *Foul and the Fragrant*.
16. See Pirogovskaya, *Miazmy, simptomy, uliki*; Classen, Howes, and Synnott, *Aroma*, 8.
17. Kravets and Sandikçi, "Marketing for Socialism," 467.
18. Similar agendas can be observed in the Second Polish Republic, which emerged when Poland gained independence after the First World War. See Krzemiński, "Krajobraz higieniczno-estetyczny miast."
19. Szpak, "Warunki sanitarne"; Nowacki, Bełdowicz, and Wilińska, *Historia polskiego przemysłu*, 119.
20. Interviews 54ALf, 64JLf, 62PSZm, and others.
21. Interview 50HJf.
22. Largey and Watson, "Sociology of Odors."
23. See Low, "Rumination on Smell"; Herz, "I Know What I Like"; Synnott, *Body Social*.
24. See Classen, Howes, and Synnott, *Aroma*, 169.
25. Synnott, *Body Social*, 195.
26. "Zapachowe legendy PRLu . . ." Perfumomania subiektywnie i ze szpileczką o perfumach, https://perfumomania.wordpress.com/2012/11/15/zapachowe-legendy-prlu-znow-mam-katar.
27. See Burszta and Grębecka, *Mówiono "Druga Moskwa,"* 57, on Polish perceptions of Russian military members' wives stationed in Poland.
28. Interview 69JDf.
29. Schlögel, *Der Duft der Imperien*.
30. Lobkovich, *Zolotoy vek russkoy parfumerii*.
31. Schlögel, *Der Duft der Imperien*, 33.
32. See Keck-Szajbel, "Shop around the Block." See also Šváb, "Consuming Western Image."
33. Interview 70AWf.
34. Interviews 71AWf, 64MWm, 60MFf.

35. Interviews 72MKm, 76LDm, 60TPm, 60PMm, 68PSZm, 63AAf ; see also Boćkowska, *To nie są moje wielbłądy*.
36. Ewa Mazgal, "Pewex, czyli pachnący sklep pełen marzeń," *Gazeta Olsztysnska*, September 12, 2015, http://gazetaolsztynska.pl/298660,Pewex-czyli-pachnacy-sklep-pelen-marzen.html.
37. Perczak, *Polska reklama*.
38. Ewa Podsiadły-Natorska, "Czym pachniało kobieta w PRLu?" *Kobieta*, December 22, 2014, https://kobieta.wp.pl/czym-pachniala-kobieta-w-prl-u-59827493 43896705a.
39. Podsiadły-Natorska, "Czym pachniało kobieta w PRLu?"
40. Nowacki, Bełdowicz, and Wilińska, *Historia polskiego przemysłu*, 122.
41. Witold Chrzanowski, "Prawie jak jeansy, prawie jak Chanel, prawie jak czop-czop, prawie dostępne . . .," TVP Tygodnik, December 14, 2018, https://tygodnik.tvp.pl/40257024/prawie-jak-jeansy-prawie-jak-chanel-prawie-jak-czopczop-prawiedostepne; Podsiadły-Natorska, "Czym pachniało kobieta w PRLu?"
42. Kraft and Steffen, *Europas Platz in Polen*.
43. Cited in Chrzanowski, "Prawie jak jeansy."
44. Pani Walewska, "Historia: 50 lat tradycji," https://paniwalewska.pl/historia; Martyna Kośka, "Historia zamknięta we flakonie: Pani Walewska i kosmteyczne cuda doktora Lustra," *IgiMag*, April 16, 2018, https://igimag.pl/2018/04/historia-zamknieta-flakonie-pani-walewska-kosmetyczne-cuda-doktora-lustra/; Joanna Szczurek, "Co wspólnego mają ze sobą perfumy Pani Walewska i kapelusz Napoleona Bonaparte?," *Avanti24*, October 2, 2019, https://avanti24.pl/Magazyn/7,150436,25260360,kosmetyki-pani-walewska-kultowa-marka.html.
45. Brzostek, *Paryże innej Europy*.
46. Neidhart, *Russia's Carnival*, 91; Fitzpatrick, "Things Under Socialism," 462–64.
47. Nowacki, Bełdowicz, and Wilińska, *Historia polskiego przemysłu*.
48. Nowacki, Bełdowicz, and Wilińska, *Historia polskiego przemysłu*, 125.
49. "Miraculum wczoraj dzis jutro," Inwentarz polsko-radziecka fabryka MIRACULUM, zespół 29/1646/0, 253, State Archive Cracow.
50. Damousi and Hamilton, "Introduction: Leaning In," 1.
51. Cited in Michal Matys, "Pani Walewska i Brutal," *Puls Biznesu*, January 27, 2012, https://www.pb.pl/pani-walewska-i-brutal-650760.
52. Pacanowska, "Początki polskich firm."
53. Drenda, *Duchologia Polska*, 166; Skąpska, *Buddenbrookowie czy piraci*.
54. Pacanowska, "Początki polskich firm."
55. Wojciech Kiermacz, "Ignacy Zenon Soszyński: Najbogatszy człowiek w PRL," *Business Insider*, https://archiwum.businsinsider.com.pl/kraj/ignacy-zenon-soszynski-najbogatszy-czlowiek-w-prl/tqbwt; Przemysław Semczuk, "Ignacy Soszynski, najwiekszy biznesmen PRL," *Newsweek*, January 6, 2010, https://www.newsweek.pl/kim-byl-najwiekszy-biznesmen-prl/8zc93bw.
56. Interview AW70f.
57. See Śliwa and Riach, "Making Scents of Transition."
58. Kostrzewski and Miączyński, "Soszyński"; Piotr Gabryel, "Imperium Soszyńskiego," *Wprost* 42 (1985): 8–12; Gabryel and Zieleniewski, *Polscy milionerzy*.
59. Nowacki, Bełdowicz, and Wilińska, *Historia Polskiego Przemysłu*, 182.
60. Matys, "Pani Walewska i Brutal"; Nowacki, Bełdowicz, and Wilińska, *Historia Polskiego Przemysłu*; see also "Miraculum wczoraj dzis jutro."
61. Pacanowska, "Początki polskich firm"; Agnieszka Brzostek, "Historia Ireny Eris: Zaczynała od metalowego garnka i jednego kremu, dziś stoi na czele koncernu," *Forsal*, September 6, 2013, https://forsal.pl/artykuly/729274,jak-irena-eris-stworzyla-imperium-kosmetyczne.html; Jan Cienski, "Inglot Is More than a Cosmetic Model: Innovative Franchising Is Behind the Success of the Polish Consumer Brand," *Financial Times*, April 17, 2012, https://www.ft.com/content/3e14ddac-87a4-11e1-8a47-00144feab49a.
62. Pacanowska, "Laboratorium na miarę XXI wieku."
63. Schlögel, *Der Duft der Imperien*, 39; see also Neidhart, *Russia's Carnival*.

Bibliography

Archival Sources
State Archive Cracow, Spytkowice, Poland: zespół 29/1646/o.

Oral History / Interviews
Sixty narrative interviews on general experiences of smell and local smellscapes, with people born between 1950 and 1975, were conducted by the author in the Polish city of Lublin between November 2018 and August 2020. Subsequent citations include the year of birth, initials, and sex of each interviewee as well as the date of the interview.

50HJf Lublin/PL, March 20, 2019.
54ALf Lublin/PL, March 18, 2019.
60TPm Lublin/PL, March 16, 2019.
63AAf Lublin/PL, February 18, 2019.
64JLf Lublin/PL, November 17, 2018.
64MFm Lublin/PL, March 29, 2019.
68PSSm Lublin/PL, December 12, 2018.
69JDf Włodawa/PL, July 5, 2020.
71AWf Lublin/PL, November 29, 2018.
72MKm Lublin/PL, January 6, 2019.
76LDm Lublin/PL, May 18, 2019.
70AWf Lublin/PL, March 25, 2019.

Published Sources
Boćkowska, Aleksandra. *To nie są moje wielbłądy*. Wołowiec: Wydawnictwo Czarne, 2014.
Brzostek, Błażej. *Paryże innej Europy: Warszawa i Bukareszt, XIX i XX wiek*. Warsaw: WAB, 2015.
Burszta, Jędrzej, and Zuzanna Grębecka. *Mówiono "Druga Moskwa": Wspomnienia Legniczan o stacjonowaniu wojsk radzieckich w latach, 1945–1993*. Krakow: Wydawnictwo Libron, 2015.
Classen, Constance. "The Odor of the Other: Olfactory Symbolism and Cultural Categories." *Ethos* 20, no. 2 (1992): 133–66.
———. *Worlds of Sense: Exploring the Senses in History and Across Cultures*. London: Routledge, 1993.
Classen, Constance, David Howes, and Anthony Synnott. *Aroma: The Cultural History of Smell*. London: Taylor & Francis, 1994.
Corbin, Alain. *The Foul and the Fragrant: Odor and the French Social Imagination*. Cambridge: Harvard University Press, 1988.
Damousi, Joy, and Paula Hamilton. "Introduction: Leaning In." In *A Cultural History of Sound, Memory and the Senses*, edited by Joy Damousi and Paula Hamilton, 1–6. New York: Routledge, 2017.
Drenda, Olga. *Duchologia Polska: Rzeczy i ludzie w latach transformacji*. Krakow: Karakter, 2016.
Engen, Trygg. *Odor Sensation and Memory*. New York: Praeger, 1991.
Fitzpatrick, Sheila. "Things Under Socialism: The Soviet Experience." In *The Oxford Handbook of the History of Consumption*, edited by Frank Trentmann, 462–64. Oxford: Oxford University Press, 2012.
Gabryel, Piotr, and Marek Zieleniewski. *Polscy milionerzy*. Poznań: Dom Wydawniczy Babicz, Harasimowicz i Spółka, 1995.
Hamilton, Paula. "The Proust Effect: Oral History and the Senses." In *The Oxford Handbook of Oral History*, edited by Donald A. Ritchie, 219–32. Oxford: Oxford University Press, 2010.
Herz, Rachel. "I Know What I Like: Understanding Odor Preferences." In *The Smell Culture Reader*, edited by Jim Drobnick, 75–94. Oxford: Berg, 2006.
Howes, David, ed. *Sensual Relations: Engaging the Senses in Culture and Social Theory*. Ann Arbor: University of Michigan Press, 2003.
Keck-Szajbel, Mark. "Shop around the Block: Trader Tourism and Its Discontents on the East German-Polish Border." In *Communism Unwrapped: Consumption in Cold War Eastern Europe*, edited by Paulina Bren and Mary Neuburger, 374–92. Oxford: Oxford University Press, 2012.
Kostrzewski, Leszek, and Piotr Miączyński. "Soszyński. Najbogatszy człowiek w PRL." In *Fortuna po polsku: Dynastie,*

sukces i pieniądze w wielkim stylu, 139–54. Warsaw: Biblioteka Gazety Wyborczej, 2015.

Kraft, Claudia, and Katrin Steffen, eds. *Europas Platz in Polen: Polnische Europa-Konzeptionen vom Mittelalter bis zum EU-Beitritt*. Osnabrück: fibre, 2007.

Kravets, Olga, and Özlem Sandikçi. "Marketing for Socialism: Soviet Cosmetics in the 1930s." *Business History Review* 87, no. 3 (2013): 461–87.

Krzemiński, Tomasz. "Krajobraz higieniczno-estetyczny miast i wsi pomorskich w dwudziestuleciu międzywojennym." *Zapiski historyczne* 77, no. 2 (2012): 35–56.

Largey, Gale Peter, and David Rodney Watson. "The Sociology of Odors." *American Journal of Sociology* 77, no. 6 (1972): 1021–34.

Levinson, Aleksey. "Povsyiudu chem-to pakhnet." In *Aromaty i zapakhi v kulture*, edited by Olga Vaynshteyn, 2:7–30. Moscow: Novoe literaturnoe obozrenie, 2010.

Lobkovich, Viktor. *Zolotoy vek russkoy parfumerii i kosmetiki, 1821–1921*. Minsk: Logvinov, 2005.

Low, Kelvin E. Y. "Rumination on Smell as a Sociocultural Phenomenon." *Current Sociology* 53, no. 3 (2005): 397–417.

———. *Scent and Scent-sibilities: Smell and Everyday Life Experiences*. Newcastle upon Tyne: Cambridge Scholars, 2008.

Luthar, Breda. "Remembering Socialism: On Desire, Consumption and Surveillance." *Journal of Consumer Culture* 6, no. 2 (2006): 229–59.

Neidhart, Christoph. *Russia's Carnival: The Smells, Sights, and Sounds of Transition*. Lanham: Rowman & Littlefield, 2003.

Nowacki, Janusz, Maria Anna Bełdowicz, and Ewa Wilińska. *Historia polskiego przemysłu chemii gospodarczej*. Warsaw: Stowarzyszenie inżynierów i techników przemysłu chemicznego, 2001.

Pacanowska, Regina. "Laboratorium na miarę XXI wieku: Firma rodzinna Dr Ireny Eris i Henryka Orfingera (1983–2010)." In *Przedsiębiorstwa podczas przemian systemowych w Polsce przełomu XX i XXI wieku. Sukcesy i porażki na rynku*, edited by Przemysław Czechanowski and Dariusz Grala, 169–92. Poznań: MK Verbum, 2013.

———. "Początki polskich firm z branży kosmetycznej w dekadzie lat osiemdziesiątych." *Rocznik dziejów społecznych i gospodarczych* 76 (2016): 473–503.

Perczak, Judyta Ewa. *Polska reklama prasowa w latach, 1945–1989: O reklamie, której nie było?* Warsaw: Dom Wydawniczy Elipsa, 2010.

Pirogovskaya, Maria. *Miazmy, simptomy, uliki: Zapakhy mezhdu meditsynoy i moralyu v russkoy kulture vtoroy poloviny XX veka*. Saint Petersburg: Izdatel'stvo Evropejskogo universiteta v Sankt-Peterburge, 2018.

———. "Odour of Chlorine in Soviet Urban Reality: Notes on the Clean and the Collective." In *Les Cinq Sens de la Ville du Moyen Âge á Nos Jours*, edited by Robert Beck, Ulrike Krampl, and Emmanuelle Retaillaud-Bajac, 199–210. Tours: Presses Univ. François-Rabelais, 2013.

Plamper, Jan. "Sounds of February, Smells of October: The Russian Revolution as Sensory Experience." *American Historical Review* 126, no. 1 (2021): 140–65.

Romaniello, Matthew P., and Tricia Starks. *Russian History through the Senses: From 1700 to the Present*. London: Bloomsbury Academic, 2016.

Saunders, Nicholas J., and Paul Cornish, eds. *Modern Conflict and the Senses: Killer Instincts?* Florence: Routledge, 2017.

Schlögel, Karl. *Der Duft der Imperien: Chanel No 5 und Rotes Moskau*. Munich: Carl Hanser, 2020.

Skąpska, Grażyna, ed. *Buddenbrookowie czy piraci: Polscy przedsiębiorcy okresu głębokich przemian*. Krakow: Towarzystwo autorów i wydawców prac naukowych, 2002.

Śliwa, Martyna, and Kathleen Riach. "Making Scents of Transition: Smellscapes and the Everyday in 'Old' and 'New' Urban Poland." *Urban Studies* 49, no. 1 (2012): 23–41.

Smith, Mark M. *Sensing the Past: Seeing, Hearing, Smelling, Tasting, and Touching in History.* Berkeley: University of California Press, 2007.

———. *The Smell of Battle, the Taste of Siege.* New York: Oxford University Press, 2015.

Švab, Alenka. "Consuming Western Image of Well-Being: Shopping Tourism in Socialist Slovenia." *Cultural Studies* 16, no. 1 (2002): 63–79.

Synnott, Anthony. *The Body Social: Symbolism, Self, and Society.* London: Routledge, 1993.

Szpak, Ewelina. "Warunki sanitarne w powojennej Polsce: Zarys problemów i dynamiki zmian (1945–1970)." In *Polska, 1944/45–1989: Studia i materiały,* edited by Jerzy Eisler and Tomasz Szarota, 277–99. Warszawa: Instytut Historii PAN, 2014.

Vannini, Phillip, Dennis Waskul, and Simon Gottschalk, eds. *The Senses in Self, Society, and Culture: A Sociology of the Senses.* New York: Routledge, 2014.

Weismann, Stephanie. "Es liegt was in der Luft: Geruchslandschaften der Volksrepublik Polen im Wandel." In "Verstörte Sinne," edited by Ulrike Krampl and Regina Schulte. Special issue, *L'homme* 31, no. 2 (2020): 73–94.

CHAPTER 3

Beyond the Bamboo Curtain

Sensing the Chinese Cultural Revolution

Cyril Cordoba

In the early 1970s, an old proverb became one of the guiding principles of the international propaganda disseminated by the People's Republic of China (PRC): "It is better to see something once than to hear about it a thousand times." In other words, despite the isolationist context of the Chinese Cultural Revolution, the Maoist leadership sent the following message, amplified by organizations such as the state travel agency Lüxingshe: "Do not trust the lies of the Western mass media and come judge for yourselves the great achievements of the PRC." Addressed to foreigners living on the other side of the Bamboo Curtain—the geopolitical barrier separating China from the Western Bloc—this appeal underscored how important it was to personally experience the "noisy and colorful" Cultural Revolution in order to truly understand and appreciate the upheaval.[1] But the "ocularcentrism" of the phrase neglected the role of the other senses, especially hearing, in the production of meaning and knowledge about Red China by foreign travelers.

In her work on the origins of sightseeing, Judith Adler demonstrates how, from the sixteenth century onward, tourists increasingly regarded the eye as superior to the ear in their efforts to describe new environments.[2] In his pivotal work on the "tourist gaze,"[3] John Urry also insists on the hegemony of vision in the appropriation of the unknown. He describes vision as "the organizing sense within otherwise multi-sensual encounters."[4] Furthermore, while many researchers have shown how famous guests were tricked by flamboyant Maoist hospitality techniques, only a few have considered how ordinary people perceived and experienced China using senses other than sight.[5] As this chapter argues, soundscapes[6] proved to be just as important as landscapes in Western perceptions of the Chinese Cultural Revolution. Inspired by the growing body of literature at the crossroads between sensory studies[7] and tourism research,[8] I will use a rich corpus of ego-documents obtained from oral history interviews and research in private archives (including notebooks, audiotapes, private correspondence, photographs, and films) to explain how both the visual and the sonic environments of the Cultural Revolution influenced Westerners' understanding of these ten years of political turmoil.

To do so, I will first present three written accounts of the late 1960s by Swiss citizens who were invited to or worked in the PRC during the first phase of the Cultural Revolution. I will demonstrate how these people, who did not speak or understand Chinese, tried to make sense of a state of civil war by relying on what they saw and particularly on what they heard. Second, I will analyze the visual and audio material produced by several Western tourists who took part in group trips to the PRC during the 1970s. Along with the standard photographs and amateur films produced by foreign travelers, the audiotapes recorded by some of the visitors reveal a great deal about the rigid mechanisms governing guided tours in China.

China from Within

Between 1966 and 1968, three Swiss couples visited the PRC as "foreign friends" of the regime. The first two—the Golays and the Jaccards*[9]—were invited by the Chinese People's Association for Friendship with Foreign Countries (CPAFFC), a body specially conceived by the Maoist government to develop international "people-to-people" relationships and increase China's influence and prestige abroad.[10] The third couple, the Grieshabers, lived and worked in the PRC for a number of months in order to be close to their daughter, who had been hired as a proofreader for Beijing Foreign Languages Press some years earlier. Each of these couples recorded their impressions of China on different media, but they all privileged written texts, which were authored solely by the men despite the use of "we" to evoke an experience shared by husbands and wives.

The first male author, Jean Grieshaber (a Latin teacher), used his hotel stationery to write letters to his colleague Paul-Henri Jeanneret (a high school director) between 1966 and 1967. The second, Bernard Golay (a watchmaker), scribbled during the winter of 1967 in a small notebook illustrated with official photographs of the Cultural Revolution (presumably a gift from his hosts). The third, Victor Jaccard (also a watchmaker), recounted his 1968 stay in the PRC in memoirs written many years later, in 2016. All three were "foreign friends" (*wàiguó péngyou*) of Beijing, a term used to designate neither Maoists nor communist "comrades" but people interested politically or culturally in China, who could help promoting it abroad. Despite their formal differences, these three sets of documents share many similarities, especially their descriptions of completely new sensory environments.

The most prominent feature of these accounts is their authors' insistence on the incompatibility between their own perceptions of events and their portrayal in Western media outlets such as Voice of America. In other words, for the Swiss travelers, seeing the Cultural Revolution firsthand was clearly more informative than hearing about it a thousand times. Contradicting the general depiction of the situation as a civil war, one of the visitors stated, "We can see with our own eyes that everything is happening calmly, without excitement, and with a kind of disciplined enthusiasm, and that everybody seems to be smiling and relaxed."[11] Grieshaber, in particular, insisted on distancing himself from the Western mass media and frequently used the expression "with our own eyes" to explain, among other things, that "the tremendous protests have nothing in common with the 'hysteria,' 'rage,' or 'chaos' that our press speaks about. On the contrary, everything looks like a party, a happy festival, accompanied by a multitude of flags, masses of flowers, and garlands."[12] The turmoil in the streets of Beijing was undeniable, but the "feeling" of those who witnessed it differed significantly from the analyses of international reporters. This discrepancy was one of the reasons Grieshaber felt the need to assure his correspondent that they were not the "victims of collective hallucinations,"[13] even if he admitted that the situation was hard to decipher for anyone who did not understand Chinese.

If the Swiss relied on their Chinese colleagues and guides to translate the dazibaos in the streets (the word *dazibao*, meaning "large-character poster," was not picked up by Western media until months later), what struck them the most was how the Red Guards appropriated urban spaces: "In all the main roads of Beijing, they put up enormous signs in two or three parallel lines and transform the sidewalk into large corridors. These signs are covered

Fig. 3.1   Gazing at the colorful other: red and blue in a tourist's photo taken at Tiananmen Square on April 8, 1976.

with mural newspapers and countless caricatures denouncing the mistakes of 'the Chinese Khrushchev and other party heads who went down the path of capitalism,' to quote the official phrase."[14] Unable to judge the stakes of the political struggles unfolding before their eyes, the visitors focused on empirical data collected in the midst of "dense, swarming crowds."[15] They observed an "abundance of paper, color, and glue"[16] on the posters, flags, and Little Red Books waved by the Red Guards; the iconic color of communism became a ubiquitous rallying symbol in Chinese cities.[17] The bright colors of the propaganda material also impressed the Swiss friends of the PRC, especially when they were welcomed by singing and dancing crowds before visiting model institutions (see fig. 3.1).

Sensory Overload

Even so, sight was not the principal sense used by the couples to decipher the complex reality of the Chinese Cultural Revolution, which was as much auditive as it was visual. Unlike the former Swiss ambassador Fernand Bernoulli (1955–1958), who considered Chinese music a mixture of strident and discordant sounds ("Nowhere else in the world have I heard such cacophony"[18]), the three couples admired revolutionary operas and ballets such as *The White-Haired Girl* and *The Red Detachment of Women*, which Jiang Qing (Mao Zedong's fourth wife) promoted as "model works."[19] Jaccard wrote that the Chinese plays were reminiscent of "Molière, with the irony that [Bertolt] Brecht admired so much" and described Chinese theater as "Piccolo Teatro to the 100th."[20] For his part, Golay noted modestly, "Perfection! Easy to understand, moving, great quality (Western) music, songs, and dances." He found one film particularly good because "the good guys and the villains cannot be confused."[21] Although the Grieshabers wrote that their "ears [were] not yet accustomed" to Chinese music, they expressed their appreciation of the bold renewal of classic Peking opera.[22] However, beyond the sounds they heard as attentive audience members (given to aesthetic judgments), the sensory aspect that they most frequently described in their accounts of the Chinese Cultural Revolution was the loud, rich sonic environment consisting of drums, cymbals, and revolutionary chants.

According to their writings, the soundscape of Chinese cities consisted of a never-ending "concert of horns, as deafening as they [were] ineffective."[23] Suggesting that radios and loudspeakers had become "revolutionary crusaders' weapons" during the Cultural Revolution,[24] they dwelled in their texts on the constant noise in Beijing's streets (not the constant *sounds*, a word without the negative connotation of invasiveness).[25] The visitors described roads swarming with people and a mind-numbing hubbub ("a deafening racket [with] loudspeakers blaring day and night")[26] and underlined the nuisance caused by this "verbal and acoustic delirium, the chaos day and night with loudspeakers, people everywhere with flags, in every corner."[27] However, all of these descriptions demonstrate that, although the three Swiss couples found themselves in a country undergoing tremendous upheaval, they evidently did not witness any acts of violence. This paradox cannot be attributed to the determination to lie but rather to the apparent effectiveness of the techniques of Chinese hospitality, designed to completely hide negative aspects of the Cultural Revolution from foreigners.[28]

Another factor should be considered to understand how Westerners dealt with the Cultural Revolution: physical exhaustion. Often inebriated or hungover from the 110-proof Maotai liquor they had downed with their Chinese guests, worn out from the relentless visits ("At this pace, they'll kill me!" wrote Jaccard),[29] or numbed by the heavy, "humid, and sticky heat,"[30] the foreigners often found themselves dazed during their stays in the PRC.[31] Of course, it must also be noted that the bustle of large cities was unfamiliar to visitors from a small and quiet country like Switzerland. However, even the cosmopolitan Chinese-Belgian writer Han Suyin explained in her autobiography that she suffered from panic attacks during that period. She described her mental state as "a sweat, a clamminess, a wrenching of spirit; the sweat of fear and the babble of terror from my mouth."[32]

After experiencing the excitement of the early Cultural Revolution, the three couples returned to Switzerland as active and enthusiastic supporters of Beijing. As Jaccard summed up in his retrospective account, "Of course, in our passionate youth, we became Maoists."[33] Confronted with the Western media's "lies" about the PRC and feeling a debt of gratitude to the regime that had welcomed them so cordially, they created the first China friendship associations, dedicated entirely to promoting the country.[34] These groups, which were supported by Beijing, organized a wide range of events in close cooperation with the CPAFFC, including conferences, exhibitions, movie screenings, and Beijing opera tours. In the 1970s, they became extremely popular thanks to a new kind of activity: guided tours of the PRC, which attracted hundreds of travelers each year.

Showcasing a Showcase

In the 1970s, the easiest way for Westerners to travel to the PRC was through a friendship association. After the Sino-American rapprochement of 1971–72,[35] these organizations enjoyed a near-monopoly on Chinese visas thanks to their privileged relations with Beijing.[36] The guided tours they organized attracted diverse groups, not necessarily left-wing, though the participants studied in this research are progressive white-collar Europeans and Americans. The travelers, whether they were active supporters of China or mere tourists in search of exoticism, usually brought back propaganda material from the Beijing Foreign Languages Press, including brochures, art books, and postcards that showcased the regime's great achievements (e.g., dams, train stations, auditoriums, and stadiums). However, the friends of the PRC also created their own "constructed ... representations" of China with their cameras.[37]

For example, in the 1970s, three Swiss friends of China[38] took photos that generally focused on the natural scenery (without any human-made structures), the daily life of the Chinese (e.g., practicing their morning tai chi), and the architectural remains of the imperial era. They sought to capture a certain aesthetic and show the natural and cultural resources in the best light possible and as "representative" of the PRC. This divergence from the official images, which presented nature as mastered by humans and a modern society free of ancient practices, was one of the few liberties taken by the friends of Beijing, who generally respected the Maoist orthodoxy in "telling the truth" about China.

Before the trips began, the friendship associations generally placed limits on the scope of creativity and recalled that "only members ... who adopt[ed] a friendly attitude towards China [could] register for the trips."[39] Participants were encouraged to photograph women doing men's jobs, Westerners and Chinese in mixed groups, and the differences between the old and the new China. One internal document of the US-China People's Friendship Association advised the travelers to take "pictures that *say* something about China or U.S.-China friendship [and that are] visually attractive, too, of course."[40] Influenced by the official promotional material depicting China in a positive light,[41] these photographs were generally taken in color, which, though more costly, was deemed by amateur photographers to be more realistic.[42] The Kodachrome photos, which were later projected onto screens in slideshows, were richly saturated with brilliant and vibrant blues, reds, and browns that reflected the bright colors of Maoist propaganda posters.

A number of tourists also brought motion-picture film with them, and the 8 mm amateur movies they shot typically showed a specific part of their itinerary (e.g., down the Yangtze River) or documented their entire stay. A participant interviewed for this research agreed to share one of these "video travel diaries" with the author.[43] The movie was shot at eye level with a still frame and often focused on intersections teeming with a never-ending flow of bicycles and bullock carts. It also showed close-ups of pagodas and the ornamentation of imperial temples. Traditional Chinese music was added as an accompaniment. This contrasted with the regime's official productions, which often used a God's-eye view (a wide high-angle shot) to spectacularly show large infrastructure projects such as canals and factories.

Less frequently, the makers of these films, while traveling by train, car, or boat, shot the rural landscapes passing by. Sometimes, a narrator intervenes—usually during visits to model institutions—and mouths the official line. For example, in the aforementioned film, the tourists are shown arriving in Dazhai while a voice-over explains that the agricultural settlement (referred to as a "production brigade"[44]) symbolizes "the unlimited power of man to tame nature. Dazhai shows how, without tools or state financing, it is possible to transform an unproductive region into a fertile landscape."[45]

In several segments, this amateur movie shows crowds gathering around the tourists (easily recognizable by their large hats and sunglasses). Like Michelangelo Antonioni in *Chung Kuo,* a documentary that had been made a few years earlier,[46] the Swiss tourist filmed motionless Chinese people looking curiously at the camera.[47]

Although the visual material produced by Western visitors to China says a great deal about the visitors' interests and expectations, it does not really allow us to understand the mechanisms of the guided tours organized by the CPAFFC during the Cultural Revolution. Fortunately, other types of documents exist, and these documents provide access to the encounters between the Chinese and their foreign friends.

Taping the Revolution

Like many other visitors to the PRC in the 1960s and the 1970s, the Swiss tourist Michel Zaugg* and the American Elinor Brelsford brought cassette recorders with them to collect "sound souvenirs" from China.[48] In addition to filling multiple notebooks with factual data, Zaugg and Brelsford, who were active supporters of the regime, recorded approximately twelve hours of audio material each during their stays between 1973 and 1977.[49] Ninety percent of the material consists of typical official speeches delivered by what some visitors called "robot cadres" in model institutions such as factories, schools, prisons, and hospitals.[50]

The speeches were made by Chinese workers, teachers, or doctors and then translated by one of the guides accompanying the tourists throughout the country. But since neither Zaugg nor Brelsford understood Chinese, they recorded only the French and English parts of the talks. What really interested them were slogans such as "integrate theory with practice" or "serve the people" or metaphorical expressions (e.g., "thousands of neck yokes are heavy, but nothing compared to the world revolution").[51] Such phrases were an efficient way to "tell the truth" about China in the West (in local newspaper articles or during public lectures) after the trip had ended.[52]

Because of the rigid rules the Chinese had to obey when it came to oral expression,[53] the most interesting parts of these audiotapes are in fact the marginal situations, such as the unexpected answers given by hosts or the background noises. For example, a few awkward silences and nervous laughs can be heard, usually in question-and-answer sessions, when there were misunderstandings between the tourists and their interlocutors. Yet all of the participants in the guided tours took part in preparatory meetings organized by the friendship associations to avoid asking "stupid questions."[54] They were coached not only on what they could ask but also on the possible responses: "'Are there layoffs?' To this question, the answer will be no. But if we ask a question about assignments, recruitments, transfers, etc., we are more likely to have a better approach to the problem."[55] Despite these precautions, it seems that some exchanges with the Chinese went awry. For example, in 1973, a group of tourists tried several times to obtain a detailed answer to the question of why equality between men and women was one of the priorities of the Maoist regime. None was forthcoming—either because their host was ill prepared or because he simply did not understand what the foreigners wanted to hear. The group ultimately lost patience and had to accept an embarrassed response: "Because here, it is a socialist country."[56]

Beyond documenting their hosts' speeches, the tapes brought back by Zaugg and Brelsford offer fascinating samplings of the rich soundscapes of the PRC in the 1970s. When listening to the recordings of their visits to factories and schools, we can hear machines or playing children as a first layer of sound in the background. Even more interesting, these recordings document the hustle and bustle of Chinese city streets: a mix of horns, conversations, and transistor radios that one Swiss traveler described as "background noise à l'italienne" (Italian cities representing the stereotypical noisy environment for Swiss audiences).[57] Even if, by then, the Cultural Revolution had moved beyond its civil war phase, street bands and demonstrations at which propaganda songs were sung were a large part of the sonic environment experienced by the tourists. In most of the cities they visited, such as Beijing, Shanghai, Nanjing, Tianjin, and Guangzhou, the constant politicization of public space (e.g., through denunciation campaigns) clearly contributed to their perception of the period as "a revolution within the revolution."

By contrast, when the tourists visited people's communes or iconic sites such as the former residence of Mao Zedong in Shaoshan, the Dazhai production brigade, or the Daqing oil field, the dominant sound was chirping birds and buzzing insects. This suggests that, despite the growing acoustic presence of state propaganda in the countryside as a result of the expansion of rural wired broadcasting,[58] certain parts of China experienced less state control of the sonic environment. The other parasitic noises on the tapes include the constant clicking of teacups, as the visitors were constantly being offered tea while they listened patiently to their hosts. In 1976, one traveler described this sonic environment as "the very soft purr of the recorder placed on the table and the jingling of the porcelain lids on the teacups."[59]

Conclusion: Bring China Home

As I noted in the introduction to this chapter, sight was considered by the Maoist regime to be the most important sensory medium through which outsiders could discover, appreciate, and understand China. The regime's confidence in the role of visual perceptions can also be observed in the efforts by Beijing Foreign Languages Press to distribute richly illustrated propaganda material on a global scale.[60] However, as I have shown, hearing proved to be every bit as important as sight for the friends of the PRC who were trying to make sense of the Cultural Revolution. Despite the sensory overload in this period of crisis—and despite the rigid rules governing encounters with their Chinese friends—most Western travelers enjoyed their stay in the PRC and tried to communicate their experiences to their fellow citizens by bringing back objects that stimulated more than these two senses.

During promotional activities such as photographic exhibitions and amateur movie screenings, friends of China displayed tiger balms, chopsticks, and dried mushrooms to convey an idealized image of the PRC. Before the start of a slideshow and talk about a trip to Beijing, for example, the organizers played traditional music in the background and sold Chinese products such as tea and papercutting art. The attendees scrutinized portraits of Mao Zedong on the walls and banners celebrating friendship with the Chinese people. The room was filled with the pleasant smells of jiaozi (Chinese ravioli), spring rolls, and burning incense. In this context, all the negative aspects of trips to the PRC were suppressed, with no mention of dysentery, pollution, heavy traffic, bad smells, unpleasant food, dilapidated buildings, or trash.[61]

Along with ideological bias, many sensory elements colored the positive assessments of the Chinese Cultural Revolution made by Western travelers. Together with the political appeal of Maoism, sensory seduction and exoticism have played a significant role in the development of intimate relationships between Beijing and its foreign friends.[62] By considering the history of emotions and the body,[63] we can better understand the collective guided tours of China, which brought strangers to the other side of the world in precarious hygiene conditions for a two- to four-week stay. Given how meticulously travelers described every dish they ate in China despite the deprivation experienced by the majority of Chinese during these years,[64] the potential "soft power" of Chinese food seemed particularly high.[65] This is something that Victor Jaccard hinted at when describing his first encounter with the PRC in 1963: "I would return to China just to eat such a delicious Peking duck."[66]

Notes

1. Pang, "Colour and Utopia," 264.
2. Adler, "Origins of Sightseeing."
3. Urry and Larsen, *Tourist Gaze 3.0*.
4. Urry, as quoted in Larsen, "Geographies of Tourism Photography," 244.
5. Hollander, *Political Pilgrims*; Hourmant, *Au pays de l'avenir radieux*.
6. This chapter will not discuss this term's prescriptive connotation, as originally conceptualized by R. Murray Schafer in *Soundscape*. For additional insights, see Kelman, "Rethinking the Soundscape"; Samuels et al., "Soundscapes." Instead, I will use "soundscape" as a synonym for "sonic landscape," following Candau and Le Gonidec, *Paysages sensoriels*; Le Guern, "Discipline qui ne fait pas de bruit?"
7. Jütte, *History of the Senses*; Howes, *Sensual Relations*; Jay, "In the Realm of the Senses," 312; Granger, "Histoire des sensibilités."
8. Coates, "Strange Stillness of the Past"; Agapito, Mendes, and Valle, "Exploring the Conceptualization."
9. Pseudonyms, marked with an *, have been used for interviewees who wished to remain anonymous.
10. Brady, *Making the Foreign*; Cagdas, *Reaching the Distant Comrade*.
11. Correspondence from Jean Grieshaber to Paul-Henri Jeanneret, August 26, 1966, fonds Madeleine et Paul-Henri Jeanneret (PHJ) 102/47, Bibliothèque de la Ville de La Chaux-de-Fonds (BV), La Chaux-de-Fonds, Switzerland.
12. Correspondence from Jean Grieshaber to Paul-Henri Jeanneret, December 11, 1966, fonds Madeleine et Paul-Henri Jeanneret (PHJ) 102/47, Bibliothèque de la Ville de La Chaux-de-Fonds (BV), La Chaux-de-Fonds, Switzerland.
13. Correspondence from Jean Grieshaber to Paul-Henri Jeanneret, March 25, 1967, fonds Madeleine et Paul-Henri Jeanneret (PHJ) 102/47, Bibliothèque de la Ville de La Chaux-de-Fonds (BV), La Chaux-de-Fonds, Switzerland.
14. Correspondence from Jean Grieshaber to Paul-Henri Jeanneret, September 16, 1966, fonds Madeleine et Paul-Henri Jeanneret (PHJ) 102/47, Bibliothèque de la Ville de La Chaux-de-Fonds (BV), La Chaux-de-Fonds, Switzerland.
15. Correspondence from Jean Grieshaber to Paul-Henri Jeanneret, August 26, 1966, fonds Madeleine et Paul-Henri Jeanneret (PHJ) 102/47, Bibliothèque de la Ville de La Chaux-de-Fonds (BV), La Chaux-de-Fonds, Switzerland.
16. Correspondence from Jean Grieshaber to Paul-Henri Jeanneret, March 25, 1967, fonds Madeleine et Paul-Henri Jeanneret (PHJ) 102/47, Bibliothèque de la Ville de La Chaux-de-Fonds (BV), La Chaux-de-Fonds, Switzerland.
17. Fengyuan, *Linguistic Engineering*.
18. Fernand Bernouilli, *Souvenirs et impressions d'une Mission diplomatique en Chine*, 1959: 32, E2500#1990/6#210, Federal Archives, Bern, Switzerland.
19. Mittler, *Continuous Revolution*.
20. *Connaissance de la Chine, Histoire (1963–2016)*: 13 and 16, personal archives of Victor Jaccard (VJ).
21. Notebook no. 1, November 26, 1967, and December 2, 1967, personal archives of Martine Golay.
22. Correspondence from Grieshaber to Jeanneret, December 11, 1966, PHJ, BV. On this common appreciation, see Kraus, *Pianos and Politics*.
23. Correspondence from Grieshaber to Jeanneret, March 25, 1967, PHJ, BV.
24. Li, "Revolutionary Echoes," 41.
25. Cheyronnaud, "Endroit tranquille"; Morat and Ziemer, *Handbuch Sound*.
26. *Connaissance de la Chine*: 22, VJ.
27. Interview with Victor Jaccard, March 1, 2017.
28. Lovell, "Uses of Foreigners."

29. *Connaissance de la Chine*: 17, VJ.
30. Correspondence from Grieshaber to Jeanneret, August 26, 1966, PHJ, BV.
31. "Whether it was the miracles of herbal medicine, unfamiliar and 'exotic' foods and beverages, or the allure of utopian revolutionary projects that one hoped could really address human sufferings, it was easy enough to 'trip out' on a visit to China." Murray, Link, and Pickowicz, *China Tripping*, 3.
32. Suyin, *My House*, 424.
33. *Connaissance de la Chine*: 28, VJ.
34. Cordoba, *China-Swiss Relations*.
35. Kazushi, "Re-examining the End"; Milwood, *Improbable Diplomats*.
36. Shaw, "Telling the Truth"; Perry, *Saluting the Yellow Emperor*; Kaixuan, "Miroir chinois"; Yuxi, *Les relations Québec-Chine*.
37. Albers and James, "Travel Photography," 140.
38. Michel Zaugg*, Bernard Monnet*, and Marie-Claude Rimaz, three members of Swiss friendship associations with China whom the author met between 2016 and 2021.
39. National coordination information pack, 1977, 002-CP-S09-SS115-D029-SD004, fonds Charles Philipona (CP), Archives contestataires (AC), Carouge, Switzerland.
40. Guide by *New China* (US-China People's Friendship Association magazine), 1970s, folder 30.5, MssCol 6176, New York Public Library, New York, NY.
41. Stylianou-Lambert, "Tourists with Cameras."
42. Kempf, "Couleur du réel"; Boulouch, *Le ciel est bleu*.
43. This movie was converted to a DVD and transmitted to the author. It was shot during a trip to around fifteen Chinese cities between July 22 and August 13, 1977, organized by a Swiss friendship association. On the expression "video travel diary," see Argod, "Carnet de voyage."
44. Dazhai village was a vast expanse of agricultural terraces celebrated by Chinese propagandists as an example of the hard work and determination of the Chinese workers. In fact, it owed its success to the extensive financial support of the state, the logistical support of the army, and fabricated statistics.

An additional model project was Daqing oil field.
45. *Regards sur la Chine*, directed by Michel Junod (Geneva: Connaissance de la Chine), personal archives of Bernard Monnet*.
46. Michelangelo Antonioni, dir., *Chung Kuo* (Radiotelevisione Italiana, 1972).
47. Maoz, "Mutual Gaze."
48. Bijsterveld and Jacobs, "Storing Sound Souvenirs."
49. The recording devices were held by the tourists, who remained stationary. The voices of the Chinese hosts sometimes sound quite distant but are always understandable.
50. Correspondence from the leader of the US-China People's Friendship Association to a delegation leader, February 16, 1990, folder 15.1, MssCol 6176, New York Public Library.
51. Notebook no. 2, April 14, 1974, personal archives of Michel Zaugg (MZ).
52. Until the late 1970s, foreigners were required to declare all recording devices (including cameras, movie cameras, typewriters, and Dictaphones) to the Chinese customs authorities.
53. Fengyuan, *Linguistic Engineering*.
54. Report on the national coordination, summer 1977, 002-CP-S09-SS115-D029-SD004, CP, AC.
55. Tour leader guide: 5, 1980, box 14, fonds Régis Bergeron (J343), Archives départementales de la Seine–Saint-Denis, Bobigny, France.
56. Untitled tape, July 7, 1973, MZ.
57. Philippe Abravanel, "Pékin, mardi 6 avril 1976," *Domaine public* 362 (May 20, 1976).
58. Li, "Revolutionary Echoes."
59. Jean Wille, "Une visite à Pékin," *Journal du Jura* (September 11 and 12, 1976), 14.
60. Cagdas, *Reaching the Distant Comrade*.
61. On the phenomenon that only positive smells were preserved, see Jenner, "Follow Your Nose?"
62. For example, Westerners' gaze on Chinese women revealed many fantasies tinged with Orientalism, which also fueled tourism in the People's Republic of China. See Huang, *Gender Legacy of the Mao Era*; Lee, "East Asian 'China Doll' or 'Dragon Lady'?"

63. Corbin, Courtine, and Vigarello, *Histoire du corps*; Plamper, *History of Emotions*; Courtine et al., *Histoire des émotions*.
64. Henningsen, "Narrating Sweet Bitterness."
65. Yang, *Gifts, Favors, and Banquets*.
66. *Connaissance de la Chine*: 9, VJ.

Bibliography

Archival Sources

Archives contestataires, Carouge, Switzerland: Charles Philipona (002_CP).
Archives départementales de la Seine-Saint-Denis, Bobigny, France: Régis Bergeron (J343).
Bibliothèque de la Ville de La Chaux-de-Fonds, La Chaux-de-Fonds, Switzerland: M. and P.-H. Jeanneret (PHJ/102/47).
Federal Archives, Bern, Switzerland: E2500#1990/6#210.
New York Public Library, New York, NY: USCPFA (MssCol 6176).
Personal archives of Martine Golay, Victor Jaccard*, Bernard Monnet*, Marie-Claude Rimaz, and Michel Zaugg*, Switzerland.

Audiovisual Sources

Antonioni, Michelangelo, dir. *Chung Kuo*. 1972. Radiotelevisione Italiana.
Interview with Victor Jaccard*, March 1, 2017.
Personal archives of Bernard Monnet* and Michel Zaugg*.

Published Sources

Adler, Judith. "Origins of Sightseeing." *Annals of Tourism Research* 16, no. 1 (1989): 7–29.
Agapito, Dora, Júlio Mendes, and Patrícia Valle. "Exploring the Conceptualization of the Sensory Dimension of Tourist Experiences." *Journal of Destination Marketing and Management* 2, no. 2 (2013): 62–73.
Albers, Patricia C., and William R. James. "Travel Photography: A Methodological Approach." *Annals of Tourism Research* 15 (1988): 134–58.
Argod, Pascale. "Le carnet de voyage audiovisuel ou cinématographique: Genre intermédial, quête et diffusion du voyage 'authentique.'" *Téoros* 30, no. 1 (2011): 119–27.
Bijsterveld, Karin, and Annelies Jacobs. "Storing Sound Souvenirs: The Multi-Sited Domestication of the Tape Recorder." In *Sound Souvenirs*, edited by Karin Bijsterveld and José van Dijck, 25–42. Amsterdam: Amsterdam University Press, 2009.
Boulouch, Nathalie. *Le ciel est bleu: Une histoire de la photographie couleur*. Paris: Textuel, 2011.
Brady, Anne-Marie. *Making the Foreign Serve China: Managing Foreigners in the People's Republic*. Lanham: Rowman & Littlefield, 2003.
Cagdas, Ungor. *Reaching the Distant Comrade: Chinese Communist Propaganda Abroad (1949–1976)*. PhD diss., State University of New York, 2009.
Candau, Joël, and Marie-Barbara Le Gonidec, eds. *Paysages sensoriels: Essai d'anthropologie de la construction et de la perception de l'environnement sonore*. Paris: CTHS, 2013.
Cheyronnaud, Jacques. "Un endroit tranquille: À propos du 'bruit,' marqueur de reproche." *Communications* 1, no. 90 (2012): 197–214.
Coates, Peter A. "The Strange Stillness of the Past: Toward an Environmental History of Sound and Noise." *Environmental History* 10, no. 4 (2005): 636–65.
Corbin, Alain, Jean-Jacques Courtine, and Georges Vigarello, eds. *Histoire du corps*. Vol. 3. *Les mutations du regard: Le XXe siècle*. Paris: Seuil, 2006.
Cordoba, Cyril. *China-Swiss Relations during the Cold War, 1949–1989: Between Soft Power and Propaganda*. London: Routledge, 2022.
Courtine, Jean-Jacques, Bruno Nassim Aboudrar, Stéphane Audoin-Rouzeau, and Antoine de Baecque, eds. *Histoire des émotions*. Vol. 3. *De la fin du XIXe siècle à nos jours*. Paris: Seuil, 2017.
Fengyuan, Ji. *Linguistic Engineering: Language and Politics in Mao's China*.

Honolulu: University of Hawaii Press, 2004.
Granger, Christophe, ed. "L'histoire des sensibilités au XXe siècle." *Vingtième siècle, Revue d'histoire* 3, no. 123 (2014).
Henningsen, Lena. "Narrating Sweet Bitterness: Tasting and Sensing the Chinese Cultural Revolution." In *Sensing China: Modern Transformations of Sensory Culture*, edited by Shengqing Wu and Xuelei Huang, 174–98. London: Routledge, 2022.
Hollander, Paul. *Political Pilgrims: Travels of Western Intellectuals to the Soviet Union, China and Cuba, 1938–1978*. New York: Oxford University Press, 1981.
Hourmant, François. *Au pays de l'avenir radieux: Voyages des intellectuels français en URSS, à Cuba et en Chine populaire*. Paris: Aubier, 2000.
Howes, David. *Sensual Relations: Engaging the Senses in Culture and Social Theory*. Ann Arbor: University of Michigan Press, 2003.
Huang, Xin. *The Gender Legacy of the Mao Era: Women's Life Stories in Contemporary China*. New York: State University of New York Press, 2018.
Jay, Martin. "In the Realm of the Senses: An Introduction." *American Historical Review* 116, no. 2 (2011): 307–15.
Jenner, Mark S. R. "Follow Your Nose? Smell, Smelling, and Their Histories." *American Historical Review* 116, no. 2 (2011): 335–51.
Jütte, Robert. *A History of the Senses: From Antiquity to Cyberspace*. Oxford: Blackwell, 2004.
Kaixuan, Liu. "Le miroir chinois: Les attitudes françaises face à la Chine dans les milieux politique, diplomatique, intellectuel et médiatique, de 1949 au milieu des années 1980." PhD diss., Sciences Po Paris, 2019.
Kazushi, Minami. "Re-examining the End of Mao's Revolution: China's Changing Statecraft and Sino-American Relations, 1973–1978." *Cold War History* 16, no. 4 (2016): 359–75.

Kelman, Ari Y. "Rethinking the Soundscape: A Critical Genealogy of a Key Term in Sound Studies." *Senses and Society* 5, no. 2 (2010): 212–34.
Kempf, Jean. "La couleur du réel: La photographie couleur(s) a-t-elle un sens? (États-Unis, 1960–1990)." *Revue française d'études américaines* 3, no. 105 (2005): 110–24.
Kraus, Richard Curt. *Pianos and Politics in China: Middle-Class Ambitions and the Struggle over Western Music*. New York: Oxford University Press, 1989.
Larsen, Jonas. "Geographies of Tourism Photography: Choreographies and Performances." In *Geographies of Communication: The Spatial Turn in Media Studies*, edited by Jasper Falkheimer and André Jansson, 243–61. Göteborg: Nordicom, 2006.
Lee, Joey. "East Asian 'China Doll' or 'Dragon Lady'?" *Bridges: An Undergraduate Journal of Contemporary Connections* 3, no. 1 (2018): 1–6.
Le Guern, Philippe. "Une discipline qui ne fait pas de bruit? Remarques sur la construction des *sound studies*." *Politiques de communication* 1 (2017): 5–30.
Li, Jie. "Revolutionary Echoes: Radios and Loudspeakers in the Mao Era." *Twentieth-Century China* 45, no. 1 (2020): 61–75.
Lovell, Julia. "The Uses of Foreigners in Mao-Era China: 'Techniques of Hospitality' and International Image-Building in the People's Republic, 1949–1976." *Transactions of the Royal Historical Society* 25 (2015): 135–58.
Maoz, Darya. "The Mutual Gaze." *Annals of Tourism Research* 33, no. 1 (2006): 221–39.
Milwood, Pete. *Improbable Diplomats: How Ping-Pong Players, Musicians, and Scientists Remade US-China Relations*. Cambridge: Cambridge University Press, 2022.
Mittler, Barbara. *A Continuous Revolution: Making Sense of Cultural Revolution Culture*. Cambridge: Harvard University Press, 2012.

Morat, Daniel, and Hansjakob Ziemer, eds. *Handbuch Sound: Geschichte—Begriffe—Ansätze.* Stuttgart: J.B. Metzler, 2018.

Murray, Jeremy A., Perry Link, and Paul G. Pickowicz, eds. *China Tripping: Encountering the Everyday in the People's Republic.* Lanham: Rowman & Littlefield, 2019.

Pang, Laikwan. "Colour and Utopia: The Filmic Portrayal of Harvest in Late Cultural Revolution Narrative Films." *Journal of Chinese Cinemas* 6, no. 3 (2012): 263–82.

Perry, Johansson. *Saluting the Yellow Emperor: A Case of Swedish Sinography.* Leiden: Brill, 2012.

Plamper, Jan. *The History of Emotions: An Introduction.* Oxford: Oxford University Press, 2015.

Regnier, Faustine. *L'exotisme culinaire: Essai sur les saveurs de l'autre.* Paris: PUF, 2004.

Samuels, David W., Louis Meintjes, Ana Maria Ochoa, and Thomas Porcello. "Soundscapes: Toward a Sounded Anthropology." *Annual Review of Anthropology* 39 (2010): 339–45.

Schafer, R. Murray. *The Soundscape: Our Sonic Environment and the Tuning of the World.* Rochester: Destiny Books, 1993.

Shaw, Alistair. "Telling the Truth About People's China." PhD diss., Victoria University of Wellington, 2010.

Stylianou-Lambert, Theopisti. "Tourists with Cameras: Reproducing or Producing?" *Annals of Tourism Research* 39, no. 4 (2012): 1817–38.

Suyin, Han. *My House Has Two Doors.* London: Jonathan Cape, 1980.

Urry, John, and Jonas Larsen. *The Tourist Gaze 3.0.* Thousand Oaks: Sage, 2011.

Wu, Shengqing, and Huang Xuelei, eds. *Sensing China. Modern Transformations of Sensory Culture.* London: Routledge, 2022.

Yang, Mayfair Mei-hui. *Gifts, Favors, and Banquets: The Art of Social Relationships in China.* Ithaca: Cornell University Press, 1994.

Yuxi, Liu. *Les relations Québec-Chine à l'heure de la Révolution tranquille.* Montreal: Presses de l'Université de Montréal, 2022.

CHAPTER 4

Sensual Sirens

Gendering Berlin's Cold War Telephony

Mark Fenemore

The crackling phone line blurs what is public and private, distant and intimate, with intriguing ambiguity. Sampling the voices of international operators, Das Modul's 1995 song "Das Fraeulein vom Amt" speculates about the mysterious, erotic energy radiated by such alluring enigmas:

> Are you blond or brunette,
> conceited or kind?
> Are you shy or coquettish?

Asking "Can you see through men?," the song alludes to the male mind's peculiar interpretation of female telephonic voices as dream-inducing, mysterious muses.[1] With a whispering tone seemingly designed to seduce, in this ditty, the acousmatic—audible but unseen—honey tongues of the female operators are bewitching. Trying to imagine the body matching the intonation, male listeners associate a particular voice with a specific but elusive physicality. Knowingly or unknowingly, this ambiguity inspires attraction, suggestion, and preoccupation.

From the beginnings of telephony, female operators were objects of tantalizing fascination. Distant but close enough to whisper, these putative "sirens" were inscrutable but enticing. Especially for adolescents, the immediacy of hearing other human voices, particularly those of the opposite sex, was exhilarating. Ethereal yet immediate, the siren voices conjured up fantasies of sweet-but-forbidden delectation, and they were often depicted as seductive in contemporary photography. As a thirteen-year-old phone phreak (or illicit telephonic tinkerer), Evan Doorbell experienced the messages recorded by telephone operators in his vicinity as racy come-ons. Fascinated by the regional variations in their accents, which he interpreted as sultriness, he became an unauthorized anthropologist of the phone system, spending hours recording his findings.[2] Imagine, then, that underneath their crisp, immaculate uniforms, the soft-voiced sirens were wearing stockings and suspenders, and you have some inkling of the explosive erotic charge sparked by operators of the East Berlin police switchboard in 1951 in the minds of prurient callers. If the arrangement of electromagnetic circuits connecting the two halves of a divided city was an expression of physics, the human part of the network provided lessons in chemistry and biology, firing the imaginations of users. The opaque but enticing "Fräulein vom Amt," as the German "hello girl" was popularly known, was still intriguing male imaginations enough in 1954 to form the subject of a West German film.[3] It chronicled the rags-to-riches life story of telephonist-turned-singer Gisela Beyer (see fig. 4.1).

There are two possible approaches to the study of Cold War telephony: one focuses on surveillance (as an expression of dystopia/totalitarianism), the other on gender (with a particular interest in the imagined sexiness of the telephonists' voices). Both have potential purchase for a history of the senses, or of sensuality, as expressed through sound. Despite talk of hired seduction and prostitution, a truly sensate history of espionage (and monitoring) has yet to be written.

Surveillance studies is an emerging field. While European preoccupations with privacy often relate to Nazi-era abuses, in-depth historical assessments of wiretaps in dictatorships are strangely missing. Despite telephonic surveillance's presence in the popular imagination, there is limited concrete historical analysis of the practice in either the Third Reich or the German Democratic Republic (GDR).[4] Berlin was, of course, of crucial importance as an arena for telephone tapping. The Soviets officially "discovered" the British-American tunnel wired up to their telephone exchange (and code-named Operation Gold) on April 21, 1956. In subsequent decades, the ECHELON

Fig. 4.1 Female phone operators were eroticized in an iconic 1954 German movie with Renate Holm, *Fräulein vom Amt*. Photo excerpt from "Illustrierte Film-Bühne," no. 2382, 1954, 4 (Verlag für Filmschriften, Hebertshausen).

listening station, perched on the Teufelsberg, recorded telecommunications throughout Eastern Europe.[5]

In early 1950s Berlin, a would-be all-encompassing panoptic vision was fatally undermined by socially conservative (but unquestioned) gendered hiring practices. This meant that, while supposed to be efficacious and impregnable, the system of reporting and surveillance possessed all too human flaws. Demonstrating both protohacking and an early use of social engineering, this case sheds light on why the East German authorities felt it necessary to disconnect the city's hitherto-unified telephone network in May 1952. While today we view them with suspicion, at the time, sexualized notions ascribed to the system of telephonic connection and based on gender went largely undisputed.

The fragments of this case allow the possibility of an ethnographic microhistory of Cold War Berlin based on the "new cultural history" model. With her studies of lewd cuckoldry and imposture, Natalie Zemon Davis suggested that different, gendered studies of the lower classes (and thus both their imaginary and lived worldviews) are possible.[6] The behavior such studies uncover is not necessarily laudable or edifying. Those who infringe rules and deliberately transgress boundaries—the silver-tongued tricksters, impostors, and dissimulators—often prove not to be. But our task, as cultural historians, is one of "capturing otherness" in the past.[7] Rather than proscribe views in other centuries that we find objectionable, we need to develop a gender history that focuses on how men and women concretely interacted in the past.[8] Written records tend to silence or look away from such interactions or to present them merely from a dominant, hegemonic standpoint. This necessitates reading them "against the grain." This chapter is an attempt to listen to the "voice of the (gendered) machine," albeit one that is, at times, impudent, garbled and distorted. For some historians, the "fictional" qualities of the story are off-putting. The "motivations and values of ordinary people in the past" can appear jarring and alien.[9] This form of cultural history requires inventiveness held in check, as far as possible, by the fragmentary and ambivalent voices of the past.

In the case of telephony in 1951, how do we define this electromagnetic communication? Following the panopticon model, we can view it as an object of fear and trepidation. But from a gender-history perspective, albeit one recording and reflecting sexist, patriarchal values, we can also see it as seductive and alluring.[10] Cold War sensory historians tend to focus more on fear than on seduction.[11] Nevertheless, a good deal of the consumer and cultural policies deployed in Berlin was about seducing waverers and enemies. To refer to Steve Goodman, we need an "ecology of seduction" as well as of fear.[12]

The Lighter Side of Surveillance

In most scholarly studies, surveillance suggests a top-down, one-way power dynamic. We associate such scrutiny and monitoring with inescapable and irreversible processes of collective intimidation and repression. We assume that strategies of (overt and covert) observation are generally effective in cowing the population, whose members dutifully submit to the goals of the system of control.[13] In Jeremy Bentham's formulation of the panopticon, the prisoners were fatally weakened by their inability to predict whether they were being observed, moment to moment, by the guards. In a different context, Franz Kafka stressed the dehumanizing and disorienting effects of technology when harnessed to bureaucracy.[14]

As early as the 1940s, George Orwell imagined a two-way device that operated like a panoptical machine. This screen allowed Big Brother to spy obtrusively on the living room of every citizen.[15] Michel Foucault expressed similar concerns about panoptic surveillance tools being used to discipline the masses.[16] However, Orwell and other dystopian soothsayers failed to anticipate how much fun later generations would associate with being monitored by their screens. Few could foresee a population so bored that they would willingly embrace the mass erosion and destruction of privacy.[17] Surveillance has become worse than anything imagined by Bentham, Orwell, or Foucault, in large part because we code it as fun.

Sex and sensuality played an important role in Cold War espionage.[18] Both sides recognized the value of beautiful women acting as "honey traps." One elaborate scheme worked by having attractive women lure a target into a shop just over the border in West Berlin.[19] East Germany specialized in sending glamorous secretaries across the Cold War frontier. A number of them rapidly became indispensable in the Bonn ministries. As well as sending female agents, espionage chief Markus Wolf deployed "Romeos" to seduce lonely West German women in important positions.[20] These handsome male agents were trained to be highly attentive lovers—in essence, men who were too good to be true. Although Chancellor Willy Brandt had a female Stasi lover, who entertained his Bonn circle in the 1950s, his political downfall actually came in 1974, when his male secretary, Günter Guillaume, was revealed to be a double agent.[21]

A number of scholars have suggested that the preoccupation with a rigid, sinister, dark, and effective panopticon overlooks and negates the possibility of resistance.[22] The French Marxist sociologist Henri Lefebvre, for example, pointed to the existence of "cracks, chinks and gaps," allowing users partially to escape or to engage with surveillance in unexpected and creative ways. Enlarging the fissures creates interstices for adept rule-breakers to pass through.[23] For every user who is cowed by the evidence of surveillance, others seek to evade, trick, or undermine it.[24] These minor acts of individual evasion and defiance can negate the system's capacity for control. As historians Patrick Major and Rana Mitter argue, with its cold civil war, Germany was a key battleground between East and West.[25] Nevertheless, in spite of the tension, many people had not yet chosen sides. In a decade-long battle to win hearts, minds, and stomachs in Germany,[26] material longings were important. But yearnings could also be intangible, imaginary, or unrealizable.

Even though it was a civil war, the two sides were not, at first, distinct. In Berlin at least, both powers possessed sizable fifth columns (people who lived in one part of the city but whose politics or lifestyle more closely matched that of the other side). Every day hundreds of thousands crossed the border, going from the sector in which they lived to the one in which they worked. Until August 1961, the frontier was porous and largely invisible: a curtain made of nylon rather than iron.[27]

The Police Telephone Exchange in East Berlin: Gendered Communication

In 1951, telephony was a "new, old technology," creating a uniquely gendered network of audio communication in divided Berlin. Before systems of automated dialing were developed, behind each telephone jack there was a living, breathing, sensual human being. Beneath the sound and the fury of the propaganda war, there was space for more nuanced public-private expressions of shared sonic community. With a sweet, angelic "speaking voice," the female telephonist was responsible for connecting caller to caller via the right plug.[28] Even without automation, the telephone network represented the closest thing to a computerized system accessible to the general public. For those with curiosity and nous, it was a challenge to crack.

From the early 1900s, the German Post Office exclusively selected girls as telephonists because it deemed them less boisterous and unpredictable than teenage boys. In addition to their "natural" submissiveness, essential for serving the machine, recruiters looked for a pleasant manner, clear enunciation, and perfect diction in High German. Yet experts feared that these young women, at the cutting edge of discordant societal acceleration, could act as conduits for nervous energy. Exposed to the sensory overload of the electrified metropolis, they could lapse into "hysteria."[29] Opening up a new arena of sensual interaction challenged existing notions of decorum and proper behavior. From the beginning, male users habitually sexualized the operators. In part, this reflected the practice of hiring unmarried young women on the basis of their soft voices and friendly politeness.

Telephony blurred the boundaries between the genders with its confusing amalgamation of "intimacy at a distance."[30] In the United States in the 1920s, the "hello girls" even provided personal wake-up services. Some male callers deliberately gained gratification by dialing the unknown, invisible women while they themselves were naked. Berlin-based psychologist Fritz Giese assumed that the delicate belles who were exposed to so many male voices would of necessity become less innocent. He engineered an experiment in which he secretly watched them leaf through a book of erotic images. Although far from scientific, this early psychosocial study linked exposure to telephony with aberrant desire.[31] In both West and East Germany, well into the 1950s, telephonists could be dismissed for even the faintest whiff of impropriety. They had to be polite even when rebuffing obtrusive male callers: "We always try to be friendly, while nevertheless pointing out that he has misbehaved."[32]

In theory, telephonists were subject to extreme levels of surveillance and control. Supervisors routinely walked up and down the switchboard with headsets, controlling "their" girls' tone, dress, demeanor, and body language. Representing peak Taylorism, they could monitor every single move, gesture, and word made by the human switches. Nevertheless, nighttime callers found bored operators less reined in and more willing to chat.

Cold War sirens are typically coded as either seductive or predictive of destruction.[33] Thanks to contemporary understandings of correct behavior, the East Berlin police switchboard was highly gendered. On the one hand, this involved the imposition of patriarchal controls. On the other, service in the People's Police rendered young women modern in their relative economic independence. In Berlin in 1951, the telephonists provided an interface between callers and the police hierarchy. They could handle anything from cats stuck in trees to reports of missing children. By relaying descriptions of suspicious behavior, they could spark a police investigation that in turn could trigger Stasi attention. Calling the hotline provided citizens with a renewed opportunity to denounce their neighbors, colleagues, friends, and former lovers for unwise comments made when drunk, exuberant, or angry.[34] The exchange was the bottom rung of a crucial security apparatus and the most visible part of the surveillance iceberg. Yet at this stage, there was no block on people calling the switchboard from West Berlin. The phone network was much denser in the capitalist sectors, and most Berliners still saw the two halves of the city as inseparable. Even at the height of the Cold War, in their eyes, what Germans shared trumped what divided them.

What If Users of a Technology Ignore Its Rationale and Reverse Its Power Dynamic?

In theory, the call centers of the People's Police (coded as "communications" hubs) formed a closed-off and firewalled gateway. Outsiders needed skill and nous to tap into them. However, what for some seemed like a forbidding panopticon was, for Wolfgang, an adventure playground.[35] He was a mischievous twenty-year-old with free time and an unguarded phone in his guard unit in Smuts Barracks, located in Spandau within the British sector of West Berlin. Starved of entertainment, he willfully took the "red pill." Embarking on a wild journey into the vortex of early 1950s Stalinism, he deliberately tied himself to the mast. For him, having an auditory peep behind the Iron Curtain represented freedom, far away from humdrum realities. More Walter Mitty than James Bond, he spun an elaborate web of deception designed to bolster his allure. Waltraud, one of the first telephonists he chatted up, said that she had found it strange that he "always wanted to see" her People's Police identity card. She had no idea what his intention was, but he kept asking for the names of her colleagues and superiors. When challenged, he told her that he "had his sources."

Combined with his skills as a sweet talker, his insouciance led to a tumultuous roller coaster ride of emotional crossed wires, not least in the form of overlapping offers of engagement. Another one of his conquests, Erika, wrote, "After a short time, I introduced him to my parents because he had expressed the intention of marrying me. At first, he didn't tell me what he did for a living, but eventually I found out that he was a secret agent with the FBI (French Security Service) [sic]."[36] On one of their dates, he had taken her to the French barracks, the Quartier Napoléon, where an officer had saluted him. This convinced her that his hints about having fought in Indochina and acting as an agent for the French must have been true. Lillian worked at a different switchboard, but Wolfgang also told her that he was a lieutenant for the French in Frohnau.

Davis suggested that we might be as interested in the "perhapses" and "may-have-beens" as what actually happened. Our goal, as historians, is to decipher what is going on.[37] Capturing the specificity of an alien culture is difficult because of the distorted lens through which the imaginary world happened to be recorded. The world Wolfgang created for himself was ambiguous, ambivalent, fluid, and unpredictable. Ascertaining Wolfgang's actual role or function was consequently difficult. The frequent misspellings of "Watchman Service" in the Stasi reports and the suggestions that this meant that he was a "British mercenary" indicate that the Stasi did not have the foggiest idea what his day job entailed. It is a sign of the Stasi's relative helplessness that the officers recorded that he wore a dark green uniform and was armed with an English carbine. The best understanding we have is that he was employed as a watchman (or security guard) at Smuts Barracks next to Spandau Prison. The purpose of this base was to provide ready-for-action Hussar-driven armored cars, but Wolfgang's role was chiefly to guard supplies. The story that he was injured in a scuffle with the People's Police at the border, near Staaken, fitted the Stasi's understanding of the Western Allies deploying German mercenaries as agents provocateurs, but it would have been an extraordinary (not to say illegal) deployment. Generally, Wolfgang stole telephone time from his employer: "When I was off duty, I used my free time to make phone calls. It was always in the two hours that I had free before I had to go on guard duty again."[38]

The Stasi began looking for him on July 24, 1951, but did not capture him until August 10. To lure him in, they spread a rumor among Erika's colleagues that she had been admitted to hospital. When he sought to visit her, he was obliged to show his identity card, and they promptly arrested him. He had known his latest fiancée for just fourteen days. Thanks to the stories he had told her and others, when they arrested him, the Stasi officers were under the misapprehension that he was working as a French agent. It appears true that Wolfgang had spent four weeks with the Foreign Legion in Innsbruck in March 1946. In one version of his story, he lied about his age, saying that he was twenty-four, not sixteen, before deserting. In another, the medical examiner declared him "unfit for service in the tropics."

Despite his limited technological know-how, Wolfgang was a proto "phone phreak."[39] Like the pioneer hackers who later emerged in the United States, he was driven by a desire to see if he could make the technology do things for which it was not designed. In 1951, the telephone network straddling Berlin formed part of the largest electromechanical machine in the world. Exploring its mysteries was fascinating for a special subset of (mostly male) users. Phreakers were driven by the prankishness that had earlier made boys unsuitable as operators. Wolfgang intuitively learned about the capabilities of the telephone network by playing with it and its human switches. Curious about how far he could venture without getting caught, he loved exploring forbidden territory; it was an activity he associated with real risk and danger. Before the advent of tone dialing, the best way to manipulate the system was to "pretext" the operator through effective patter. Following the panopticon paradigm, we tend to see female operators as "pawns of social control," closely regulated by society. On occasion, however, they could act as subversive mavericks who flouted rules and transgressed sociopolitical boundaries. Expected to be passive and docile, they could instead manifest an unruly consciousness within the impersonal machine.

Davis legitimately asks, "In historical writing, where does reconstruction stop and invention begin?"[40] Disentangling truth from fiction is not easy. Essentially, in the case of Wolfgang, Waltraud, and Erika, we are left with traces of a defunct emotional community that was based on shared sensory experiences but remained subterranean and largely unrecorded. The sensate left a powerful residue in the sensibilities and behaviors of the actors concerned, but it did not leave much trace in the historical record. In other words, we have the emotional translation but not the original sensory transcript or text. Partly this is because Wolfgang and his (girl)friends were engaged in deception. Yet it is also because our record of the sensory experience is secondhand and mediated through a bureaucratic police organization that was largely uninterested in the sensate. Far from giving Wolfgang a "clean hearing," the Stasi set the agenda for the interrogations. The officers decided what did and did not become part of the record according to their own (alien) system of meaning.[41] Some details are pin-sharp; others are frustratingly blurry. We can assume that Wolfgang's voice must have been persuasive, convincing, and authoritative because of the dramatic series of events that ensued. We do not have a precise account of the tone or even of the words he used.

It is as difficult to determine Wolfgang's "true identity" in the twentieth century as it was to determine Arnaud du Tilh's in the sixteenth.[42] Bumping along the bottom of the job market, Wolfgang was looking for a form of employment that would give him an air of excitement and mystery. In March

1950, he spent a day working for a detective agency based in Stalinallee. He joined the guard unit on December 12, 1950, because he was in a desperate financial situation. Other people in the past are other. Sometimes, in Wolfgang's interrogation file, the truth seems more bizarre than the fiction. Wolfgang denied that he had met with French agents in a strip club. Yes, he said, he had been to such a burlesque café in the French sector, but he had gone there for entertainment with his sister and his uncle Fritz. He insisted that his links to the French authorities, which he had been keen to stress to his girlfriends, were nothing more than "pure boastfulness" and bravado.

Capricious and willful, Wolfgang seems to have begun probing the police exchange on his own initiative. It is possible that, even at this early stage, he was working at the lower levels of the Western intelligence hierarchy, feeding tidbits of information to one or more of the Allies in return for petty cash. Saying that he had been commissioned to trick the telephone operators into revealing the names and home addresses of their superiors, he referred to a bunkmate called Horst B. According to this version of his story, it was Horst who made the first contacts and then set Wolfgang up on dates with Erika and the other girls, because Horst was already engaged and no longer needed their numbers. Horst B. came from East Berlin and said that he could expect fifteen years in Siberia if he dared to set foot in the Eastern sector again. In another version, Horst was Wolfgang's guard post commander who gave him low-level intelligence assignments. He encouraged him to call the Weissensee, Lichtenberg, Prenzlauer Berg, and Friedrichshain precincts and emboldened him to get the names of the heads of the inspectorates. He supposedly also paid Wolfgang a pack of English cigarettes to deliver an envelope to a People's Policeman in the underground toilets at Alexanderplatz. Sometimes, however, Wolfgang introduced himself as Horst. It is possible, then, that Horst B. was merely Wolfgang's alter ego, his Tyler Durden. Or he could genuinely have been a shadowy Svengali. Such is the ambiguity in the records. Although he clearly mixed business with pleasure, the geographical spread and systematic nature of Wolfgang's analog attack suggests that the calls were more about the former than the latter. Nevertheless, if Wolfgang was an agent, he was probably a rogue one.

In terms of the history of emotions, the effects of Wolfgang's affectations fundamentally altered the narrative. Nevertheless, a large part of his seduction was based on exaggerations, obfuscations, and outright lies. We can juxtapose the ease with which he lied to his conversation partners with his subsequent, much more urgent, need to lie to his interrogators. Wolfgang's skill in convincing others to pass on information happened to be similar to the modus operandi of intelligence agencies.[43] Like him, both phreaks and spooks commonly used insider jokes to establish rapport in cold calls. However, in the realms of catfishing and social engineering, it is legitimate to ask if unmediated sensory perceptions really exist.

Any network with a human component is vulnerable to a social-engineering attack. In the context of a phone system, social engineering commonly involves wheedling (or tricking) information out of unsuspecting employees. In the process of chewing the fat, Wolfgang built up an intimate understanding of the network and its flaws. Without any discernible political motivation, he became an expert in the internal workings and office politics of the police exchange. To get past the operators' defenses, he used a mixture of catfishing and blagging. Demonstrating a sophisticated understanding of the exchange's inner dynamics, he combined boasts and delusions of grandeur with jokes and friendly curiosity. Those in charge realized that a particular stranger was endeavoring to make conversation with the female comrades working on the switchboard. His conversations stood out as "political in content" and always ended with what they termed "vituperative jokes about the GDR."[44] Erika described his first call to her as entertaining; he already knew her name and important details about her social standing, preferences, and tastes. His interpersonal skills closely resembled those of US social-engineering pioneer Denny Teresi but without the latter's technical capabilities.[45] Wolfgang appears to have been engaged in an unauthorized, do-it-yourself, one-man campaign of "sensory warfare." He embodied an intersensorial version of what Cold War historian Dayton Lekner terms "heart warfare."[46]

Something about his voice and personality gave him a knack for disarming and befriending the young women in uniform. The closeness in age allowed Wolfgang to allay their suspicions. In spite of the geopolitical disparities, his sonar ping produced a strong echo. Blackmail or threats repeated in the daytime were no match for his suave seduction at night. He found the police girls happy to gossip about their colleagues and superiors. In a few cases, he even managed to unlock their hearts, turning strangers into lovers.

Socially engineering the exchange offered access to a (sonic) secret society. Wolfgang's skill in disarming the operators exploited their boredom and curiosity as well as their nonchalance about the rules. In 1951, for adolescents starved of entertainment, the police switchboard was the closest thing they had to the intimacy and immediacy of a social network. Operators had always been a nexus for gossip and news. Despite being subject to intensive surveillance during the day, they were far from cowed. Left to their own devices, late at night, they frequently rebelled. Many of them were living a double life, working for the Stalinist "man" but shopping, socializing, and dancing in the Western sectors. Although ostensibly first-line defenders of state socialism, they nevertheless flirted with all the forbidden fruit that capitalism (and Western boyfriends) had to offer.[47] Wolfgang's target audience was also, to some extent, implicitly engaged in sensory warfare. The telephonists were expected to be both beautiful and fragrant because of the way they spoke on the phone. For those working on the switchboard, there seems to have been some pressure to meet the ideal in callers' imaginations.

Wolfgang's overtures were effective because of the wider backdrop of "sensual deprivation" in early 1950s Berlin. As a tout, he instinctively knew how to "sell with color," as Victoria Phillips put it.[48] In many ways, he was an exceptional operator. His charm on the phone blinded at least two of the girls to his glaring shortcomings. Though he was no oil painting, he was attractive and persuasive enough for them to want to marry him. His mastery of the telephone clearly influenced his listeners profoundly, but the aural love triangle was a complicated set of entangled relationships.

We mainly associate intelligence gathering with professional government agencies like the CIA, KGB, or SIS. All three operated in Berlin in the early 1950s with varying degrees of success. However, as many as eighty different agencies were active in the divided city at the height of the Cold War.[49] Some were private-sector subcontractors who in turn employed ad hoc agents and couriers on a piecemeal basis. Wolfgang was in the habit of flashing an FBI badge to get out of trouble. Although it cannot be ruled out, he does not appear to have worked for any bona fide Western intelligence agency in 1951. Rather, he appears to have been an enthusiastic amateur, driven by a combination of curiosity and chutzpah to probe for weaknesses in the border-straddling telephone system. Nevertheless, the fact that he went straight back to espionage in 1957, after his release from prison (in the process earning himself a life sentence), suggests that this was a deliberate career move rather than a passing fancy.[50]

This case proves the maxim that the weakest part of any security system is its human component. The lowest rung of the East German system of domination was no exception. Such was Wolfgang's gravitas and the (audible) allure he managed to project that several of the police girls became putty in his hands. Nevertheless, in femme fatale Erika, Wolfgang seems to have met his match. Her Russian father had died at Stalingrad (apparently fighting on the German side). Worried by her behavior, her God-fearing Polish mother and Hungarian stepfather sent her to a convent. Congenitally incapable of staying on the straight and narrow, she managed to transition from a "Home for Wayward Young Women" to employment in the People's Police. Although he had advised her against joining because of his own negative experiences of the force's "strict military tone," her brother told her what to stress in her police application. Counting in her favor was the fact that she had been arrested four times in the French sector during the UGO Putsch, the strike by railwaymen in the Western sectors in May 1949. Erika was clearly resolute in defending her "side" when called upon to do so. After she joined the police, however, the Stasi noted that she had had "a number of love affairs" with male members of the People's Police.

Two paths of self-destruction converged: the bad boy, would-be foreign legionary, and gentleman spy encountered his ex-convent-school, mysterious other woman. Intoxicated by the love triangle in which he had become entangled, he failed to see that she was actually his nemesis. Toward the end, both sets of parents threatened to call the authorities if the strikingly unsuitable couple persisted in seeing each other. Wolfgang's mother could not stand Erika, seeing her as responsible for his slide into debauchery. A row occurred when he sought to pick up his possessions while still in her "evil clutches." This led his parents to call the West Berlin police, who briefly arrested Erika. Such was his infatuation that it was only a matter of time before he fell into the Stasi's lap.

Conclusion: Cold War Sirens

In postwar East Germany, telecommunications technology was supposed to assist the work of everyday surveillance and policing. In deploying sensual and seductive sirens in pursuit of such goals, gender concerns appear to have trumped security. Leaving the vital communications hub unsupervised at unsociable hours proved a dangerous strategy. Following an Odyssean inner logic, the sirens began luring unwary Western voyagers onto the Cold War rocks. Despite their security training and indoctrination, the switchboard girls proved to be low-hanging fruit for someone who could put on a suave and debonair phone manner.

In a democratic system, by exposing flaws, hackers can paradoxically help strengthen privacy and security. Wolfgang sought personal gratification and gain rather than endeavoring to reveal the system's flaws or abuses.

One way for the Stasi to neuter or tame Wolfgang's power would have been to recruit him as a double agent, but the Stasi could not guarantee that he would manifest any lasting loyalty to their system. Although his techniques were not that dissimilar to their own, they saw him merely as an enemy spy to be crushed.

In the end, the gendered hiring practices proved a fatal Achilles' heel, transforming the switchboard from an impregnable top-down panopticon into a synoptical bottom-up Trojan horse. In consequence, despite its harsh ambitions, the Stalinist surveillance regime proved light years away from effectively policing its operators' morals. Wolfgang's actions show that resistance to surveillance can be highly dynamic, permitting agency in ways not recognized by a would-be totalizing panopticon model. Despite being an outsider and an enemy, through exceptional idiosyncrasy and sheer force of personality, he was able, briefly, to rewrite the power dynamic. A few months later, blaming espionage, the East German authorities severed the city's phone network.[51] In itself, this is a fitting tribute to Wolfgang's skill in hacking (or socially engineering) the exchange. Creating a feedback loop in the network of auditory surveillance, Wolfgang's activity enlarges our understanding of the Cold War. This particular arena of sound warfare was inextricably linked to sexualized, auditory notions of gender. Proving that, on its own, the gendered voice can form a powerful object of desire (and fantasy), the case also underlines that the Stalinists were less proficient in "operant conditioning" than first believed.

Our interpretations remain fragile and tentative. Some imbroglios put our skills as cold-case detectives to the test. But, by definition, a sensory history of the Cold War has the potential to offer a more egalitarian view of history. Vivid and colorful stories can be as salient and meaningful as their opposite. Although the Stasi's distorted "acoustic mirror" contains holes and contradictory evidence, it nevertheless allows us to recreate an ethnographic microhistory of Cold War Berlin.[52] I have sought to make evident the limitations of the material and the deliberate "crafting and shaping" required to unlock its meaning. Albeit packaged in half-truths and lies, Wolfgang, Waltraud, and Erika's messy love triangle stresses the importance of sensual attraction in gendered studies of surveillance and espionage (with technology facilitating and sparking attraction between young men and women in the past). It also stresses the extent to which those of both sexes, involved in surveillance and deception, were savvy operators, canny and complicit, rather than mere dupes. If Wolfgang was skilled in telling his listeners what they wanted to hear, the girls acted as lures for his aberrant behavior. Although young ladies with taste and decorum need do little for boys to consider them mysterious and alluring, the telephonists represented the pinnacle of (sensual) sophistication in 1951 Cold War Berlin.

Notes

1. Das Modul, "Fraeulein vom Amt."
2. For a unique ethnography of sound, see Evan Doorbell, "How I Became a Phone Phreak," posted on November 19, 2017, by Curt Rowlett, YouTube video, 52:20, https://www.youtube.com/watch?v=suqsJzb7_IA.
3. See Carl-Heinz Schroth, dir., *Fräulein vom Amt* (West Germany: Burg-Film, 1954).
4. See Wiesen, Zatlin, and Zimmerman, "Forum."
5. Murphy, Kondrashev, and Bailey, *Battleground Berlin*, 205–37.
6. See Davis, *Return of Martin Guerre*; Davis, *Fiction in the Archives*.
7. Burke, *What Is Cultural History?*, 38.
8. Davis, "'Women's History,'" 89.
9. Finlay, "Refashioning of Martin Guerre," 553.
10. Marvin, *When Old Technologies Were New*, 84.
11. See Biess, *German Angst*.
12. See Goodman, *Sonic Warfare*.
13. See Bentham, *Panopticon Writings*.
14. See Kafka, *Trial*.
15. See Orwell, *1984*.
16. See Foucault, *Discipline and Punish*.
17. Here Orwell's former teacher, Aldous Huxley, was more farsighted with his depiction of soma and feelies. See Huxley, *Brave New World*.
18. See Michael Dobbs, "Sexpionage: Why We Can't Resist Those KGB Sirens," *Washington Post*, April 12, 1987.
19. See Blake, *No Other Choice*, 169–70.
20. Central Intelligence Agency, "Romeo Spies: Intelligence and Operations," June 4, 2018, https://www.cia.gov/stories/story/romeo-spies/.
21. See Miard-Delacroix, *Willy Brandt*, 56–57; Michels, *Guillaume*.
22. Geesin, "Resistance to Surveillance," 19, 22.
23. Lefebvre, *Critique of Everyday Life*, 127.
24. See Gilliom, "Resisting Surveillance," 72.
25. See Major and Mitter, "East is East," 9.
26. See chapter 1 in this volume.
27. See Péteri, "Nylon Curtain"; Castillo, "Nylon Curtain."
28. Fleeger, *Mismatched Women*, 8.
29. Although the possibility of injury was real, talk of "hysteria" was patently balderdash. Siegert, "Das Amt des Gehorchens"; see also Killen, *Berlin Electropolis*.
30. Hutchby, *Conversation and Technology*, 81, 83.
31. See Giese, *Berufspsychologische Beobachtungen*, 57–60, as cited in Killen, *Berlin Electropolis*, 197–99.
32. See Klaudia Deus, *Lokalzeit Bergisches Land*, "Das Fräulein vom Amt," originally aired January 2013 on Westdeutscher Rundfunk, posted on January 5, 2013, by lokalzeitjunkie, YouTube video, 4:21, https://www.youtube.com/watch?v=LMeIhFNfuxo.
33. See Bull, "Introduction: Sound Studies," xxviii. Cf. Bull, *Sirens*. The dangerousness authorities attribute to women is both political and highly symbolic. See Grendi, "Ripensare la microstoria," 545.
34. See Gellately, "Denunciations," 947.
35. I first read his file in connection with a study of kidnappings in 1950s Berlin. See Bundesarchiv (hereafter BArch), MfS AU 1046/58, Vols. 1–4.
36. Kommando-Stelle PVP an MfS, "Anrufe einer englischen Dienststelle an VP-Dienststellen," July 7, 1951, BArch, MfS AU 1046/58, Vols. 1, 7.
37. Davis, *Return of Martin Guerre*, viii, 49.
38. Vernehmung K., October 1, 1951, BArch, MfS AU 1046/58, Vol. 1, 125–31.
39. Lapsley, *Exploding the Phone*, 306.
40. Davis, "On the Lame," 572.
41. See Stasi file on Wolfgang K., BArch, MfS AU 1046/58, Vols. 1–4.
42. Davis, "On the Lame," 572.

43. See Rositzke, *CIA's Secret Operations*, 74.
44. Kommando-Stelle PVP an MfS.
45. Like a number of early phreaks, Teresi was blind. His authenticity depended in large part on an expertly authoritative performance of gender.
46. See chapter 5 in this volume.
47. It is not that surprising that, despite their economic independence, the telephonists were largely pre-feminist. A recent and not particularly popular imposition, state socialism did not properly address women's emancipation until after the 1953 uprising and then in ways that diverged from Western-style feminism.
48. See chapter 1 in this volume.
49. See Fenemore, *Fighting the Cold War*, 170.
50. Cf. "Lebenslänglich Zuchthaus für Menschenhändler," *Neues Deutschland*, April 21, 1957.
51. Cf. "First Phone Calls Since '52 Link East and West Berlin," *New York Times*, February 1, 1971.
52. Thompson, "Gendered Sound," 109.

Bibliography

Archival Sources
Bundesarchiv, Berlin, Germany: BArch, MfS AU 1046/58, Vols. 1–4.

Audiovisual Sources
Deus, Klaudia. *Lokalzeit Bergisches Land.* "Das Fräulein vom Amt." Originally aired January 2013 on Westdeutscher Rundfunk. Posted on January 5, 2013, by lokalzeitjunkie. YouTube video, 4:21. https://www.youtube.com/watch?v=LMeIhFNfuxo.
Doorbell, Evan. "How I Became a Phone Phreak." Posted on November 19, 2017, by Curt Rowlett. YouTube video, 52:20, https://www.youtube.com/watch?v=suqsJzb7_IA.
Das Modul. "Fraeulein vom Amt." *Musik mit Hertz*. Urban 529 002-4, 1995, cassette album.
Schroth, Carl-Heinz, dir. *Fräulein vom Amt.* 1954. West Germany: Burg-Film.

Published Sources
Bentham, Jeremy. *The Panopticon Writings*. Edited by Miran Božovič. London: Verso, 1995.
Biess, Frank. *German Angst: Fear and Democracy in the Federal Republic of Germany*. Oxford: Oxford University Press, 2020.
Blake, George. *No Other Choice: An Autobiography*. London: Jonathan Cape, 1990.
Bull, Michael. "Introduction: Sound Studies and the Art of Listening." In Bull, *Routledge Companion to Sound Studies*, xvii–xxxii.
———, ed. *The Routledge Companion to Sound Studies*. London: Routledge, 2018.
———. *Sirens*. London: Bloomsbury, 2020.
Burke, Peter. *What Is Cultural History?* 2nd ed. Cambridge: Polity Press, 2008.
Castillo, Greg. "The Nylon Curtain: Architectural Unification in Divided Berlin." In *Berlin Divided City, 1945–1989*, edited by Philip Broadbent and Sabine Hake, 46–74. Oxford: Berghahn, 2010.
Davis, Natalie Zemon. *Fiction in the Archives: Pardon Tales and Their Tellers in Sixteenth-Century France*. Cambridge: Polity, 1987.
———. "On the Lame." *American Historical Review* 93, no. 3 (1988): 572–603.
———. *The Return of Martin Guerre*. Cambridge: Harvard University Press, 1983.
———. "'Women's History' in Transition: The European Case." *Feminist Studies* 3, no. 3/4 (1976): 83–103.
Fenemore, Mark. *Fighting the Cold War in Post-Blockade, Pre-Wall Berlin: Behind Enemy Lines*. London: Routledge, 2020.
Finlay, Robert. "The Refashioning of Martin Guerre." *American Historical Review* 93, no. 3 (1988): 553–71.
Fleeger, Jennifer. *Mismatched Women: The Siren's Song Through the Machine*. Oxford: Oxford University Press, 2014.

Foucault, Michel. *Discipline and Punish: The Birth of the Prison.* Translated by Alan Sheridan. London: Allen Lane, 1977.

Geesin, Beverly. "Resistance to Surveillance in Everyday Life." PhD diss., University of York, 2012.

Gellately, Robert. "Denunciations in Twentieth-Century Germany: Aspects of Self-Policing in the Third Reich and the German Democratic Republic." *Journal of Modern History* 68, no. 4 (1996): 931–67.

Giese, Fritz. *Berufspsychologische Beobachtungen im Reichstelegraphendienst.* Leipzig: Barth, 1923.

Gilliom, John. "Resisting Surveillance." *Social Text* 23, no. 2 (2005): 71–83.

Goodman, Steve. *Sonic Warfare: Sound, Affect, and the Ecology of Fear.* Cambridge: MIT Press, 2010.

Grendi, Edoardo. "Ripensare la microstoria?" *Quaderni storici* 29, no. 86 (1994): 539–49.

Horwitz, Jamie. "1984." *Film Comment* 20, no. 1 (1984): 25–28.

Hutchby, Ian. *Conversation and Technology: From the Telephone to the Internet.* Cambridge: Polity, 2001.

Huxley, Aldous. *Brave New World.* London: Chatto & Windus, 1932.

Kafka, Franz. *The Trial.* Translated by Willa and Edwin Muir. Harmondsworth: Penguin, 1935.

Killen, Andreas. *Berlin Electropolis: Shock, Nerves, and German Modernity.* Berkeley: University of California Press, 2006.

Lapsley, Phil. *Exploding the Phone: The Untold Story of the Teenagers and Outlaws Who Hacked Ma Bell.* New York: Grove Press, 2013.

Lefebvre, Henri. *Critique of Everyday Life.* Vol. 3. London: Verso, 2005.

Major, Patrick, and Rana Mitter. "East is East and West is West? Towards a Comparative Socio-Cultural History of the Cold War." In *Across the Blocs: Cold War Cultural and Social History,* edited by Patrick Major and Rana Mitter, 1–18. London: Frank Cass, 2004.

Marvin, Carolyn. *When Old Technologies Were New: Thinking About Electric Communication in the Late Nineteenth Century.* New York: Oxford University Press, 1988.

Miard-Delacroix, Hélène. *Willy Brandt: Life of a Statesman.* Translated by Isabelle Chaize. London: I. B. Tauris, 2016.

Michels, Eckard. *Guillaume, Der Spion: Eine deutsch-deutsche Karriere.* Berlin: Ch. Links, 2013.

Murphy, David E., Sergei A. Kondrashev, and George Bailey. *Battleground Berlin: CIA vs. KGB in the Cold War.* New Haven: Yale University Press, 1999.

Orwell, George. *1984.* London: Secker & Warburg, 1949.

Péteri, György. "Nylon Curtain—Transnational and Transsystemic Tendencies in the Cultural Life of State-Socialist Russia and East-Central Europe." *Slavonica* 10, no. 2 (2004): 113–23.

Rositzke, Harry A. *The CIA's Secret Operations: Espionage, Counterespionage, and Covert Action.* New York: Reader's Digest Press, 1977.

Siegert, Bernhard. "Das Amt des Gehorchens: Hysterie der Telefonistinnen oder Wiederkehr des Ohres, 1874–1913." In *Armaturen der Sinne. Literarische und technische Medien, 1870–1920,* edited by Jochen Hörisch and Michael Wetzel, 83–106. Munich: Fink, 1990.

Thompson, Marie. "Gendered Sound." In Bull, *Routledge Companion to Sound Studies,* 108–17.

Wiesen, Jonathan, Jonathan Zatlin, and Angela Zimmerman, eds. "Forum: Surveillance in German History." *German History* 34, no. 2 (2016): 293–314.

PART II

PARTITION, PROPAGANDA, SENSORY BORDERS

CHAPTER 5

Breaking the Aquatic Sound Barrier

Hearing Yourself and Your Enemy Across the Taiwan Strait

Dayton Lekner

From 1975 to 1977, while performing compulsory military service, the young Taiwanese Wang Yiwen was stationed on the island of Jinmen, a mere twelve hundred meters from Communist China. From his aquatic front line, Wang could see across the divide cleaved in 1949 when the Chinese Communist Party had claimed the mainland and the Nationalists, in retreat to Taiwan, had managed to retain this tiny group of islands just off the coast of Fujian. Despite its ideological, national, and military binaries, the border remained sonically porous. As Wang recalls:

> Apart from the shelling on both sides of the [Taiwan] Strait, regardless of whether it was day or night, you could hear the shouts and music from the other side resounding across the sky, especially in the middle of the night. In fact, after a while, I really didn't pay attention to what they were talking about. It always accompanied us during our work, rest periods, and life. But I can still clearly feel that sense of the "sonic domain" (*sheng yu*) of the time and place. Sometimes when I hear broadcasts resounding around a large space,

the echoes are somewhat similar and it takes me back to hearing the "heart war calls."[1]

These "heart war calls" were signals from large speaker installations on the Chinese coast. Despite clear ideological goals, the "shouts and music"—once amplified, relayed across the water, and scattered among the rocky headlands of Taiwan—left only diffuse impressions on Wang. This diffusion, from ideological opposition to human voice and finally to quotidian and even otherworldly reception, belies Cold War binaries, exposes plural ways of hearing, and is the focus of this chapter.

In 1949, following a civil war between the Chinese Communist Party (CCP) and the Chinese Nationalist Party (KMT, Kuomintang), a rupture occurred in which the Communists held the mainland and its six hundred million inhabitants, and the KMT fled to Taiwan. Each regime claimed to be the rightful ruler and heir to China, both as a nation-state and as a culture. Undergirding these claims were the military and political heft of the two primary Cold War foes—the Soviet Union supporting the Communists and the United States supporting the Nationalists. Military skirmishes continued to break out. In the Battle of Guningtou in October 1949, the Nationalists managed to defend the islands of the Jinmen archipelago in the Taiwan Strait. In the Second Taiwan Straits Crisis in late 1958, the CCP again shelled the islands and again failed to claim them. The result was a Cold War front line in which the Jinmen Islands just offshore remained under Nationalist rule and became the base for up to one hundred thousand troops. Despite ethnic and familial bonds and geographical proximity, the aquatic front line thus established ultimately crystallized into a threshold of friend-foe dichotomies and opposing ideologies.

From 1953 to 1992, speaker towers located on the headlands of both Xiamen (China) and Jinmen (Taiwan) broadcast sound at high volumes across this Cold War divide. Separated by a distance of as little as twelve hundred meters, these towers were one of the few channels of communication between the Communists and the Nationalists for much of the era. In principle, and according to central directives, the speakers were frontline weapons in the battle between communist and "free" China. In practice, however, they piped sounds at high volume but inconsistent clarity across the strait with mixed results. Like other forms of sonic propaganda deployed by the United States in Korea and Vietnam—and across Europe in the Second World War—weather, terrain, and interference from other sounds often determined whether an audience heard a message as written. Political messages were repeated in the hope that listeners would gradually piece together a coherent meaning. As the relay of semantic content was unreliable, tone of voice became critical. Songs, the melodies of which carried better than the semantics of Communist or Nationalist tenets, were used. In songs and vocal messages, divisions between the two sides broke down as each reached out with the other's songs, tone of voice, and dialect.

Previous sonic studies of China during this era have noted the authoritarian goals of sonic infrastructure.[2] This chapter, based on primary interviews, memoir, and archival sources, explores such goals as they were translated into sounds and disseminated. It addresses central policy; the binaries of ideological division; the broadcast of such messages under geographical, sonic, and linguistic constraints; and the perception of the messages by their target audiences and those caught in the sonic crossfire. It examines how the processes of speaking, making sound, and being heard break down under such conditions, and it gives primary consideration to the contingencies and plural modes of hearing. I make three arguments: First, in the sonic back-and-forth across the Taiwan Strait, what began as ideological opposition for both sides soon became an exercise in the physics and psychoacoustics of signal and reception. Second, while initially opposed, each side at once responded to the other's calls, even mimicking them at times, but finally marked out a national voice in opposition to but in conversation with its foe. Finally, in the impulse, diffusion, and reception of these Cold War signals, we see that a sonic focus can decenter dominant narratives and reveal plural and shifting temporalities, boundaries, and experiences.

Impulse: Establishing a Sonic Front Line

The first station was established by the People's Republic of China (PRC) on Jiaoyu Island two kilometers north of Mashan on the main island of Jinmen. It used an array of nine 250-watt speakers called the "nine-headed bird."[3] Stations were then set up along the Chinese coast, first in Xiangshan and then in Shimaotou and Baishi Paotai. After the Taiwan Straits Crisis of 1958, a master controlling station was built on Hulishan. The KMT responded with stations of its own in corresponding locations, first in Mashan, then in Hujingtou on Lieyu Island, then on Dadan Island, and finally, in 1967, on Guningtou.[4] A sonic arms race ensued, with regular upgrades of the audio technology in each side's towers, as each side sought to dominate the

Fig. 5.1 Sonic weaponry at the aquatic frontier: Beishan broadcasting tower in Guningtou, Taiwan, 2020. Photo: Dayton Lekner.

soundscapes, render political propaganda more audible, and drown out enemy broadcasts (see fig. 5.1).

Once the speaker installations had been built, the concrete and steel structures required human operators: announcers to provide their voices, technical operators to manage the equipment, and station managers to handle intelligence gathering and oversee operations. Both sides favored female broadcasters.[5] In Taiwan, this preference was institutionalized from 1954 as the first wave of broadcasters were drawn from the Young Women's Task Force of the Ministry of National Defense.[6] Women from this unit, in most cases recent high school graduates, were sent to Jinmen, where they carried out duties that included singing military songs, teaching political classes, publishing periodicals, and serving as broadcasters in the speaker towers.[7] Those who ended up serving as announcers in Jinmen often served their country with only their voice. Chen Xinmei, who began working on Lieyu Island on June 6, 1958, recalled that other recruits were engaged in education and cultural work, visited bases to rally troops, taught political classes, or were engaged in intelligence gathering but that announcers "knew nothing about this kind of work. We were always in the speaker towers, just broadcasting to the bandits every day."[8] Across the waves in Xiamen, female broadcasters were also the norm but not the rule. One of the men to take on the role was Wu Shize, who in 1953 was twenty-three years old and working as a cultural instructor in the People's Liberation Army. The majority of KMT soldiers stationed on Jinmen spoke Hokkien, a Min language that was widespread in southeastern China and Taiwan. Wu, who was fluent in the language, was transferred to the broadcasting group and became the first person to broadcast to Jinmen in Hokkien.[9]

Voices: Communist and Nationalist Vocalization

There are historical reasons for these divergent approaches to staffing and "voicing" the towers. While China and Taiwan had become territorially distinct only five years earlier, ideological and cultural differences that went back to the founding of the CCP resulted in markedly different approaches to the relationship between national and individual voices and thus to the staffing of the stations and to the act of "calling." Both Mao Zedong (with his thick Hunanese accent) and Chiang Kai-shek (with a Ningbo twang) were ruled out as possible national voices for cross-strait transmission. The system required a pure, clear vocal impulse if it was to retain maximal intelligibility on the other side. How could this be achieved? Paulina Hartono has given us insight into the origins and development of the Chinese socialist broadcast voice. She highlights the key role of Soviet theater practitioner Konstantin Stanislavski as a model for the ideal broadcaster who conveys not only the intellectual content of propaganda but also the emotional energy stirred by the revolution.[10] This approach created broadcasters in Xiamen who were politically educated, informed about developments in Taiwan, and encouraged to add their own emotion to a state voice.

The female model for Nationalist broadcasters during the Cold War emphasized a different relationship among text, body, and voice. Her name was Tokyo Rose, and she was not a single announcer but an interchangeable group of Japanese women who broadcast in coquettish voices in English to Allied GIs in the Pacific theater during the Second World War.[11] Indeed, the Taiwan announcers were given the nickname "Heart War Roses" in allusion to their Japanese progenitors. This prototype of a feminine siren voice then coalesced with the broader Nationalist goal of preserving a Chinese culture that the Nationalists claimed to be in the process of being polluted on the mainland. The model voice was therefore not of an individual who passionately embraced the ideology of the KMT but an idealized "national voice" (*Guoyu*) that was both clear and precise and at the same time continued the vocal practices of late dynastic and Republican China.[12] A closer examination of the vocal practices of each side reveals that it was the Communists who encouraged individuals to add the contours of their own voices to those of the party voice, structuring the party voice with their own feeling, and it was the Nationalists who ruled out such idiosyncratic vocal artifacts.

The two sides' divergent recruitment and deployment strategies for personnel are also reflected in the approach that each side's announcers took to their work. While Chen Xinmei worked alone—institutionally isolated from those who had received political or military training—Chen Feifei, who broadcast from Xiamen from 1955 onward and became one of the PRC's most famous Cold War announcers, recalls group study sessions of texts such as "We Must Liberate Taiwan" and "Peaceful Reunification of the Motherland" as well as updates on major changes to central policy in Taiwan.[13] In Taiwan such in-depth study was exclusive to the writers of broadcasting scripts, including Mr. Chang, who worked in Taipei and sent recordings and scripts at regular intervals to Jinmen.[14]

These same divergences in institutional culture meant that the broadcasters on each side of the strait were granted different freedoms to improvise.

In the PRC, many who served as the voices of these large arrays of speakers took liberties with their broadcasts. Wu Shize recalls how he decided to use his own voice in announcements even when recorded material had been provided.[15] Tian Wangong, who worked as an announcer at the same station as Wu Shize, remembers making up lines based on what he and others had observed through their binoculars: "Sometimes when the defenders of Jinmen were clearly at work on defensive fortifications and out digging tunnels, we'd call out to them: 'Digging fortifications again? Don't be so hard on yourselves!'"[16] On Jinmen, on the other hand, every word was to be read for the microphone precisely as it had been written at the Institute for the Heart War in Taipei.[17] Tong Limei, who began broadcasting at the speaker walls in Jinmen in 1979, recalled that "the manuscript was approved at a higher level. You couldn't do this yourself.... We relayed news that had been copied down from radio broadcasts from Taipei. It was also officially authorized. If you misread anything, it was a serious issue."[18]

Whatever the scope for improvisation, both sides adhered to a disciplined set of messages that changed only incrementally over time. These messages were preceded by a standard opening such as "KMT officers and soldiers, compatriots in Kinmen, the Fujian frontline People's Liberation Army will now begin its broadcast to Kinmen."[19] The primary message conveyed from the Jinmen speaker walls was the cruelty and ineptitude of the CCP regime. Thus, as at the US-funded broadcaster Radio Free Asia, which was founded in 1951 on the model of Radio Free Europe, many of the broadcasts were made up of news reports that were strategized, researched, and written in Taipei. A "heart warfare topic meeting" was held at the Ministry of National Defense on a weekly basis, and Taiwanese heart warfare experts, academics, and military leaders discussed what should be broadcast to Xiamen. Each script had to adhere to principles laid out in the handbook *Composing Scripts for Heart War Calling*, including integrity in conveying the truth, kindness in tone and sympathy for the other side, affirmation to avoid ambiguity and specious information or make offers that cannot be made good on, and care in adhering to national policy without wavering.[20]

Apprehending the Towers

Other Cold War sounds predated those of the towers. Beginning with the Battle of Guningtou in 1949, cross-strait artillery (sporadic until the Second Taiwan Straits Crisis of 1958 but then a regular feature of life until 1978) shaped the listening practices of those on both sides.[21] For those growing up in Jinmen in the 1950s and 1960s, however, the sounds of shells snapped one into a different mode of hearing. At an event held in Taipei in 2020 to commemorate the 1958 Taiwan Straits Crisis, Hang Shenghe spoke about the sounds that all Jinmen residents of the time knew and were imprinted indelibly in memory. "Shooooooo," he mimicked into the microphone, and "Booooom" replied the crowd of older Jinmen locals. Hang went on to discuss the necessity of telling apart the sounds of a shell that would pass overhead and one that might land near you: "Fefefefe."[22] Among those who lived through heavy waves of shelling, it was sound that made the enemy and their weaponry, indistinct on the visual horizon, real and immediate.

And it was within this percussive and threatening soundscape that the speaker towers fought for the attention of a captive audience. Wu Shize recalls, "The two places were so close together that even if [people] didn't want to listen [to the speakers], there was no choice."[23] Dai Hongyan, who also lived in Xiamen, held the same opinion, stating that the speaker broadcasts were "characterized by a sort of compulsion—when the speaker sounded, you heard it whether you wanted to or not."[24]

The response to this compulsion was an attempt by the authorities on both sides to either render their troops and civilians deaf to enemy broadcasts or to interfere with these broadcasts with their own sounds. On Jinmen, this took the form of ersatz earplugs made from cotton wool or the beating of gongs and drums.[25] Indeed, such sonic interference was the original impulse for the establishment of speaker towers on Jinmen, and the towers were used in this way throughout the Cold War—piping music to interfere with CCP propaganda and inadvertently providing a score to the vocal performance from Xiamen. Over on the mainland, the CCP had strict regulations forbidding people to listen to Taiwanese radio or speaker broadcasts. Not listening to KMT broadcasts led the list of the "Four Don'ts" of enemy propaganda: "Don't listen, don't look, don't consider, don't repeat."[26] A similar approach was taken in Taiwan. Chen Feifei remembers often seeing through her binoculars KMT soldiers looking blankly at the mainland—"obviously listening to the broadcast." She recalls seeing a man in an officer's uniform shoo enlisted troops who were listening off the beach and then sitting down on the shore to listen himself.[27]

The actions of the officer, which Chen Feifei interpreted as an indication of the irresistible quality of her words, were in fact most likely representative of the intelligence gathering undertaken by both sides. While troops and civilians on Jinmen and Xiamen were forbidden to listen to the broadcasts, each side assigned specific individuals to serve as the ears of the state, just as the announcers served as its mouth, and to record the messages piped over the waves. Chen Feifei recalls, "We had a dedicated person to record the content of their broadcasts. We also went to listen from time to time to get a sense of what they were up to."[28] In Taiwan, the KMT also had dedicated "intelligence officers" who alone were responsible for recording the CCP broadcasts.[29] Transcripts were then sent to military leadership in Taipei and eventually filtered down to scriptwriters such as Mr. Chang.

Outside this circuit of a state voice speaking to a state ear, however, the sounds of the speaker towers were apprehended in more unpredictable ways. The semantics of the ideological battle broke down as the signals became diffuse over time and distance. Words written in Beijing and Taipei, broadcast several kilometers through the mouths of announcers and the technology of the enormous speaker walls, crossed the strait, echoed off waves, and then commingled with the daily lives of those living in Xiamen and Jinmen. A key variable was clarity. In much of Jinmen, the content of CCP broadcasts was hardly discernible. Fan Yilin, who worked on Dadan Island from 1985 to 1987 (at the peak of broadcast power and clarity for both sides), recalls that "no matter what our or their side said, my impression was that none of it was clearly audible and you only had a rough idea [of the message]."[30] Mr. Chang confirms this, noting in an interview that the broadcasts he heard gave him the feeling that someone was trying to speak to him and make an attempt at communication but that what they said was unclear.[31] This lack of clarity meant that many listeners simply tuned out, and the broadcasts became part of what J. Martin Daughtry describes as an "audible inaudible zone," which emerges as experience teaches one to distinguish between meaningful sounds that may have an impact on or even threaten one's life and those that can be ignored.[32]

But not listening actively to the words that were broadcast did not equate to an absence of effect. Rather, the lack of intelligibility meant that it was the rhythm, texture, and tone of the broadcasts that were notable to listeners in Jinmen and Xiamen. Once the broadcast towers were in operation, new sounds marked time for the people of Jinmen and Xiamen. Dai Hongyan remembers that in Xiamen they would operate their towers on a regular schedule for twenty-three hours a day and that "the broadcast shouting battle between the two sides became both a lullaby and wakeup call for soldiers in Jinmen and Xiamen."[33] Mr. Wang, who began working as a schoolteacher on

Lieyu Island in 1973, recalls that "everyday at mealtimes (breakfast at seven thirty, lunch at noon), they started to broadcast Hokkien songs. They knew exactly when we ate." He remembers that they would play the Taiwanese folk song "Nongcun qu" (Village tune), explaining, "All the soldiers were based in the area of lower land behind the school, and when they heard that song play, they would line up and march in time with their metal chopsticks and bowls."[34] Thus, Mr. Wang's experience of the broadcasts across the strait was integrated into his daily life, as mainland broadcasts helped to mark out the rhythms of life in opposition territory.

The Gendered Tone of a Siren Voice

Tone of voice also played a key role. One female resident of Xiamen recalls working near the coast, often hearing the announcements from Jinmen, and noting the softer tone of voice and the music played as both mingled with the sounds of live fire: "At that time, I loved to listen, working in the fields, turning my ears to the water, and craning my neck to listen—it felt so exotic."[35] The exotic call of Taiwanese broadcasts was not always well received, however. A PRC defector questioned by Taiwanese defense officials noted that the use of soft-voiced female announcers and popular songs was unsettling to much of the mainland audience.[36] Well into the 1970s, those listening in Xiamen were often struck by the soft tone of the broadcasts from Taiwan. In his memoir, Chen Zhiping remembers that, prior to the 1980s, most people in China were accustomed to a crisp broadcasting style, which he equates with North Korea today—"strict and impassioned."[37] They did not know what to make of the gentler tones of voice that drifted across the strait.[38] In interviews with announcers from Taiwan, most noted this same discrepancy: the feeling of being scolded by their counterparts on the one hand and replying in a warmer voice on the other.[39] This was not a fixed state of affairs, however, and both Mr. Wang and Mr. Chang recall the back-and-forth between the two sides as each adjusted their own voice depending on what they heard from the other.[40] The result was that the tone and rhythms of the two sides' broadcasts grew ever closer over the years.

As the semantic import of the messages fell away through either a lack of clarity or excessive repetition to the point of noise,[41] such tones became central to what was being conveyed. With the semantic meaning lost, listeners interpreted the voice of the opposing side and, based on this, the character of their enemy.[42] But the performance of gender in voice was also shaped by other factors. Equally important was the dual nature of the audience of the Taiwanese broadcast towers. CCP broadcasts had a captive audience of up to one hundred thousand KMT troops and only a limited population on the mainland that lived near the coast.[43] The KMT broadcasts served audiences of both CCP troops and civilians in Xiamen, as well as a huge population of KMT troops stationed on Jinmen, representing up to a third of the Republic of China's standing army. The broadcasters I interviewed were acutely aware of their twin role as both soldiers in the "heart war" against their ideological enemies and morale-boosting cheerleaders for their own troops.[44] The troops serving on Jinmen at the time were equally aware of the presence and voices of these young women, against the overwhelmingly male makeup of the population under martial law.[45]

This meant that the young female "Heart War Roses" in Taiwan were simultaneously performing two contrasting vocal models. They spoke in a siren voice to call to their errant compatriots on the other shore, luring them over. And they also spoke to the Nationalist troops stationed on the Jinmen Islands, who missed home and particularly their girlfriends, mothers, and wives. That all of the Taiwanese broadcasters were, by regulation, precluded from having a boyfriend or husband reinforced the broadcasters' position as an idealized feminine presence. They were separated from the troops in Jinmen, with demarcations of space and time keeping members of different genders apart. So it was only their voices, ostensibly directed out across the strait but also turned inward toward their own troops, that provided the troops with a sonic specter of femininity. Mladen Dolar writes that the human voice serves as "a bodily missile which has detached itself from the source, emancipated itself, yet remains corporeal."[46] Indeed, on both sides, the role of the voice was corporeal and communicative, refusing to play a simple role in the ideological battle.[47]

Sounds from the "Other Side"

Other specters were also in play. For both sides, the other shore was a mysterious place, at once frightening and alluring. Hokkien culture has a tradition of superstition surrounding the sea, with widespread stories of apparitions or ghosts appearing on the beach or just offshore.[48] Interviewees in Jinmen often spoke of ghosts as something they did not see but occasionally heard. During the Cold War, this relationship with the water became fused with the cross-strait struggles and the voices from the other shore. Many interviewees remembered hearing the broadcasts with fear, finding the voices themselves haunting.[49] Some explicitly connected the nighttime broadcasts with local ghost stories.[50] These local religious beliefs mingled with what Michel Chion refers to as the power of the acousmêtre, a voice whose source is never seen.[51]

Such ghosts represented the partial breach of a mortal divide. In 1949, a parallel division of families took place across the Taiwan Strait, as sons were cut off from their parents, grandparents, and native soil. It was only via the sonic medium of the broadcasts that communications could be made. As Wu Shize recalls, the Xiamen broadcasting team made good use of this situation. The broadcasters found out that one of the officers on Jinmen was from Hunan and his mother was still in his hometown, so they sent a team to record her voice. The mother's voice was then piped over the speakers back to Jinmen.[52] This tactic was also used against the broadcasters themselves. The Xiamen broadcasters located the family of Tang Lizhu, who had worked as an announcer in Jinmen from 1955 to 1958. Dai Hongyan recalls that they broadcast letters from Tang's aunt, and her nephew's voice was recorded with a message indicating that Tang's extended family was all alive and happy.[53] Even if family members did not appear personally, the pull from relatives on the mainland was a constant for those who had come over during or at the end of China's civil war (1945–49).[54]

These were sonic reunions, or yearnings for reunion, from a division cleaved in 1949 or before. However, during the Cold War, a new way of crossing to the other side was made possible as defectors from both sides either returned home or fled from it. These people then added to the voices from beyond that were piped back to their point of departure. Perhaps the most famous case is that of Guo Kunren, who swam from Xiamen to Jinmen, received an education in Taiwan, then moved to the United States, and eventually served as an interpreter for Deng Xiaoping's 1979 visit to the United States. On the night of July 19, 1968, Guo and his brother took to the water at Dadeji Beach on Gulangyu Island, swimming across to Dadan Island without flotation devices. Guo's own voice then joined those of other friends and relations piped across the strait. Guo's classmate in Xiamen, Zheng Qiwu, remembers that while the news of Guo's defection was still spreading in Xiamen, Guo's voice itself had floated back across the strait, with Guo calling on his classmates to "struggle for freedom." Zheng writes that Guo went on to name individual classmates, and he waited in terror for his own name to be announced by the voice of his friend and now national villain.[55]

Echo: The Towers over Time

These are listening vignettes that give us a pointillistic picture of how the speaker walls affected the daily lives on Xiamen and Jinmen. But what about the long-term effects of the presence of these towers and the high-volume sounds they emitted on those who lived and worked within their range? The overwhelming response I received when interviewing residents who lived close to the coast and thus under the sonic umbrella of both KMT and CCP towers is that they simply grew accustomed to the all-pervasive sounds of propaganda from the other side, which were mixed with military and subsequently popular songs from their own. Some said that at first they could not sleep, and Mr. Wang, teaching on Lieyu Island, had to lower the pitch of his teaching voice so as not to share a pitch with the voices of female announcers from the other side.[56] However, after several months, residents adjusted to the volume, tone, and rhythms of the broadcasts.

Although counterintuitive, the long-term impacts of hearing the towers seem far greater for those who spent shorter periods exposed to them. In Taiwan, these people were most often the men who served on Jinmen during their compulsory military service. For them, the sounds of the towers are connected to memories of the Cold (and not so cold) War, to the extremes of battle, and to the act of remembering itself. In 1973 and 1974, Tan Yuanhan served on Jinmen and was stationed at Queshan in the northeast of the main island. He said, "The first thing I recall after reporting for duty was walking out of the tunnel and hearing extremely loud music and shouting. This went on day and night. I asked another soldier, 'What unit is that making all the racket?' He replied, 'That's the Communists calling!'" Tan's base was just south of the Mashan broadcasting station, and his night patrol took him near the villages that surrounded Mashan. He recalls that "the sound was so loud that I couldn't believe that the people or troops who lived here could sleep at night."[57] For Cai Jinjian, on coastal defense duty in Jinmen from 1977 to 1980, a dominant memory is the sounds of live fire. The changing soundscape also determined his sense of time, since he heard the defensive fire during the day and the Mashan broadcasts at night. However, as with many soldiers, he cannot recall what was said in the broadcasts.[58]

What those who served on Jinmen do tend to recall are songs. In contrast to the assault to the senses that accompanied duty on the front line, as young troops sought to stifle their homesickness and physical discomfort, the pop songs broadcast mark moments of emotional release. At the end of

1979, Li Zhengxiong was stationed near Mashan. He recalled, "Every day, from morning to evening, the broadcast towers on the mainland broadcast Coco Fang's 'Mending the Split Net' (*bu po wang*). Standing guard there, I couldn't keep from crying."[59] Indeed, memories of such songs allow the men to locate moments of their own service along a collective timeline. Chen Jinlang recalls, "In the winter of 1982, when Gao Lingfeng sang 'A Fire in Winter' (*dongtian li de yi ba huo*), I was serving as a sentry at the Houbian coastal defense station. It was an area most exposed to the cold winter. The freezing wind blew against the sentry post. From time to time, I'd faintly hear an 'A Fire in Winter' broadcast. Gao Lingfeng sang with indescribable beauty, a heartbreaking beauty. At this moment it felt like a raging fire warmed me, illuminating me."[60] Eventually, though, it was not individual songs or individual sources of sound, such as machine gun fire or broadcast music or voice, but the entire soundscape that characterized the memories of those who had served in Jinmen.[61] Here we see the impact not only of individual sounds but also of what Wang Yiwen, whose recollection opened this chapter, calls a "sonic domain." A sonic domain summons a time and place not through a sonic impulse but through the contours of its reverberation through space, recreating the echo of a memory for the listener.

Conclusion: Sonic Ruptures of Place and Time

The speaker walls on opposing sides of the Taiwan Strait transmitted sounds that carried diametrically opposed ideological messages but hewed ever closer to one another in rhythm and tone. As Mr. Wang and Mr. Chang point out, the two sides were engaged in a decades-long "sounding out" process—listening to the other side and adjusting volume, tone, and rhythm accordingly. In many accounts of the towers, the people who worked in them mention the gradual development of a *mo qi*, a term that literally means a "silent understanding" but in practice describes a relationship in which one gleans the state and intent of the other through sustained, long-term interactions that are never spoken of explicitly. It seems counterintuitive to write of a *mo qi* in this case, which was anything but silent, but in fact it is an apt description of the state of two nations attempting to interact through the technologically advanced but communicatively crude physics and psychoacoustics of amplified voice over distance.

At the same time, while the two sides were forming this relationship, each was defining itself through the observation and exaggeration of subtle differences between its voice and that of the other side. Chen Feifei describes the role of each side as "putting on a rival show." Rivalry was indeed key, but it necessitated difference. While the two sides responded to one another, mimicked patterns of voice, and drew closer in some respects (notably, the use of Hokkien and eventually Taiwanese songs), on each coast broadcasters and scriptwriters sought to show difference and in the process created divergent national voices. Conveyed in tone, cadence, and message, the broadcasts hinted at communication with the other side but were simultaneously focused inward, on the national self. The feedback loop of speaking to the other side, hearing its voice, and sending back a slightly adjusted version of one's own, all over the course of four decades, became implicit in the gradual cultural drift that would separate the two Chinas and cleave a fissure that would become more difficult to repair than the ideological rupture of the Cold War itself.

With respect to those who apprehended the sound of the towers but were not directly involved in the towers' operation, we see the splintering of the rationale of political propaganda into quotidian experiences of daily, and even religious, life. For a vast number of people who lived within the acoustic range of these towers in Jinmen and Xiamen, what began in Taipei and Beijing as a political tenet became instead a tone of voice, a time of day, or the sense of an enemy somewhere too far away to see. Or it transformed into the voice of one's kin or native place, also coming from somewhere out of reach for everyone but the bravest or the foolhardiest. Songs chosen to instill fear or show the strength of the CCP's or KMT's resolve served as the rhythm for a march, piqued interest, or became an eerie reminder of the world on the other shore, rendered uncanny by its mixture of sonic proximity and ideological distance. Friedrich Kittler, in his book *Gramophone, Film, Typewriter*, draws parallels between military and civilian life—particularly as regards the application of media technology, which was developed for military use, to our quotidian existence.[62] Given Michael Szonyi's emphasis on the "militarization of the civilian society" on Jinmen during the Cold War, it would seem natural to follow both Kittler and Szonyi and view the reception of the broadcasts, particularly as their tone softened over time and drew increasingly on popular music, as examples of this relationship and a broader "military-entertainment complex."[63] But reactions to the broadcasts also suggest that influence was not unidirectional and that as diffusion reached its peak and words became unintelligible, the sounds of the broadcasts broke free of their military and political origin to coalesce with daily and spiritual life.

We began with a set of borders between both nation-states and states of emotion. These borders were rendered porous as the binaries of ideology broke down and became diffuse across and within the Taiwan Strait. In auditory acts, those in Jinmen and Xiamen drew closer even as they fought each other with sonic weapons. However, temporal boundaries were also crossed: Cold War initiatives and acts by newly formed states were apprehended within older modes of listening in which familial voices coalesced with beliefs of folk religion and ghost stories, and acts of listening transcended and left behind initial acts of sound-making. Heonik Kwon has called for a "decomposition of the Cold War"—a treatment of the period as both anthropology and history—arguing that an understanding of how "peripheral" groups experienced the era is central to "putting into perspective the way in which the exemplary center conceptualizes the nature of this history and also in the sense that struggles between the image of the whole and representation of the parts are critical to the understanding of the global Cold War."[64] In considering the acts of hearing in Jinmen and Xiamen, we see both the complexity and the potential of such an aspiration and its execution. To listen to this history is not to neglect the major "key" of the era but to note that its oscillations created resonances within other preexisting harmonic structures and that these, while consequent to the initial impulse, were heard, felt, and lived as primary.

Notes

1. Wang Yiwen, comment on a Facebook discussion started by Lai Shujuan, September 12, 2020, https://www.facebook.com/groups/520415718345316/permalink/1166866103700271/.

2. See Li, "Revolutionary Echoes"; Lei and Sun, "Radio Listening."

3. He Shubin 何书彬, "Xiamen jiao yu dao: 'Duitaixi'—haixia shangkong de guangbo zhan" 厦门角屿岛："对台戏"—海峡上空的广播战 (Jiaoyu Island, Xiamen: "A rival show"—The broadcast war over the strait), http://mjlsh.usc.cuhk.edu.hk/book.aspx?cid=6&tid=161&pid=1272.

4. See Chen Chaofu 陳朝福, "Xinzhan hanhua mantan" 心戰喊話漫談 (A talk about heart war calls), Jinmen ribao 金門日報, August 25, 2014, https://www.kmdn.gov.tw/1117/1271/1275/242917/.

5. The gendered voices operating on both sides of the divide are noted throughout this essay. Space prohibits further discussion, which is forthcoming in a sustained study of gender and voice in broadcasting in greater China.

6. See Lin 林美華, Qingting zhandi de shengyin: Jinmen de zhandi guangbo (1949–1992) (Listening to the sounds of a battlefield: Broadcasting in wartime Kinmen [1949–1992]), 57.

7. Lin 林美華, Qingting zhandi de shengyin, 57.

8. Interview with Chen Xinmei 陳信妹, "Liu yue liu ri fei jinmen xin zhan hanhua zai gui shan" 六月六日飛金門 心戰喊話在龜山 (June 6 flight to Jinmen, heart war calling at Mt. Gui), 口述歷史-戰爭回憶-榮民文化網, https://lov.vac.gov.tw/zh-tw/oralhistory_c_2_158.htm?5.

9. Shubin 何书彬, "Xiamen jiao yu dao."

10. Hartono, "'Good Communist Style.'"

11. On Tokyo Rose, see Shibusawa, "Femininity, Race and Treachery."

12. On late dynastic theories and practices of voice, see Zeitlin, "From the Natural to the Instrumental."
13. Fu Ningjun 傅寧軍, "'Ditai' de shengyin—qing zhuyi, xianzai kaishi boyin" "敵臺"的聲音—請注意,現在開始播音— 中國知網 (The voice of the "enemy station"— Please pay attention, the broadcast will now begin), *Yu hua* 雨花, no. 3 (2015).
14. Author's interview with Mr. Chang, New Taipei City, August 13, 2020. Names have been changed when requested by interviewees.
15. Shubin 何书彬, "Xiamen jiao yu dao."
16. Tian Wangong, as quoted in Shubin 何书彬, "Xiamen jiao yu dao."
17. Guo Yuan, as quoted in Lin, *Qingting zhandi de shengyin*, 61.
18. Tong Limei, as quoted in Lin, *Qingting zhandi de shengyin*, 61.
19. Dai Hongyan, as quoted in "Xin zhan" 心战 (Heart war), *Zhongguo Zhou kan* 中國周刊, September 9, 2013.
20. As reported in Chen, "Xinzhan hanhua mantan." *Composing Scripts for Heart War Calling* is a handbook distributed by the Ministry of Defense. Here I rely on Chen's discussion, as the handbook is relatively inaccessible to scholars today.
21. Szonyi, "Cold War on the Ground."
22. Hang Shenghe, talk at conference Ba er san zhanyi jinian zuotan hui 八二三戰役紀念座談會 (August 23 battle memorial conference), followed by interview with the author, Taipei, August 23, 2020.
23. Wu Shize, as cited in Shubin 何书彬, "Xiamen jiao yu dao."
24. Dai Hongyan, as quoted in "Xin zhan."
25. Shubin 何书彬, "Xiamen jiao yu dao."
26. Chiang, *Lengzhan jinmen: Shijie shi yu diyu shi de jiaozhi* (Cold War Kinmen: The interweaving of world history and regional history), 48.
27. Chen Feifei, as quoted in Shubin 何书彬, "Xiamen jiao yu dao."
28. Interview with Chen Feifei, as quoted in "Ni jianguo neng wanli chuan yin de guangbo ma? Ta jiu zai Xiamen" 你见过能万里传音的广播吗? 它就在厦门 (Have you ever seen a broadcast that can transmit sound over great distance? It's in Xiamen), Wenwu chuanqi 文物传奇, May 13, 2017, https://www.sohu.com/a/140319901_781216.

29. Xue Zusen, as quoted in Chiang, *Lengzhan jinmen*, 148.
30. Fan Yilin 范義彬, as quoted in Chiang, *Lengzhan jinmen*, 152–53.
31. Author's interview with Mr. Chang, Jinmen, September 3, 2020.
32. Daughtry, *Listening to War*, 77–92.
33. Dai Hongyan, as quoted in "Xin zhan."
34. Author's interview with Mr. Wang, Jinmen, September 3, 2020.
35. Chiang, *Lengzhan jinmen*, 154.
36. Weishi, *Dalu shehui xinli yu xin zhan fanying*, 16.
37. Chen Zhiping, as quoted in Chiang, *Lengzhan jinmen*, 154.
38. Chen Zhiping, as quoted in Chiang, *Lengzhan jinmen*, 154.
39. Author's interview with Ms. Qin, Ms. Zhang, and Ms. Chang, Taipei, August 19, 2020.
40. Author's interviews with Mr. Chang and Mr. Wang, Jinmen, September 3, 2020.
41. On such repetition, see Goodman, "Propaganda and Sound."
42. On modes of hearing voice, see, for example, Lagaay, "Between Sound and Silence"; Weidman, "Voice."
43. Many note that broadcasts from Jinmen were not audible a few kilometers inland or in the city at all.
44. Author's interview with Ms. Qin, Ms. Zhang, and Ms. Chang, Taipei, August 19, 2020.
45. Chen Shucha, as quoted in Lin, *Qingting zhandi de shengyin*, 58.
46. Dolar, *Voice and Nothing More*, 73.
47. There is clearly much more to explore with respect to the gendering of voice. Further work is planned.
48. For one pertinent example, see Szonyi, "Virgin and the Chinese State."
49. Author's interview with Mr. Lin, Jinmen, September 2, 2020.
50. Author's interview with Ms. Yang, Jinmen, September 7, 2020.
51. Chion, Murch, and Gorbman, *Audio-Vision*, 129.
52. Wu Shize, as quoted in Shubin 何书彬, "Xiamen jiao yu dao."
53. Dai Hongyan, as quoted in "Xin zhan."
54. See, for example, the story of Deng Wenjin in Chiang, *Lengzhan jinmen*, 81.

55. Zheng Qiwu 郑启五, "1968 Nian 7 yue 19 ri de heiye . . ." 1968年7月19日的黑夜 . . . (The night of July 19, 1968 . . .), 2019, http://mjlsh.usc.cuhk.edu.hk/Book.aspx?cid=4&tid=5220.

56. Author's interview with Mr. Wang, Jinmen, September 3, 2020.

57. Tan Yuanhan, Facebook post and communication with the author, August 24, 2019, and August 25, 2020, https://www.facebook.com/permalink.php?story_fbid=3238815566156360&id=100000838456187.

58. Cai Jinjian, Facebook discussion, September 9, 2020, https://www.facebook.com/groups/520415718345316/permalink/1166866103700271.

59. Li Zhengxiong, Facebook discussion, August 23, 2020, https://www.facebook.com/thomas.kao.7/posts/10158531345774038.

60. Chen Jinlang, Facebook post, August 28, 2020, https://www.facebook.com/groups/520415718345316/permalink/1154657071587841/.

61. Nicole Huang refers to the soundscapes of the Mao era as "total soundscapes," as they pervaded "a highly politicized society where every corner of social life was thoroughly saturated with centrally ordained and politically charged sound bytes." I attempt here to show the heterodoxy of hearing in such "total soundscapes." See Huang, "Listening to Films," 190–91.

62. Kittler, *Gramophone, Film, Typewriter*.

63. Lenoir, "All but War Is Simulation."

64. Kwon, *Other Cold War*, 7.

Bibliography

Oral History / Interviews
Mr. Chang, Jinmen, September 3, 2020.
Mr. Chang, New Taipei City, August 13, 2020.
Mr. Lin, Jinmen, September 2, 2020.
Ms. Qin, Ms. Zhang, and Ms. Chang, Taipei, August 19, 2020.
Mr. Wang, Jinmen, September 3, 2020.
Ms. Yang, Jinmen, September 7, 2020.

Published Sources
Bull, Michael, ed. *The Routledge Companion to Sound Studies*. Abingdon: Routledge, 2019.
Chiang, Bo-wei. *Lengzhan jinmen: Shijie shi yu diyu shi de jiaozhi*. Jinmen: Jinmen guojia gongyuan guanli chu, 2017.
Chion, Michel, Walter Murch, and Claudia Gorbman. *Audio-Vision: Sound on Screen*. 2nd ed. New York: Columbia University Press, 2019.
Daughtry, J. Martin. *Listening to War: Sound, Music, Trauma and Survival in Wartime Iraq*. New York: Oxford University Press, 2015.
Dolar, Mladen. *A Voice and Nothing More*. Cambridge: MIT Press, 2006.
Goodman, David. "Propaganda and Sound." In Bull, *Routledge Companion to Sound Studies*, 90–98.
Hartono, M. Paulina. "'A Good Communist Style': Sounding Like a Communist in Twentieth-Century China." *Representations* 151, no. 1 (2020): 26–50.
Huang, Nicole. "Listening to Films: Politics of the Auditory in 1970s China." *Journal of Chinese Cinemas* 7, no. 3 (2013): 187–206.
Kittler, Friedrich A. *Gramophone, Film, Typewriter*. Translated by Geoffrey Winthrop-Young and Michael Wutz. Stanford: Stanford University Press, 1999.
Kwon, Heonik. *The Other Cold War*. New York: Columbia University Press, 2010.
Lagaay, Alice. "Between Sound and Silence: Voice in the History of Psychoanalysis." *e-pisteme* 1, no. 1 (2008): 53–62.
Lei, Wei, and Wanning Sun. "Radio Listening and the Changing Formations of the Public in China." *Communication and the Public* 2, no. 4 (2017): 320–34.
Lenoir, Tim. "All but War Is Simulation: The Military-Entertainment Complex." *Configurations* 8, no. 3 (2000): 289–335.
Li, Jie. "Revolutionary Echoes: Radios and Loudspeakers in the Mao Era." *Twentieth-Century China* 45, no. 1 (2020): 25–45.
Liang, Weishi 梁蔚實, ed. *Dalu shehui xinli yu xin zhan fanying* 大陸社會心理與心戰反應, 心戰參考資料. Taibei: Unclear, 1968.
Lin, Meihua. *Qingting zhandi de shengyin: Jinmen de zhandi guangbo*

(1949–1992). Jinmen: Guoli Jinmen jishu xueyuan, 2009.

Morat, Daniel, ed. *Sounds of Modern History: Auditory Cultures in 19th- and 20th-Century Europe*. New York: Berghahn, 2017.

Shibusawa, Naoko. "Femininity, Race and Treachery: How 'Tokyo Rose' Became a Traitor to the United States after the Second World War." *Gender and History* 22, no. 1 (2010): 169–88.

Szonyi, Michael. "The Cold War on the Ground: Reflections from Jinmen." *Journal of Asian Studies* 75, no. 4 (2016): 1041–48.

———. "The Virgin and the Chinese State: The Cult of Wang Yulan and the Politics Of Local Identity of Jinmen (Quemoy)." *Journal of Ritual Studies* 19, no. 1 (2005): 87–98.

Weidman, Amanda. "Voice." In *Keywords in Sound*, edited by David Novak and Matt Sakakeeny, 232–45. Durham: Duke University Press, 2015.

Zeitlin, Judith T. "From the Natural to the Instrumental: Chinese Theories of the Sounding Voice Before the Modern Era." In *The Voice as Something More: Essays Toward Materiality*, edited by Martha Feldman and Judith T. Zeitlin, 54–76. Chicago: University of Chicago Press, 2019.

CHAPTER 6

Listening to the Voices of Exile

Radio Free Europe in Romania

Andreea Deciu Ritivoi

The opening sounds of the Romanian First Rhapsody by George Enescu are well known to classical music lovers, but they acquired a special meaning for many Romanians during the Cold War. The first bars of Enescu's rhapsody were the sonic signature of Romanian broadcasts of Radio Free Europe (RFE). For decades, RFE penetrated the Iron Curtain to deliver anti-communist political commentary and news reports along with literary and artistic analyses and historical reportage broadly informed by a pro-Western, pro-American, anti-communist cultural canon. RFE was financed by the United States and was broadcast from Germany into all of the Soviet satellite countries. Now entering its eighth decade of existence, RFE remains one of the most significant organizations created during the Cold War to protect democracy worldwide. Its initial Cold War mission was to propagate Western political ideas in the Soviet Bloc to populations that lived under communist dictatorships and were held captive to ideological dogma. The voices of RFE, which broadcast in the local language of each country it served, were often the voices of political exiles.[1] Some of the exiles who acted as key figures at RFE were prominent intellectuals who had left their countries when the communist regimes ascended to power. Later on, some dissidents joined the RFE staff upon defecting.[2] Listening to these exiles, RFE audiences heard calls to oppose communism and the Soviet Union that they did not regard as the propaganda of a foreign nation. That these calls were issued by familiar voices speaking in their own language made a significant difference. Through the voices of the exiles, the West transmitted to Eastern Europe messages of political empowerment without getting directly involved in regime change in the region.

In this chapter, I will investigate the relationship between the listening practices of Romanian audiences and the way in which RFE broadcasts used the voices of exiles who asserted their political autonomy from the official diplomatic stance of the United States during the Cold War. This official US stance was the Western logos of the Cold War, and RFE embodied this logos. It came alive through the Eastern European émigrés staffing RFE. They gave voice to a vision of political transformation that emerged from within Eastern Europe rather than from their American supervisors. They promoted the logos of Western democracy, but they did so in the voice of their nations.

My approach is informed by a broader philosophical concern with the relationship between *logos* and *voice*. Adriana Cavarero has argued that an "exclusive interest in the Said corresponds to the central role of a logos understood as an intelligible order that represents, expresses, signifies, designates, duplicates, and organizes the objective order of beings."[3] To analyze the political dynamic of the Cold War with a focus on the actual voices of those who spoke its arguments and strategies is to move beyond that intelligible order into a clandestine space where competing agendas fought and exploited each other. Logos, if we follow Cavarero, "concerns itself with saying, but not with the human world of singular voices that, in speaking, communicate the speakers to one another. Rather, this Saying becomes an abstract, anonymous logos—a code, a system. Chained to speech, but indifferent to the vocal, reciprocal communication of the speakers themselves, logos ends up moving toward a realm of mute, visible, present signifiers that come to constitute its origin and its fulfillment."[4] I define *listening practices* as the way in which individuals engage not only with the Said but also with the Saying, in Cavarero's terms, and as the way in which they engage not only with content and information but also with physical characteristics such as tone, timbre, and accent in the overall context of the quality of sound, dependent on the listening device, setting, and socialization anchored around the listening experience.

The Cold War was not just an ideological conflict but also an embodied experience. The ideological conflict was embedded in, and in turn shaped, a cluster of feelings such as fear and anxiety and physical states such as hunger and cold. As Joanna Bourke has argued, "Assaults on the senses are not incidental to the warring enterprise. Mobilizing human and animal sensibilities are intrinsic components of militarization. From the moment war is declared, the sensual worlds of all protagonists are marshaled to the cause."[5] Sensory-based approaches to the Cold War have revealed lesser-known aspects of how individual agents experienced the conflict, from smells to sounds, and in so doing they have helped us acquire a more nuanced understanding of the Cold War as a lived experience. Scholars who study this conflict from a sensory perspective have also helped us move beyond some of the conceptual impasses of ideology-based approaches, such as responsibility, truthfulness, and manipulation. In the propaganda battles of the Cold War, what individuals on each side assumed was true depended significantly on what they could evaluate with their bodies and senses: the communist propaganda bragged of record-breaking agricultural production, but hungry stomachs knew this was a falsehood without having to analyze claims or find rival sources of information.[6]

The audible played an important part in this process, especially given socialist state control over print material and the lack of a public sphere for open political dialogue and deliberation. Listening to RFE became the basis for a different type of political sphere, one based on close networks of trust. What kind of listening practices did the RFE broadcasts encourage and make possible? And what was the overall effect of Eastern Europeans listening to RFE? I aim to address these questions, focusing on one particular case, that of the Romanians, and evaluating how listening to RFE changed the Romanians' political behaviors.

My reconstruction of the listening practices of RFE audiences is in part speculative, insofar as it tries to recreate a lived experience indirectly. It makes use of informal interview data and personal communications along with scholarly sources and documentary media evidence. Conceptually and methodologically, my approach is informed by Alain Corbin's reminder that "the objective measurement of the frequency, form, and intensity of auditory messages"—among which I include RFE broadcasts—"does not allow us to reconstitute their impact upon the individual who heard them. The reception of such messages is determined at once by the texture of the sensory environment, the modes of attention brought to bear on the environment, and the procedures of decipherment."[7] While it is hard (and risky) to generalize, I will discuss the sensory environments in which Romanian audiences listened to RFE and how the audiences' attention was guided by the voices of the exiles to arrive at a particular understanding ("decipherment") of the messages they received.

The RFE Logos

In July 1950, RFE went on air using a 7.5 kW shortwave transmitter located near Frankfurt, West Germany.[8] This overseas location, while necessary for technical reasons related to broadcasting limitations at the time, symbolically affirmed the democracy-by-proxy approach underwriting the station's entire mission.

George Kennan, a diplomat with extensive experience with Russia and the father of the Cold War containment doctrine, played a key role in devising the political strategy behind RFE. In an April 30, 1948, memo to the Office for Policy Coordination (OPC), which was a covert operation wing of the CIA, Kennan argued that the United States was "handicapped by popular attachment to the concept of basic difference between peace and war, by a tendency to view war as a sort of sporting contest outside of all political context."[9] In his view, the new realities of the postwar political arena required policies unencumbered by the distinction between war and peace. In the same document, Kennan proposed that both "white propaganda" (clandestine support of "friendly" foreign elements) and "black psychological warfare" (support for underground resistance) were needed in order to oppose the Soviet Union. His strategy of indirect intervention relied on former Eastern European statesmen who had fled their countries. According to him, they had experienced American democracy firsthand and could share their experience and newfound convictions with their own people. The refugees were to be a proxy for American democracy.

The selection, recruitment, and supervision of the exiles was placed under the patronage of a front organization called the National Committee for Free Europe, formed in June 1949 under the leadership of former undersecretary of state Joseph Grew as chairperson and State Department official DeWitt Poole as executive secretary. Its board members included General Lucius Clay, General Dwight Eisenhower, Hollywood film giant Cecil B. DeMille, CIA director Allen W. Dulles, media mogul Henry Luce, and former attorney general Francis Biddle.[10] In the statement in which he presented the organization to the press, Grew explained the mission entrusted to the Eastern Europeans, saying, "These exiles and refugees will become independent witnesses to the worth of our American endeavor. Then, if we enable them to communicate by radio or printed word with their peoples in the Eastern European homelands, their messages will not be formed on theory and hypotheses but living substance. They can testify to what the trial of freedom and democracy in the United States has brought."[11] On August 26, 1948, Kennan's plan was approved by the State Department.[12] The meeting notes show that the State Department officials worried that the exile community was fragmented into various factions vying for power, each claiming to be the true spokesperson of its nation. Indeed, the voices of the exiles formed a dangerous political cacophony. On April 4, 1949, FBI director J. Edgar Hoover discussed the role of the Soviet Bloc émigrés with Frank Wisner, director of OPC, and other American diplomats. Hoover supported Kennan's plan but insisted on an American committee overseeing the émigrés, arguing that the enterprise's success was entirely dependent on "the character and activity of the small group at the center which would really direct the operation."[13] Under the direction of this small group of American citizens, the exiles were meant to be a propaganda tool to expose the ills and perils of communism. RFE was part of a larger American political vision that subsumed, or even erased, the political autonomy of the exiles as well as their nations.

The secret political patronage at the basis of RFE reflected the workings of Cold War propaganda and the power dynamic of a state that exploited refugees in the name of the common cause. The State Department deemed it appropriate to control the exiles because it was acting within a political ontology that advanced its self-interest as a global concern. RFE did not give the exiles control over the broadcasts, thus denying them national autonomy as representatives of their countries even as it publicly recognized them as the voices of their nations. The sound of their own voices was the exiles' main political asset. RFE targeted an audience that tuned in to listen to broadcasts in their native languages and in the voices of their fellow nationals.[14] However, they heard an American political perspective on the events in their lives, regardless of whether they realized it. If Kennan and other State Department officials sought to make the exiles into a mouthpiece for the US government, the exiles asserted their autonomy by adapting to the listening conditions of their audiences and developing a direct, unmediated relationship of trust with them.

The State Department expected and allowed some degree of autonomy for the exiles. RFE was expected to become more effective than the Voice of America in promoting American interests beyond the Iron Curtain, precisely because it involved exiles.¹⁵ At the same time, American control was tight. Only five months after launching its broadcasts, RFE was already under pressure to ensure that the American staff had the final say over content. In a letter to W. H. Jackson, deputy director of the CIA, Wisner wrote, "Emphasis has shifted from the use of distinguished political and intellectual exiles, whose personal prejudices and protracted absence from their native lands render them of questionable current value, to timely news items and commentary slanted to accomplish Radio Free Europe's purposes."¹⁶

The March 16, 1950, memo for Horace Nickels at the Office of Eastern European Affairs, Department of State, lists by category the "type of information desired" for RFE broadcasts: "economic" (including food, clothing, wage increases, public construction, currency devaluation, retail prices, and water shortages); "education" (from the ratio of teachers to students to the political manipulation of schools); "political" (with an emphasis on the collectivization and nationalization of property); "religion" (denunciations of the lack of religious freedom); "labor" (including the use of "enslaved" or forced "voluntary" labor); "culture" (especially the lack of entertainment); society (such as societal conformity to Communist Party demands); and, finally, more personal factors such as unpublished news, street conversations, contact with the West among the general population, and demographic information (from addresses and phone numbers to sports interests, food preferences, pets, and favorite jokes, phrases, songs, books, and clothing).¹⁷ The exiles already had such information, but their role, as carefully plotted in this scenario, was to deliver it in the categories mentioned above. The United States did not want individual testimony by a witness but rather a detailed political ethnography cutting across individuals and hence voices and carefully circumscribed by areas of life, beliefs, behaviors, and values that could be listened to, seen, smelled, and tasted.

Hearing was of course crucial for the radio. When tuning in to RFE broadcasts, listeners heard a distinctive broadcasting voice often defined by a particular timbre, intonation, and enunciation. Over time, this voice became easily recognizable to the audience, especially since the same major anchors were featured consistently throughout the week. By speaking in distinctive voices, the exiles could appear more credible to their audiences. They could convey the views of the American government and make these views resonate with the beliefs of the audiences.

In the early days of RFE, the sensory environment of Eastern European radio audiences was shaped by a distinctly Soviet sound that was associated with the official radio speakers heard in the workplace, schools, and other institutions. This Soviet sound capitalized on silence, especially in film, while experimenting with linguistic differences by briefly allowing various languages from the Soviet republics to gain a voice in cinema before moving on to a more common representation of the omniscient voice—usually a masculine one—as the source of the logos.[18] The RFE broadcasts to Romania experimented with voices in important ways. Listeners grew accustomed to voices like those of writer Virgil Ierunca and his wife Monica Lovinescu, the latter of whom had a distinctive smoking-inflected husky voice that became iconic for the Romanian RFE station; or the voice of historian Vlad Georgescu, which exuded confidence and authority; or "the extraordinary voice, penetrating and subtle, of Nöel Bernard," the director of the Romanian language desk.[19] These voices participated in a discourse rivaling that of the Soviet sonic regime of truth. They sounded more cosmopolitan than regional and were eloquent in a sense recognized as European and old-style (that is, pre-communist). Sound gave the broadcasters legitimacy and authority, even though the content and ideological direction of the radio were controlled by the American government.

The RFE broadcasts not only provided listeners with information and ideological arguments but also invited them to participate in a political drama. Radical political changes employ theatrical elements. Melissa Feinberg has examined how the communist show trials organized throughout the satellite states after the Second World War established, as their historical precedents had done in Moscow in the 1930s, a climate of submission. The accused—prominent public and political figures—complied with the requirement to sign and perform in court a full confession of the crimes with which they were being charged, regardless of whether they had committed them. "The public act of confession," Feinberg explains, "was the physical sign of the party's power to shape the world in which it operated and to create the truth it desired. Whether or not that truth was believable was secondary to the fact that it was obeyed."[20] To Romanian audiences tuning in to RFE broadcasts, RFE was the very voice of the truth.[21] Voice and logos, in Cavarero's terms, merged. In listening to this truth, the average Romanian attained a political transcendence of sorts and achieved symbolic rather than concrete liberation.

In the 1970s, when the US government came under pressure from Senator William Fulbright and others to eliminate funding for RFE, letters sent by listeners from behind the Iron Curtain were used to make the case that the radio broadcasts were a lifeline for those inside Eastern Europe. "It happens quite often that I am unable to hear your station because of the jamming," wrote a listener from Czechoslovakia to the Czech broadcasting station. "At such moments, I feel like smashing the radio, as if the wooden box were to blame, and I almost cry in helpless rage. It seems to me that somebody wants to tear me away by force from my good friends. Be with us, as we remain with you."[22]

Beyond the content of the ideas or facts being conveyed, the experience of listening to the RFE broadcasts created an alternative space of political engagement. People usually tuned in at night (or after hours), secretly, mostly in the privacy of their homes, with the audio turned down so as not to be heard by neighbors who might report to the police the illegal activity of engaging with Western propaganda.[23] At the same time, the practice of listening to RFE was hardly a secret: one knew who else was tuning in every night. "Listeners engaged in small acts of revolution merely by creating safe spaces for listening, constructing antennae when necessary, tuning in, and adjusting their dials. In this way, listeners joined émigrés in the unique territories of imagined home nations constructed via RFE broadcasts"[24] (see fig. 6.1).

In stark contrast to the official radio broadcasts of the communist regimes, usually blasted in public spaces or the workplace, RFE programs were listened to privately, and the experience was hidden from others and shared only within one's trusted networks. While democratic public spheres are built upon open deliberation and dialogue, discussing RFE broadcasts posed serious dangers and required a level of trust that created intimate political networks. Through these networks circulated other kinds of information as well, including books and music that had entered illegally from the West and introduced democratic concepts and ideas that challenged communism.[25] The political community that emerged in this way was united by an underground resistance of ideas rather than by active opposition, but the American sponsors of the broadcasts assumed, or hoped for, a natural extension of ideas into practice. Risking imprisonment and persecution, struggling to make out the voices speaking to them through RFE despite the jamming that rendered them almost unintelligible at times, the Eastern European audiences grew in numbers to an estimated 25 percent of the population by the 1980s.[26] RFE's political proselytizing was focused not only on increasing adherence to Western political values but also on emboldening a population that no longer expected Western support to help it act upon what were or what it took to be its own beliefs.

Fig. 6.1   Covert listening techniques imagined by Radio Free Europe / Radio Liberty Cold War broadcasters during the Crusade for Freedom, 1965. Hoover Institution Library & Archives, Washington, DC, Radio Free Europe / Radio Liberty corporate records, box 2427. © Radio Free Europe / Radio Liberty, Inc.

The RFE broadcasts were not limited to political commentary. Some of the most popular broadcasts, including music programs, had no obvious political content. RFE's sound signature was markedly different from that of official Romanian programs. It used classical music where the Romanian state-sponsored programs often used Romanian country music. Even when classical music was featured on the radio in Romania, it was contained and isolated in a particular type of broadcast dedicated to the genre of classical music, such as Iosif Sava's Musical Soirée (Serata muzicala). As a sound signature, the classical music featured by RFE emphasized its difference from the sound of Romanian state-sponsored radio. RFE also played contemporary Western music that was unavailable, if not explicitly banned, on state socialist radio.[27] While the regular programs on state radio discussed agricultural production and industrialization in the socialist economy and featured mainly Romanian country music or local pop music stars, RFE broadcasts blended music for all tastes and generations with political commentary.

Not only did RFE play classical music more often than Romanian radio, but it also featured discussions about classical music in other broadcasts. In 1956, RFE commentator Nöel Bernard interviewed American-born violinist and conductor Yehudi Menuhin, who had studied with George Enescu and had gone on to become one of the most famous musicians of the age.[28] The conversation between Bernard and Menuhin was not just about music but also about cultural status. The relationship between Enescu and Menuhin symbolized an internationally known and respected Romania, which RFE claimed to represent.

RFE also featured contemporary music that was rarely heard inside Romania. For generations of Romanian teenagers and young adults, the electrifying sound of the Rolling Stones, the Beatles, and Queen was part of RFE's auditory landscape. These listeners tuned in to RFE not for political commentary but for the latest hits from New York, California, and London. The political role of American and British popular music has been documented in other contexts, most notably East Germany after the Second World War.[29] Listening to music was a way to transcend national and local boundaries and tap into a youthful global spirit that defied clear political affiliation. As Călin-Andrei Mihăilescu puts it, generations of Romanians came of age with the beats they heard on Cornel Chiriac's RFE broadcasts.[30] In an interview with Queen's John Deacon and Roger Taylor broadcast on November 12, 1974, Chiriac spoke in a relaxed, informal manner intended for an audience that wanted to be entertained rather than politically edified.[31]

The fact that music became the recognizable signature of RFE suggests that listening to the station was an emotional experience as well as a way of receiving information. It was this holistic experience (as opposed to facts or evidence incriminating communist regimes) that created an encounter of minds not only among Eastern European audiences, the exiles, and the United States but also among the listeners. Philosopher Jean-Luc Nancy argues that "to listen is to be straining toward a possible meaning, and consequently one that is not immediately accessible."[32] By tuning in to the RFE broadcasts, Eastern Europeans sought a political truth that reflected their lived experience and countered the socialist dogma to which they were subjected regularly.[33] They sought this alternative truth *with their senses*, from the sounds they were trying to make out to the movement of bodies at dance parties, where teenagers listened to pop music and rock 'n' roll courtesy of RFE.

Straining toward a possible different meaning, to paraphrase Nancy, became a form of soft dissidence, unfolding clandestinely through listening to RFE. This clandestine status made the listening experience politically transgressive and therefore transformative. Speaking to secret listeners behind the Iron Curtain, the exiles could transport their audience from the present in which they lived their lives of economic privation and political oppression in the communist dictatorship into a "sonic time," to use Éric Méchoulan and David F. Bell's term. Sonic time "forces us to make our conception of the present more complex."[34] In offering an escape from a dreary and suffocating present, the voices of the exiles brought back to life a past that was a political fantasy of freedom and democracy in wartime, a fantasy that made it possible to imagine a future without communism.

Listening Spaces

Because listening to RFE was an illicit activity, the spaces where people tuned in were private, domestic, and concealed from others. In such private spaces, the sounds of RFE, including music, voices, and the noises of pauses and interruptions associated with the quality of the transmission, became the auditory background of everyday, even intimate, life. Those who listened to RFE had to be cautious when engaging in discussions about the broadcasts and especially when deciding who they discussed them with. "Sotto voce" conversations about RFE, as Călin-Andrei Mihăilescu puts it, created a public political discourse that was only partly audible, positioned somewhere between asides and direct statements.[35]

The listening experience was impacted by the uneven audibility of the broadcasts, which could at times be good quality and at others badly jammed by the communist authorities.[36] The distorted sound caused by jamming became a part of the auditory experience and encouraged attentive and involved listening. The listener had to infer words even if only bits could be fully heard or infer meanings without hearing fully articulated messages.

For younger Romanians, RFE broadcasts formed more of a sonic background than a voice they listened to consciously and intently. Mihăilescu describes this background sound as an "echo" that accompanied the voices of adults who commented on the RFE broadcasts.[37] "In the actuality of listening," Mechoulan and Bell note, "the sound track is both a presence and an echo."[38] For the younger generations, the presence and echo of RFE meant persistent exposure to tones, timbres, and even pronunciations that were markedly different from those that formed the overall sound of the Romanian spoken in the listeners' everyday environments. Mihăilescu emphasizes the distinct way in which one of the main RFE Romanian broadcasters, Ioana Măgură, pronounced the word *Suedia* (Sweden), modulating the diphthong *-ue* as in *suede* in contrast to the more common pronunciation that separated the vowels (*Su-edia*).[39] Such nuances marked the voices of RFE broadcasters as different from those a Romanian heard every day at work, at school, on the street, in movie theaters, or in stores. Hearing the voices of RFE became a way to imagine a better Romania, a country free of oppression as well as material deprivation.

Listening to RFE also became a way to create and guard one's community of trusted fellow citizens, to sort out reliable friends from feared strangers, and to define one's political and—more broadly—cultural, social, and artistic views and tastes. People listened with family members and with very close, trusted friends because of the danger involved in being known as an RFE listener. To be exposed as an RFE listener could lead to being interrogated by the Securitate (Romanian secret police) and placed under surveillance, which could in turn result in imprisonment.[40]

RFE broadcasts did not simply instill political beliefs in a propagandistic effort to inspire and cultivate opposition to the communist regime. More broadly, RFE encouraged a way of thinking that was different from and nonconforming with the beliefs and views officially sanctioned and socialized inside Eastern Europe. RFE listeners were, or believed themselves to be, independent thinkers and actors in a time and place where independence was by definition politically subversive. They were friends—for some literally but for many symbolically—with the RFE personalities Nöel Bernard, Cornel Chiriac, Vlad Georgescu, Virgil Ierunca, and Monica Lovinescu. These were strong figures with voices that sounded authoritative and confident and sometimes arrogant and assertive. However, the arrogant voices of the RFE speakers were also reassuring, commanding the attention and assent of their audiences. In 1977, when a 7.2 magnitude earthquake hit Romania, killing more than one thousand people and wounding more than eleven thousand (most in the capital city of Bucharest), the president of the country, Nicolae Ceaușescu, could not be reached immediately for comment because he was on a trip to Africa. This meant there were no official communications to the population just after the quake, because they could not first be vetted by Ceaușescu. RFE became the default source of information for Romanians desperate to track down relatives and find out if they were still alive.[41] RFE journalists delivered official updates on the number of casualties, offered encouragement, handled inquiries about particular people, conveyed personal messages, and, most importantly, sought to keep the Romanian public calm during the panic of the disaster. Tuning in to RFE became a way of openly connecting to others at a tragic time for many Romanians.

Hearing the "Truth"

Jean-Luc Nancy asks, "What does it mean for a being to be immersed entirely in listening, formed by listening or in listening, listening with all his being?"[42] This philosophical question acquires special significance in regard to the Romanian listener who tuned in to RFE every night not only to connect with trusted journalists but also to experience truth as a form of being. RFE gave such listeners a political ontology.

As Gelu Ionescu, former RFE journalist for the Romanian desk, has noted, RFE listeners were impressed with the accuracy and timeliness of the information.[43] In a period when news traveled much more slowly than it does today, RFE journalists were able to produce timely commentary on developments in Romania, appearing to respond immediately to events. Through such prompt interventions, RFE created a close connection to its listeners and presented itself as a part of their world, attuned to their challenges, sharing their worries, and voicing concerns the listeners themselves could not express freely.

How was it possible for RFE to have fast access to the events and situations unfolding behind the Iron Curtain? In addition to maintaining a vast correspondence with listeners, RFE broadcasters were in contact with visitors who managed to secure passports and visas that allowed them to go on short trips abroad. Since information reached RFE from its listeners, one could argue that, in a way, these listeners were hearing their own views and ideas in the RFE broadcasts, while also indirectly transmitting them to many others. This dynamic of transmission complicates the simplistic model of propaganda dissemination that sees RFE as the mouthpiece of the US government. The listeners were not passive recipients of messages; rather, they often generated these messages themselves.

The ties between some of the RFE broadcasters and listeners were often bolstered by close-knit networks of personal friends. In the 1960s and 1970s, as the number of defections from Eastern Europe increased, some of the newly arrived migrants who were seeking employment with RFE relied on their personal connections among the RFE staff to join the broadcasting service. In some cases these friendships resulted in the strategic employment of high-quality journalists, but over time they also influenced hiring decisions that overlooked quality for mere linguistic competence.[44] Regardless of how capable they were as journalists, the émigré broadcasters cultivated a relationship with their listeners that positioned the broadcasters more as friends than as experts. Listening to RFE as one listens to a friend shaped the auditory experience by making it more oriented to tone and emotions than content.

Tuning in to the RFE broadcasts, Romanians sought an alternative political perspective to the one that had become dogma in their country. However, that perspective was not simply news from abroad. Rather, for many of them, it was already their own vision, which they heard validated every time they tuned in to RFE.[45] The broadcasts followed the protocol of topics established by the station's American sponsors but fleshed out these topics into arguments that emerged from information and sometimes even just rumors from informants in Romania.[46] This circulation of knowledge from Romania to RFE and then back to Romania reveals a logos based more on trust than on the accuracy of the information. However accurately informed they might have been, the RFE broadcasters sounded above all trustworthy to their audiences.

Listening to RFE was politically emancipatory on moral and emotional levels but a poor substitute for political practice. As Ioana Macrea-Toma has shown, the larger the number of RFE listeners in a country, the smaller the number of concrete political activities directed against the communist regimes.[47] Through their involvement with RFE, the exiles were positioned at the nexus of a militaristic logos of regime change and a utopian vision of spontaneous democratization. Viewed in their countries as vehicles of accurate information, the exiles became the agents of this awaited and imagined democratization. RFE listeners believed the information and arguments they heard on RFE, but more importantly, they also believed the implicit salvationist rhetoric of the broadcasts.

"The Americans are coming!"—this was a well-known catchphrase in Romania during the early period of the Cold War, especially before the Hungarian Revolution of 1956 and the Prague Spring of 1968. Eastern Europeans continued to hope that the West would come to their aid if they tried to emancipate themselves from Soviet influence or, more ambitiously, oust their own communist regimes. As is well known, the United States never intervened directly in any attempt by an Eastern European country to overturn its regime. If "radio is *distant* sound,"[48] as Mechoulan and Bell remind us, the distance between the Eastern European listeners and the US politicians who designed RFE as a propaganda tool remained a safe one as far as the Americans were concerned. The Americans and the exiles were far from the sites of conflict and suffering, no matter how often these sites were evoked in RFE broadcasts. RFE broadcasters, however, were not always safe at their jobs. During the late 1970s and the 1980s, the Romanian dictator Ceaușescu forced "a vengeful war" on RFE.[49] On February 21, 1981, the RFE headquarters in Munich, Germany, was the target of a fifteen-kilogram bomb made of the Romanian-made explosive nitropenta. The attack was attributed to the Securitate and the terrorist Carlos, known as "the Jackal." Four employees were injured, some of them severely. The building sustained major damage and had eventually to be demolished.[50] The communist regimes saw RFE as an enemy and tried to annihilate it by any means. RFE was part of the Cold War of words and voices, but it suffered its share of violent "hot war" attacks, as the fight against the broadcasts eventually let into attacks with poison and explosives.

Conclusion

Analyzing the sound of RFE and the listening practices of its audiences, as I have briefly done here, can reveal a political realm that could remain invisible without such analysis, hiding from us the subtle dynamics of power that complicate the common image of the Cold War as a fight between the

United States and the Soviet Union or a liberation mission to restore the freedom of captive nations. The US Cold Warriors assigned the exiles the role of proxies for American democracy. Yet the exiles did not offer their fellow citizens proximity to the West. Instead, through RFE, the exiles maintained their emotional proximity to their homelands. Neculai Constantin Munteanu, one of the broadcasters for the Romanian section of RFE, reflected on how deeply immersed in a Romanian world the broadcasting émigrés were, even as their everyday lives unfolded in the materially comfortable setting of a Western city like Munich.[51] The émigrés not only did the talking, but they also listened to their listeners, both symbolically and concretely, taking phone calls and reading letters from audience members.

One way to measure the political impact of RFE—which is recognizably hard to measure—is not through its role in ending communism but rather through its role in creating listening practices that shaped political beliefs. The sound environment of RFE promoted and benefited from private and transnational networks of trust within a society living in constant mistrust. Trust, from a political perspective, can shape a democratic polity in which strangers can associate with and rely on one another for their economic, political, and social needs. RFE functioned as a marker of trust, both by creating a relationship of trust between listeners and the broadcasters and by differentiating between those one could trust enough to discuss RFE broadcasts, and in some cases listen alongside with, and those one could not. According to Gerard Hauser and Chantal Benoît-Barné, "As conditions that bind us to partners who are marked by difference increase in scope and complexity, we lose our capacity to understand the basis for our partner's actions or their level of commitment to common goals. This diminished capacity raises trust as a paramount problem for civil society."[52] In totalitarian societies, individuals live in constant fear of surveillance. Suspicion becomes the norm, as trust recedes deeply into the private sphere. But in Romania, mistrust in the public sphere was counterbalanced by a high degree of trust in certain people. These bonds of trust were often created around sharing news first heard on RFE. Totalitarianism—at least in the communist Eastern European version—resembled traditional societies organized around bonds of kinship and tight-knit circles of friends and associates on whom one could count for the basic necessities of existence. RFE political kinship played a key role in creating an alternative political space in which individuals could discuss their political views safely. In Adam Seligman's view, in such a political space, trust is based on clearly visible "obligations, responsibilities, and mutuality. . . . The corollary to this is that whatever is outside of the system is totally unknown and hence dangerous."[53] Romanians listening to RFE had to be careful about admitting to strangers—who were potential informants and spies—that they were RFE listeners, and this continued vigilance pushed them more deeply into private spaces, among friends and relatives, where they thought they could speak up without fear of consequences. This privatization of political discourse had long-term consequences for a society that would later, after the collapse of communism, have to learn how to engage in political behaviors openly and transparently.

Cavarero reminds us that "the price for the elimination of the physicality of the voice is . . . first of all, the elimination of the other, or, better, of others."[54] If we eliminate, or do not engage directly, with the voices of RFE broadcasts and the listening practices of their audiences, we risk failing to appreciate fully their struggles and their accomplishments, which are difficult to assess in the complicated political drama of the Cold War. This essay hopes to be a contribution to much-needed additional research on those who gave their voices to RFE.

Notes

1. See Holt, *Radio Free Europe*.
2. See Miller, "Inside Radio Free Europe / Radio Liberty."
3. Cavarero, *For More Than One Voice*, 29.
4. Cavarero, *For More Than One Voice*, 43.
5. Bourke, "Afterword: War on Senses," 245.
6. See Urban, *Radio Free Europe*.
7. Corbin, *Village Bells*, 293.
8. See Johnson, *Radio Free Europe*.
9. George Kennan, "George F. Kennan, 'The Inauguration of Organized Political Warfare,'" April 30, 1948, Entry A1 558-B, Record Group 59, Policy Planning Staff/Council, Subject Files, 1947–1962, Box 28, History and Public Policy Program Digital Archive, National Archives and Records Administration, Washington, DC, obtained by Brendan Chrzanowski, https://digitalarchive.wilsoncenter.org/document/208714.
10. See Johnson, *Radio Free Europe*.
11. Quoted in Holt, *Radio Free Europe*, 35.
12. "US Government Officials Discuss Émigré Broadcasts to Eastern Europe," August 26, 1948, CIA Mandatory Declassification Review Document #C05458947, History and Public Policy Program Digital Archive, obtained by and contributed to the Cold War International History Project (CWIHP) of the Wilson Center by A. Ross Johnson, http://digitalarchive.wilsoncenter.org/document/114321. Cited in Johnson, *Radio Free Europe*, 13.
13. "Memorandum of Conversation with Mr. J. Edgar Hoover, Director, Federal Bureau of Investigation, 10:00 am, Monday, 4 April 1949 [Approved for Release, March 2009]," April 19, 1949, CIA Mandatory Declassification Review Document #C01441000, History and Public Policy Program Digital Archive, obtained by and contributed to the CWIHP by A. Ross Johnson, https://digitalarchive.wilsoncenter.org/document/114324. Cited in Johnson, *Radio Free Europe*.
14. See Puddington, *Broadcasting Freedom*.
15. See Pomar, *Cold War Radio*.
16. Cummings, *Radio Free Europe's "Crusade for Freedom*," 46.
17. "Memorandum for Mr. Horace Nickels, 'Support for Radio Broadcasting Program to Satellite Nations' [Approved for Release, March 2009]," March 16, 1950, CIA Mandatory Declassification Review Document #C01441003, History and Public

Policy Program Digital Archive, obtained and contributed to the CWIHP by A. Ross Johnson, https://digitalarchive.wilsoncenter.org/document/114334. Cited in Johnson, *Radio Free Europe*.
18. See Salazkina, introduction to *Sound, Speech, Music*, 7.
19. Vladimir Tismaneanu, "RFE's Romanian Service Opened Our Eyes," Radio Free Europe, August 1, 2008, https://www.rferl.org/a/RFEs_Romanian_Service_Opened_Our_Eyes/1187792.html.
20. Feinberg, *Curtain of Lies*, 34.
21. Nagat, "Ceaușescu's War."
22. "Listening in on Radio Free Europe," letter to the editor, *New York Times*, March 26, 1972.
23. Nagat, "Ceaușescu's War."
24. Haas, "Communities of Journalists," 46.
25. See Reisch, *Hot Books*.
26. See Parta, *Discovering the Hidden Listener*.
27. See Mogoș and Berkers, "Navigating the Margins."
28. Nöel Bernard, "1956—Yehudi Menuhin: Am Respirat Împreună in Zilele Acelea la Bucuresti," Radio Free Europe, April 1956, https://moldova.europalibera.org/a/27723585.html.
29. See Mrozek, "G.I. Blues and German Schlager."
30. Călin-Andrei Mihăilescu, personal communication, February 1, 2021.
31. See Eugen Tomiuc, "Memories of a Romanian Icon," Radio Free Europe / Radio Liberty, August 1, 2008, https://www.rferl.org/a/Memories_Of_A_Romanian_Icon/1187788.html.
32. Nancy, *Listening*, 6.
33. See Nagat, "Ceaușescu's War."
34. Mechoulan and Bell, "Are Sounds Sound?," 11.
35. Mihăilescu, personal communication.
36. See Parta, *Discovering the Hidden Listener*.
37. Mihăilescu, personal communication.
38. Mechoulan and Bell, "Are Sounds Sound?," 9.
39. Mihăilescu, personal communication.
40. See Nagat, "Ceaușescu's War."
41. See Alexandru Solomon, dir., *Cold Waves* (Germany: Geppert Productions, 2007).
42. Nancy, *Listening*, 7.
43. Gelu Ionescu, personal communication, January 15, 2021.
44. Gelu Ionescu, personal communication, January 15, 2021.
45. See Urban, *Radio Free Europe*.
46. Ionescu, personal communication.
47. See Macrea-Toma, "Radio Free Europe in Paris."
48. Mechoulan and Bell, "Are Sounds Sound?," 35 (emphasis added).
49. Cummings, "'RFE/RL Will Continue To Be Heard.'"
50. In 2023, a Munich-based exhibition revealed the real life-and-death risks to which RFE employees were exposed. See Bodo Mrozek, "Ausstellung zu Radio Free Europe: Bomben gegen Radiowellen," *Tagesspiegel*, February 5, 2023, https://www.tagesspiegel.de/kultur/ausstellung-zu-radio-free-europe-bomben-gegen-radiowellen-9287235.html.
51. See Alexandru Solomon, dir., *Cold Waves* (Germany: Geppert Productions, 2007).
52. Hauser and Benoît-Barné, "Reflections on Rhetoric," 266.
53. Seligman, "Trust and Civil Society," 20.
54. Cavarero, *For More Than One Voice*, 46.

Bibliography

Archival Sources
National Archives and Records Administration, Washington, DC: Record Group 59.
Wilson Center, Washington, DC: Digital Archive.

Audiovisual Source
Solomon, Alexandru, dir. *Cold Waves*. 2007. Germany: Geppert Productions, 2007.

Published Sources
Bourke, Joanna. "Afterword: War on the Senses." In *Modern Conflict and the Senses*, edited by Nicholas J. Saunders and Paul Cornish, 375–78. London: Routledge, 2017.
Cavarero, Adriana. *For More Than One Voice: Toward a Philosophy of Vocal Expression*. Translated and with an introduction by Paul Kottman. Stanford: Stanford University Press, 2005.

Corbin, Alain. *Village Bells: Sound and Meaning in the Nineteenth-Century French Countryside*. Translated by Martin Thom. New York: Columbia University Press, 1998.

Cummings, Richard. *Radio Free Europe's "Crusade for Freedom": Rallying Americans Behind Cold War Broadcasting, 1950–1960*. Jefferson: McFarland, 2010.

———. "'RFE/RL Will Continue To Be Heard': Carlos the Jackal and the Bombing of Radio Free Europe / Radio Liberty, February 21, 1981." Radio Free Europe / Radio Liberty Press Room, April 14, 2020.

Feinberg, Melissa. *Curtain of Lies: The Battle over Truth in Stalinist Eastern Europe*. Oxford: Oxford University Press, 2017.

Haas, Susan D. "Communities of Journalists and Journalism Practice at Radio Free Europe during the Cold War (1950–1995)." PhD diss., University of Pennsylvania, 2013.

Hauser, Gerard, and Chantal Benoît-Barné. "Reflections on Rhetoric, Deliberative Democracy, Civil Society, and Trust." *Rhetoric and Public Affairs* 5, no. 2 (2002): 261–75.

Holt, Robert. *Radio Free Europe*. Minneapolis: University of Minnesota Press, 1958.

Johnson, Ross A. *Radio Free Europe and Radio Liberty: The CIA Years and Beyond*. Stanford: Stanford University Press, 2010.

Macrea-Toma, Ioana. "Radio Free Europe in Paris: The Paradoxes of an Ethereal Opposition." MA thesis, Central European University, 2008.

Mechoulan, Eric, and David F. Bell. "Are Sounds Sound? For an Enthusiastic Study of Sound Studies." *SubStance* 49, no. 2 (2020): 3–29.

Miller, Stephen. "Inside Radio Free Europe / Radio Liberty." *Partisan Review* 70, no. 1 (2003): 74–84.

Mogoş, Petrică, and Pauwke Berkers. "Navigating the Margins between Consent and Dissent: Mechanisms of Creative Control and Rock Music in Late Socialist Romania." *East European Politics and Societies* 32, no. 1 (2018): 56–77.

Mrozek, Bodo. "G.I. Blues and German Schlager: The Politics of Popular Music in Germany." In *Made in Germany: Studies in Popular Music*, edited by Oliver Seibt, Martin Ringsmut, and David-Emil Wickström, 122–34. New York: Routledge, 2021.

Nagâţ, Germina. "Ceauşescu's War Against Our Ears." In *Cold War Broadcasting: Impact on the Soviet Union and Eastern Europe*, edited by A. Ross Johnson and Eugene Parta, 229–38. Budapest: Central European University Press, 2010.

Nancy, Jean-Luc. *Listening*. New York: Fordham University Press, 2007.

Parta, Eugene R. *Discovering the Hidden Listener: An Assessment of Radio Liberty and Western Broadcasting to the USSR during the Cold War*. Stanford: Hoover Institution Press, 2007.

Pomar, Mark G. *Cold War Radio: The Russian Broadcasts of the Voice of America and Radio Free Europe / Radio Liberty*. Lincoln: Potomac Books, 2022.

Puddington, Arch. *Broadcasting Freedom: The Cold War Triumph of Radio Free Europe and Radio Liberty*. Lexington: University Press of Kentucky, 2003.

Reisch, Alfred A. *Hot Books in the Cold War: The CIA-Funded Secret Western Book Distribution Program Behind the Iron Curtain*. Budapest: Central European University, 2013.

Salazkina, Masha. Introduction to *Sound, Speech, Music in Soviet and Post-Soviet Cinema*, edited by Lylia Kaganovsky and Masha Salazkina, 1–18. Bloomington: Indiana University Press, 2014.

Seligman, Adam. "Trust and Civil Society." In *Trust and Civil Society*, edited by Fran Tonkiss, Andrew Passey, Natalie Fenton, and Leslie C. Hems. London: Palgrave Macmillan, 2000.

Urban, George R. *Radio Free Europe and the Pursuit of Democracy: My War Within the Cold War*. New Haven: Yale University Press, 1997.

CHAPTER 7

Hearing Korea, Seeing Cuba

NO-DO as Sonic and Visual Propaganda in Francoist Spain

José Manuel López Torán

It is truly difficult to understand the course of modern history if we ignore its periodic wars. Modern warfare has an important characteristic that distinguishes it from all previous warfare: in addition to its technical and tactical advances, modern warfare has been affected by the degree to which it uses propaganda. Mass society demands coverage of the progress of war, and governments use manipulative tactics when planning large-scale persuasive (dis)information campaigns. The aim is to influence public opinion at a time when mass support is essential to overcome the global impact of each individual armed conflict.[1] Propagandists have realized the importance of emotions and the senses, and to make their messages even more effective, they often attempt to engage both directly. To do so, they use media research to distribute their messages. Sensory propaganda that provides immersive experiences through audiovisual and other forms of media represents a huge advance over the paper propaganda used in the late nineteenth century.

For around four decades, the Spanish state-controlled agency Noticiario y Documentales (News and Documentaries, or NO-DO for short) produced cinema newsreels that were the only official source of audiovisual information for Spaniards seeking to learn about current events. Cinemas were required to screen NO-DO newsreels before movies, and throughout its existence, the organization produced more than four thousand such programs. It is worth noting that, in 1956, there were an estimated three thousand television sets in all of Spain, most of which were located in Madrid (by comparison, there were sixty million in the United States). It took several years for television sets to become widespread in Spanish homes. In the 1960s, the figure grew significantly to eight hundred and fifty thousand, a remarkable number but still relatively low for a population of more than thirty million.[2]

For this reason, NO-DO newsreels were by far the most widespread means of social communication. They were especially popular because the cinema was an important form of entertainment not only in cities but also in rural areas.[3] However, the rigid control exerted over content by Francisco Franco's dictatorship completely altered the information the population received. Nevertheless, thanks to the NO-DO newsreels, Spaniards could "travel" thousands of miles and witness events around the world from a movie theater near home. According to NO-DO's own motto, NO-DO "put the whole world within reach of all Spaniards."

From a chronological perspective, the Franco dictatorship emerged parallel to the Cold War, and this made the NO-DO newsreels one of the few audiovisual sources available to the Spanish population in a context of global uncertainty. At the start of the Cold War, newsreels played a prominent role in many Western countries; Spain was no exception in this regard. However, NO-DO did not have extensive experience in the production of documentaries, and it soon began obtaining material from other newsreel producers—including Gaumont, Metro News, and Fox News—in order to solve this problem.[4] The short audiovisual programs brought the international conflicts of the Cold War closer to millions of Spaniards, providing sounds and images of combat thousands of kilometers away.

This chapter seeks to show how these newsreels influenced the population by presenting a very biased view of the wars. It also explores how the images and sounds created a more direct experience for viewers. In order to achieve these two objectives, I carefully analyzed dozens of newsreels released during two relevant Cold War events—the Korean War and the Cuban Missile Crisis.[5]

As is commonly known, two of the "warmest" locations in the first stage of the Cold War were Korea and Cuba, and the conflicts in these countries constitute two of the most interesting case studies. My decision to adopt a twelve-year chronology is based on the significance of these two episodes during the Cold War. Furthermore, both conflicts played an important role in Francoist propaganda, since they coincided with the first stage of Franco's dictatorship, when censorship and control over content was stronger and the regime's foreign policy changed most dramatically. It is precisely this period in which the bilateral relations between Spain and the United States were reconfigured after having grown more distant in the previous years. This was a crucial moment that shaped developments in the following decades. As far as NO-DO is concerned, it has been noted that the information NO-DO provided to Spanish viewers about both events was entirely aligned with Franco's strategy of US-Spanish rapprochement and with the complete rejection of communism and the Soviet Union. Several common strategies have been identified in the coverage of both conflicts, a fact that makes it possible to establish a continuum between them that is interesting and necessary to analyze.

NO-DO as Sonic and Visual Propaganda in Francoist Spain

The world that emerged from the Second World War was strongly polarized. The two superpowers that established themselves after the war—the United States and the Soviet Union—deployed their resources to create strong spheres of influence and expand their power throughout the globe. Francoist Spain, having retained its neutrality during the war and shown sympathy for the Axis powers, remained in a difficult position, isolated from the rest of Europe and outside the Western Bloc led by the United States.[6] Nevertheless, after the initial phase of the postwar period, the global political situation underwent a notable change that led to a reorganization of international relations. In fact, the 1950s marked a significant shift in the Franco regime's relations with the world to which the outbreak of the Korean War was closely linked. At a time when the Eastern and Western Blocs were heading toward a new armed conflict, Spain positioned itself as a crucial space where Western Europe could be defended from the spread of Soviet influence.[7]

With these geostrategic developments, Spain indirectly entered the uncertainties of the Cold War period, and the Franco regime saw the necessity of providing the Spanish population information about the events taking place in this new context. To do so, it used numerous resources such as the press and radio; however, NO-DO newsreels assumed a special role, because as audiovisual media they combined the advantages of images and sounds and effectively influenced the senses of sight and hearing. From this point onward, NO-DO was responsible for reporting on the large number of events that took place within the Spanish borders and also abroad. As far as international developments go, there is little doubt that the Cold War and its various related episodes were long one of the main topics in NO-DO's programming. In this sense, NO-DO positioned itself as a true reporter of everything related to the Cold War climate of insecurity and as an extraordinary channel through which the Spanish population was able to experience the images and sounds of war, something that aroused substantial interest among the population.

Wars have always fascinated people; however, for centuries they were perceived as distant events accessible only to those who participated directly in the battles. This situation started to change radically when combat became portable due to gradually emerging new media. Thanks to these new resources, war was brought into people's homes, and the barbarism of armed confrontation was transmitted over the globe. Among all new media, audiovisual media provided an especially immersive experience by incorporating image and sound. This revolution transformed war propaganda into a multisensory experience by giving people access to a sound reality that had previously been restricted to those experiencing the conflict firsthand. As R. Murray Schafer has pointed out, "The soundscape of the world is changing. Modern man is beginning to inhabit a world with an acoustic environment radically different from any he has hitherto known."[8] This observation is fully applicable to the world of armed conflict, since modern wars are characterized by a high degree of industrialization and the incorporation of large, powerful weapons that have completely modified the soundscape of war.

It is difficult for those who have participated in armed conflict to forget what they saw, heard, and smelled. All of these feelings and senses seem to be exclusive and difficult to understand for those who have not directly experienced the horrors of war. However, we can certainly ask whether it is possible to transport the atmosphere beyond the actual location of the events and reproduce their sensory effects. Proof that this is possible can be found in various media, since they allow images and sounds to "travel" thousands of kilometers and bring large groups of people close to the epicenter of a conflict. Specifically, the images and sounds of war make two journeys: the first through space itself and the second from the reality of war to its representation in media. Soldiers' experience is reduced to flat black-and-white images, and only certain images are selected for use by camera operators, producers, and directors. Sounds are transformed into reproductions, recorded by microphones, and sometimes amplified, or they are replaced by more dramatic sounds, reproduced by (back then, mono) speakers, and deprived of a large part of their spatial component. Music is added to induce certain emotions, and it connects the images from abroad with other cinematic traditions, such as the use of symphonic arrangements and popular melodies. There are various ways in which film can generate feelings of tension or produce bodily responses. Media theorist and sensory studies scholar Laura Marks, for example, explains in her work on touch that sight can induce additional bodily responses such as stomach pain or even skin reactions like goosebumps, hair standing on end, and the sensation of freezing or sweating.[9] Generating such sensations is exactly what NO-DO did with news from the Cold War and the fighting that took place far away from Spain.

In addition to these visual and auditory methods, the spaces in which NO-DO newsreels were presented contributed to the perception of the episodes reported on.[10] The cinemas that screened the short films provided a series of advantages that were ideal for amplifying the effects of the propaganda, since they made the experience much more immersive. The size, volume, and darkness of the theaters contributed to this immersive effect and presumably produced sensory responses that gave viewers a particularly vivid and psychologically intense experience of the contexts shown. A number of the people I interviewed for my research mentioned that they vividly remembered the distinctive smells of these spaces and explained how they associated these smells with NO-DO newsreels. Though it might be surprising, the sense of smell thus also contributed to the sensory experience of the Cold War provided by NO-DO programs. Finally, it is worth noting that, even in small cities and villages, the cinemas seated around one thousand people each, so screenings became a social experience in which all the details could be shared with large groups of people.

In short, a space emerged that engaged the audiences' senses, translated the atmosphere of the narrated episodes, and amplified the desired effects. The senses mediated the relationship between the self and society, between mind and body, and between idea and object.[11] We can easily demonstrate that NO-DO carefully planned all the details to achieve the best results in terms of the reception of the information. The next section presents two examples of how NO-DO intentionally used newsreels to modify the relationship between the object and the audience, between the "hot" reality of war at the front and the media reality of Cold War propaganda in Spain.

Korea: The Cold War Heats Up

The Korean War was one of the first direct confrontations between the two blocs during the Cold War. It turned the region of East Asia into a chessboard on which the future of the polarized world was to be decided. As in other modern wars, the media played an important role in the dissemination of information, although this information was always determined by the propaganda interests of the respective countries. Newsreels made the war into a spectacle by offering content to a global audience, the members of which were transformed into consumers of information.[12]

For the newly created NO-DO, the Korean War—due to its broad international repercussions and the interest generated among viewers—was one of the most significant events covered in its programming. As my research has demonstrated, more than sixty NO-DO newsreels presented a wide range of situations in the Korean War, all with their corresponding sounds, including the start of a military intervention, the use of new weapons, and the liberation of prisoners of war. The exceptional nature of the screened images is beyond question. Despite their variety, it is possible to identify a common denominator among all of them: a powerful sense of anticommunism. Because of the war declared by the Franco dictatorship on communism, all the information that was gathered about the armed conflict in Korea reflected the dictatorship's firm rejection of the advance of this ideology in East Asia. In addition, the newsreels screened in Spanish cinemas projected a very positive image of the United States, showing American soldiers helping civilians, doing good deeds, and combating cruel and ruthless enemies.

Despite this biased view, the newsreels provided viewers with all sorts of experiences that are extremely interesting from a sensory perspective. For example, in the newsreel screened on October 30, 1950,[13] the US Air Force was shown carrying out "impressive bombing raids" on Korean territory. The news programs from December 10, 1951,[14] and March 30, 1953,[15] enabled viewers to "climb aboard" US planes chasing Soviet Mikoyan-Gurevich jet fighters (MiGs). The moving images taken from inside the aircraft offered a unique perspective and immersive experience, as they allowed audiences to see the war through the pilot's eyes for a few seconds, either chasing enemy planes or dodging the large columns of smoke that shot into the sky after bombs were dropped.[16] In addition, in a newsreel from July 9, 1951, audiences were transported to large warships that were preparing for the next military operation or firing cannons on enemy vessels,[17] and in another newsreel from December 29, 1952, viewers accompanied President Dwight D. Eisenhower on a voyage to Honolulu after a visit to Korea.[18]

Although the air and the water were two surprising environments to which the public was given access, it was the battlefield that was most frequently shown. Scenes of fighting soldiers constitute the most important identifiable pattern in this period. Viewers found themselves in the center of the battlefield and experienced the constant risks there while listening to the sound of bazookas, machine guns, or the impact of bombs being dropped by enemy planes.

In the different newsreels that covered the Korean War, we can detect the significant presence of sounds recorded on the battlefield as well as the reduced prominence of narration or music added during the editing period. This is an interesting element to examine since the narration and studio music that were minimized in the Korean War newsreels became essential in NO-DO's portrayal of events that took place in Cuba, as will be explained later in this chapter.

One possible explanation for this situation is that NO-DO may have wished to make the sounds that were taking place on the battlefield more direct, without distractions for the audience, so as to achieve a more immersive experience. The idea of achieving a more immersive experience is particularly evident in the news program from March 30, 1953, in which the noise of the US planes flying over the skies can be heard, and in the one from August 28, 1950, in which the deafening noise of the tanks plays a leading role in the scenes.

As the horrible effects of war were considered important for propaganda, the newsreels showed towns that had been burned to the ground and destroyed by advancing troops. The NO-DO images thus made the Spanish population realize that civilians were also victims of the war, as many lost their homes as a result of the attacks on villages and cities. A number of programs focused on this message, including the newsreel dated August 28, 1950.[19] Of course, ruined towns have long been a common propaganda theme. During the First World War, such images were widely used in what was known as "atrocity propaganda."[20] The language this propaganda used emphasized the violent acts committed by the troops, and the recurring themes included attacks on civilians and soldiers; looting, pillage, rape, and torture; and the destruction of ancient libraries, cathedrals, houses, and entire villages. Although all the nations involved in the First World War used such images, the Allies were much more successful in their campaigns, both in terms of their impact and the number of people they reached. The purpose of these campaigns was to denounce the violent acts carried out on civilians, who were portrayed as the innocent victims of barbarism. In the case of the Korean War, the cruelty of communism was shown through apocalyptic images and the sound of the flames devouring houses after fighting.

At this point, it is worth reflecting on the impact that these intense news programs might have had on Spanish society. After all, the images and sounds that NO-DO transmitted from Korea clearly generated a wide variety of emotions. This was the first time that young viewers "experienced" the atmosphere of war, and the audiovisual experience may have aroused feelings of astonishment and even excitement. Audiences that had lived through the Spanish Civil War of 1936–39 probably had very different emotional responses, however, because they had witnessed similar situations themselves fifteen years earlier in Guernica and other Spanish cities.[21] Their responses might have included bitter memories, painful flashbacks, or perhaps a sense of relief that the shocking experiences were over for them. As there are no official written testimonies about the impressions the newsreels left on audiences—taking the form, for example, of reviews of the short films or letters to producers—it is difficult to gauge their impact. During a period when the regime had tight control over the population, there was no place for viewers to express such opinions about official audiovisual media.

War brings not only destruction but also death. On December 10, 1951, one of the most shocking newsreels of the Korean War was screened.[22] It showed dozens of bodies piled up in trenches and arranged in rows for identification. The title of one section, "The Crimes of Communism," is a clear indication of the producers' intention to denounce these murders by the enemy. The footage was accompanied by a number of explanations in English, including "It is a sign of the horror behind the communist lines" and "Both soldiers and civilians were murdered in cold blood." In Francoist Spain, showing the cruelty of communism was a fundamental strategy used to justify not only the crusade against the Soviet threat but also, on a secondary level, the atrocities that Franco had committed against communists in the Spanish Civil War not long ago. Such images made it possible to effectively carry out this plan (see fig. 7.1).

The desire to denounce the evils of communism motivated not only the images of ruins and dead bodies but also those of prisoners. The newsreels that probably had the greatest emotional impact include those that presented the testimonies of prisoners of war, who described the horrors they faced

Fig. 7.1 Seeing the horrors of war in a Spanish news reel from NO-DO: body count at the Korean front, 1951. Film still provided by Filmoteca Española. Noticiario NO-DO, no. 466 B, 953. Photo © Filmoteca Española.

during their time in captivity. The aim was to show the actions taken by the communist regime against the South Koreans and further demonize the Soviet Bloc. By presenting these first-person testimonies and allowing the audience to see faces and hear voices, the newsreels ensured the messages were communicated even more effectively. Visual and auditory information has a powerful impact on multiple sensory levels. Cinema, as an audiovisual experience, provides a way to approach the "other" through an identification process that binds every viewer to what is being shown on screen. The shock effect makes viewers keenly aware of the unfolding event. By using the senses of sight and hearing, the films were once again able to engage the emotions of those who watched the brief news programs.

Similarly, these newsreels repeatedly used images of children. This was not a novelty for war propaganda, since in previous armed conflicts such images had also been included to illustrate the plight of innocent victims of enemy actions or to highlight the good deeds of other soldiers. For example, in a newsreel dated March 9, 1953,[23] a group of Korean children are shown receiving clothes from American soldiers while the narrator offers the following moving explanation: "These children, who at their young age have known nothing but calamity and hardships, are receiving the warm support of the United States in an act of Christian charity." In addition, the newsreel from April 20, 1953,[24] presents a large group of schoolchildren receiving gifts from another group of soldiers.[25] Inevitably, these images of children shocked viewers, so the strategy was used especially often during the last year of war, when the effects of the fighting became all the more evident. NO-DO provided the Spanish people with images and sounds of the Korean War over a period of three years.

The Cuban Missile Crisis Through the NO-DO Lens: Communist Alert in the Caribbean

The 1960s began with another "hot" chapter of the Cold War, the Cuban Missile Crisis in October 1962. The confrontation caused panic throughout the world, as it was considered a dangerous international security emergency. The first episode of one of the greatest crises between the two superpowers took place in April 1961, after the Bay of Pigs invasion. On this occasion, from May 1 to 8, 1961, NO-DO produced three newsreels. The first, N 956 A, is dedicated to the consequences of the Cuban conflict abroad. It shows "the protests promoted by the communist machine in East Berlin" while mentioning that, in other countries, people were "demonstrating in support of those who believe that Cuba should not become a threat to world peace and security as a satellite of the Soviet Union." Although both demonstrations were covered, the differences between the two descriptions reveal the regime's official position.[26]

N 956 B shows emotionally charged images taken after the attack on Cuba, including shots of smoking buildings and several structures bombed to ruins. As part of the same strategy identified in the programs about Korea, this newsreel also includes footage of the planes deployed in the air operation and the bombs dropped on Cuban soil. In terms of sonic propaganda, while the narrator describes the accusations exchanged between Fidel Castro's supporters and the participants in the attack, tense music plays in the background that makes the scene seem more aggressive than it would otherwise.[27] Sound is thus clearly harnessed to indirectly persuade viewers to take a certain position on events. The music pieces are not superfluous elements but part of a deliberate propagandistic strategy. They were instrumental in creating a specific atmosphere for each situation and were written especially for NO-DO by composers such as Manuel Parada.[28]

The coverage of the first phase of the Cuban conflict closes with images of women visiting revolutionary headquarters in Miami in search of information about men who had taken part in the "attempt to liberate their country" and had gone into exile for fear of repression by the Castro regime. By including these brief scenes of crying mothers and wives, the program attempts to present a negative view of the actions taken by the Cuban leader against opponents of his policies. Although the narrator does not offer any assessment of Castro, viewers can reach their own conclusion by contrasting the scenes of the Cuban leader refusing to release prisoners of war (also accompanied by tense background music) with the tranquil scenes of the meeting held by President John F. Kennedy and Dwight D. Eisenhower at Camp David to analyze the international situation.[29]

The second major phase in this crisis began with missile deployments in 1962. The installations were discovered in photographs taken by a US spy plane, which further escalated tensions with Cuba. The most dangerous day of the confrontation was so-called Black Saturday on October 27, when a U-2 spy plane was shot down over Cuba by a Soviet missile, killing the pilot. Although it turned out that the downing of the plane was in violation of Nikita Khrushchev's orders, tensions reached the breaking point. That same day, to end to the crisis, the Soviet leader proposed dismantling the nuclear missile bases in Cuba in a communication to Kennedy. In exchange, Khrushchev obtained a guarantee that the United States would not invade Cuba or support operations to that end and that it would dismantle nuclear missile bases in Turkey. The crisis was thus overcome, and direct conflict was averted once again.[30]

Because these last few events were quickly resolved, references to them have been discovered in only five NO-DO newsreels, produced between November 5 and December 3. They report on the outcome of the crisis and the alleviation of the fears of a new war. The newsreels clearly take the side of the United States, rejecting the form of communism established in Cuba under Castro. Despite the fact that attention had shifted from East Asia to the Caribbean, the underlying idea was thus the same: communism was a threat to world peace, and vigilance was needed to stop its global expansion.

While the sounds of tanks and weapons were crucial to the coverage of the Korean War, narration and footage play more prominent roles in the films about Cuba. In other words, the sensory portrayal of the Korean War in

NO-DO propaganda relied to a greater extent on hearing, whereas coverage of the Cuban crisis relied more on sight. Thanks to the newsreels, the Spanish people were able to closely follow the rapid development of the Cuban crisis with all the attendant military and diplomatic actions. Once again, airplanes and ships formed two of the preferred backdrops for the films. For example, the three newsreels from November 5, 1962,[31] show the aerial reconnaissance of Russian missile bases on the Caribbean island and allow viewers to follow the US ships sent to Cuba in the event that a military intervention was necessary. The accompanying music and the narrator's explanations served to heighten the viewers' anxiety and suspense—precisely the effect propaganda was supposed to have. Staged in this way and dramatized by music, the threat was perceived as all the greater by audiences.

These three newsreels also show images of demonstrations against US actions in the streets of Havana. According to the narrator, these protests were an attempt by Cuban leaders to resolve the tense situation by "making noise." The negative message about the protests that had been incited by the Cuban leaders, as well as the images and sounds, performed the function of casting communism in an unfavorable light.

As one might expect, the propaganda also included footage of the missiles themselves, as people were eager to see the "mysterious threat" that had altered the course of international relations. The newsreel dated November 26, 1962, for example, shows the weapons being transported on the decks of large ships while the United States monitored the disarmament process (see fig. 7.2).[32] The different descriptions of the Soviet and American missiles are noteworthy. In one of the newsreels from May 1962, the Soviet missiles are referred to as "deadly weapons," whereas the Titan missiles are proudly described as "the most modern and effective retaliatory weapons of the United States." In other words, whereas Soviet weapons were meant to kill, the American missiles served a punitive purpose in response to aggression from other nations.

The news cycle came to an end on December 3, 1962, with the lifting of the Cuban embargo. This last step on the path toward international stability was presented as the successful conclusion of efforts to avoid what threatened to become a direct armed confrontation. The newsreel released on that day describes developments as "the first time that journalists had resumed contact with Kennedy since the beginning of the crisis in Cuba, which had almost provoked a world war." The film takes a different tone and uses a calmer narrative and music in order to convey the relief experienced in international politics.

Fig. 7.2 Aerial view of the Cuban Missile Crisis from NO-DO, 1962. Film still provided by Filmoteca Española. Noticiario NO-DO, no. 1038 A, 247. Photo © Filmoteca Española.

In short, while the Cuba crisis was not a direct military confrontation and did not involve the "hot" combat seen in Korea, it produced tensions that were felt by the Spanish public. In addition, this crisis quickly attracted the attention of the Spanish population as it was perceived as one of the most dangerous chapters of the Cold War.

Conclusion

This study pursued two objectives: first, it examined examples of newsreels and how the senses were engaged in propaganda about "hot" confrontations in the Cold War; second, it demonstrated how different techniques were employed to achieve a certain effect on viewers during two important international events, the Korean War and the Cuban Missile Crisis. As expected, NO-DO showed exactly what Franco's censors believed would satisfy national interests, and it became a powerful tool to spread the regime's ideology. It brought the Cold War into the cinemas of Spain and presented the most important events of the war to millions of people who did not generally have access to other multisensory communication media such as television.

As described above, one of the main advantages of the newsreel is that it remained popular as a medium throughout the Cold War. It provided an interesting range of news and—as a means of propaganda—transmitted numerous images and sounds to a population eager to learn about what was going on in the world. The main difference between NO-DO newsreels and other forms of media, such as newspapers and photographs, is that the newsreels incorporated moving images and sound. These two elements were intentionally used to provide a more immersive experience of the narrated events. They were carefully selected to shape people's opinions about events and convince them to support or oppose certain ideas. Their effects were enhanced by the spaces in which NO-DO programs were shown, since the environment of the movie theater made it easier to directly address the viewers' senses. Although the effect on viewers is no longer demonstrable, it can be concluded that NO-DO's strategy contributed to effectively conveying the atmosphere of the narrated episodes.

As regards my second research objective, in analyzing the strategies employed by NO-DO, I found certain similarities in the coverage of the two episodes that were separated by a decade. These similarities are of interest to anyone wishing to learn how Spaniards experienced the conflicts of the Cold War through mediated and modified sensory stimuli. For example, there was a tendency during both crises to preserve the original sounds and not erase any details that could be useful for sensory reception, such as the noise of planes. Similarities can also be seen in the types of images used, such as the prevalent aerial scenes of airplanes and boats shot using the camera perspectives described above. Finally, music also played an important role in many of the newsreels analyzed here. The narrator's comments were rarely neutral but rather reinforced the main objective of the short films, which was to fight communism. The commentary linked the events in Asia and Latin America to European and even domestic tensions during the Cold War. At the same time, though, we find a number of differences between the two episodes. For example, while the generally accepted narrative of media history is that of a trajectory of development to multisensory "multimedia," this case study shows that sounds were less important to later media representations of Cuba than they were to representations of Korea. Here I have sought to establish how these strategies addressed specific senses for specific propaganda goals. In short, NO-DO manipulated the process of communicating with Spanish audiences so as to make the transmission of propaganda through newsreels more effective.

As discussed above, sensory perception is fundamental to our experience of reality, and propaganda has the ability to modify that experience to suit specific interests. Against this backdrop, one can conclude that in both situations, with respect to the experiences created by NO-DO's sounds and images, sensory stimuli were the ammunition used to evoke and manipulate emotions.

Notes

1. See Jowett and O'Donnell, *Propaganda and Persuasion*.
2. See Rueda, "La televisión en España," 55.
3. For more on NO-DO, see Abella and Cardona, *Años del No-Do*; Rodríguez, *El NO-DO*; Tranche and Sánchez-Biosca, *NO-DO*.
4. Most of the images from the programs analyzed in this chapter were taken from these international agencies. See Atkinson, "Newsreels as Domestic Propaganda."
5. Since 2015, the section dedicated to Filmoteca Española on RTVE's website offers in open access the complete NO-DO archives, including 6,573 documents and 1,719 hours of video. All the links provided in the chapter 7 notes were checked for the last time on February 18, 2021.
6. See Botero, *Ambivalent Embrace*; Elizalde and Delgado, *España y Estados Unidos*.
7. See Niño, "Dilemas de la propaganda americana," 157.
8. Schafer, *Soundscape*, 3.
9. See Marks, *Touch*, vii–xii; also Elsaesser and Hagener, *Film Theory*.
10. See Rodríguez, *El NO-DO*.
11. See Bull et al., "Introducing Sensory Studies."
12. See Bakogianni and Hope, *War as Spectacle*, 10.
13. Cf. No. 408 A (4:03–5:09), Noticiarios NO-DO Collection, Filmoteca Española fonds, Madrid, Spain (hereafter NO-DO), https://www.rtve.es/filmoteca/no-do/not-408/1487403/.
14. Cf. No. 466 A (6:15–6:35), NO-DO, https://www.rtve.es/filmoteca/no-do/not-466/1470681/.

15. Cf. No. 534 B (2:58–3:46), NO-DO, https://www.rtve.es/filmoteca/no-do/not-534/1468934/.
16. However, it must be noted that although these scenes allowed audiences to take part as spectators, other elements made the experience of the pilots much different than the audiences' experience: smells, weightlessness, dizziness, the struggle against wind, the sensations provoked by the movement of the waves, and the presence of real danger.
17. Cf. No. 444 A (5:39–6:58), NO-DO, https://www.rtve.es/filmoteca/no-do/not-444/1487200/.
18. Cf. No. 521 A (1:50–2:35), NO-DO, https://www.rtve.es/filmoteca/no-do/not-521/1468802/.
19. Cf. No. 399 A (7:50–10:09), NO-DO, https://www.rtve.es/filmoteca/no-do/not-399/1467603/.
20. See Lasswell, *Propaganda Technique*.
21. For insights into how the Spanish population might have perceived the bombing of Guernica, see Cueto, *Guernica en la escena*.
22. Cf. No. 466 B (9:16–10:09), NO-DO, https://www.rtve.es/filmoteca/no-do/not-466/1470676/.
23. Cf. No. 531 A (2:33–3:36), NO-DO, https://www.rtve.es/filmoteca/no-do/not-531/1468738/.
24. Cf. No. 537 A (1:17–2:44), NO-DO, https://www.rtve.es/filmoteca/no-do/not-537/1468936/.
25. On the Cold War politics of gifts, see chapter 1 of this book.
26. Cf. No. 956 A (6:10–7:12), NO-DO, https://www.rtve.es/filmoteca/no-do/not-956/1470442/.
27. Cf. No. 956 B (2:05–3:36), NO-DO, https://www.rtve.es/filmoteca/no-do/not-956/1470430/.

28. See Málaga, "Manuel Parada."
29. Cf. No. 957 A (3:01–4:06), NO-DO, https://www.rtve.es/filmoteca/no-do/not-957/1470437/.
30. See George, *Cuban Missile Crisis*; Carradice, *Cuban Missile Crisis*.
31. Cf. No. 1035 A, B, and C (7:29–9:38), NO-DO, https://www.rtve.es/filmoteca/no-do/not-1035/1471500/.
32. Cf. No. 1038 A (2:36–3:24), NO-DO, https://www.rtve.es/filmoteca/no-do/not-1038/1486450/.

Bibliography

Audiovisual Source
Filmoteca Española, Madrid, Spain: Noticiarios NO-DO Collection, Nos. 399 A; 408 A; 444 A; 466 A and B; 521 A; 531 A; 534 B; 537 A; 956 A and B; 957 A; 1035 A, B, and C; 1038 A.

Published Sources
Abella, Rafael, and Gabriel Cardona. *Los años del No-Do: El mundo entero al alcance de todos los españoles*. Barcelona: Destino, 2008.
Atkinson, Nathan S. "Newsreels as Domestic Propaganda: Visual Rhetoric at the Dawn of the Cold War." *Rhetoric and Public Affairs* 14, no. 1 (2011): 69–100.
Bakogianni, Anastasia, and Valerie M. Hope. *War as Spectacle: Ancient and Modern Perspectives on the Display of Armed Conflict*. New York: Bloomsbury Academic, 2015.
Botero, Rodrigo. *Ambivalent Embrace: America's Troubled Relations with Spain from the Revolutionary War to the Cold War*. London: Greenwood Press, 2001.
Bull, Michael, Paul Gilroy, David Howes, and Douglas Kahn. "Introducing Sensory Studies." *Senses and Society* 1, no. 1 (2006): 5–7.
Carradice, Phil. *The Cuban Missile Crisis: Thirteen Days on an Atomic Knife Edge, October 1962*. Barnsley: Pen & Sword Military, 2017.
Cueto, Elena. *Guernica en la escena, la página y la pantalla: Evento, memoria y patrimonio*. Zaragoza: Prensas de la Universidad de Zaragoza, 2017.
Elizalde, María Dolores, and Lorenzo Delgado. *España y Estados Unidos en el siglo XX*. Madrid: CSIC, 2005.
Elsaesser, Thomas, and Malte Hagener. *Film Theory: An Introduction through the Senses*. New York: Routledge, 2010.
George, Alice L. *The Cuban Missile Crisis: The Threshold of Nuclear War*. New York: Routledge, 2013.
Jowett, Garth, and Victoria O'Donnell. *Propaganda and Persuasion*. Thousand Oaks: SAGE, 2006.
Lasswell, Harold. *Propaganda Technique in the World War*. New York: Peter Smith, 1927.
Málaga, Álvaro. "Manuel Parada: Un músico para el cine." *Salamanca: Revista de estudios*, no. 42 (1999): 279–90.
Marks, Laura U. *Touch: Sensuous Theory and Multisensory Media*. Minneapolis: University of Minnesota Press, 2002.
Niño, Antonio. "Los dilemas de la propaganda americana en la España franquista." In *Guerra fría y propaganda: Estados Unidos y su cruzada cultural en Europa y América Latina*, edited by José Antonio Montero and Antonio Niño, 155–96. Madrid: Biblioteca Nueva, 2012.
Rodríguez, Saturnino. *El NO-DO, catecismo social de una época*. Madrid: Editorial Complutense, 1999.
———. "El NO-DO, cuando el cine deja de ser fábrica de sueños para ser máquina de comunicados." *Sociedad y utopía: Revista de ciencias sociales*, no. 11 (1998): 15–32.
Rueda, José Carlos. "La televisión en España: Expansión y consumo social, 1963–1969." *Anàlisi: Quaderns de comunicació i cultura*, no. 32 (2005): 45–71.
Schafer, R. Murray. *The Soundscape: Our Sonic Environment and the Tuning of the World*. Rochester: Destiny Books, 1993.
Tranche, Rafael R., and Vicente Sánchez-Biosca. *NO-DO: El tiempo y la memoria*. Madrid: Cátedra-Filmoteca Española, 2018.

CHAPTER 8

The Smell of the Berlin Wall

Olfactory Border Management at the Inner-European Frontier

Bodo Mrozek

When the Berlin Wall was erected in 1961, it consisted mainly of solid materials: bricks, concrete, barbed wire, spotlights, and watchtowers. During the first days of the physical partitioning of Germany, which was part of a more extensive borderline in a global conflict, it became obvious that the confrontation had entered a new historical phase. The inner-German border was largely a green one that passed through forests and fields, but in Berlin, it cut directly through the cityscape—through streets, neighborhoods, congregations, and even a cemetery. The wall was not yet finished when several incidents demonstrated that a large part of the German population was not willing to accept the new front line in the Cold War. The first spectacular escapes by soldiers and construction workers, who made the quick, life-threatening jump into the Western sectors, not only foretold the deadly conflict to come but were also captured in iconic photographs that became weapons in a war of images. This propaganda war has been broadly analyzed by historians and media scholars, and images were not the only weapon.[1] On the Western side of the border, radio stations and human rights activists began disseminating their messages from mobile loudspeakers directly across the Berlin Wall.[2] The East German authorities fought back with similar audio devices.

Soviet supersonic military jets went "on the air" and destroyed numerous windows in West Berlin buildings as they broke the sound barrier and took sonic warfare to a higher level. The role of sonic and visual sensory experience in the conflict is obvious, but was there an olfactory dimension as well? In other words, did the Berlin Wall *smell*? And if so, what did it smell like?

This chapter examines the micropolitics of the enforced partition of Europe by concentrating on olfactory conflicts at the inner-German border and beyond. In public memory, this frontier—especially the 160 kilometers of the Berlin Wall—symbolizes a highly militarized, deadly, and impenetrable barrier. However, what the field of borderland studies emphasizes in general is also true of this barrier: border zones are highly complex products and factors in cultural, social, and temporal processes. They are dynamic spaces that undergo change. They are zones not only of division but also of (mostly unwanted) transit. In recent years, historical research has focused on the surprising amount of informal traffic at the Cold War's frontiers.[3] What is true for human border crossers is even more relevant for other unwanted border transgressors. Animals, plants, water, and even air acted as transnational factors that resisted the artificial barriers and required intense border management.[4] These nonhuman "actants," as they are called in actor-network-theory (ANT), were part of the border networks formed by the interaction of humans with human-built objects and environmental factors.[5] How was the human sensorium involved in the connection and association of these factors? Combining approaches from sensory studies, border(land) studies, and ANT in the field of Cold War history, this chapter explores the role of olfaction. Smell, I argue, was the most unexpected factor in these processes, and in several events, smell even caused diplomatic conflicts that extended from everyday experience to the highest level of politics.

Phantom Stenches? The Smell of Death at the Berlin Wall

In November 1963, just two years after the construction of the Berlin Wall, a creepy incident occurred at the newly militarized Berlin border. In Bernauer Strasse, along a stretch of the wall that had been the scene of several spectacular escapes by East Berlin citizens, nosewitnesses noticed an extremely unpleasant smell. As a letter writer explained to the West Berlin health senator, it was the smell of death. A memo from the West Berlin police station in the Wedding district notified the administrative authorities that "in recent days, due to the weather, a smell of decay has been perceptible, sometimes weak, sometimes more intense, coming from the former tunnel system at Stettiner Station at the corner of Gartenstrasse and Bernauer Strasse."[6] The suggestion was that it came from corpses.

In olfactory history, the smell of death is described as perhaps the most extreme sensation.[7] In almost every culture, the necessity of burying the dead is the basis of civilization. The smell of human decay, often described as "sweet" and "musk-like," is considered scandalous and must be avoided at all costs, because it reminds the living of the (culturally suppressed) finitude of life. The strong emotions and affects triggered by the gas emitted by decaying bodies are usually described as extreme disgust. The rotting corpse has been characterized as "presumably the paradigm of the disgusting object" and as the origin of the affect of disgust.[8] Another response is fear, which has its roots in older, long-disproved but persistent ideas of a ptomaine, a poison developing in and dripping out of dead bodies. While studies from the life sciences claim that these sensory and emotional reactions to decay are anthropologically or even genetically universal, the field of cultural studies has emphasized changes in sensibilities about decay over centuries and different historical situations. In his analysis of the theme of corpse decay in war novels, literary scholar Frank Krause argues that the smell of death is often used to describe a status of alarm; it is also the first sign of emergency rule and a harbinger of war.[9]

In Berlin in 1962, the experience of the Second World War was still fresh in the minds of the contemporaries. They had strong memories of the smell of dead, decaying bodies in destroyed buildings, victims of urban warfare in the final battles in Berlin, and humans as well as animals lying dead in bomb craters. When horses had died, people had quickly emerged from their homes, equipped with knives to save the meat before it could go bad, as hunger was one of the scourges of wartime Berlin. With these memories still alive, West Berlin health officials were just as alarmed as the passersby who had detected the alleged "smell of death" at the Berlin Wall. They conducted several inspections and confirmed the statements by local residents. During their olfactory investigations, though, they were unable to locate the source of the spooky smell. "It might possibly come from the S-Bahn tunnel at Stettiner Station or from a sewer pipe," they guessed. The street in question was intersected by the newly erected border facilities and ended abruptly at the wall. In January 1964, the source of the smell was still unknown. An additional memorandum notes that the West Berlin police were informed, but since their jurisdiction ended at the border, they were unable to trace the smell to its source. To evaluate and clarify the origins of the smell, the report states, it was necessary to work with the East German health authorities. In this period, just after the construction of the wall, relations between the authorities in East and West Berlin were at a low point, making it difficult to resolve the delicate matter. The West Berlin investigators agreed to bring in the appointed technical commissioner—and exercise "the highest discretion."[10] The incident was even more delicate because Bernauer Strasse was the scene of several spectacular escapes. Local residents had climbed out of windows to reach West Berlin territory, and a soldier in the German Democratic Republic's (GDR) National People's Army was photographed jumping over barbed wire at the border. The headlines in this period referred to the many successful and several deadly attempts to escape the Soviet sector of Berlin, including those through tunnels.

The digging of a tunnel required meticulous planning, extensive preparation, and carefully guarded secrecy. It was the most time-consuming method of escape and could take weeks, if not months, of work. Between 1961 and 1981, around forty tunnels were built, most starting from Western territory, some from the East.[11] Several hundred East Germans escaped by crawling on their hands and knees through dark and narrow passageways that had been quietly dug beneath the border, while guards stationed in towers overhead scoured the landscape with binoculars for escapees taking the overland route. A large number were caught. At least four people died in tunnels—two Western escape helpers and two GDR border guards.[12] In the period in which the smells were reported, tunnel escapes were all over the news. In May 1962, a dozen elderly East Germans escaped by walking upright through a "senior citizens' tunnel" that was 32 meters long and 1.75 meters high. One tunnel to the West Berlin district of Neukölln was discovered before it was finished. In September, a group of twenty-nine GDR citizens were welcomed by an NBC news team after escaping through the 120-meter-long "Tunnel 29" from Bernauer Strasse, the same street where the smells would be detected only three months later.[13] With events like these widely reported in the West, it was certainly plausible to assume the stench came from dead bodies underneath the ground.

In March 1964, the West Berlin Sanitation Department finally contacted the Reichsbahn (East German Railway), which was responsible for maintaining the tunnel system that partly ran under West Berlin. In a confidential report, the authorities were notified of the Reichsbahn's reply: during an inspection of the tunnels in late January, no smells or "deposits" had been detected. The Reichsbahn therefore recommended waiting for further complaints from local residents. A letter from the Sewage Department described the technical construction of the canal system and came to the same conclusion. The vertical tunnels on East Berlin soil were open and subject to permanent monitoring. Offensive smells seemed "very unlikely."[14] On this final note, the records were closed, but one question remains: What had the residents who reported "the smell of death" actually apprehended?

Although it might have been dead animals, possibly rats, the reports by the Sanitation Department do not point to this mundane explanation. One possibility is a phenomenon known in sensory studies as "phantom sensations." Today, everyone is familiar with such sensations in the form of wrongly sensed phone vibrations, which people believe they feel even when their phone is not in their pocket. Research has shown that cognitive processes can cause sensations in the body. In other words, the *idea* of a sensation can be so strong that it is ultimately sensed. It is worth considering whether the everyday news about spectacular tunnel escapes, shots fired from watchtowers, and—in the notorious 1962 case of eighteen-year-old escapee Peter Fechter—a shot and dying body lying for hours in the no-man's-land of the Berlin Wall stimulated the imagination of local residents to such an extent that they sensed corpses with their noses—or at least associated perceived sensations with ideas about the border as a deadly zone.

Invisible Border Crossers: Transnational Smell Conflicts

Olfaction at the inner-German border was not always a product of pure imagination. In November 1974, thirteen years after the erection of the Berlin Wall, a resident of the green district of Mariendorf in West Berlin, upon leaving his home, noticed a strange odor in the air that immediately had intense consequences. As he explained, the smell caused nausea and even vomiting. In a letter to the East Berlin authorities, he described it as "so pungent it penetrates even closed windows and doors." He was not the only one thus affected. The stench was present on several days, lasting for hours, and made it impossible to open school windows.[15] The next day, a West Berlin paper reported on the unpleasant experience, describing how residents of several West Berlin districts suffered from the odor.[16] The reporter pointed to the usual suspect, suggesting that sewage plants were the origin. However, the suspected location of the emitter was rather unusual: it was presumed to be in the political East, far behind the highly militarized border to West Berlin. The next day, another West Berlin paper picked up the story, speculating on other possible sources, including carcass disposals or chemical plants in the nearby East German district of Teltow. The persistence of the smell was described as exceptional since odors of this intensity were unusual in this green part of Berlin.[17] The November winds were suspected of blowing the smell across the border. After all, 40 percent of the time, they blew from the south of Berlin, in the surrounding GDR, to West Berlin in the north.

It was even more difficult to identify the origin because characterizations by the affected people varied from "burned cabbage" to "boiling glue." Most found it hard to describe what they perceived—a common problem with smells. As smell studies emphasize, there is no common formalized system that allows people to precisely categorize olfactory experiences in distinct terms—terms like those used for taste (sweet, sour, bitter, salty, sharp, and umami). According to anthropologist David Le Breton, smell is "the least diversified sense in language": "Even though we are able to discriminate thousands of odors, we stumble over our words to describe or communicate them to others."[18] As a result, the immediately alarmed city authorities set out to analytically "sniff" the unknown olfactory particles in the air. Engineers from the Department of Air Monitoring used measurement vehicles to technically examine the characteristics and extent of the problem. However, although their technical equipment was able to detect corrosive gases such as sulfur dioxide and carbon monoxide, it could not precisely determine the smells.[19] The engineers suspected amines from the ammonia family as the main source of the disturbance—an indication that chemical plants, which a West Berlin internal note identified as near Teltow, were to blame.[20] In early December, the phenomenon intensified. Local authorities received more than one hundred complaints, several of which described unpleasant visceral effects that ranged from headaches to vomiting.

In an official memorandum, the West Berlin civil servant in charge of the matter urged that the East German authorities be informed and put under pressure to resolve the situation.[21] Attached to the memorandum is an olfactory map that shows numerous lines crossing the southern border between East and West Berlin and ending in numbered marks that can be individually studied. These marks show the dates and precise locations of the engineers' measurements and form what is described as a "scent wedge" that cuts deeply into West Berlin territory. The map provides a picture of a border area that was heavily penetrated by unknown nonhuman agents

Fig. 8.1 Olfactory map visualizing border-crossing scent nuisances in the south of West Berlin, November 25–December 4, 1974. Landesarchiv Berlin, B Rep 002, No. 24845.

that were well suited to intensify not only sensory but also political conflict (highlighted in yellow, see fig. 8.1).

The local civil servant was the driving force behind efforts to put the problem on the political agenda. In a number of letters and encrypted memos, he urged the federal government to include the topic in its German-German negotiations.[22] Ultimately, in a report marked urgent and confidential, the governing mayor of West Berlin, Klaus Schütz, tried to persuade the West German chancellor to bring the matter to the attention of the Federal Republic of Germany's (FRG) permanent mission in the GDR.[23] However, the permanent representative Günter Gaus refused to address the noxious issue: he feared that doing so would endanger the general negotiations between the two German states and urged that the GDR would act "increasingly restrictive" as regards such questions.[24] (The West German ambassador to East Germany was officially called a permanent representative because East Germany was not recognized as an independent state—a result of the Hallstein doctrine.[25]) Further commentary in the West Berlin press described the diplomatic and legal complexity of the problem. Regional environmental protection in greater Berlin lacked sufficient regulation, one newspaper complained. At the same time, the paper called for a treaty between the FRG and the GDR to supplement the Four Powers Agreement on Berlin, which had been signed by the American, British, French, and Soviet powers in September 1971. The absence of an environmental protection treaty was blamed for the powerlessness of the West Berlin authorities: because German-German relations were a national matter, the West Berlin senator for environmental affairs had to lodge a formal request in the FRG capital of Bonn in order to initiate diplomatic negotiations. However, attempts to enforce environmental protection regulations in the divided city of Berlin without a treaty were "like keeping a burst pipe shut with your bare hands," lamented Günter Matthes, columnist for the West Berlin *Tagesspiegel*. Berlin was not the only affected area, he wrote. The industrial region of Leuna in East Germany smelled to him "like the devil's grandmother," a sensory indicator that raised serious concerns about the GDR's ability to tackle its environmental issues. At the time, West Berlin's energy policy was based on transports of Soviet coal and oil through the GDR. Referring to these transports as the political Achilles' heel that threatened West Berlin's independence, Matthes sought to explain the "contract-less smell" in the context of the larger geopolitical conflict.[26]

In 1979 complaints about unpleasant smells in the southern part of West Berlin once again intensified.[27] Correspondence between the *Tagesspiegel* and several local residents reveals that twenty thousand were now affected; the complaints from 1974 are also mentioned.[28] In March, a formal resolution was drafted by the West Berlin senator for health and environmental protection. It laid the foundation for an "air pollution control plan" that aimed to reduce emissions, especially sulfur dioxide, in the air above the "exposed territory" of Berlin. Initial measures included an emission register and the provision of particular actions for a substantial reduction of emissions, based on the Federal Emission Control Act (Bundes-Immisionsschutzgesetz), which was now in effect in West Germany. In June the offensive smells were the subject of negotiations between the permanent mission of the FRG and the GDR Ministry of Foreign Affairs. According to internal reports, though, they had little effect. Since East Germans were strictly prohibited from coming close to the restricted zone of the border facilities, which was regarded as a military secret and hardly mentioned in the East German press, most complaints came from West Berlin. Meanwhile, though, East Berlin citizens were now complaining about smells from the West. In a letter to the West Berlin mayor that contained a nearly identical description of the physical effects of these smells, an East Berlin citizen pointed to an industrial plant in the West Berlin district of Reinickendorf and mentioned noise pollution from Tegel Airport in West Berlin.[29] As a result, several press articles reported on the "dicke Luft" (literally "thick air") between East and West,[30] a German phrase that describes tensions between two parties. They also referred to "Berlin air" as an object of local pride, praised in a traditional Berlin song from around 1900.[31]

On the occasion of the first (and last) face-to-face meeting between Erich Honecker and Helmut Schmidt, the GDR and FRG heads of state, respectively, the West Germany paper *Die Welt* ran the headline "Chancellor to Discuss also Bad Smells with Honecker."[32] This time the appeal for better air was initiated by the Bavarian governor Franz Josef Strauß, a conservative Cold War warrior who had complained about smells similar to "cat dung" crossing the southwestern border in the triangle between Czechoslovakia (ČSSR), the GDR, and the West German state of Bavaria, a matter destined to play a role in FRG-ČSSR-GDR relations from the late 1970s to the late 1980s.[33] Smell had become an issue at the highest level of political exchange between the rival German states and within the larger confrontation between the blocs.[34] The smell events of the 1970s and 1980s were perhaps the most urgently discussed sensory incidents at the Berlin Wall. Others—as the first example suggests—were perhaps only imagined sensations. But were smells also deliberately used to police the border?

Policing the Border: Animal Sensoria and Smell Barriers

Smell definitely played a significant role in securing the inner-German border. For example, dogs were used from an early stage to detect fugitives. The history of the usage of animal sensoria in conflicts is long and includes not only birds as early detectors of gas attacks and the navigational abilities of pigeons and dolphins but above all dog noses.[35] As in other states, both the police and the military in the GDR used and trained dogs, but little serious research has been conducted on dogs in the GDR security forces.[36] Dogs have about twice as many olfactory receptors as humans,[37] and their ability to track human smells was an integral part of the training dogs received before serving in the police force—and later in the border troops.[38] In 1963 the first seventy-two dogs went through training in the police force's dog school in Pretzsch, where they learned to sniff out fugitives at border checkpoints.[39] From the mid-1960s onward, dogs were deployed in the border zone, which

Fig. 8.2 Smell barrier: West German intelligence photo of the inner-German border in 1969. Image courtesy of Bundesarchiv/SELKE, Germany, B 206-1915 BND.

in areas outside Berlin was partly fortified with landmines and self-shooting shrapnel devices. They were attached by a two-and-a-half-meter-long leash with a ring to a fifty- to one-hundred-meter-long cable overhead, and they were badly fed and given water by soldiers who came in by jeeps but otherwise left on their own.[40] These poor creatures did not undergo special sniff training. That was reserved for the border troops' trained detection dogs, whose abilities to recognize individuals with their noses were proudly demonstrated to state guests during excursions to the border.[41] Those dogs were trained to recognize butric acid, "as humans transpire this substance," an internal document on service dogs explained.[42] In 1989, the GDR's canine corps consisted of a total of 857 dogs. This meant that sniffing was an important weapon in policing the border and preventing escapes, but did the border itself smell?

The question might sound absurd, but in fact it did. In May 1969, when agents from the West German foreign intelligence service (Bundesnachrichtendienst) were routinely observing the inner-German border in the state of Lower Saxony, their cameras captured an unusual image. On the eastern side of the double wire-mesh fence at the "green border," military personnel in full chemical protective suits, gloves, and gas masks were busy attaching strange objects directly to the fence at knee height. Close-ups later revealed that these objects were transparent bottles about twenty-five centimeters high, filled with a dark brown liquid. Forty-centimeter wicks were dipped into this liquid, their long ends woven into the barbed wire of the fence. These mysterious new devices were installed over a 7.3 kilometer stretch at the border. From the wicks, the unknown liquid (allegedly turpentine) evaporated, causing a "strong smell." In a secret report, the West German foreign intelligence service expressed its suspicion that the bottles functioned as a "scent barrier" to prevent wildlife from crossing the border (see fig. 8.2).[43]

In fact, wild animals constituted a significant problem for the border troops, as they triggered the electric alarm systems when crossing the demarcation line. Deer, boars, and foxes were therefore the targets of special hunting squads led by officers from the People's Army and tasked with "military wildlife shooting": killing whatever wildlife moved into their crosshairs without regard for hunting seasons or the protection of pregnant does or hinds.[44] Often the bodies of these animals were left to rot in the borderlands, the smell of decay attracting scavengers. Despite the hunters' efforts, the false alarms remained an urgent problem in the GDR and elsewhere. In Hungary, forty to sixty soldiers responded whenever a signal wire triggered an alarm. This number could easily increase to four hundred if the reason for the alarm was not detected within an hour. Due to wildlife and birds, the number of false alarms ran to around four thousand a year, leading to high costs and frustration among border units, whose soldiers were further demoralized because they were deployed against their fellow citizens.[45] As a result, border-crossing animals became more than just a side effect of the political partition. According to historian Frank Wolff, they were a major reason for the border weariness of Hungarian leaders in the mid-1980s, who ultimately ordered the demilitarization of the border.[46] The smell barriers had turned out to be ineffective in preventing animals from crossing the demarcation line.

Olfactory Warfare: Sprays and Powders

Another smell event shows that additional volatile substances were used in border management. The term *border management* refers to the maintenance and improvement measures designed to protect zones that are usually imagined as fortified hermetic partitions but are in fact often "messy meeting points rather than neat divisions," as borderland studies emphasize.[47] In May 1987, such a messy encounter took place at the section of the Berlin border that cut through the district of Kreuzberg. Passersby in the West noticed a sharp smell from the border that immediately caused physical reactions—"a dry cough, nausea, and headache."[48] Their suspicion was that some kind of gas had been released by the GDR border troops. Around sixty residents signed and sent a petition to the mayor that included photographic documentation of chemical activities. According to a press article, a nearby retirement home and a kindergarten were affected, and many children suffered mucosal irritation, burning eyes, and general malaise.[49] The article contains a statement from one resident, who complained about the ruthlessness of the border soldiers. In the past, these soldiers had used traditional sickles and scythes to clear grass and underbrush, but now they had switched to a toxic brew of chemicals. These toxins were also used on the property of the East German Reichsbahn, whose lines ran through West Berlin territory. Citizens' initiatives from West Germany raised concerns about specific weed killers and cited the Seveso disaster in July 1976, when an explosion at a Roche chemical plant in the Lombardy region in northern Italy exposed twelve thousand residents to the highly toxic dioxin TCDD (2,3,7,8-Tetrachlorodibenzo-p-dioxin).[50] The accident contaminated large areas of the region, killed thousands of animals, and affected the health of hundreds of people. With these images in mind, local residents found it particularly disturbing to see Reichsbahn personnel using gas masks while spraying their chemicals.[51]

In 1976, the mayor of West Berlin wrote to the Reichsbahn president, complaining about the nuisance and declaring it to be the result of weed-killing activities on railroad property that affected residents of the West Berlin forest Grunewald. One focus of his complaint was the noxious smell of the activities: "Pesticides have the negative characteristic of smelling particularly bad. Many people have an allergic reaction to malodorous substances," the mayor wrote in his protest note.[52] Selest, the substance used, was an extremely volatile ester formulation, and he appealed to the Reichsbahn to use salts instead.

But powders can also cause problems. Some years after the Selest incident, a fine white powder blew over the wall into the West Berlin district of Marienfelde. Once again, the West Berlin Police suspected that the GDR had used an unknown substance as an herbicide in its border management efforts in order to guarantee its guards on their towers a clear view of (or shot at) potential escapees.[53] "What Is the Reason for the Frightening White

Powder Sprayed Near the Wall?" ran the headline over a photo of a gardener displaying white spots on the leaves of his homegrown rhubarb.[54] In 1984 two West Berlin police officers on a border patrol reported that they were engulfed by a large white cloud of powder blown from two trucks passing by on the other side of the border. They tried to escape the smelly clouds by jumping into their car but could not help inhaling the potentially poisonous chemicals. One policeman had to seek medical care for a numb feeling in his mouth, burning skin, and a sore throat.[55] During the period of détente that began in the mid-1970s, it was possible to bring up incidents such as these in bilateral negotiations. The GDR authorities cooperated on environmental issues and in many cases were willing to accept Western technical know-how, including methods to desalinate the Werra River or filters for exhaust air from industrial plants.[56] However, these late smell conflicts at the inner-German border remained largely unresolved as they took place in the last phase of the division of Germany. Only months after the last reported incidents, inner-German border fortifications were dismantled—at first symbolically by hammer-wielding participants in the peaceful revolution, then by heavy construction equipment. In the broader process of the transformation, the smellscapes of the border were finally blown away.

Conclusion

As part of his smellscape concept, J. Douglas Porteous distinguishes between smell marks and smell events that eventually form olfactory landscapes. Although volatile, these olfactory landscapes can be perceived as typical and memorable.[57] The borders of the Cold War cut through landscapes and cityscapes. Analyses of the smellscapes of the border regimes confirm what sensory studies have already formulated about odors: they "cannot be readily contained, they escape and cross boundaries."[58] The smell events analyzed above confirm in a literal sense what borderland studies have always emphasized about demarcations: instead of being the hermetic lines of division that they are often imagined as, they are in fact areas of permeability. As such, border regimes were unable to partition the atmospheres in the East and the West (despite the strong indication that in both parts of Germany, distinguishable smellscapes developed in everyday life, consumerism, and the environment).[59] Furthermore, border facility management and militarization measures created their own perceptible zones. Because smellscapes change over time, several olfactory events can be identified that were initially detected by only a small number of people. These events drew attention from the media and the authorities, were debated in public, and eventually led to political action. The use of chemical pesticides in the border zones can be understood as part of *olfactory warfare* during the Cold War.[60] This broader conflict included the use of military gas and herbicides in the "hot wars" of Vietnam, CS (2-chlorobenzalmalononitrile) gas against domestic protests, and olfactory forensics when dealing with internal opposition in the GDR.

The peculiarity of olfactory perception is that we have only a limited vocabulary to describe it, even though—or perhaps because—the human nose has thousands of olfactory receptors (yet the human tongue has only a small number and variety of tastebuds).[61] This peculiarity plays an important role in the transborder smell conflicts studied above. Many individual complaints are based on an obvious fear, which can grow stronger if the nature and source of the olfactory nuisance remain unclear. And fear was a central factor in the security thinking of the Cold War.[62] In several smell conflicts, this emotion was intensified by disgust, a sensorial state that is difficult to bear. Finally, as the events of the Cold War demonstrate, smell events have the power to intensify not only fear but also political conflict. Even natural factors such as changing climate conditions or wind directions, which are a problem for every border architect, have the potential to play a political role by endowing volatile smells with an unexpected function in a conflict. From an ANT perspective, these nonhuman *actants* were involved in creating complex and constantly changing networks. The reluctance of officials to act on behalf of the people making the complaints might indicate that they attached less importance to sensory problems than to more obvious military dangers. Or the sensory problems might in fact have been regarded as dangerous accelerants to political conflict.

The false alarms triggered by animals in border areas were one reason Hungary finally demilitarized its border zones. And in 1989, it was above all in Hungary where East Germans gathered to apply for political asylum or directly cross the now-demilitarized border on their way to the FRG via Austria. The pressure these escapes put on the GDR regime is today considered a major factor in the eventual fall of the Berlin Wall. It would be an overstatement to say that animals in the Hungarian border zone were a key factor (or *actants*) in the process that ended the Cold War in Central Eastern Europe, but the end of the Hungarian border regime was undoubtedly a major step in the chain reaction that finally led to the collapse of state socialist regimes. In conclusion, one might say that smell was not only a problem but also a tool in border management—though mostly an unsuccessful one. Control was one of the main objectives of the Cold War border regimes, but smells, one can summarize, are more of a problem than a tool in policing borders. They are extremely difficult to control.

Notes

1. See Cull, "Reading, Viewing, and Tuning in." For the visual dimension of the global Cold War, see the chapters by Victoria Phillips, Cyril Cordoba, and Markus Mirschel in this volume.
2. See Stöver, "Der Sound des Kalten Krieges"; Stratenschult, "Lasst Euch nicht verhetzen!"
3. See Fenemore, *Fighting the Cold War*; Skalski, "Socialist Neighborhood."
4. Astrid M. Eckert speaks of "transboundary nature." See Eckert, *West Germany*, 159–99.
5. See Latour, *Reassembling the Social*.
6. See Bezirksamt Wedding von Berlin, Abt. Gesundheitswesen—Gesundheitsamt, Betr.: Geruchsbelästigung an der Sektorengrenze, November 28, 1963, Landesarchiv Berlin (hereafter LAB), B Rep 002, Nr. 24845. (This and all the following quotations from archival documents have been translated from German by the author.)
7. On the smell of decay, see Corbin, *Foul and the Fragrant*, 19, 33–34, 121–22, 164, 203.
8. McGinn, *Meaning of Disgust*, 13.
9. See Krause, *Geruchslandschafen mit Kriegsleichen*, 27–32.
10. Vermerk betr.: Geruchsbelästigung an der Demarkationslinie im Abschnitt Gartenstr./Bernauer Str., Berlin, January 3, 1944, LAB, B Rep 002, Nr. 24845.
11. See Hertle, *Berlin Wall*, 73–79; Mitchell, *Tunnels*, 155–58, 199–203.
12. See Hertle, *Berlin Wall*, 73–79.
13. Hertle, *Berlin Wall*, 76–77.
14. Berliner Stadtentwässerung, An den Senator für Verkehr und Betriebe, Betr.: Geruchsbelästigung an der Demarkationslinie im Abschnitt Gartenstraße / Bernauer Straße, January 7, 1964, LAB, B Rep 002, Nr. 24845.
15. See "An die Behörden der DDR, Betr.: Geruchsbelästigung," November 28, 1974, LAB, B Rep 002, Nr. 24845, not numbered.
16. See "Gestank kommt aus dem Osten," *Berliner Morgenpost*, November 28, 1974, 1.
17. L. H., "Die Gerüche kommen aus der DDR: Seit Tagen Gestank im Süden Berlins—Beschwerden nur über Senatskanzlei," *Der Tagesspiegel*, November 29, 1974.
18. Le Breton, *Sensing the World*, 139.
19. A general problem with chemical detection, described in detail in Christy Spackman's chapter in this volume.
20. Der Regierende Bürgermeister von Berlin an den Senator für Bundesangelegenheiten in Bonn, Berlin, December 5, 1974, LAB, B Rep 002, Nr. 24845, not numbered.
21. See Der Senator für Gesundheit und Umweltschutz an die Senatskanzlei, betr.: Großräumige Geruchsbelästigungen im Süden Berlins sowie an der Grenze zur DDR, notes from November 25, 1974, and December 4, 1974, with map, LAB, B Rep 002, Nr. 24845.
22. For example, see der regierende buergermeister von berlin an den senator fuer bundesangelegenheiten, verschluesselt eilt, December 5, 1974, LAB, B Rep 002, Nr. 24845.
23. See Fernschreiben, Der regierende Bürgermeister von Berlin an den Senator für Bundesangelegenheiten, Betr.: Schäden und Gefahren an den Sektorengrenzen und an der Demarkationslinie—Einschaltung der Ständigen Vertretung, hier: Geruchsbelästigung aus der DDR, December 5, 1974, LAB, B Rep 002, Nr. 24845.
24. SKzl [Senatskanzlei] I B, Betr.: Geruchsbelästigung aus der DDR, Berlin, December 19, 1974, LAB, B Rep 002, Nr. 24845.
25. On the shifts within the Hallstein doctrine in relation to the global Cold War, see Gray, *Germany's Cold War*.

26. [Günter Mat]thes, "Am Rande bemerkt: Der vertraglose Gestank," *Der Tagesspiegel*, December 8, 1974.
27. See Betr.: Geruchsbelästigung in der Gropiusstadt und Umgebung, February 14, 1979, LAB, B Rep 002, Nr. 2484.
28. See Betr.: Geruchsbelästigung in der Gropiusstadt und Umgebung, February 14, 1979, LAB, B Rep 002, Nr. 2484.
29. See Herrn Regierenden Bürgermeister von Berlin Herrn Dr. Stobbe, Berlin, August 28, 1979, LAB, B Rep 002, Nr. 2484.
30. "Bei Ostwind herrscht 'dicke Luft' im Kiez," *Berliner Morgenpost*, December 19, 1979; "So schlecht ist die Berliner Luft," *Spandauer Volksblatt*, January 12, 1980.
31. See Morat, "Berliner Luft"; Binger, *Himmel, Rauch und Care-Pakete*, 7.
32. Peter Schmalz, "Kanzler soll mit Honecker auch über üble Gerüche reden," *Die Welt*, July 27, 1980.
33. See Mrozek and Olšáková, "Die Katzendreckgestanks-Affäre."
34. See Möller, Schöllgen, and Wirsching, *AAPD*, doc. 30, n. 26; doc. 32, n. 28.
35. See Steinbrecher, "Fährtensuche."
36. Except for the fake paper claiming that the border dogs were the biological descendants of the Nazi regime's concentration camp dogs. The paper was intended as disguised criticism of both progressive animal studies and conservative totalitarianism theory. See Oltermann, "Human-Animal Studies Academics Dogged by German Hoaxers," *The Guardian*, March 1, 2016, https://www.theguardian.com/world/2016/mar/01/human-animal-studies-academics-dogged-by-german-hoaxers; Heitzer and Schultze, *Chimära Mensura*.
37. See Salesse, "Odorat des animaux," 88–93, 92.
38. See Hauptverwaltung Deutsche Volkspolizei, "Richtlinien über den Einsatz und die Führung von Diensthunden," Berlin 1960, 6–9, Bundesarchiv, Koblenz, Germany (hereafter BArch), DO1/87176.
39. See Zollverwaltung der Deutschen Demokratischen Republik, Stellvertreter des Ministers des Innern, "Ausbildung von Diensthunden für die Zollverwaltung durch die Zentralschule der Deutschen Volkspolizei in Pretzsch," February 22, 1963, BArch, DO1/94303.
40. According to journalist Marie-Luise Scherer, who wrote a literary reportage on border dogs. See Scherer, *Die Hundegrenze*, 86.
41. Scherer, *Die Hundegrenze*, 74–75.
42. See Gröschner, "On Long Leashes," 168.
43. "DDR Grenzsperranlagen an der IDG—Geruchssperre," May 9, 1969, BND-Archiv, BArch, B 206/1915.
44. See Scherer, *Die Hundegrenze*, 59–61.
45. See Wolff, *Die Mauergesellschaft*, 881.
46. See Wolff, *Die Mauergesellschaft*, 882.
47. Deleixhe, Embinska, and Iglesias, "Securitized Borderlands," 640.
48. Bundesminister des Innern für Umwelt, Naturschutz und Reaktorsicherheit, betr.: Geruchsbelästigungen aus der DDR in Berlin, September 15, 1987, LAB, B Rep 002, Nr. 24845.
49. See "Chemie-Wolke aus Ost-Berlin bereitet Übelkeit," *Berliner Morgenpost*, August 8, 1988.
50. See Landesverband Bürgerinitiativen Umweltschutz NRW [North Rhine-Westphalia] e.V., Rhein-Ruhr-Aktion gegen Umweltzerstörung, Projektgruppe Biozidbekämpfung an den Senator für Gesundheit und Umweltschutz [West] Berlin, Neuenrade, June 15, 1977, LAB, B Rep 016, Nr. 478.
51. See Vermerk betr.: Unkrautbekämpfungsaktion der Deutschen Reichsbahn auf ihrem Gelände in Berlin West, June 28, 1977, LAB, B Rep 002, Nr. 24845.
52. Einschreiben an den Präsidenten der Reichsbahndirektion Berlin, October 18, 1976, LAB, B Rep 016, Nr. 478.
53. See polizeipraesidium [West] berlin an sen[ator] f[ür] stadtentwicklung und umweltschutz: von ddr-gebiet hueruebergewehtes, vermutlich pflanzenschutzmittel [Telex], October 6, 1981, LAB, B Rep 004, Nr. 3532.
54. Undated, enclosed with LAB, B Rep 004, Nr. 3532.
55. See Der Senator für Inneres, Anlage: Bericht, July 16, 1984, LAB, B Rep 004, Nr. 3532.
56. See Eckert, *West Germany*, 173, 191; Mrozek and Olšáková, "Die Katzendreckgestanks-Affäre."
57. See Porteous, "Smellscape."
58. Classen, Howes, and Synnott, *Aroma*, 6.

59. See the overview by Grapa, "Une Histoire de l'Allemagne de l'Est par l'olfaction," *Regards sur la RDA et l'Allemagne de l'Est: Un carnet des germanistes du CEREG* (blog), Université Paris Nanterre et Université Sorbonne Nouvelle, January 4, 2023, https://allemagnest.hypotheses.org/3170#more-3170.

60. See Mrozek, "Bewaffnete Organe."

61. See Touhara, "Olfactory Receptor Functions."

62. See Miard-Delacroix and Wirsching, "Emotionen und international Beziehungen"; Biess, *German Angst*, 95–129, 298–307; Greiner, Müller, and Walter, *Angst im Kalten Krieg*.

Bibliography

Archival Sources

Bundesarchiv, Koblenz, Germany: BArch B 206/1915; BArch B 295/7433, 7434, 7435, 7436, 7438; BArch DO1/87176, 94303.

Landesarchiv Berlin, Berlin, Germany: LAB B Rep 002, No. 24845, No. 24846, No. 24846 F, No. 2847, No. 3527; LAB B Rep 004, No. 3532; LAB B Rep 016, No. 478.

Published Sources

Biess, Frank. *German Angst: Fear and Democracy in the Federal Republic of Germany*. Oxford: Oxford University Press, 2020.

Binger, Lothar. *Himmel, Rauch und Care-Pakete: Eine Geschichte der Luft*. Berlin: Jovis, 1998.

Braverman, Irus. "Passing the Sniff Test: Police Dogs as Surveillance Technology." *Buffalo Law Review* 61 (2013): 81–168.

Classen, Constance, David Howes, and Anthony Synnott. *Aroma: The Cultural History of Smell*. London: Routledge, 1994.

Corbin, Alain. *The Foul and the Fragrant: Odor and the French Social Imagination*. Cambridge: Harvard University Press, 1986.

Cull, Nicholas J. "Reading, Viewing, and Tuning in to the Cold War." In *Cambridge History of the Cold War*, edited by Melvyn P. Leffler and Odd Arne Westad, 2:438–59. Cambridge: Cambridge University Press, 2010.

Deleixhe, Martin, Magdalena Embinska, and Julien Iglesias. "Securitized Borderlands." *Journal of Borderland Studies* 34 (2019): 639–47.

Eckert, Astrid M. *West Germany and the Iron Curtain: Economy, Culture and Environment in the Borderlands*. Oxford: Oxford University Press, 2019.

Fenemore, Mark. *Fighting the Cold War in Post-Blockade, Pre-Wall Berlin: Behind Enemy Lines*. Routledge Studies in Modern European History 71. London: Routledge, 2020.

Gray, William Glenn. *Germany's Cold War: The Global Campaign to Isolate East Germany, 1949–1969*. Chapel Hill: University of North Carolina Press, 2003.

Greiner, Bernd, Christian Th. Müller, and Dierk Walter, eds. *Angst im Kalten Krieg*. Studien zum Kalten Krieg 3. Hamburg: Hamburger Edition, 2011.

Gröschner, Annett. "On Long Leashes: About Dogs and Their Handlers." In *Inventarisierung der Macht: Die Berliner Mauer aus anderer Sicht / Taking Stock of Power: An Other View of the Berlin Wall*, edited by Annett Gröschner and Arwed Messmer, 166–71. Berlin: Hatje Cantz, 2016.

Heitzer, Enrico, and Sven Schultze, eds. *Chimära Mensura? Die Human-Animal Studies zwischen Schäferhund-Science Hoax, kritischer Geschichtswissenschaft und akademischem Trendsurfing*. Berlin: Vergangenheitsverlag, 2018.

Hertle, Hans-Hermann. *The Berlin Wall Story: Biography of a Monument*. 2nd ed. Berlin: Ch. Links, 2016.

Krause, Frank. *Geruchslandschaften mit Kriegsleichen*. Göttingen: V&R Academic, 2016.

Latour, Bruno. *Reassembling the Social: An Introduction to Actor-Network-Theory*. Oxford: Oxford University Press, 2005.

Le Breton, David. *Sensing the World: An Anthropology of the Senses*. London: Bloomsbury, 2006.

McGinn, Colin. *The Meaning of Disgust*. Oxford: Oxford University Press, 2011.

Miard-Delacroix, Hélène, and Andreas Wirsching. "Emotionen und internationale Beziehungen im Kalten Krieg." In *Emotionen und internationale Beziehungen im Kalten Krieg*, edited by Hélène Miard-Delacroix and Andreas Wirsching, 1–24. Schriften des Historischen Kollegs 104. Munich: De Gruyter Oldenbourg, 2020.

Mitchell, Greg. *The Tunnels: Escapes Under the Berlin Wall and the Historic Films the JFK White House Tried to Kill*. New York: Broadway Books, 2016.

Möller, Horst, Gregor Schöllgen, and Andreas Wirsching, eds. *Akten zur Auswärtigen Politik der Bundesrepublik Deutschland (AAPD), 1983*. Vol. 1. *1. Januar bis 30. Juni 1983*. Edited by Mechthild Lindemann, Ilse-Dorothee Pautsch, Tim Geiger, and Matthias Peter. Munich: Oldenbourg, 2014.

Morat, Daniel. "Berliner Luft: Zur Karriere einer Stadthymne." *Moderne Stadtgeschichte* 1 (2017): 20–33.

Mrozek, Bodo. "Bewaffnete Organe: Sensory Warfare." *Merkur: Zeitschrift für europäisches Denken* 75, no. 871 (2021): 49–58.

Mrozek, Bodo, and Doubravka Olšáková. "Die Katzendreckgestanks-Affäre: Grenzüberschreitende Geruchskonflikte zwischen der Bundesrepublik, der ČSSR und der DDR (1976–1989)." *Vierteljahrshefte für Zeitgeschichte* 71, no. 2 (2023): 311–49.

Paul, Gerhard, and Ralph Schock, eds. *Sound des Jahrhunderts: Geräusche, Töne, Stimmen 1889 bis heute*. Bonn: bpb, 2013.

Porteous, J. Douglas. "Smellscape." In *The Smell Culture Reader*, edited by Jim Drobnick, 89–106. Oxford: Berg, 2006.

Salesse, Roland. "L'odorat des animaux." *Nez: La Revue olfactive* 7 (2019): 88–93.

Scherer, Marie-Luise. *Die Hundegrenze*. Berlin: Matthes & Seitz, 2018.

Skalski, Michael. "A Socialist Neighborhood: Cross-Border Exchanges Between Poland, East Germany, and Czechoslovakia, 1969–1989." PhD diss., University of North Carolina at Chapel Hill, 2017.

Steinbrecher, Aline. "Fährtensuche: Hunde in der frühneuzeitlichen Stadt." *Traverse: Zeitschrift für Geschichte / Revue d'histoire* 15 (2008): 45–59.

Stöver, Bernd. "Der Sound des Kalten Krieges: Charakteristische Hörerlebnisse in einem globalen Konflikt." In Paul and Schock, *Sound des Jahrhunderts: Geräusche, Töne, Stimmen 1889 bis heute*, 320–25.

Stratenschult, Eckart D. "Lasst Euch nicht verhetzen! Der Lautsprecherkrieg in Berlin." In Paul and Schock, *Sound des Jahrhunderts: Geräusche, Töne, Stimmen 1889 bis heute*, 432–35.

Touhara, Keiichi Yoshikawa Kazushige. "Olfactory Receptor Functions." In *Handbook of Olfaction and Gustation*, edited by Richard L. Doty, 109–22. 3rd ed. Hoboken: Wiley, 2015.

Westad, Odd Arne. *The Cold War: A World History*. New York: Basic Books, 2017.

Wolff, Frank. *Die Mauergesellschaft: Kalter Krieg, Menschenrechte und die deutsch-deutsche Migration, 1961–1989*. Berlin: Suhrkamp, 2019.

PART III

MIND CONTROL, COVERT OPERATIONS, OVERT WARFARE

CHAPTER 9

Hallucinated Sensations

Brainwashing and Mind Control in Psychochemical CIA Experiments

Walter E. Grunden

In the 1950s and 1960s, during the height of the Cold War, the CIA experimented with hypnosis, sensory deprivation, and hallucinogenic drugs such as LSD-25 (D-lysergic acid diethylamide, LSD) in order to obtain operative control over human beings. Prompted by fears that communist nations had developed a new technique to "brainwash" political prisoners, the CIA sponsored a series of projects, the most notorious of which was code-named MKULTRA, in order to perfect a means of mind control that could be used to extract information from enemy assets more effectively and to "program" its own agents for highly sensitive missions. Such agents would be conditioned to act on cue and then forget all facets of their mission and training. These "Manchurian candidates," as they came to be popularly known, were likened to robots and zombies—that is, to organisms that could be manipulated to do a master's bidding unwittingly and against their will. In tandem with these CIA experiments, the US Army conducted research into various psychochemicals in order to test their potential efficacy as nonlethal incapacitating agents. Such programs attempted to discover new, less lethal ways of conducting warfare by attacking the senses, disorienting or incapacitating the mind, and, ultimately, controlling the enemy. Even after it became clear that no new communist technique for brainwashing had been developed, however, the CIA continued to conduct mind control experiments using military research into psychochemicals as a smoke screen to extend the MKULTRA program, at least until its ostensible termination in 1973. Cold War national security imperatives thus trumped medical ethics and the law by providing the CIA and US military services with the pretexts necessary to engage in clandestine research that was otherwise illegal.

Academics seem reluctant to investigate the matter and have left the subject largely to journalists and a handful of freelance writers. Since the 1979 publication of the groundbreaking exposé *The Search for the "Manchurian Candidate"* by former State Department officer and author John Marks—without whose relentless efforts to obtain documentation through numerous Freedom of Information requests the details of this program may never have come to light—too few studies have been produced that merit serious attention.[1] In the history of the senses field, military subjects are gaining increasing attention; however, Cold War intelligence, and particularly warfare, is still a terra incognita.[2] This chapter attempts to bridge the two fields and thereby fill a critical gap in the scholarship by exploiting primary source material in which MKULTRA research and concerns related to the history of the senses intersect.[3] What did Project MKULTRA discover about mind control, mind-altering drugs, and such drugs' impact upon the senses? Did the program reveal the secret of brainwashing, and were the CIA operatives of MKULTRA ultimately able to create a "Manchurian candidate"?

Brainwashing and Hypnosis

In February 1953, the communist regime of the Democratic People's Republic of Korea (DPRK) released film footage of captured US Air Force pilots confessing to crimes against humanity in the Korean War, including the conduct of biological warfare against Chinese and North Korean military units.[4] Members of the US intelligence community watched in dismay as the men stiffly and robotically uttered their false confessions. How had the communists turned them? Had they succeeded in developing a true form of "brainwashing"? The films conjured up images of the Moscow show trials conducted under Joseph Stalin in 1936–38, in which a "long parade of high-level Bolshevik leaders" confessed to a litany of crimes and conspiracies that were obviously false.[5] The films also invoked memories of Cardinal József Mindszenty, who had been arrested for speaking out against the dissolution of religious orders in the Hungarian People's Republic and tried by the socialist regime for conspiracy and treason. During his trial in February 1949, he appeared wide-eyed and dazed and confessed to all the crimes for which he stood accused. The intelligence community in the United States watched the televised trial with concern and puzzled over how the Hungarian regime had apparently been able to force Mindszenty to confess against his will. Alarmed, they "felt they had to know how the Communists had rendered the defendants zombielike."[6]

In the wake of the Mindszenty trial, the CIA turned first to hypnosis as a possible explanation for these robotic behaviors. On April 5, 1950, Sheffield Edwards, chief of the CIA's Office of Security, proposed the formation of "special interrogation" teams to develop and employ novel questioning methods when vetting and debriefing intelligence agents and defectors. The impetus for the creation of such teams, Edwards stated, stemmed from "the recent spy trials in Hungary and other satellite countries." Each team was to include a psychiatrist and a polygraph expert with training in hypnosis. According to Edwards's proposal, the teams would "utilize the polygraph, drugs, and hypnotism to attain the greatest results in interrogation techniques."[7] On April 20, 1950, in order to coordinate the research conducted in these areas by various agencies, CIA director Roscoe Hillenkoetter initiated Project BLUEBIRD, which merged all related activities into one program. BLUEBIRD would be the agency's first official project dedicated to the study of behavior control and hypnosis.

When Allen W. Dulles joined the CIA in January 1951 as deputy director for planning, he took a keen interest in the agency's ongoing work in hypnosis. A former spymaster at the Office of Strategic Services (OSS) during the Second World War, Dulles was a staunch anti-communist and was open to innovations in intelligence gathering that would give the United States an edge over the Soviet Union and its Communist Bloc allies.[8] Dulles soon turned his attention to Project BLUEBIRD. Upon reviewing the nascent project, he concluded that BLUEBIRD would benefit from better coordination and greater oversight of its research. In July 1951, he recruited Dr. Sidney Gottlieb, a chemist and research associate at the University of Maryland, to head the program.[9]

It was around this time that research shifted from a defensive to an *offensive* posture. From the beginning of the Cold War there were grave concerns about what would happen should a US intelligence asset fall into Soviet hands. How could such assets protect themselves from revealing deep secrets under interrogation? There was interest not only in determining the best defense against various interrogation methods but also in learning how to enhance the methods already known and to discover methods still *unknown* for eliciting information involuntarily. In August 1951, Dulles implemented changes to BLUEBIRD that transformed it from a mere research project into an "operations" unit, which he designated Project ARTICHOKE. A memorandum dated January 25, 1952, reflects the mission's decisive switch to an offensive stance, asking, "Can we get control of an individual to the point where he will do our bidding against his will and even against such fundamental laws of nature such [sic] as self-preservation?"[10]

The new mission statement of ARTICHOKE allowed for "the use, both for *offensive* and defensive purposes, of special interrogation techniques—primarily hypnosis and truth serums," by agents in the field. Similar work was already underway in the US Navy under Project CHATTER, an Office of Naval Intelligence program launched in 1947 that focused on identifying and testing drugs suitable "for use in interrogations and in the recruitment of agents."[11] ARTICHOKE now subsumed the agendas of both BLUEBIRD and CHATTER, and it incorporated research into hypnosis enhanced by the application of select pharmaceuticals. The new charter clearly extended the mission beyond the laboratory to active operations in the field.

Thus, ARTICHOKE continued the "fieldwork" begun by BLUEBIRD, much of which was conducted abroad in areas occupied by US military forces, such as West Germany and Japan. According to Marks, many of the ARTICHOKE subjects were "the flotsam and jetsam of the international spy trade," including "individuals of dubious loyalty, suspected agents or plants, [and] subjects having known reason for deception, etc." More "benign" experiments were ostensibly conducted in the United States on volunteers who had given "informed consent."[12] By summer 1952, ARTICHOKE had begun to show real promise in using a combination of drugs and hypnosis, or "narco-hypnosis," in the preparation of subjects for interrogation. A CIA memo dated July 1952 reveals that two Russian agents were interrogated with desired effects using a combination of sodium pentothal and Desoxyn—a type of methamphetamine—with hypnosis. It states, "In both cases, the subjects talked clearly and at great length and furnished information which the case officers considered extremely valuable."[13] At last, ARTICHOKE seemed to be producing tangible results.

Allen W. Dulles became director of the CIA in February 1953. His leadership introduced an increasingly aggressive posture toward the Soviet

Union, which was reflected in the programs that came under his purview, especially those researching human behavior and mind control. Dulles was concerned that the Soviets were pursuing research in the same fields and feared the United States may be falling behind, suggesting a growing "mind control gap" in research. On April 10, 1953, Dulles delivered an impassioned speech titled "Brain Warfare" in Hot Springs, Virginia, before the National Alumni Conference of the Graduate Council of Princeton University. In this oratory, Dulles outlined the threat communism posed to the United States and presented a rationale for taking greater measures to combat Soviet efforts in psychological warfare. As he stated, "The Soviets are now using brain perversion techniques as one of their main weapons in prosecuting the Cold War." Their approach, he explained, was twofold: mass indoctrination to produce a docile populace and "the perversion of the minds of selected individuals." These latter victims, he alleged, were subjected to treatment that "deprived [them] of the ability to state their own thoughts. Parrot-like[,] the individuals so conditioned can merely repeat thoughts which have been implanted in their minds by suggestion from outside." Dulles extended the threat to include China, noting that the Chinese had coined the term "brainwashing" to describe such a process of conditioning, which, he concluded, "seems aptly to describe this phase of brain warfare."[14]

How far would one need to go to take control of another person's mind, Dulles wondered. Could a human being be "programmed" to commit an act unwittingly and against their will? Only an expanded and enhanced research program could reveal the answers to such provocative questions. Morse Allen, a former BLUEBIRD director, argued that in operational terms it was now necessary to proceed to the next level. According to him, this meant that "terminal experiments" were now needed to determine "how well the technique worked in the real world."[15] Under the leadership of Allen W. Dulles, the CIA was about to embark upon the most ambitious program for the investigation of mind control to date.

MKULTRA and CIA Mind Control Experiments

On April 13, 1953, Dulles established Project MKULTRA for the purpose of investigating and developing "chemical, biological, and radiological materials capable of employment in clandestine operations to control human behavior."[16] MKULTRA subsumed and enhanced the mission of ARTICHOKE. Dulles allotted the program a start-up budget of $300,000 and granted its doctors and scientists greater latitude for innovative areas of research. Inspired by the aforementioned DPRK propaganda footage released in February 1953, Dulles was determined to discover how the communists were seemingly able to brainwash even these well-trained and patriotic American prisoners of war (POWs). Dr. Sidney Gottlieb was charged with finding out. For the next two decades, Gottlieb would oversee the CIA's foray into brainwashing and mind control research as the director of Project MKULTRA.

Dulles afforded Gottlieb wide latitude in his research, which encompassed "various fields of psychology, psychiatry, sociology, anthropology, and graphology"—and which utilized drugs, radiation, electroshock, and an array of "harassment substances" and "paramilitary devices and materials."[17] As a US Senate Intelligence Committee investigation revealed in 1977, the research and development of materials to be used by MKULTRA for altering human behavior consisted of three phases: "First, the search for materials suitable for study; second, laboratory testing on voluntary human subjects in various types of institutions; third, the application of MKULTRA materials in normal life settings."[18]

A top priority for Dulles and Gottlieb remained unraveling the mystery of brainwashing, at which the communists seemed to excel. Just how much this perception resulted from filmed visual accounts of "confessions" of US POWs in Korea and the Mindszenty trial, or from portrayals of the Soviets in American culture, cannot be easily determined. Most Americans, influenced by popular periodicals and films of the early 1950s, tended to believe that "modern methods of thought control and terror had transformed the Russian people into an enslaved mob of subservient, dull, and militaristic robots." Science fiction films of the time, such as *Invaders from Mars* (1953) and later, more famously, *Invasion of the Body Snatchers* (1956), reflected "the obsession with Soviet-like conformity and regimentation" as depicted in the "slew of alien invasion, 'we'll-all-be-zombies' films," wherein the monsters were invariably "cold, calculating and completely lacking in emotion" and "showed the same robot-like traits that were said to plague Stalin's subjects."[19] Had the US intelligence community become believers in America's own cultural propaganda?

For Dulles at the time, it may have been difficult to separate fact from fiction. Of the 7,190 American POWs held captive in China, some 70 percent confessed to various war crimes or signed petitions calling for an end to the war, and many refused to recant their confessions even after returning home.[20] A memorandum dated July 15, 1953, from the Medical Branch of the Office of Scientific Intelligence to the chief of the Technical Branch of Special Operations notes that American POWs repatriated from the Soviet Union and China at the end of the Korean conflict experienced a "blank period" or "period of disorientation while passing through a special zone in Manchuria." The memo suggested that "drugging was indicated."[21] But what had happened to them there, and why had they turned against the United States? In late 1953, Dulles reached out to experts beyond the agency and recruited Dr. Harold Wolff, a neurologist at Cornell University Medical College who specialized in migraine research, as well as his colleague, Dr. Lawrence Hinkle. Together, Wolff and Hinkle launched an official investigation of the "communist brainwashing" phenomenon that took nearly three years to complete.[22]

In the meantime, Gottlieb began to investigate an array of pharmaceuticals in search of the ultimate mind control drug. He was particularly drawn to LSD, or "acid." The drug was first synthesized by the Swiss chemist Dr. Albert Hofmann at the Sandoz Pharmaceutical Corporation in 1938, but its hallucinogenic properties were not discovered until April 1943, when Hofmann accidentally absorbed some of the chemical through his skin. Hofmann described the experience as "a remarkable but not unpleasant state of intoxication": "As I sat in a dazed condition with eyes closed, there surged up from me a succession of fantastic, rapidly changing imagery of a striking reality and depth, alternating with a vivid, kaleidoscopic play of colors." A second, deliberate ingestion was less pleasant. Hofmann reported, "My field of vision swayed before me, and objects appeared distorted like images in curved mirrors." At one point he thought he had died.[23]

After Hofmann published papers on this discovery, the medical community considered the potential of the drug as a possible treatment for mental illness, while military services around the world took note of its potential as a chemical weapon.[24] In 1949, Dr. Max Rinkel, a psychiatrist in the United States, procured a small supply of LSD from Sandoz and passed it on to his associate, Dr. Robert Hyde, who decided to test it on himself and hence became the first person in America known to have experienced an "acid trip."[25] Not long after, psychiatrists and psychologists across the United States became intrigued by the new drug and began to experiment with it on their own. Among them was a young clinical psychologist and Harvard professor, Dr. Timothy Leary, who subsequently became the "acid guru" and icon of the 1960s counterculture movement.

Isolation Box and Sleep Chamber: Sensory Deprivation

Although the CIA first became interested in LSD in the late 1940s, it only undertook serious investigations of the drug in the early 1950s, when intelligence reports suggested that the Soviet Union had begun "intensive efforts" to produce LSD and appeared to have attempted to buy up the world's available supply. As one CIA officer explained, "We were literally terrified, because this was the one material that we had ever been able to locate that really had potential fantastic possibilities if used wrongly."[26] The chief of the medical staff of the CIA wrote in 1952, "There is ample evidence in the reports of innumerable interrogations that the Communists were utilizing drugs, physical duress, electric shock, and possibly hypnosis against their enemies. With such evidence it is difficult not to keep from becoming rabid about our apparent laxity. We are forced by this mounting evidence to assume a more aggressive role in the development of these techniques."[27] Thereafter, research in these areas, especially on LSD, changed even more decisively "from a defensive to an offensive orientation."[28] In this heady atmosphere, Gottlieb had near carte blanche to investigate the properties and effects of LSD on the human mind and body. Gottlieb had tried the drug himself in late 1951, as had many other CIA researchers, in order to understand its impact. For Gottlieb, it was something of a revelation, and he came to believe that LSD could be "the key to mind control."[29] According to a CIA scientific intelligence memorandum dated August 5, 1954, that was likely written by Gottlieb himself:

> Of all substances now known to affect the mind, such as mescaline, harmine, and others, LSD is by far the most potent. Very minute quantities (upwards of 30 millionths of a gram) create serious mental confusion and sensual disturbances, or render the mind temporarily susceptible to many types of influences. Administration of the drug produces in an individual such mental characteristics of schizophrenia as visual or auditory hallucinations and physiological reactions of dizziness, nausea, dilation of the pupils, and lachrymation. . . . Data, although still very limited, are available which indicate its usefulness for eliciting true and accurate statements from subjects under its influence during interrogation.[30]

LSD had the additional benefit of being odorless and tasteless, and in such small doses, it was undetectable by the human eye.

But more testing was needed. Not only did CIA researchers try the drug themselves, but they also tested it on each other surreptitiously. Like fraternity house pranksters, they secretly "dosed" one another's coffee while at work and then observed the dupe's behavior. On one occasion, such secret dosing antics ended with tragic consequences. The underhanded dosing of Frank Olson, an MKULTRA researcher, resulted in his lapsing into a deep state of depression. After displaying increasingly erratic behavior, project members took Olson to New York City for a psychiatric evaluation. On November 28, 1953, at 2:30 a.m., Olson fell to his death from the tenth-story window of a hotel.[31] The Olson incident put an end to such irregular "in-house" experiments and forced MKULTRA researchers to look elsewhere for unwitting subjects. One such operation, lewdly titled "Midnight Climax" (MKULTRA Subproject 42), entailed the use of prostitutes to lure unsuspecting johns to "safe houses" wired with microphones and cameras. Once there, the prostitutes secretly dosed their prey with various quantities of LSD slipped into cocktails, and the researchers observed what followed through two-way mirrors.[32]

Across the United States and Canada, Gottlieb and the CIA enlisted numerous doctors, scientists, academics, and public and private research institutions as contractors for various MKULTRA subprojects. Many performed research for MKULTRA without knowing it. Some even engaged in human experimentation for MKULTRA, and many subjects were experimented on without their informed consent, sometimes with devastating consequences. Among the more heinous cases was that of Dr. Donald Ewen Cameron, director of the Allen Memorial Institute in Montreal, Canada, whom Gottlieb tapped for his work on behavior control. Cameron, a widely recognized psychiatrist and president of the American Psychiatric Association (1952–53), was driven to find a cure for mental illness, especially schizophrenia, and developed a number of alternative "therapies" and putative "cures" for patients at the institute, many of which were inhumane, unethical, and arguably transgressed the boundaries of torture.

Cameron believed he could cure mental illness through a process known as "depatterning," which, according to his methodology, entailed the elimination of undesired thoughts and behaviors by means of electroshock therapy, prolonged periods of drug-induced sleep, and sensory deprivation. According to Cameron's theory, once the troublesome personality had been erased, a new healthy one could be restored in its place. As Marks writes, "Here was a psychiatrist willing—indeed, eager—to wipe the human mind totally clean."[33]

New thoughts and behavior patterns, perhaps even a new personality, could be installed in the subject through what Cameron called "psychic driving." This was a process in which key words and phrases were played on a repeating tape loop while the subject remained in a deep, drug-induced sleep. The desired effect of the repetition was to create something akin to what Steve Goodman describes as an "earworm," in which a musical tune or ad jingle becomes stuck in one's head and repeats over and over again while unconsciously affecting the person's behavior.[34] Gottlieb's interest in Cameron's work was obvious. If Cameron could "reprogram" mentally ill patients, could he not also "program" spies, even assassins?

Cameron used innumerable patients at the Allen Memorial Institute as human guinea pigs for these areas of research. Most were not informed of his program's objectives—nor were their families—and none knew that they were being exploited for CIA purposes.[35] Many would not have been of sufficiently "sound mind and body" to understand the implications in any case. For those who were, psychic driving proved mostly ineffective. When the patient's own voice was used for the looped recording, for example, Cameron found that they "rarely liked the sound of their own voices" and that the recordings "often produced a defensive reaction from the patients, and some refused to acknowledge the voice as their own. Not every patient would sit still and listen to a traumatic episode of their life recited in a voice that was foreign-sounding though uncomfortably and undeniably their own."[36] Cameron's depatterning procedure often combined sensory deprivation and select pharmaceuticals. He constructed an isolation "box" inside which subjects were deprived of all outside stimulation of the senses. On occasion, he injected subjects with curare, a paralyzing neurotoxin, to keep them immobilized.[37] His preferred drug of choice in the depatterning process, however, was LSD, which he felt held the most potential for altering a subject's personality. Cameron allegedly gave many of his subjects extremely high doses of LSD, sometimes on successive days and as often as fourteen times a month, leaving some in a veritable "zombified" state. One patient, Velma Orlikov, recalled terrifying hallucinations that elicited panic and the feeling she was losing control—as if her "bones were melting." Peggy Mielke, a nurse working under Cameron in the "Sleep Room," a wing of the institute "kept in continuous semi-darkness" and called the "Zombie Tomb" by the nursing staff, described one patient who had undergone repeated treatments combining LSD and electroshock as "the nearest person to one of the living dead" she had ever seen.[38] Precisely how the CIA may have used data from Cameron's research is unknown, but it soon became clear that "depatterning" did not work and subjecting a person to exceedingly high doses of LSD did little more than destroy their minds.

Psychochemicals and "Humane" Chemical Warfare

Meanwhile, the US Army was ramping up its own line of investigation into psychoactive agents, including not only LSD but also EA 1298 MDA (3,4-methylenedioxyamphetamine); EA 2148 PCP (1[1-phenylcyclohexyl] piperidine) or Sernyl (SN); EA 2277 QCB (3-quinuclidinyl benzilate) or Buzz (BZ); and later EA 3834, an enhanced variant of BZ. The US Army Chemical Corps rationalized this area of research as a more "humane" form of chemical warfare. Whereas prior to the end of the Second World War only two principal categories of chemical weapons existed—*harassing agents* and *lethal agents*—the objective now was to develop a third type, *incapacitating agents*, or nonlethal weapons that would render the enemy defenseless but leave them alive and without permanent injury.[39] As the authors Robert Harris and Jeremy Paxman wrote, "From the military point of view, psychochemicals appeared immensely attractive. They seemed to offer all the advantages of chemical or radiological weapons, with none of the disadvantage: no damage to property, no dead bodies, and no danger of infection."[40] They were also virtually undetectable by the ordinary human senses.

The army's psychochemical program became one of its primary research divisions in the development of nonlethal weapons. Research on EA 1298 MDA (not to be confused with MDMA, 3,4 methylenedioxymethamphetamine) began in earnest at the Edgewood Arsenal in Maryland in the early 1950s, and human trials were conducted clandestinely at the New York State Psychiatric Institute, which the army funded to the tune of $140,000 between 1953 and 1957. The accidental overdose of a tennis professional named Harold Blauer in January 1953, however, was not a promising beginning, and MDA proved difficult to weaponize.[41] Investigation into MDA was eventually phased out, but the search for the ideal incapacitant continued. In 1959, the Chemical Corps began to investigate EA 2148 PCP (SN) and EA 2277 QCB (BZ). Testing of SN, originally of interest due to its somnolent effect and its potential as an incapacitant, revealed that higher doses such as those required for weaponization produced the opposite results: erratic and violent behavior. Better known by its street name "Angel Dust," the drug left subjects less sensitive to pain but fully awake and hyperenergetic. According to one chemical warfare expert, "If Agent SN had been used under combat conditions, the results may well have not been the 'somnolence' envisioned, but more like something out of the movie *Night of the Living Dead*." Although approved for manufacture, these "Agent SN munitions were never produced."[42]

Similarly, BZ and its variants proved undesirable as incapacitants. Called "Buzz" because of the "mental aberrations it purportedly caused," BZ was expensive to synthesize, difficult to weaponize as a reliable munition, and impractical for wide-area dispersal. The effective dosage rate required in the field also came perilously close to the lethality index of some nerve agents. Moreover, its side effects, including paranoia and mania, could render the enemy unpredictable, and these symptoms were known to last beyond recovery. Perhaps the final factor in the decision to discontinue the development of BZ in its weaponized form was that it could be easily counteracted with simple prophylactic measures, such as using "several layers of folded cloth over the nose and mouth." Worse yet, its "visible white agent cloud warned of its presence," giving the enemy ample time to react. The US Army declared BZ "obsolete" in 1977.[43] The army's foray into developing psychochemicals as incapacitating agents had apparently run its course.

"Manchurian Candidates" and Zombie Assassins

By the mid-1950s, CIA research into exploiting hypnosis and LSD for brainwashing and behavior control was turning up mixed results at best. Still, Morse Allen, once the primary overseer of hypnosis investigation for BLUEBIRD and ARTICHOKE, remained confident that it was possible to create a programmed assassin or "Manchurian candidate," as such a person later came to be known thanks to the popular 1958 novel of the same name by Richard Condon and the film adaptation released in 1962.[44] To prove his point, in February 1954, Allen personally hypnotized two of his secretaries and ordered one to shoot the other. The pistol used in this dangerous stunt was unloaded, fortunately, but this outrageous display apparently sufficed to impress his superiors. Yet there was no way of knowing for certain if this technique would be operationally viable in a "real-world" situation. For a programmed assassin to be truly effective, the subject would have to respond to a predetermined cue to execute the command to act and then forget that they had done anything at all.

Brainwashing was one thing, and perhaps even achievable as an extreme form of conventional indoctrination, but it was much more complicated to program a person through hypnosis, LSD, and psychic driving and then produce amnesia to spontaneously wipe out all memory of the event so as to eliminate the possibility of the perpetrator implicating the CIA. Nonetheless, CIA director Dulles still believed it possible. In late 1954, Dulles charged Gottlieb with the task of producing a veritable "Manchurian candidate."[45] Projects BLUEBIRD and ARTICHOKE had begun to explore the efficacy of narco-hypnosis, but this was only one avenue that appeared promising. Gottlieb and MKULTRA researchers considered many other equally exotic technologies in their quest to control human behavior and to create the ultimate assassin. These included sonic waves to induce a hypnotic trance, microwave radiation to stimulate or destroy brain tissue, radio and television to induce mass hypnosis, and brain-implanted electronic devices to control movement.[46] Such projects bordered on science fiction.

When Wolff and Hinkle finally submitted the results of their three-year study of brainwashing in August 1956, their report left Dulles less sanguine about its possibilities. Wolff and Hinkle concluded that neither the Soviets nor the Chinese had developed any novel method or technology for brainwashing. Nor did they appear to have used hypnosis, any specific drug, or any combination thereof to achieve their objectives. Instead, they applied commonly known conventional methods of indoctrination, including isolation, humiliation, and other forms of mental duress. In short, it appeared that neither the Soviets nor the Chinese had produced, or were capable of producing, a zombie assassin. While this came as something of a relief to Dulles and Gottlieb, it was not quite what they had expected to hear. The Wolff-Hinkle report substantially undermined any arguments that the CIA could now muster to rationalize continuing this line of research, as there was not likely any "mind control gap" after all.[47] Yet MKULTRA research was not terminated for several more years, and the question remains: Did the CIA ever succeed in creating a real, live Manchurian candidate?

The assassination of President John F. Kennedy in Dallas, Texas, on November 22, 1963, and the subsequent murder of his alleged assassin Lee Harvey Oswald by nightclub owner Jack Ruby, raised a seemingly infinite number of questions that in popular culture boiled over into elaborate conspiracy narratives implicating everyone from Cuban dictator Fidel Castro to the Russians to the Mafia (Cosa Nostra) to the CIA itself. And Condon's film, released just one year before, only added to the level of paranoia and suspicion building in the national zeitgeist.[48] Given the complexity of the assassination and the confusion that ensued from media coverage of it, many

Americans seemed unwilling to accept the verdict of the Warren Commission, which concluded in September 1964 that a lone gunman, Lee Harvey Oswald, had killed the president.

Consequently, in March 1967, when a mysterious twenty-four-year-old man was arrested in Manila for conspiring to assassinate Philippine president Ferdinand Marcos and revealed under the influence of hypnosis and "truth serum" (presumably sodium amytol) that he had been involved in an assassination plot four years prior, the Philippine National Bureau of Investigation (NBI) took note. The mystery man, identified as Luis Angel Castillo, stated that he had been "hypno-programmed to kill a man riding in an open car," and although he "did not know the identity of his target, the scene of his supposed 'hit' was Dallas, Texas. The date was November 22, 1963."[49] The NBI was skeptical but cautious, so they contacted the FBI, which requested that the NBI interrogate Castillo further. A professional hypnotist was summoned to conduct the questioning, and Castillo endured hours of interrogation under hypnosis, during which the hypnotist identified what he called four distinct "zombie states," each with a separate identity. The final NBI report on Castillo described him as a bona fide hypno-programmed "zombie" and implicated him in the Kennedy assassination. But for reasons that remain unexplained, the NBI released Castillo after concluding its report. He purportedly returned to the United States, was picked up by the FBI again for interrogation, and, although sentenced to six years in prison on charges of robbery in June 1971, was inexplicably released again in August that year. He was not seen thereafter.[50]

So far as is known, CIA research into mind control using hypnosis and various hallucinogens did not produce an effective brainwashing technique, and many aspects concerning the link between the senses and the mind remained a mystery even to the most advanced and well-funded scientists and physicians in the Western world. Nor did the US Army Chemical Corps succeed in developing a psychochemical agent that would serve as an effective next-level incapacitating agent. Although LSD, MDA, SN, and BZ initially seemed promising, and most had the added benefit of not being detectable by the human senses, the effects they had on the mind made them less than ideal for this purpose. These attempts to develop chemical weapons not only to temporarily incapacitate the mind but also to control it often resulted only in irreparably damaging or *destroying* the mind, ultimately producing not programmable human robots but mental *zombies* and proving that no one yet really understood how to manipulate the senses to repattern a person's thinking or behavior.

What becomes clear after an examination of the CIA's and the US Army's research into brainwashing, psychochemical incapacitating agents, and mind control during the early years of the Cold War is that giving such state institutions carte blanche to do whatever was necessary to defeat communism invariably led to violations of the Nuremberg Code and people's fundamental human rights, the full extent of which remains unknown to this day. Without regulatory oversight, Project MKULTRA researchers committed some practices somewhat comparable to those previously known by Nazi doctors during the Second World War. These revelations were only made when hundreds of pages of CIA documents—the so-called "family jewels" created under Dulles—were discovered in the shake-up of the intelligence community in 1974, leading to Congressional hearings led by Vice President Nelson Rockefeller and later Senator Frank Church.[51] Just how much CIA protocols, practices, and culture may have changed as a result of this public scrutiny cannot be determined, but it is certain that MKULTRA serves as the ultimate example of what was possible when exploring the realm of the senses during the Cold War.

Notes

1. Marks, Search for the "Manchurian Candidate." Among the more reliable accounts are Kinzer, Poisoner in Chief; Albarelli, Terrible Mistake; and Gillmor, I Swear by Apollo.

2. On sensory histories of general warfare, see Bodo Mrozek's introduction to this volume.

3. Studies that examine the subject matter through the lens of critical theory are noticeably lacking. An analysis of MKULTRA through the interpretive frame of Foucault's biopower or biopolitics, for example, waits to be written. Unfortunately, such an effort is beyond the scope of this chapter.

4. For an example of such footage, see the DPRK propaganda film U.S. Germ Warfare in Korea, posted on June 28, 2011, by PublicResourceOrg, YouTube video, 21:59, https://www.youtube.com/watch?v=gGP1q2vVoas. Claims that the United States engaged in biological warfare during the Korean War have never been convincingly substantiated and were likely part of a Chinese propaganda campaign. See Leitenberg, "False Allegations."

5. Scheflin and Opton, Mind Manipulators, 14–15, 77–78, 87–94.

6. Marks, Search for the "Manchurian Candidate," 23.

7. Chief of Inspection and Security Staff to Director of Central Intelligence, "Subject: Project BLUEBIRD," April 5, 1950, Central Intelligence Agency (hereafter CIA), Washington, DC, Freedom of Information Act Electronic Reading Room, General CIA Records, CREST Files, Document #: RDP83-01042R000800010003-1.

8. On the role of the Dulles family in Cold War activities, see chapter 1 of this volume.

9. See Kinzer, Poisoner in Chief, 8–9, 38–39.

10. Scheflin and Opton, Mind Manipulators, 120.

11. Project MKULTRA, The CIA's Program of Research in Behavioral Modification: Joint Hearing Before the Select Committee on Intelligence and the Subcommittee on Health and Scientific Research of the Committee on Human Resources, 95th Cong. 67–68 (1977).

12. These "volunteers" were typically college students. See Marks, Search for the "Manchurian Candidate," 33–34.

13. Bowart, *Operation Mind Control*, 102–3.
14. Allen W. Dulles, "Brain Warfare: Summary of Remarks by Mr. Allen W. Dulles at the National Alumni Conference of the Graduate Council of Princeton University, Hot Springs, Va.," April 10, 1953, CIA, Freedom of Information Act Electronic Reading Room, General CIA Records, CREST Files, Document #: RDP80R01731R001700030015-9.
15. Marks, *Search for the "Manchurian Candidate,"* 34–35.
16. Project MKULTRA, 69.
17. Project MKULTRA, 70.
18. Project MKULTRA, 70. The "MK" designation indicated projects undertaken by the CIA's technical services staff. Other related projects sharing the "MK" designation included MKDELTA, which investigated the effects of selected drugs in interrogations and as harassing agents; MKNAOMI, which investigated toxins for biological warfare applications; and MKSEARCH, which entailed the weaponization of aspects of MKULTRA research.
19. Many such low-budget horror films of the day had a decidedly anti-communist subtext. See Smith, "American Nightmare."
20. See Marks, *Search for the "Manchurian Candidate,"* 134.
21. Memorandum reproduced in Ross, *CIA Doctors*, 35.
22. Marks, *Search for the "Manchurian Candidate,"* 134–36.
23. Hofmann, *LSD*, 1–15.
24. See Bowart, *Operation Mind Control*, 75–78; Marks, *Search for the "Manchurian Candidate,"* 3–5.
25. Lee and Shlain, *Acid Dreams*, 19–20.
26. Project MKULTRA, 72–73.
27. Project MKULTRA, 73.
28. Project MKULTRA, 73.
29. Kinzer, *Poisoner in Chief*, 60–61.
30. "Scientific Intelligence Memorandum: Potential New Agent for Unconventional Warfare," Office of Scientific Intelligence, August 5, 1954, 1, CIA, Freedom of Information Act Electronic Reading Room, General CIA Records, CREST Files, Document #: RDP83-01042R000800010006-8.
31. Whether Frank Olson committed suicide by jumping or was deliberately pushed out of the window remains uncertain. For an official account of the Olson incident, see Project MKULTRA, 74–79. On CIA clandestine dosing and the Olson incident, see also Marks, *Search for the "Manchurian Candidate,"* 79–93, 99–108; Kinzer, *Poisoner in Chief*, 108–28, 141–49; Albarelli, *Terrible Mistake*.
32. Concerning "Operation Midnight Climax" and its mastermind, George Hunter White, see Marks, *Search for the "Manchurian Candidate,"* 107; Scheflin and Opton, *Mind Manipulators*, 134–41; Kinzer, *Poisoner in Chief*, 141–49.
33. Marks, *Search for the "Manchurian Candidate,"* 142.
34. Goodman, *Sonic Warfare*, 141–48.
35. Marks states that even Cameron himself may not have known that the CIA was funding his research, support for which "came through a conduit, the Society for the Investigation of Human Ecology." See Marks, *Search for the "Manchurian Candidate,"* 141–42.
36. Gillmor, *I Swear by Apollo*, 48.
37. Marks, *Search for the "Manchurian Candidate,"* 146–48.
38. From the deposition of Velma Orlikov, in Thomas, *Secrets and Lies*, 182–88, 203. She is identified as "Val" Orlikov in Marks, *Search for the "Manchurian Candidate,"* 148–49.
39. See Kirby, "Paradise Lost."
40. Harris and Paxman, *Higher Form of Killing*, 192.
41. Harris and Paxman, *Higher Form of Killing*, 191–92.
42. Kirby, "Paradise Lost," 2.
43. BZ was rumored to have been considered for use in the American war in Vietnam, but whether it was actually tested there remains uncertain. Kirby, "Paradise Lost," 3. On some of the other physical and cognitive effects of BZ, see Harris and Paxman, *Higher Form of Killing*, 192–93.
44. Seed, *Brainwashing*, 106–33.
45. Marks, *Search for the "Manchurian Candidate,"* 194–205.
46. See Bowart, *Operation Mind Control*, 261–74.
47. Marks, *Search for the "Manchurian Candidate,"* 136–39. For the full report, see Lawrence E. Hinkle Jr. and Harold G. Wolff,

Communist Interrogation and Indoctrination of "Enemies of the State": Analysis of Methods Used by the Communist State Police (A Special Report), August 1956, CIA, Freedom of Information Act Electronic Reading Room, General CIA Records, CREST Files, Document #: RDP65-00756R000400020008-8.

48. See Seed, *Brainwashing*, 106–109.
49. Bowart, *Operation Mind Control*, 171–78.
50. Bowart, *Operation Mind Control*, 181.
51. Marks, *Search for the "Manchurian Candidate,"* 220–21.

Bibliography

Archival Sources

Central Intelligence Agency, Washington, DC: Freedom of Information Act Electronic Reading Room, General CIA Records, CREST Files.

Audiovisual Sources

Frankenheimer, John, dir. *The Manchurian Candidate*. 1962. M.C. Productions.
Menzies, William Cameron, dir. *Invaders from Mars*. 1953. National Pictures.
Siegel, Don. *Invasion of the Body Snatchers*. 1956. Allied Artist Pictures.
U.S. Germ Warfare in Korea. DPRK propaganda film posted on June 28, 2011, by PublicResourceOrg. YouTube video, 21:59. https://www.youtube.com/watch?v=gGP1q2vVoas.

Published Sources

Albarelli, H. P., Jr. *A Terrible Mistake: The Murder of Frank Olson and the CIA's Secret Cold War Experiments*. Walterville: Trine Day, 2009.
Bowart, Walter. *Operation Mind Control*. New York: Dell, 1978.
Gillmor, Don. *I Swear by Apollo: Dr. Ewen Cameron and the CIA-Brainwashing Experiments*. Montreal: Eden Press, 1987.
Goodman, Steve. *Sonic Warfare: Sound, Affect, and the Ecology of Fear*. Cambridge: MIT Press, 2010.
Harris, Robert, and Jeremy Paxman. *A Higher Form of Killing: The Secret History of Chemical and Biological Warfare*. New York: Random House, 2002.
Hofmann, Albert. *LSD: My Problem Child*. New York: McGraw-Hill, 1980.
Jütte, Robert. *A History of the Senses: From Antiquity to Cyberspace*. Translated by James Lynn. Cambridge: Polity Press, 2005.
Kinzer, Stephen. *Poisoner in Chief: Sidney Gottlieb and the CIA Search for Mind Control*. New York: Henry Holt, 2019.
Kirby, Reid. "Paradise Lost: The Psycho Agents." *CBW Conventions Bulletin* 71 (May 2006): 1–5.
Lee, Martin A., and Bruce Shlain. *Acid Dreams: The Complete Social History of LSD; The CIA, the Sixties, and Beyond*. New York: Grove Press, 1985.
Leitenberg, Milton. "False Allegations of U.S. Biological Weapons Use during the Korean War." In *Terrorism, War, or Disease: Unraveling the Use of Biological Weapons*, edited by Anne L. Clunan, Peter R. Lavoy, and Susan B. Martin, 120–43. Stanford: Stanford University Press, 2008.
Marks, John. *The Search for the "Manchurian Candidate": The CIA and Mind Control*. New York: W. W. Norton, 1979.
Ross, Colin Ross. *The CIA Doctors: Human Rights Violations by American Psychiatrists*. Richardson: Manitou, 2006.
Scheflin, Alan W., and Edward M. Opton Jr. *The Mind Manipulators*. New York: Paddington Press, 1978.
Seed, David. *Brainwashing: The Fictions of Mind Control*. Kent: Kent State University Press, 2004.
Smith, David A. "American Nightmare: Images of Brainwashing, Thought Control, and Terror in Soviet Russia." *Journal of American Culture* 33, no. 3 (2010): 217–29.
Taylor, Kathleen. *Brain Washing: The Science of Thought Control*. Oxford: Oxford University Press, 2004.
Thomas, Gordon. *Secrets and Lies: A History of CIA Mind Control and Germ Warfare*. Old Saybrook: Octavo Editions, 2007.

CHAPTER 10

To Inform and Deceive

Sensory Approaches in the Military Propaganda of Cold War Germany

Carsten Richter

The confrontation between East and West Germany during the Cold War reestablished compulsory military service as the new normal in men's lived biographies.[1] As a result, millions of draftees experienced specific sets of sensory practices exclusive to the modern military. In terms of the draftees' sensorium,[2] these practices were marked by want, refinement of their senses, overstimulation, and dullness. With the border between the rivals marking the European front line of two antagonistic global systems armed to the teeth with conventional and nuclear weapons, the confrontation was carried out for the most part through a propaganda war that peaked between 1960 and 1972.[3]

In this chapter, I will argue that the nature of the military domain's sensory aspects was exploited by the military propaganda of the German Democratic Republic (GDR) and the Federal Republic of Germany (FRG) to gain a military advantage for wartime. Military propaganda differs from other forms of propaganda in its character as a weapon of war: it is focused on military-related topics, aims to either boost or undermine support for all matters defense-related, and relies not just on positive but also negative messaging. It usually originates from the military itself or from intelligence services. While it mainly addresses audiences serving in the armed forces with the ultimate goal of fostering dissent, disobedience, and desertion, it usually aims at entire societies.[4] Both the draft and the use of propaganda were an integral part of the Cold War, with the former mostly characterized as a war *on* the senses and the latter constituting a war *through* the senses. While evidence that military propaganda had the desired effects on its target audiences remains largely elusive, there is ample proof of its unintended effects on the respective military organizations. But it paints an uneven picture: whereas West German soldiers experienced propaganda mostly as background noise, East German soldiers suffered severely from its effects. These effects contributed to alienating East German soldiers from the ruling regime; a similar impact cannot be found among their Western counterparts.

In terms of historical sources, this chapter draws primarily on archival documents from the Militärarchiv (Federal Military Archives) in Freiburg and the Stasi Records, both of which are held by the Bundesarchiv (German Federal Archives). This material provides unique insights into how each side perceived the military propaganda war and its Cold War context, meaning its own realm and that of the other side. It allows us to track the actions taken by each side to maintain control of its own "sensory collectives" and interfere with those of the other side.

In terms of its theoretical approach, this chapter draws on the domain-based concept of influences on the sensorium developed by David Howes and Constance Classen. It makes the case that the military and its specific set of sensory practices constitute a noteworthy form of "life of the senses in society."[5] It uses and expands Steve Goodman's far-reaching concept of "sonic warfare" to include "sensory warfare" and its effects on human targets and the structures they form.[6] As for empirical insights into the sensory dimension of the military domain, these are to some extent covered in the literature dealing with the experience of battle,[7] but they receive scant attention in the literature addressing peacetime proceedings. The specifics of the West German experience during the Cold War seem to have been ignored in academic literature so far, but Rüdiger Wenzke, Torsten Diedrich, and Jochen Maurer have provided important accounts of everyday life in the Nationale Volksarmee (NVA, National People's Army) of the GDR and its Grenztruppen (Border Guards).[8]

I will start by taking a look at how the militaries of both Cold War German states shaped their constituents' sensorium through sensory practices and collective sensory experiences. I will go on to show how military propaganda attempted to exploit these sensory aspects of the military domain. This will take me to my final argument on how propaganda harmed the targeted structures not so much by successfully appealing to soldiers as by evoking a disproportionate and misguided organizational reaction.

Despite numerous objections to rearmament, the confrontation of Western democracy and Soviet communism quickly brought about the emergence of new German militaries. In the East, the Soviets' drive for power and their puppet government's weakness necessitated a rapid buildup of paramilitary police forces that were soon transformed into a military in all but name. In 1955, the FRG established its own armed forces, the Bundeswehr, and passed laws for a national draft just months afterward. Only then did the GDR make its military official, capitalizing on the propagandistic value of merely responding to an alleged Western aggression. The East German draft followed in 1961, when the construction of the Berlin Wall made it all but impossible for draft dodgers to flee to the FRG. The length of service for draftees in West Germany was initially set at eighteen months but was reduced to fifteen in the 1970s. In the GDR, it was eighteen months throughout the Cold War. During this time, both German states claimed the power to control its constituents' bodies, shaping them and thus their sensorium to meet its needs.

Despite all the differences between the Bundeswehr and the NVA—and despite all the internal differences and variations over time—the sensory experiences of draftees were quite similar in two respects.[9] First, their basic training was geared toward conditioning them to fight as infantrymen, which meant subjecting them both to sensory want and overstimulation. Second, their subsequent service period was meant to maintain and expand this conditioning in their respective specializations. This latter phase was marked by dull repetitiveness and alternation between idleness and overload. These sensory characteristics made draftees receptive to propagandistic targeting.

A War on the Senses: Conditioning Young Men for the Infantry

"The first constancy of a soldier is constancy in enduring fatigue and hardship. Courage is only second. Poverty, privation and want are the school of the good soldier."[10] This quotation from Napoleon Bonaparte comes from a time when warfare was conducted by men in colorful uniforms who fought in formations on open fields to allow their commanders a clear view of the situation. Conditions changed drastically in the twentieth century. Modern warfare is marked by the "emptiness of the battlefield": cover, camouflage, and dispersion have replaced dense formations and bright colors because of the increased firepower of modern weaponry.[11] Hence, turning young civilians into infantrymen means teaching them to "sense" the battlefield. Seeing and hearing skills are trained so infantrymen can spot the enemy amid natural or built surroundings while hiding from enemy eyes. Recruits are taught to discern friend from foe by the appearance and sounds of their arms and machinery. And they are drilled until they know their weapons through and through, which entails managing a complex interplay of sensory and motoric skills. Shooting lays claim to a soldier's entire mind and body: he needs to be strong and stable physically to withstand the recoil that threatens to ruin his aim. He must coordinate his arms and hands in a way that brings the gun sight delicately in line with his eyes, avoiding any tremors in a life-and-death situation full of intimidating noise. His index finger must detect the trigger and then pull it as smoothly as possible, lest the movement ruin the shot. His ears must bear the noise of this shot without causing the instinctive flinch of the body, which can also interfere with his aim. To reload and clean the weapon, his hands must instinctively know the location and shape of the magazine, magazine pockets, and other parts of the weapon. He must know how to assemble these parts in the light of day or the dark of night, in the relative calm of a shooting range or in the barrage of sensory impressions during battle.

Such refinements of the senses and their separation from the mind by means of drilling are in contrast to the habituation to overwhelming sensations. Habituating the recruit to continuous physical and mental strains and a hostile environment continues to be a cornerstone of basic training in all militaries today. Recruits learn to bear the discomfort and pain of carrying heavy weights over long distances and then to engage in the physically demanding exercises of combat training. Blisters, abrasions, and bruises combined with sore muscles make for a painful full-body experience. Year-round, only tents and perhaps a campfire provide shelter and warmth against the weather. Nights that are shortened and interrupted by alarms and sentry duty deprive the recruits of sleep, numbing their senses when it is crucial for them to remain alert. Hunger and thirst are part of the entire ordeal, which is meant to enable recruits to continue fighting no matter what the circumstances.

Sensory Dullness: Life in the Barracks

During the Cold War, the strains of basic training, which lasted two to three months, were followed by a year or so of dullness and repetition. While the working hours in military service were meant to inspire discipline and maintain soldiers' high skill level, disorganization and negligence often caused delays that then had to be made up for. For the soldiers, this led to a frustrating alternation between idleness and overload. Barracks were usually no joy to look at: most were of a plain design and had been constructed from cheap materials before the war. The sanitation facilities were often in a deplorable state. While both the East and West German militaries invested in better accommodations, the accommodations were a source of discontent for generations of soldiers.[12]

As the lowest-ranking members of the military, draftees usually lived in crowded rooms with up to sixteen others, though four to eight was the standard by the end of the Cold War. Living so close together meant a constant assault on the senses. One West German draftee describes in his diary how, when his peers took their boots off, the whole room quickly filled with the "obtrusive smell of cheesy feet." When he returned from a duck-and-cover drill, he noticed the room smelled like "sheep shit"—only to realize that the smell was emanating from his own jacket as he had been crawling in dung the night before.[13]

Soldiers experienced dullness in gustatory respects as well. While not necessarily ill tasting, meals were not meant to be enjoyed but to provide energy. In the NVA, every soldier was supposed to receive forty-one hundred calories per day—testimony to the enormous physical demands on their bodies. These calories came in the form of an ever-repeating cycle of meals that included a dish nicknamed "dead grandmother" (black pudding, sauerkraut, salted potatoes), a variety of stews, and the occasional schnitzel. Breakfast and dinner consisted of bread, marmalade, a little butter, and some cold cuts or cheese. For drinks, there was tea made in large vats. Meals were eaten unit by unit, with limited time for the conscripts to get their food and eat it before mealtime was over. Thus, the comfort usually provided by food was lessened by the dullness of repetition and the limited options of industrial kitchens. Mealtime was also cut short and made into yet another joyless part of the day by the necessity of feeding a large number of people in a limited time.[14]

The East German Experience: An Atmosphere of Distrust and Disillusion

Military service in the GDR not only contributed to the national defense effort but also intended to mint loyal citizens by cultivating "sozialistische

Soldatenpersönlichkeiten" (socialist soldierly personalities).[15] It is worth taking a look at some of its special features and their effects on life in the military, as these features arguably caused severe friction between draftees and the political and military leadership.

First of all, the Soviet military doctrine to which the NVA adhered demanded a constant high level of readiness, with 85 percent of troops available in the barracks at all times. Maintaining this state of readiness was all-important and the overall goal of the soldiers' service. For East German draftees, this meant even less time off to recover than their West German counterparts. Weekend passes were limited, and soldiers could only leave the barracks on Saturday afternoon and Sunday. But even outside the barracks, they had to wear their uniforms. Border guards were only permitted to leave the military grounds under the supervision of a superior. East German draftees were not even permitted to have civilian clothes in their lockers, as such clothes were seen as enabling desertions.[16] This prohibition stood in stark contrast to the rules for West German soldiers, who were not only allowed to wear civilian clothes in their spare time but also had one more day off each week.

Furthermore, the East German soldiers' free time was often filled with work performed for the ruling socialist party, the Sozialistische Einheitspartei Deutschlands (SED), or for affiliated organizations. This additional work was expected of them, and not performing it could raise the suspicion of a lack of loyalty to the ruling ideology. This suspicion, in turn, could bring draftees to the attention of the GDR's secret service, the Stasi. The military was full of Stasi informants—there were far more informants per soldier than per civilian in the GDR[17]—and this likely caused an atmosphere of suspicion and distrust among soldiers. Even slight deviations from the regulations could result in severe disciplinary actions or courts-martial. The soldiers' media consumption was regulated, and all Western media were banned. The atmosphere of distrust and pressure to do the party's bidding caused many draftees to experience disillusionment with their socialist ideals and the party's actions.[18] While this finding is seemingly contradicted by the sheer volume of transgressive and even criminal behavior mentioned below, it can be explained by two observations: alcohol played an important role in transgressions, and disillusionment about the military made soldiers not care anymore.

For those serving as border guards, the disillusionment was even greater when they realized they were not so much protectors of their homeland against foreign invaders as they were prison guards for their countrymen. They were ordered to shoot unarmed civilians who attempted to cross the border illegally into the West.[19] It goes without saying that there was nothing even close to this experience in the Bundeswehr.

In addition, the constant pressure and disillusionment made the draftees turn on each other. It was not long before the emergence of the EK-Bewegung (*Entlassungskandidaten-Bewegung*), an unofficial movement of draftees in the final six months of their service who began terrorizing younger conscripts in hazing rituals and forcing their work on them. The NVA leadership was acutely aware of this problem but ultimately helpless. The EK-Bewegung took advantage of the fact that practically all superiors left the barracks after 5 p.m. and were otherwise overwhelmed with their extensive duties. The noncommissioned officers who remained had the task of maintaining order, but they were often outnumbered and overpowered.[20]

Locked up in often intolerable conditions with little free time, many draftees turned to alcohol to numb their senses or enhance moments of pleasure. While excessive alcohol consumption can be found in all militaries, and certainly in the Bundeswehr as well, it became a severe threat to the crucial state of readiness of the GDR military. Alcohol was a key factor in most of the rampant crime committed by East German soldiers. The most common violations were violent attacks on civilians and other soldiers, absences without leave, and desertion. A ban on alcohol in all barracks proved largely ineffective.[21]

As a part of the general propaganda war between the FRG and the GDR, each side's military served as both a distributor and target audience of propaganda. The aim was to drive a wedge between the opponent's military and society, and between the military and its leadership, thus weakening the military's will to fight. An additional goal was to increase the will to fight of one's own military. In terms of the sensorium, this meant influencing perceptions, ideally to the point of controlling them. The two propaganda machines exploited the specific sensory wants of their target audiences when disseminating their messages.

Western Music, Eastern Goals: GDR Radio Broadcasts Targeting the Bundeswehr

The GDR's propaganda against the Bundeswehr took many forms, the most notorious being Deutscher Soldatensender 935 (DSS 935), a radio broadcasting service established in 1960.[22] Conditions for this type of propaganda were very favorable: tuning in to radio broadcasts had become a popular activity in Germany. With falling prices for radios and the increasing purchasing power of the population, it became common in the 1960s for even teenagers to own one or more sets. The invention of the transistor decreased the size of the radio, which promoted its use.[23] Thus, soldiers spent their off-duty time (and often enough on duty) listening to broadcasts when and where they wanted: alone or in groups, in communal areas, in the semi-privacy of their rooms in the barracks, or off military grounds. The possibilities for superiors to rein in this media consumption were fairly limited: they had no legal basis for prohibiting media consumption outside service hours, and the prevalence of radios made it virtually impossible to hold consumption in check. Furthermore, the proliferation of radios contributed to the emergence of a distinct youth culture in which pop music and rock 'n' roll played a foundational role.[24] Exploiting this kind of music to reach target audiences became a standard tool in the radio propaganda of both East and West Germany.[25]

Few did this as successfully as DSS 935. Its focus on "hot" Western dance music was crucial in making it an institution, as Bundeswehr deserters told the Stasi.[26] In 1966, a West German military intelligence study found that DSS 935 was one of the two most popular radio stations among soldiers.[27] Fifty percent of soldiers regularly tuned in to DSS 935 to indulge in escapism, the essence of pop music.[28] Thus having caught the Bundeswehr soldiers' attention, DSS 935 began using propaganda messages to sway them. Posing as a representative of the soldiers' interests to their leadership, DSS 935 broadcast a mix of truths, half-truths, and outright falsehoods about grievances in the Bundeswehr. Reports focused on desertions, abuses of power, and other grievances and were mostly gathered from West German newspapers. A prime example is a broadcast from 1964 that specifically addressed a unit in the town of Ebern, Bavaria. A deserter from this unit allegedly stated:

> I will go to the GDR because I have seen in the Bundeswehr that what I have written about as a reporter in Würzburg for the newspaper *Mainpost*. I knew the Würzburgian doctor Herterich, and I know how this honorable doctor was threatened and pressured due to his calling-out of former members of the Nazi establishment in the judiciary. I have now experienced myself that the Bundeswehr is ruled by the old spirit, as ombudsman [Wehrbeauftragter; CR] Heye said.

The acting platoon leader corporal Knöchel for example is one of those, who in our first month as draftees addressed us only as "pigs." For these people we are only animals to be drilled, like Heye said. And that is why I'm going over there.[29]

This report is a compilation of a variety of themes often employed to deliver the core message: West Germany is a Nazi state, and one must leave it in order to be on the right side of history. The message was peppered with hints at news stories that were well known and widely discussed in the West German public sphere, such as the Heye report and the fate of Dr. Herterich, which lent credibility. While the report had the name of the unit wrong, Corporal Knöchel and his misdemeanor might well have been real: the Bundeswehr had a serious problem with instructors crossing the line of abuse, especially in the 1960s. Also, DSS 935 knew its messages were more effective if they were tailored to a specific target audience and included verifiable details.

These reports were intended to motivate listeners to write DSS 935 about their own experiences. Not only did this give listeners a sense of agency and a way to express their grievances, but it also left the impression on many that DSS 935 was actually a West German institution for Bundeswehr soldiers, possibly even affiliated with the soldiers' ombudsman in the West German parliament. DSS 935 promoted this myth by concealing its real location on the outskirts of East Berlin and providing its audience with an address that included what looked like a West Berlin zip code.[30] Even personnel with security clearances, who were explicitly warned about such methods of extracting information, were among those fooled by this ruse.

It is difficult to understand how this impression, mentioned in the Bundeswehr intelligence service study, could have come about. Other sources point out that the soldiers were well aware that they were listening to East German propaganda.[31] The content and diction of the reports were too obvious to the critical listener. DSS 935 even promised to warn soldiers of upcoming alarm exercises—hardly something a West German radio service would do. However, soldiers did not mind. They just wanted their music entertainment.

DSS 935 also began connecting soldiers with East German women as pen pals. In this way, GDR propaganda exploited one important aspect of sensual deprivation in barracks: there were hardly any women around. This deprivation was especially acute as draftees were young adolescent men shaped by the military, an institution of hypermasculinity. Further evidence that GDR

TO INFORM AND DECEIVE 193

Fig. 10.1 Attracting the Western male gaze: the caption to this photo in this 1972 issue of GDR military propaganda magazine *Rührt Euch* offers a high-quality version of the photo in exchange for valuable personal data. Photo: Deutsche Nationalbibliothek.

propaganda consciously exploited this situation is the use of erotic images in magazines targeting Bundeswehr soldiers—a striking feature, given that such images were banned in the GDR itself. The depiction of women in GDR propaganda varied so as to cater to every conceivable taste: various body types in various states of undress, ranging from playful to artisan, but always appealing to heterosexual men's carnal desires.[32] Figure 10.1 gives an example of this and also reveals its purpose: the caption offers the image as a decorative print free of charge, requiring only the intended recipient's address—an address that would end up on the GDR's vast and ever-growing mailing list for propaganda.

Bundeswehr officials were alarmed. One report attributed several desertions to DSS 935 broadcasts, which was a particularly desirable effect from the GDR's perspective.[33] Deserters had a high level of credibility concerning conditions in the military, and this credibility was regularly exploited by propagandists on both sides. According to the Bundeswehr's military intelligence service, the main effect of propaganda was to disrupt the military order and erode the standing of the Bundeswehr among youth. It feared this could lead to larger numbers of draftees objecting to service on grounds of conscience, a central problem for a conscription force. In addition, the Psychologische Kampfführung (PSK, Psychological Warfare Division), which was tasked with counterpropaganda, was afraid that draftees and young people might believe the Bundeswehr had been subverted by communist agents on a large scale. This would have been a sign of weakness that contradicted the goal of presenting a strong fighting spirit.[34]

To stop the threat of DSS 935, the Bundeswehr weighed a ban on the station, but this was quickly ruled out. The West German constitution guaranteed all citizens the right to free information, and soldiers were no exception. So the PSK produced a brochure to counter DSS 935 propaganda, reframe it, and change soldiers' perceptions. The PSK exposed the broadcaster for what it was—an East German propaganda tool—and described its methods as so primitive as to be repulsive to West German soldiers, even though this ran contrary to its own findings. More importantly, it emphasized that many had called for a ban but that this was neither needed nor wanted. After all, a ban would be incompatible with West German democracy, which the PSK described as much too strong to be affected by this sort of propaganda.[35] In other words, the PSK communicated that the leaders of the Bundeswehr had confidence in their soldiers, the resilience of democracy, and the rule of law. In this way, the PSK convincingly countered the main theme of GDR propaganda, that is, that the FRG was a fascist authoritarian regime and the Bundeswehr was the tool with which it subjugated its citizens. The brochure also attempted to reframe the practice of listening to DSS 935 for its music, explaining that soldiers should tune in to other broadcasters because DSS 935, unlike West German radio stations, did not compensate artists. However, there were few alternatives among the rather conservative, exclusively state-run West German broadcasters.[36] Ultimately, it was only a treaty signed in 1972 that put an end to DSS 935. Even so, the effectiveness of the station's propaganda remains questionable. It failed in its stated goal of driving up the number of deserters. Its only discernible effect was to keep some Bundeswehr officials alert and preoccupied and to help some soldiers escape the dullness of life in the barracks.

Targeting Soldiers, Hitting the Regime: PSK Leaflet Drops

To challenge the GDR's initiative in the propaganda war, the Bundeswehr tasked the PSK, its psychological warfare division, with targeting the NVA and Border Guards. Reaching them proved difficult, though. The GDR went to great lengths to maintain maximum control over its soldiers' minds and bodies, isolating them from the civilian world and controlling their media consumption to every extent possible. However, these efforts were mostly fruitless: Western media were favored among GDR audiences,[37] and young men were already accustomed to these media outlets when they were drafted. It was risky for soldiers to tune in to Western broadcasts while in the barracks. However, evidence from Stasi files and the accounts of former soldiers show that doing so was nevertheless a common practice.[38]

In order to avoid putting their target audiences in harm's way with radio broadcasts, the PSK resorted to mass drops of leaflets via hydrogen balloons, a method already in use by the propaganda offices of West German political parties.[39] Drawing on these parties' experience, the PSK dropped large numbers of leaflets, brochures, newspapers, and even whole books near East German military units. The more elaborate materials mimicked official East German newspapers in their layouts, and the PSK took pains to keep up with changes. It went so far as to use imported GDR paper to make the fake newspapers look and feel more like the original.[40] Reports by dissidents were made to look like official service books. They were printed on especially thin paper to reduce their weight and maximize the drop size, or on special pharmaceutical paper that made them resistant to rain, to which many of the dropped materials were exposed until found. Officially, this camouflage was intended to protect soldiers from punishment, as they could plausibly deny knowing that they were in possession of propaganda. The camouflage could also serve to fool readers, at least initially, rendering the readers open for arguments (see fig. 10.2).

The PSK's objective was to establish a propaganda platform that would deliver a strategic advantage in case of war. It proceeded to drive a wedge between the soldiers and their military and political leadership by providing a counternarrative to GDR propaganda. This narrative focused on creating a new image of the conflict between East and West Germany with verifiable information. The aspect of truthfulness was considered to be of strategic importance: there needed to be a high level of trust in the information to ensure its effectiveness and build a sense of community between East and West Germans. This would guarantee a "devastating effect on the NVA fighting power in the event of war."[41]

Despite the extreme security measures taken by the GDR, the PSK was well informed about its target audience's situation and how best to exploit

Fig. 10.2 Deceiving sight and touch: forged Western military propaganda papers delivered to the GDR like this 1964 issue of *Volksarmee* looked and felt like the poor-quality originals but displayed NVA deserters enjoying superior FRG products. Image courtesy of Bundesarchiv/SELKE, Germany, BW 64/638.

it. More than one thousand East German soldiers had defected before the construction of the Berlin Wall. Even after the wall was finished, a significant number of deserters made their way to West Germany. They provided PSK debriefers with all the details they needed.[42] This was why the PSK focused on the economic situation of West Germans and their extensive consumption opportunities, peppering its propaganda with matter-of-fact criticism of SED policies. Statistics were used to show the evolution in West German workers' incomes, which topped those of most other countries' workers by far.[43] There was low inflation in the West and a larger range of goods and services that people could spend these higher earnings on. Price lists of cars, motorcycles, and vacations abroad were also included to remind soldiers of the modern luxuries they were missing out on because their government was unable to deliver them on a comparable scale. Consequently, PSK propaganda also encouraged East German soldiers to desert their units and make their way to West Germany, presenting stories of some who had made it. In the example given, the first page provides stories of successful cross-border deserters, some of them with their wives and children. The stories focused on how the lives of the deserters had improved economically: they had higher wages that they could spend on travel to foreign countries like Spain and Italy, flats with furniture of high quality, and shopping trips. Images of the seemingly radiantly happy protagonists of the stories with status symbols of the time—fine suits, coats, cognac—supported the stories' message. The stories put an emphasis on the jobs that the protagonists held: they were all working-class, none of them held an academic degree, and they still were able to afford this lifestyle. Smaller bits rebut GDR propaganda about deserters dying, ask finders of the pamphlet to pass it on, and offer help for those who want to desert to the West. The back of the page claims to merely copy the advertising section of a West German newspaper, relying on the advertising to suggest that West Germany offers affordable consumption on a level impossible in the GDR, especially in terms of traveling.[44]

All in all, the PSK narrative combined the freedoms of a pluralistic political system with the opportunities of modern consumption. This was the theme most likely to effectively exploit the dull and freedom-lacking sensory community of the military.[45] PSK propaganda argued in a remarkably rational way. While images played an important role in supporting and illustrating arguments, they never went below the belt: erotica was no part of it.

In the GDR, the security apparatus regarded military propaganda as a grave threat to the effectiveness and loyalty of its troops. Considered a part of generally condemned Western media, this propaganda became the scapegoat for all misconduct of military personnel, such as desertions, absences without leave, violence, political criticism, and involvement in the EK-Bewegung.[46] Wherever traces of military propaganda could be found, the regime responded by vastly increasing the network of Stasi informants in the military in an effort to keep close track of even the smallest signs of disobedience, which was punished severely.[47] Political education offensives were launched to ensure the soldiers' loyalty and identification with party rule.[48] The regime also increased its grip on the soldiers' media consumption and tried to collect dropped leaflets as quickly as possible under the supervision of trusted loyalists.

However, its ever-tightening grip worsened the already "strained socialist relations" in the NVA and Border Guards. Because criticism and opposition within the military could easily be seen as a form of disloyalty to party rule motivated by West German propaganda, the relationship between the party leadership and military personnel became trapped in a vicious cycle that produced disillusionment among soldiers. Thus, the institution that was supposed to create a power base completely in line with the SED leadership to a great extent failed in its mission, partly due to its sensory characteristics.

Conclusion

This chapter set out to explore the sensory experiences and practices specific to the military in Cold War Germany and how the military propaganda of the GDR and the FRG sought to exploit them. It showed that propaganda was widely consumed and often not recognized for what it was, as its producers had designed it to deceive its target audiences for better effect. However, propaganda did not discernably affect its target audiences in the desired way: desertions to the opponent's territory remained rather uncommon on both sides, and there is little evidence that propaganda was a driving force behind those that did occur. Still, propaganda did affect security apparatuses on both sides, triggering countermeasures that kept them occupied. In the case of the GDR, these countermeasures were far more harmful than the propaganda ever could have been, alienating soldiers from their leadership.

Thus, this chapter showed that there *is* a set of sensory experiences and practices specific to the modern military domain in which millions of men participated and, moreover, that it had unique features in both East and West Germany. This set of experiences and practices was deliberately exploited by both militaries to deliver propaganda messages that aimed to change individuals' perceptions and behavior, which were an effect of, and in turn had an effect on, the Cold War.

Notes

1. The draft applied only to the male population. Women were banned from almost all military functions except for those in medical corps. Hence, the sensory practices of the military discussed here are exclusive to men. They offer obvious connections to broader conceptions of (military) masculinity and their transfer to civil society, which go beyond the scope of this chapter. See Bickford, *Fallen Elites*; Fenemore, *Sex, Thugs and Rock 'n' Roll*.

2. Walter Ong defines the sensorium as "the entire perceptual apparatus as an operational complex." See Ong, "Shifting Sensorium," 47.

3. I would like to thank Bodo Mrozek for his kind invitation to take part in his innovative workshop "The Cold War and the Senses," which took place online October 15 and 16, 2020, and to all participants, especially Mark Fenemore, for valuable comments.

4. For a discussion of the military use of propaganda, see Taylor, *Munitions of the Mind*, 1–16.

5. Howes and Classen, *Ways of Sensing*, 1–13, especially 12.

6. In Goodman's conceptualization, the term *structure* denotes built structures, and it aims to show that sounds affect much more than living beings. However, I will use the term exclusively in the sense of structures as expressions of organizations, as these are more relevant to the subject of this chapter. See Goodman, *Sonic Warfare*.

7. See Grossman, *On Killing*; Smith, *Smell of Battle*.

8. See Diedrich, "Gegen Aufrüstung"; Wenzke, "Zwischen 'Prager Frühling' 1968"; Wenzke, *Ulbrichts Soldaten*; Maurer, *Halt—Staatsgrenze!*

9. I am focusing on draftees as opposed to longer-serving personnel in order to shed light on the specific military experience of a greater share of the population and to emphasize the fact that the military and civil society were linked through a constant exchange of people. While longer-serving personnel shared the draftees' experience of basic training and the same set of sensory practices, most of their service time differed in significant ways. Because of this, longer-serving personnel will be addressed separately throughout this chapter.

10. Quoted in Grossman, *On Killing*, 66.

11. Biddle, *Military Power*, 3.

12. Wenzke, *Ulbrichts Soldaten*, 207–14.

13. Wolfgang M., Tagebuch, 1980/81, in Bundesarchiv (hereafter BArch), BW 1/12877, Freiburg, Germany, as quoted in Nübel, *Dokumente*, 662–63.

14. See Wenzke, *Ulbrichts Soldaten*, 215–18.

15. Fenemore, *Sex, Thugs and Rock 'n' Roll*, 118–31, 184–205.

16. See Wenzke, *Nationale Volksarmee*, 91, 94.

17. See Diedrich, "Gegen Aufrüstung"; for figures about Stasi informants, see Wenzke, "Zwischen 'Prager Frühling' 1968," 322–23.

18. See Diedrich, "Gegen Aufrüstung," 183–90.

19. See Maurer, *Halt—Staatsgrenze!*, 290–95, 361–74.

20. Maurer, *Halt—Staatsgrenze!*, 297–316; Wenzke, *Ulbrichts Soldaten*, 463–73.

21. See Wenzke, *Ulbrichts Soldaten*, 478–84.

22. Wilke, "Radio im Geheimauftrag," delivers the best account of DSS 935 so far. Kaiser, "Soldatensender," is an attempt to continue DSS 935's propaganda work but delivers some interesting details based on Kaiser's own insights. Kaiser was a member of the DSS staff from 1960 to 1968 and contributed to its work until 1972.

23. See Weber, *Das Versprechen mobiler Freiheit*, 85–160, especially 119–41.

24. For an extensive analysis of this phenomenon, see Mrozek, *Jugend—Pop—Kultur*.

25. See Mrozek, "G.I. Blues and German Schlager"; Fischer, "Schlagerkrieg im Äther."

26. See Information über die Wirksamkeit konterpropagandistischer Maßnahmen der 14. Verwaltung des MfNV und anderer gegen die NATO-Politik Westdeutschlands gerichteter Publikationen auf den Personalbestand militärischer Organe des Gegners, Berlin, October 18, 1963, BArch, MfS HA I 5866, BStU, Berlin, Germany, 446–47, 452–53. Unfortunately, DSS playlists survived in neither the archives of the BStU nor those of the Bundeswehr, so specifics like particularly heavily played artists and a sound analysis cannot be delivered.
27. See "Erfahrungsbericht der MADGrp WB I über die offene Zersetzung des DSS 935," July 1966, BArch, BW 1/65817, Freiburg, Germany, quoted in Nübel, *Dokumente*, 387–90 (hereafter cited as "Erfahrungsbericht").
28. See Fischer, "Schlagerkrieg im Äther," 44.
29. BPA, Aktenvermerk, August 26, 1964, BArch, BW 2/20169, Freiburg, Germany (translated by the author), 1.
30. "Erfahrungsbericht," 387–90.
31. See loose questionnaires, BArch, BW 2/20169, Freiburg, Germany.
32. Not enough GDR print propaganda has survived to analyze this aspect in more detail.
33. See Vermerk, July 13, 1961, BArch, Fü B VII 9, BW 2/6974, Freiburg, Germany.
34. See Verfügung, August 17, 1967, BArch, Fü S VII 6, BW 2/20169, Freiburg, Germany.
35. See "Der Deutsche Freiheitssender 904" (DFS 904), BArch, BW 2/20257, Freiburg, Germany. While the headline deals with another East German propaganda broadcaster, the arguments in this study explicitly extend to DSS 935 as well. The Bundeswehr treated DFS 904 and DSS 935 as practically identical because they had the same origin, purpose, and even transmitter.
36. The other radio station favored by soldiers was Radio Luxemburg, which allegedly also played music without paying royalties. Designing its programs around pop music and the emerging DJ culture, it succeeded in reaching young target audiences, especially the so-called baby boomers, and increasing advertising revenue. See Jehle, *Welle der Konsumgesellschaft*, 235–49.

37. See Kuschel, *Schwarzhörer*, especially 188–202.
38. See Teilstudie (Aktivität Nr. 4) zum Thema: "Die bewusste Ausnutzung spezifischer Besonderheiten der Wirkungsweise von Rundfunk und Fernsehen in der ideologischen Diversion des Gegners gegen die NVA: Die aus der Entwicklungstendenz dieser Massenmedien sich ergebenden Schlussfolgerungen für ihre wachsende Rolle im Rahmen der psychologischen Kriegführung der 70er Jahre," BArch, MfS HA I 15616, Berlin, Germany, 14–15; Diedrich, "Gegen Aufrüstung," 173–74; Maurer, *Halt—Staatsgrenze!*, 326.
39. See Buschfort, *Parteien im Kalten Krieg*, 129–35. On military aspects of the propaganda war with leaflets, see Bliembach, "Worte als Waffen"; Drews, *Die Psychologische Kampfführung*.
40. See interview with Lieutenant Colonel Bernhard Ickenroth, August 2003, as quoted in Drews, *Die Psychologische Kampfführung*, 198.
41. "Sozialwerk NVA," January 14, 1963, BArch, Fü B VII 9, BW 2/25465, Freiburg, Germany.
42. See BArch, BW 2/25464, 156–57; Anl. 14, BW 2/25465, Freiburg, Germany; Aussagen eines geflüchteten SED-Funktionärs, November 17, 1969, BW 2/7080, Freiburg, Germany.
43. See *Mitteldeutsche Arbeiterzeitung*, no. 1, 1968, BArch, BW 64/638, Freiburg, Germany.
44. See *Volksarmee*, no. 3, 1964, BArch, BW 64/638, Freiburg, Germany.
45. On consumer culture in the GDR and how it affected attitudes toward the regime, see Merkel, *Utopie und Bedürfnis*.
46. See Dokumentation: Die politisch-ideologische Diversion und andere Formen der Feindtätigkeit gegen die NVA und die Grenztruppen der DDR sowie ihre Auswirkungen in den Truppenteilen und Einheiten, Berlin, December 1974, BArch, MfS HA I 1999, Berlin, Germany, 118–54.
47. See Studie zum Gesamtproblem des Einschleusens von Hetzschriften mittels Ballons durch Spezialeinheiten der Psychologischen Kampfführung der Bundeswehr im Zusammenhang mit dem Auftrieb von Radiosonden und anderen Ballons für

meteorologische Zwecke durch die Meteorologischen Dienste beider deutscher Staaten, BArch, MfS ZOS 1180, Berlin, Germany, 68–69. For a detailed account of the Stasi's work in the Border Guards, see Maurer, *Halt—Staatsgrenze!*, 117–32.

48. See Einzel-Information über erkannte Formen und Methoden der Organisierung von Grenzdurchbrüchen durch feindliche Elemente an den Staatsgrenzen West und Berlin der DDR, unter Ausnutzung und Hinzuziehung von Angehörigen der Grenzsicherungskräfte der DDR, BArch, MfS HA I 15783, Berlin, Germany, 163–66; Beschluss des Sekretariats der Politischen Hauptverwaltung, August 29, 1983, BArch, MfS ZAIG 7887, Berlin, Germany, 26–28.

Bibliography

Archival Sources

Bundesarchiv, Germany: Abteilung Militärarchiv, Freiburg—BArch BW 1/12877, BW 1/65817, BW 2/20169, BW 2/20257, BW 2/25464–65, BW 2/6974, BW 2/7080, BW 64/638; Stasi Records, Berlin—BArch MfS HA I 15616, MfS HA I 15783, MfS HA I 1999, MfS HA I 5866, MfS ZAIG 7887, MfS ZOS 1180.

Published Sources

Bickford, Andrew. *Fallen Elites: The Military Other in Post-Unification Germany*. Stanford: Stanford University Press, 2011.

Biddle, Stephen. *Military Power: Explaining Victory and Defeat in Modern Battle*. Princeton: Princeton University Press, 2004.

Bliembach, Eva. "Worte als Waffen: Flugblattpropaganda im Kalten Krieg." In *Propaganda in Deutschland*, 235–54.

Buschfort, Wolfgang. *Parteien im Kalten Krieg: Die Ostbüros von SPD, CDU und FDP*. Berlin: Christoph Links, 2000.

Diedrich, Torsten. "Gegen Aufrüstung, Volksunterdrückung und politische Gängelei: Widerstandsverhalten und politische Verfolgung in der Aufbau- und Konsolidierungsphase der DDR-Streitkräfte, 1948–1968." In *Staatsfeinde in Uniform? Widerständiges Verhalten und politische Verfolgung in der NVA*, edited by Rüdiger Wenzke, 31–196. Berlin: Christoph Links, 2005.

Diesener, Gerald, and Rainer Gries, eds. *Propaganda in Deutschland: Zur Geschichte der politischen Massenbeeinflussung im 20. Jahrhundert*. Darmstadt: Primus, 1996.

Drews, Dirk. *Die Psychologische Kampfführung / Psychologische Verteidigung der Bundeswehr: Eine erziehungswissenschaftliche und publizistikwissenschaftliche Untersuchung*. Self-published, Mainz, 2006.

Fenemore, Mark. *Sex, Thugs and Rock 'n' Roll: Teenage Rebels in Cold-War East Germany*. Monographs in Germany History 16. New York: Berghahn, 2009.

Fischer, Jörg. "Schlagerkrieg im Äther: Schlager und Politik im DDR-Rundfunk der 1960er Jahre." *Info 7*, no. 3 (2014): 44–47.

Goodman, Steve. *Sonic Warfare: Sound, Affect, and the Ecology of Fear*. Cambridge: MIT Press, 2010.

Grossman, Dave. *On Killing: The Psychological Cost of Learning to Kill in War and Society*. New York: Back Bay Books, 2009.

Heinemann, Winfried. *Die DDR und ihr Militär*. Munich: Oldenbourg, 2011.

Howes, David, and Constance Classen. *Ways of Sensing: Understanding the Senses in Society*. London: Routledge, 2014.

Jehle, Anna. *Welle der Konsumgesellschaft: Radio Luxembourg in Frankreich, 1945–1975*. Medien und Gesellschaftswandel im 20. Jahrhundert 9. Göttingen: Wallstein, 2018.

Kuschel, Franziska. *Schwarzhörer, Schwarzseher, und heimliche Leser: Die DDR und die Westmedien*. Medien und Gesellschaftswandel im 20. Jahrhundert 6. Göttingen: Wallstein, 2016.

Maurer, Jochen. *Halt—Staatsgrenze! Alltag, Dienst und Innenansichten der Grenztruppen der DDR*. Berlin: Christoph Links, 2015.

Merkel, Ina. *Utopie und Bedürfnis: Die Geschichte der Konsumkultur in der DDR*. Alltag & Kultur 6. Cologne: Böhlau, 1999.

Mrozek, Bodo. "G.I. Blues and German Schlager: The Politics of Popular Music in Germany during the Cold War." In *Made in Germany—Studies in Popular Music*, edited by Oliver Seibt, Martin Ringsmut, and David-Emil Wickström, 122–31. Routledge Global Popular Music Series 18. New York: Routledge, 2020.

———. *Jugend—Pop—Kultur: Eine transnationale Geschichte*. Berlin: Suhrkamp, 2019.

Nübel, Christoph, ed. *Dokumente zur Deutschen Militärgeschichte, 1945–1990: Bundesrepublik und DDR im Ost-West-Konflikt*. Berlin: Christoph Links, 2019.

Ong, Walter. "The Shifting Sensorium." In *The Varieties of Sensory Experience*, edited by David Howes, 25–30. Toronto: University of Toronto Press, 1991.

Risso, Linda, ed. *Radio Wars: Broadcasting during the Cold War*. London: Routledge, 2016.

Schindelbeck, Dirk. "Propaganda mit Gummiballons und Pappraketen: Deutsch-deutscher Flugblattkrieg nach dem Bau der Mauer." In *Propaganda in Deutschland*, 213–34.

Smith, Mark M. *The Smell of Battle, the Taste of Siege: A Sensory History of the Civil War*. Cary: Oxford University Press, 2014.

Taylor, Philip M. *Munitions of the Mind: A History of Propaganda from the Ancient World to the Present Day*. Manchester: Manchester University Press, 2003.

Weber, Heike. *Das Versprechen mobiler Freiheit: Zur Kultur- und Technikgeschichte von Kofferradio, Walkman und Handy*. Bielefeld: Transcript, 2008.

Wenzke, Rüdiger. "Die Fahnenflucht in den Streitkräften der DDR." In *Armeen und ihre Deserteure: Vernachlässigte Kapitel einer Militärgeschichte der Neuzeit*, edited by Ulrich Bröckling and Michael Sikora, 252–87. Göttingen: Vandenhoeck & Ruprecht, 1998.

———. *Nationale Volksarmee: Die Geschichte*. Munich: Geramond, 2014.

———. *Ulbrichts Soldaten: Die Nationale Volksarmee, 1956 bis 1971*. Berlin: Christoph Links, 2013.

———. "Zwischen 'Prager Frühling' 1968 und Herbst 1989: Protestverhalten, Verweigerungsmuster und politische Verfolgung in der NVA der siebziger und achtziger Jahre." In *Staatsfeinde in Uniform? Widerständiges Verhalten und politische Verfolgung in der NVA*, edited by Rüdiger Wenzke, 199–428. Berlin: Christoph Links, 2005.

Wilke, Jürgen. "Radio im Geheimauftrag: Der Deutsche Freiheitssender 904 und der Deutsche Soldatensender 935 als Instrumente des Kalten Krieges." In *Zwischen Pop und Propaganda: Radio in der DDR*, edited by Klaus Arnold and Christoph Classen, 249–66. Berlin: Christoph Links, 2004.

CHAPTER 11

Sniffing the Enemy

Chemical Detection During the Vietnam War

Christy Spackman

In a 1971 operational report on lessons learned in the period ending October 31, Captain Dennis S. Pogany of the 1st Cavalry Airborne Division of the US Army noted that "electronic gadgetry is over relied upon by American forces in Vietnam. Too often it is the only means used for collecting information." Pogany pointed to electronic intelligence being gathered from "Red Haze, SLAR [side-looking airborne radar], Sniffer, Sensors, and URS's [user readout simulators]." Of the various forms of electronic intelligence detailed, the sniffer stands apart—first, for its constant use ("largely due to its availability") and second, for its reliance on a sense not often explicitly trained for use in combat: olfaction.[1]

The American conflict in Vietnam, often referred to as the Vietnam War in the United States, is generally understood to have occurred from 1954 to 1975. Historians note that the war's beginning and end are fuzzy: the conflict grew out of earlier US entanglements in Franco-Vietnamese politics during the First Indochina War, with large-scale US troop mobilization occurring in the early 1960s.[2] Unlike previous wars waged by the United States, conflict in Vietnam challenged conventional military attitudes and approaches. Metrics previously used to evaluate progress, soldier effectiveness, and success failed in the face of the Viet Cong counterinsurgency and the densely jungled terrain where much of the conflict occurred.[3] The US military increasingly turned its attention to technology as a means of overcoming the challenges encountered in Vietnam. As Barton Hacker, a historian of armed forces at the Smithsonian Institution, notes, the mid to late twentieth century is characterized by a distinct elaboration of military innovations. These include the further development of nuclear arms and their delivery systems, adoption of helicopters and other airborne modes of surveillance, and new sensor networks to help identify truck roads and personnel trails.[4] Technologies developed for and used in Vietnam fundamentally transformed how US forces fought war.[5]

Innovations in electronics played an especially critical role in remaking conventional ways of waging war.[6] The adoption of applied electronics (e.g., precision guidance technologies and information processing), Hacker suggests, was a complete revolution in the conventional approach to warfare—an "automation" of the battlefield that could use "new technology to locate, track, and target the enemy."[7] The sniffer—also known as the General Electric Ordnance Department E63 detector, the personnel manpack, the XM-2 personnel detector, or, colloquially, the "people sniffer"—and other forms of "electronic intelligence" highlighted by Pogany in his 1971 report fall under Hacker's categorization of military innovations. Unlike nuclear arms and their delivery systems, however, the sniffer seems a mere blip in the history of twentieth-century war. "It has not yet provided truly accurate intelligence," Pogany critiqued, noting that "twice responding to particularly intense sniffer readouts the results were totally negative." Pogany's remark is not echoed by a later report on the use of analysis to reinforce military judgment submitted to the Department of the Army in 1974 by Lieutenant General Julian J. Ewell and Major General Ira A. Hunt Jr. Instead, Ewell and Hunt saw the sniffer as a successful technology, but one whose successful use was influenced by differences in terrain. No matter the success or failure of the sniffer as a mode of electronic intelligence gathering, those working to innovate in policing and military fields, as well as in more mundane fields such as environmental monitoring and industrial food production, remain interested in the possibility of an electronic nose. These devices, which are constantly in development, are touted as technological objects capable of either working alongside or, in more recent capital-raising campaigns, replacing human noses in the effort to make sense of and bring order to the world.

This chapter examines how different forms of linking the human sensorium to instruments and in turn turning instruments into stand-ins for the human sensorium enacted a micropolitical effort to shape combat abroad and conflict at home during the latter years of the Vietnam War. I draw on declassified military reports, scientific reports, and mass media publications to examine how advances in the scientific understanding of olfaction's characteristics shaped Cold War sensing practices (defined below) in the closing years of conflict. I am especially interested in the role played by olfaction, a relatively "weak" sensing practice embedded in the "sensate regimes of war"—the ways that sensing is transformed and mobilized in the conduct of war.[8] In calling olfaction weak, I purposefully follow a well-established history of arranging the senses into a hierarchy that prioritizes vision and hearing over touch, gustation, and olfaction.[9] This is not to say that I think olfaction a weak sense; I do not. Rather, I acknowledge that olfaction continues to be an underexamined sensory mode that nonetheless defines experiences of conflict. This is true *even* as warfare is increasingly conducted at a distance, and even if the olfactory cues smelled increasingly reflect one's own body rather than the entire battlefield.

Olfaction is central to how many humans make sense of and communicate about the world. It is also a mode of sensory engagement whose potential for sensing environments, be they political, personal, environmental, or on the combat field, remains to be fully realized.[10] Despite the technological, scientific, and physical challenges posed by efforts to mechanize and weaponize sniffing as a sensing practice, the Limited Warfare Laboratory, in concert with General Electric, invested significant time, money, and some level of secrecy to develop, test, and bring to field a device dedicated to sniffing. The sniffer promised to change how soldiers made sense of the battlefield.

Human and nonhuman olfaction has historically played a critical—even if underexamined—role in warfare. Dogs, for example, were used in the Second World War to alert Allied troops to enemy movement, in Vietnam to help US soldiers detect land mines or other hazards, and in Iraq to identify explosives.[11] Soldiers learn to navigate unfamiliar territory and identify others through olfactory cues ranging from campfires to cigarette butts, while seeking to minimize their own odorous traces.[12] Scholars of modern warfare have demonstrated that war's industrialization reorganized sensory experience.[13] The eerie changes to the landscape caused by trenches, land ordinances, and bombs; by the spectacular heat of Napalm; and by the sonic assault of planes, helicopters, and automatic weapons transformed human sensing. Modern warfare shifted modes of experiencing the world: masks, machines, and weapons distanced combatants from the world and the people around them, creating new encounters with the environments of conflict. New technologies of sensing such as radar, night vision goggles, and scopes further shifted sensing in conflicts from a human or human-animal activity to a constellation of human and nonhuman/nonanimal sensing practices.[14] Adoption of computer technologies such as digital population data and geographical information systems similarly changed the conduct of warfare, requiring that on-the-ground military advisers take observations of social life and translate them into a machine-readable format; this transformed military advisers and the Vietnamese officials they worked with into what Oliver Belcher terms "embodied sensors" capable of turning subjective observations into data points that informed constantly changing maps.[15] Sensing in the late twentieth century distinctly differed from its earlier iterations.

In using the phrase "sensing practices," I seek to specifically draw attention to how modern warfare extends the sensorium beyond human modes of sensing and in the process reshapes political landscapes in not only large but, perhaps more critically, minute ways. My articulation of sensing practices draws together insights from Jennifer Gabrys and Helen Pritchard, as well as from Belcher, to refer to how practices of coupling embodied sensing with technologies shift the types of knowledge produced and do so by integrating different geographical locations, materials, and even political concerns.[16] Attending to sensing practices rather than simply human sensing, Gabrys suggests, facilitates examining how different modes of experiencing the world can put in place the possibility for new forms of collective political action.[17] In the case of the Vietnam War, sensing practices extended in multiple directions, linking questions of what olfactory cues could reveal about race and identity at home with questions of how to distinguish between others and self in the war theater abroad.[18]

New Sensing Practices: Sniffing Out

Sniffing is at its most basic a sensing practice. A nose acts as the sampling device, engaging with the surrounding environment to capture and analyze volatile molecular inputs.[19] Categorization of people based on scent relies on cultural understandings of smells of the other. During the Second World

War, for example, the US Army drew on these understandings in an effort to weaponize canine olfactory abilities, presuming that by training dogs to detect US soldiers of Japanese descent, the army could in turn use those dogs to detect Japanese soldiers in the field.[20] This did not work. The possibility of even imagining a sensing device like the people sniffer came about because of a massive mid-twentieth-century rearrangement in how researchers investigated olfactory cues, a rearrangement that partially obfuscated the cultural understandings underpinning olfactory classification. Specifically, the introduction and adoption of novel research instruments such as gas chromatographs, mass spectrometers, and flame ionization detectors offered researchers significant new insights into which molecular aspects of the world gave rise to olfactory perception. The subsequent widespread adoption of standardized ways of communicating about findings reorganized olfaction into a process of detecting and identifying molecules; molecules in turn came to stand in for specific olfactory cues (e.g., benzaldehyde for cherry).[21] This twentieth-century reduction of olfactory experience to molecular signals opened the door for a new constellation of sensing practices to emerge.

A range of researchers found understanding odors as molecules a useful new sensing practice. Oil and food chemists, perfumists, and flavorists shared an interest in a molecular approach to instrumentally identifying the molecules responsible for smell. They saw this as offering new insights into the causes of unwanted odors and flavors in products and as a way of providing the steps for overcoming such olfactory or gustatory challenges. Sensing unwanted flavors and odors initially was a practice in instrumental exuberance. Journal reports of gas chromatograph and mass spectrometry readings from a range of substances highlighted the multimolecular nature of odor. However, initial enthusiasm soon encountered a tricky reality: The transformation of sensation into molecular data, despite its exciting offerings, produced flat representations of the molecular world, failing to indicate which of the molecules in a smelly mixture actually smelled. Those interested in the human sensorium and human response had to adjust their sensing practices once again. They did this by coupling humans as sensors that worked in concert with machines. What emerged was a new sensing practice in which instrumental and human sensors collaborated in the work of identifying which components of smelly mixtures actually mattered to sensing, smelling bodies.[22]

In contrast, the human side of olfaction—at least when it came to a human olfactory response—did not really matter for the development of the people sniffer. Instead, the sniffer's function as a mode of surveillance simply rested on the idea that it could distinguish among various molecular cues. Theoretically, once specific molecular cues were instrumentally identified, that information could in turn alert the sniffer's users to the presence of Viet Cong combatants. This meant that all that the people sniffer needed to do was identify a relevant molecular signal and indicate to users that it had detected something. This sensing practice carried similarities with that of a gas chromatograph-olfactometer. In both cases, the machine detected and humans responded, but the response activated by the people sniffer was distinctly different from that of the gas chromatograph-olfactometer: rather than activating an evaluation of a molecule's perceptible properties or hedonic qualities, as the gas chromatograph-olfactometer did, the sniffer activated practices of additional detection and destruction.

Declassified reports indicate that the people sniffer worked by sampling air for the presence of "carbon and ammonia, emitted by man and other sources, and compound sigma, an emission peculiar solely to man."[23] Public-facing reports, such as one 1967 *New York Times* article about the people sniffer, proclaim its capacity to "roll back the Viet Cong's jungle cover," enhancing the ability of airborne troops to interact with an otherwise invisible foe.[24] Another article points out that the sniffer allowed detection of ammonia in decomposing sweat at levels well below anything the human nose could detect, with a reported sensitivity of one part in two hundred million.[25] *Time Life* clarified that the E63 detected ammonia caused by bacteria metabolizing urea in sweat. When ammonia-containing air entered the instrument, it interacted with hydrochloric acid, causing a fog to form. The fog altered light levels shining on a photoelectric cell, "varying the amount of electric current produced" and thus changing the audible output from the E63 backpack[26] (see fig. 11.1).

While the people sniffer's most charismatic form (at least as presented in later communication with the public) was as a backpack, the most common usage, according to declassified documents, was via aerial reconnaissance.[27] The jungle canopy's limited sight lines made molecular detection desirable, while the limited capability of the human sensorium called for new sensing practices that increasingly distanced American soldiers from the on-the-ground combat the American public was losing patience with.

Racializing Science: Essentialized Olfaction

Public-facing reports such as those from the *New York Times* were careful to indicate that the people sniffer was useless around US troops due to its

Fig. 11.1 "Smelling" the enemy technically: photo of the E63 Manpack Personnel Detector, colloquially known as the "people sniffer," October 10, 1966 (photographer unknown). Courtesy of National Archives, Photographs of American Military Activities, ca. 1918–ca. 1981, no. 11-1-NA 111-SC-634782-001.

inability to distinguish friend from foe. Yet the mention of compound sigma as a molecule *unique* to human bodies calls attention to the larger research context that the people sniffer existed in. The late 1960s were a heady time for researchers interested in olfaction.

One in particular, Dr. Andrew Dravnieks of the Illinois Institute of Technology, was especially interested in human bodies' unique olfactory signatures. Dravnieks's career trajectory was shaped by war. Born in St. Petersburg in 1912, he graduated with a degree in chemical engineering from the University of Latvia in 1938. He lived in Riga during German and Soviet occupation and then immigrated to the United States to pursue a doctoral degree in chemistry at the Illinois Institute of Technical Research. After naturalizing in 1952, Dravnieks spent most of his career examining the chemistry of odors.[28] In the 1960s, Dravnieks expanded his research to participate in the home-front effort to influence US success in the Vietnam theater, having obtained funding from the US Army to determine the olfactory signatures of humans in general as well as whether humans had unique olfactory fingerprints. Dravnieks and his colleagues accomplished this by sticking people into a six-foot-long glass tube and running air over them for analysis using the new gas chromatography technology.[29] For Dravnieks, odors were chemistry in action.

Dravnieks's efforts seemed to offer a promising level of nuance to the blunt olfactory information gathered by the people sniffer. He told reporters from the Chicago-based *Muhammed Speaks* paper—a publication of the Nation of Islam—that "persons have basically two kinds of odors associated with them. There are those inherent in a person's race and those picked up from environment."[30] In other words, Dravnieks understood that people inherently carried with them molecular markers that matched not only where they lived and those they interacted with but also revealed racial characteristics on the molecular level. It is perhaps not surprising that *Muhammed Speaks* was the news outlet to give voice to the racial implications of Dravnieks's work, headlining the short article with "Whites have definite odor states scientific report," given the racialized nature of the Black nationalist agenda promoted by the Nation of Islam—a response to science supporting *white* conceptions of superiority in the same period.[31]

A 1966 report in the popular science magazine *New Scientist* similarly claimed that women and men exhibited distinct olfactory profiles; it pointed out that machine readings demonstrated white males of unmarked nationality "smelled" differently than immigrant students from India.[32] When considered alongside the people sniffer's development, Dravnieks's work reveals the US Army's interest in using sensing practices that undo human olfaction altogether by removing the human nose, while also drawing together the most human of assumptions about race. In other words, Dravnieks's efforts highlight the prevalence of an essentialized understanding of different groups of people as fundamentally "smelling" and smelling in ways that could be detected by a machine more sensitive to olfactory cues than the human nose.

Olfactory stereotyping or racism may seem an ingrained human activity. Certainly, humans from different regions, with different cultural patterns, values, or diets, offered up different olfactory cues to smelling noses. However, as Mark M. Smith points out, smell's social function in Western society has fundamentally changed over time: beginning in the late nineteenth and into much of the twentieth century, odor became something that scientists and others used not just to differentiate between groups but also to "supposedly 'detect' race and ethnicity."[33] Andrew Kettler similarly notes that olfactory othering is historically and culturally situated; it was central to maintaining extractive economic systems that used sensorial arguments to justify the commodification of enslaved black bodies.[34] Dravnieks's work thus extended a long line of efforts in Western society to disambiguate between individuals based not on a visual cue—understood here as unreliable—but rather on an olfactory cue indelibly tied to some understanding of a fundamental difference in olfaction between races.

Odorized Battlegrounds: The Smeller in Action

Different divisions in Vietnam reported different results using the people sniffer. For the 101st Airborne Division, the people sniffer primarily served as an initial detection device. A report covering the period May 1970 to January 1971 stated that "hot spots" of ammonia, carbon, and compound sigma signaled to the division that it had to follow up with "visual reconnaissance, aerial rocket and cannon artillery, CS agent [o-chlorobenzalmalononitrile, also referred to as super tear gas], air strikes, and/or insertion of troops."[35] Although the people sniffer was consistently used when requested, reports in the following year indicate that its olfactory signal could not compete with the skill of the "trained eye of the air cavalry observer."[36] Reports from the experience of the 9th Infantry Division were more positive. During one period of use, "over one half of all significant readings to which we [the division] reacted resulted in contacts." This success, however, was the result of the careful retraining of the sensing practices of the division. Rather than basing decisions simply on readings, the infantry division "relied heavily on the air cavalry to sort out our readings ... hovering over areas of significant readings seeking visual information."[37] These on-the-ground and aerial forms of sensing extended the human sensorium in ways that looked nothing like everyday practices of perception and were further enhanced by the use of CS agent to physically force any humans in the area (at least those not in bunkers) to move.

The technological challenges of the people sniffer contributed to the reshaping of sensing practices in Vietnam. Olfaction could not detect trace amounts of molecular information left behind by foes' bodies. Although research such as Dravnieks's seemed to promise a future in which instrumental sniffing could distinguish between American and Viet Cong soldiers, the on-the-ground reality was that of a blunt instrument whose readings "required careful employment and proper interpretation" before they could differentiate between residual scents and those of people active in an area.[38] A pre-1970 television report by Steve Rowan for CBS made this challenge especially clear as it took viewers into the chopper and onto the ground to better understand how the sniffer worked:[39]

> [ROWAN] Here's one way to find the enemy: fly low enough so that he'll shoot at you. But these daredevils of the 1st Infantry Division are doing much more than that. They're looking for enemy troops with the sniffer, a device that picks up the tell-tale odors of campfire smoke and urine, signaling their presence in the atmosphere like a thermometer registers the temperature. Hours at a time, back and forth over the jungle-covered areas populated only by unfriendly individuals with guns. A closer look at the sniffer with Captain Paul Gardener, Wood River Junction, Rhode Island.
>
> [GARDENER] This piece of equipment operates on the principle of just taking an air sample into it, processing some of the effluents, smells, given off by the humans, and giving you eventually a reading here on the meter.
>
> [ROWAN] With the sniffer mounted in the chopper moving at about eighty knots or so right over the treetops, does that give you enough time to pick up a smell and analyze it and get a reading on it?
>
> [GARDENER] It sure does. We find that we hit a hot spot and we have a reading on this within a matter of a couple of seconds. . . .

[ROWAN] The dial indicates there's something down there. A campfire? A group of V.C. ["Victor Charlie," the US Army code for Viet Cong]? Or a few harmless water buffalo? Well, that the sniffer doesn't know. But something. The spot is marked on the map by an observer flying overhead. The coordinates given to the artillery boards [indistinct] so they can give the area the once-over tonight.

[UNKNOWN] 000 218 these last readings are all . . .

[ROWAN] A little later, another cluster of hot spots. And someone spots a [indistinct] beneath the trees. No friendlies living in the area so permission to fire is granted. And the escorting gunships race in [sound of gunfire]. Today's mission is over. The map now contains marks indicating an area where the sniffer found evidence of human habitation. Tonight artillery will pound that area. If the V.C. are there, they'll have to move. Tomorrow the sniffer will be smelling them out again. Steve Rowan, CBS News.

Sniffing's success depended on coordination between land-based and air-based divisions, use of visual confirmation and visualizing technologies such as cameras, and even additional chemical inputs such as CS gas to force humans on the ground to move. This unwieldy assemblage divided the work of sensing into a range of different sensing practices. Sniffing in Vietnam no longer bore even a passing resemblance to smelling. Rather, sniffing coupled together multiple sensory modes that in turn decoupled any individual's sensory experience into constituent parts that had to enter into the larger assemblage of identification, detection, and analysis to function.

Politics in the Decoupled Sensorium

For a technology supposedly shrouded in secrecy and characterized by classification, the people sniffer received a surprising amount of press. From CBS news reports to articles in major newspapers such as the *New York Times* and popular periodicals like *Time* and *Popular Mechanics*, the sniffer's existence was readily available for the US-based public's consideration.[40] The timing of the declassification of the sniffer seems relevant. Between 1966 and 1967, public opinion about American involvement in Vietnam began to decline. While polling in 1966 and 1967 demonstrated continued support for the war effort, media attention to the war, and to a growing protest movement, put the war effort and the Lyndon B. Johnson administration's involvement in it on increasingly unsteady footing.

Johnson brought to his presidency an established interest in the domestic and international potential of technological innovation. Historians of science characterize the Johnson administration as especially supportive of applied science as a tool for bringing about political goals.[41] The various forms of electronic intelligence developed to assist troops in the Vietnam War aligned with these aims, seeking to give American soldiers a distinct advantage against the immediate threat of North Vietnam fighters and the extended threat of communism. More critically, the forms of technological and electronic intelligence developed offered a potential solution to what Edward Fairhead terms the "spectacle of the military body"—in other words, they increased the ability to wage warfare at a distance.[42]

Partial declassification of sensing technologies like the people sniffer entered into a civilian environment in which individual sensing was constantly being reformed. Twentieth-century innovations such as telephones, automobiles, televisions, personal cameras, and even building technologies increasingly distributed everyday sensing well beyond the confines of a human body in ways only previously hinted at. In this new world, characterized by an increase in the modes and types of sensor technologies, olfactory experience remained obdurately embedded in individual bodies until the 1960s. Sniffing required living noses attached to thinking brains. The sniffer, partially declassified, presented to the American public a testament of US technological superiority over the sensorium, a superiority that—or so the implicit promise went—could turn the war's tide toward conclusion. Olfaction entered into the larger efforts to persuade the public to support the war.

But the people sniffer did not work the way its developers and funders had hoped. Readings were too blunt to provide the precision necessary to allow effective on-the-ground identification. Reports indicate that the backpack version emitted "a faint audible tick that made it particularly unpopular and unnerving for those designated on point."[43] Success required assembling a multiplicity of sensing practices and sensors. Like the other charismatic technologies introduced to the public in the late 1960s, the people sniffer came up against an expanded home-based sensorium in which sensing extended well beyond the body. Gallup polls, death tolls, and on-the-ground reporting from the war front created their own sensory landscape. Even if the reporting was from a distance and networks edited out graphic violence or collaborated with the US government, the home-based sensorium nonetheless had an increased level of access to conflict abroad.[44] In October 1967, the new editor of *Time* and *Life*, publications both previously supportive of the effort, summed up the problem: it was tough at best to ask young Americans to die for "a highly important—but in the last analysis not absolutely imperative—strategic interest of the U.S. and the free world."[45] The society-wide expansion of sensing practices, so critical to decoupling olfaction from the body, contributed to reshaping public opinion in the United States about conflict.

Conclusion

Practices of "smelling the other" were not unique to US armed forces; indeed, some reports indicate that North Vietnamese soldiers were able to smell Americans in the jungle.[46] This is not a surprise, given differences in grooming habits and diet between opposing forces, despite efforts to minimize olfactory traces. However, the sniffer did more than simply recreate everyday human practices of smelling. Its emergence within efforts to develop and deploy new technological modes of sensing transformed the social, physiological, and cultural practices of olfaction into mechanical olfaction. The apparent objectivity of the people sniffer, and its ability to "smell" at a distance that exceeded human eyesight, obfuscated the scientific histories of essentializing olfactory molecules into racialized and gendered categories that undergirded the instrument's development. The "deployment" of the people sniffer in written and televised news reports at home further erased these histories, presenting to the consuming public a picture of olfaction as a practice that could be stripped of its cultural trappings. As such, the sniffer carries with it a cautionary tale as well as a reminder of olfaction's power: even if the sniffer did not succeed in its stated aims in helping "win" the Vietnam War, the scientific efforts supporting the sniffer's production and implementation in the battlefield reverberate into the present. Made molecular, odors came to be understood as potential biomarkers. In their most benign form, odors are biomarkers of age, disease, or disorder.[47] At the same time, when conceptualized as molecular, odors become another data stream ready for mining.[48] What ultimately gets mined, however, depends entirely on the social ideals and norms shaping scientific conduct.

Notes

1. Dennis S. Pogany, "Operational Report—Lessons Learned, 3rd Brigade (Separate), 1st Cavalry Division (Airmobile), Period Ending 31 October 1971, RCS CS FOR-65," November 13, 1971, Department of the Army, Defense Technical Information Center (hereafter DTIC).
2. See Davidson (1988); Spector (2023).
3. See Daddis, "No Sure Victory."
4. See Hacker, "Machines of War."
5. See Gibson, *Perfect War*; Shaw, "Scorched Atmospheres."
6. See Hacker, "Machines of War."
7. Hacker, "Machines of War," 274.
8. Butler, "Discourse of Terror," 109–18; McSorley, "Sensate Regimes of War."
9. See Classen, Howes, and Synnott, *Aroma*; Johansen, "Aristotle."
10. See Settles, "Sniffers."
11. See Hediger, "Dogs of War"; Lazarowski and Dorman, "Explosives Detection"; "Dogs of War," *Scientific American* 120, no. 1 (1919): 10–11.
12. See Hockey, "On Patrol"; McSorley, "Sensate Regimes of War."
13. See Saunders and Cornish, *Modern Conflict*.
14. See Leonard, "Sensorial No Man's Land"; Leonard and Breithoff, "Warfare and the Senses."
15. See Belcher, "Sensing, Territory, Population."
16. Gabrys and Pritchard, "Sensing Practices"; Belcher, "Sensing, Territory, Population."
17. See Gabrys, "Sensors and Sensing Practices." See also Helmreich, "Anthropologist Underwater"; Ballestero, *Future History of Water*; Shapiro, "Attuning to the Chemosphere."
18. I do not have the sources to treat this topic equally from the Vietnamese perspective.
19. In the English language, sniffing is also understood as a process of showing contempt or investigating. In its noun form, the sniff is an action of sampling through a nose.
20. See Callow, "Odour and Ethnicity."
21. See Gerontas, "Creating New Technologists"; Spackman, "Perfumer, Chemist, Machine."
22. See Spackman, "Perfumer, Chemist, Machine"; Spackman, "Ordering Volatile Openings."
23. Ewell and Hunt, *Sharpening the Combat Edge*, 147.
24. "U.S. Airborne Device Sniffs for Foe under Jungle Canopy," *New York Times*, May 28, 1967.
25. See "'People Sniffer' Goes to War in Vietnam," *New York Times*, July 16, 1967.
26. "Sniffing Out the Enemy," *Time* 89, no. 23 (1967): 88.
27. See Department of the Army, "Senior Officer Debriefing Report: John J. Hennessey, 101st Airborne Division—Period May 1970 to January 1971 (U)," January 15, 1971, DTIC, https://apps.dtic.mil/sti/citations/tr/AD0514578; Department of the Army, "Senior Officer Debriefing Report: Major General Thomas M. Tarpley, CG, 101st Airborne Division (Airmobile)—Period February 1971 to February 1972 (U)," July 13, 1972, DTIC, https://apps.dtic.mil/sti/pdfs/AD0521407.pdf; Pogany, "Operational Report—Lessons Learned"; Department of the Army, "Senior Officer Debriefing Report: MG John M. Wright, Jr, CG, 101st Airborne Division (Airmobile)—Period 25 May 1969 to 25 May 1970 (U)," July 10, 1970, DTIC, https://apps.dtic.mil/sti/citations/tr/AD 0510128.
28. See Editorial Board, "Tribute to Andrew Dravnieks."
29. See Dravnieks and Krostoszynski, "Human Vapors."
30. "Whites Have Definite Odor States Scientific Report," *Muhammed Speaks* 4, no. 37 (1965).
31. Ogbar, *Black Power*, 3; Tucker, *Science and Politics*.
32. Dravnieks, "Odours as Signatures."
33. Smith, "Transcending, Othering, Detecting," 381.
34. See Kettler, *Smell of Slavery*.
35. Department of the Army, "Senior Officer Debriefing: Hennessey."
36. Department of the Army, "Senior Officer Debriefing: Tarpley," 14, 41.
37. Ewell and Hunt, *Sharpening the Combat Edge*, 148–49.
38. Ewell and Hunt, *Sharpening the Combat Edge*, 148.

39. Dating for this untitled segment featuring Steve Rowan reporting on the sniffer is based on the fact that Rowan left his post as CBS's Pentagon correspondent in late 1969 or 1970. See Mudd, *Place to Be*, 80; "Vietnam War Footage 'People Sniffer' (1st Infantry)," originally aired on CBS, pre-1972, posted on October 20, 2018, ShockandAwe-USA, YouTube video, 2:47, https://www.youtube.com/watch?v=mXoNLLdJ1Tw.

40. See "'People Sniffer' Goes to War in Vietnam"; "Applied Science: Sniffing Out the Enemy," *Time*, June 9, 1967, http://content.time.com/time/subscriber/article/0,33009,843899,00.html; Wallace Cloud, "Amazing New Science Called Olfactronics: Now They'll Know You," *Popular Mechanics*, February 1968.

41. See Martini, "Chemical War"; Doel and Harper, "Prometheus Unleashed."

42. Fairhead, "Supplanting the Spectacle"; Adams, "Future Warfare."

43. Kirby, "Operation Snoopy," 20–22; McSorley, "Sensate Regimes of War."

44. See Hammond, "Press in Vietnam"; Griffin, "Media Images"; Hallin, *Uncensored War*.

45. Cited in Donovan and Scherer, *Unsilent Revolution*.

46. See Gibbons, "Intimate Sense of Smell," cited in Le Breton, *Sensing the World*, 276.

47. See Mitro et al., "Smell of Age"; Kataoka et al., "Noninvasive Analysis."

48. See Jha et al., "Human Body Odor"; Vesovic, Zlatanovic, and Teodorovic, "How Do I Smell?"

Bibliography

Archival Sources

Department of the Army, Defense Technical Information Center, Fort Belvoir, VA: 101st Airborne Division (Airmobile)—Periods 25 May 1969 to 25 May 1970 (U), May 1970 to January 1971 (U), and February 1971 to February 1972 (U); 1st Cavalry Division (Airmobile)—Period Ending 31 October 1971.

Audiovisual Source

"Vietnam War Footage 'People Sniffer' (1st Infantry)." Originally aired on CBS, pre-1972. Posted on October 20, 2018, by ShockandAweUSA. YouTube video, 2:47. https://www.youtube.com/watch?v=mXoNLLdJ1Tw.

Published Sources

Adams, Thomas K. "Future Warfare and the Decline of Human Decisionmaking." *Parameters* 41, no. 4 (2001): 57–71.

Ballestero, Andrea. *A Future History of Water*. Durham: Duke University Press, 2019.

Belcher, Oliver. "Sensing, Territory, Population: Computation, Embodied Sensors, and Hamlet Control in the Vietnam War." *Security Dialogue* 50, no. 5 (2019): 416–36.

Butler, Judith. "The Discourse of Terror." In *Weapon of the Strong: Conversations on US State Terrorism*, edited by Jon Bailes and Cihan Aksan, 109–18. London: Pluto Press, 2012.

Callow, Susannah. "Odour and Ethnicity: Americans and Japanese in the Second World War." In Saunders and Cornish, *Modern Conflict and the Senses*, 157–70.

Classen, Constance, David Howes, and Anthony Synnott. *Aroma: The Cultural History of Smell*. London: Routledge, 1994.

Daddis, Gregory A. "No Sure Victory: Measuring U.S. Army Effectiveness and Progress in the Vietnam War." PhD diss., University of North Carolina at Chapel Hill, 2009.

Davidson, Phillip B. *Vietnam at War*. Oxford: Oxford University Press, 1988.

Doel, Ronald E., and Kristine C. Harper. "Prometheus Unleashed: Science as a Diplomatic Weapon in the Lyndon B. Johnson Administration." *Osiris* 21, no. 1 (2006): 66–85.

Donovan, Robert J., and Ray Scherer. *Unsilent Revolution: Television News and American Public Life*. Cambridge: Cambridge University Press, 1992.

Dravnieks, Andrew. "Odours as Signatures." *New Scientist* 31 (September 1966): 622–24.

Dravnieks, Andrew, and Boguslaw Krostoszynski. "Human Vapors May Be

Chemical Signatures." *Chemical and Engineering News*, April 19, 1965.

Editorial Board. "A Tribute to Andrew Dravnieks." *Chemical Senses* 14, no. 1 (1989): 3–9.

Ewell, Julian J., and Ira A. Hunt Jr. *Sharpening the Combat Edge: The Use of Analysis to Reinforce Military Judgment*. Vietnam Studies. Washington, DC: Department of the Army, 1974.

Fairhead, Edward. "Supplanting the Spectacle of Sacrifice: Drone Warfare and the Anti-Spectacle of the Safe Military Body." *Media, War and Conflict*, December 12, 2019.

Gabrys, Jennifer. "Sensors and Sensing Practices: Reworking Experience Across Entities, Environments, and Technologies." *Science, Technology, and Human Values* 44, no. 5 (2019): 723–36.

Gabrys, Jennifer, and Helen Pritchard. "Sensing Practices." In *Posthuman Glossary*, edited by Rosi Braidotti and Maria Hlavajova, 394–95. Theory in the New Humanities. London: Bloomsbury Academic, 2018.

Gerontas, Apostolos. "Creating New Technologists of Research in the 1960s: The Case of the Reproduction of Automated Chromatography Specialists and Practitioners." *Science and Education* 23 (2014): 1681–1700.

Gibbons, Boyd. "The Intimate Sense of Smell." *National Geographic* 170 (1986): 324–61.

Gibson, James W. *The Perfect War: Technowar in Vietnam*. New York: Atlantic Monthly Press, 2000.

Griffin, Michael. "Media Images of War." *Media, War and Conflict* 3, no. 1 (2010): 7–41.

Hacker, Barton C. "The Machines of War: Western Military Technology, 1850–2000." *History and Technology* 21, no. 3 (2005): 255–300.

Hallin, Daniel C. *The Uncensored War: The Media and Vietnam*. Berkeley: University of California Press, 1989.

Hammond, William M. "The Press in Vietnam as Agent of Defeat: A Critical Examination." *Reviews in American History* 17, no. 2 (1989): 312–23.

Hediger, Ryan. "Dogs of War: The Biopolitics of Loving and Leaving the U.S. Canine Forces in Vietnam." *Animal Studies Journal* 2, no. 1 (2013): 55–73.

Helmreich, Stefan. "An Anthropologist Underwater: Immersive Soundscapes, Submarine Cyborgs, and Transductive Ethnography." *American Ethnologist* 34, no. 4 (2007): 621–41.

Hockey, John. "On Patrol: The Embodied Phenomenology of Infantry." In *War and the Body: Militarisation, Practice and Experience*, edited by Kevin McSorley, 93–105. London: Routledge, 2013.

Jha, Sunil K., Ninoslav Marina, Chuanjun Liu, and Kenshi Hayashi. "Human Body Odor Discrimination by GC-MS Spectra Data Mining." *Analytical Methods* 7, no. 22 (2015): 9549–61.

Johansen, Thomas. "Aristotle on the Sense of Smell." *Phronesis* 41, no. 1 (1996): 1–19.

Kataoka, Hiroyuki, Keita Saito, Hisato Kato, and Kazufumi Masuda. "Noninvasive Analysis of Volatile Biomarkers in Human Emanations for Health and Early Disease Diagnosis." *Bioanalysis* 5, no. 11 (2013): 1443–59.

Kettler, Andrew. *The Smell of Slavery: Olfactory Racism and the Atlantic World*. Cambridge: Cambridge University Press, 2020.

Kirby, Reid. "Operation Snoopy: The Chemical Corps' 'People Sniffer.'" *Army Chemical Review* (January–June 2007): 20–22.

Lawrence, Mark Atwood. *The Vietnam War: A Concise International History*. Oxford: Oxford University Press, 2008.

Lazarowski, Lucia, and David C. Dorman. "Explosives Detection by Military Working Dogs: Olfactory Generalization from Components to Mixtures." *Applied Animal Behaviour Science* 151 (February 2014): 84–93.

Le Breton, David. *Sensing the World: An Anthropology of the Senses*. Translated by Carmen Ruschiensky. New York: Routledge, 2020.

Leonard, Matthew. "A Sensorial No Man's Land: Corporeality and the Western Front during the First World War." *Senses and Society* 14, no. 3 (2019): 257–70.

Leonard, Matthew, and Esther Breithoff. "Warfare and the Senses: Archaeologies of the Senses and Sensorial Archaeologies of Recent Conflict." In *The Routledge Handbook of Sensory Archaeology*, edited by Robin Skeates and Jo Day, 281–92. London: Routledge, 2019.

Martini, Edwin A. "The Chemical War in Vietnam and the Illusion of Control." *War and Society* 31, no. 3 (2012): 264–79.

McSorley, Kevin. "Sensate Regimes of War: Smell, Tracing and Violence." *Security Dialogue* 51, no. 2–3 (2020): 155–73.

Mitro, Susanna, Amy R. Gordon, Mats J. Olsson, and Johan N. Lundström. "The Smell of Age: Perception and Discrimination of Body Odors of Different Ages." *PLOS ONE* 7, no. 5 (2012): e38110.

Mudd, Roger. *The Place to Be: Washington, CBS, and the Glory Days of Television News*. New York: PublicAffairs, 2008.

Ogbar, Jeffrey O. G. *Black Power: Radical Politics and African American Identity*. Baltimore: Johns Hopkins University Press, 2004.

Saunders, Nicholas J., and Paul Cornish, eds. *Modern Conflict and the Senses*. New York: Routledge, 2017.

Settles, Gary S. "Sniffers: Fluid-Dynamic Sampling for Olfactory Trace Detection in Nature and Homeland Security—The 2004 Freeman Scholar Lecture." *Journal of Fluids Engineering* 127, no. 2 (2005): 189–218.

Shapiro, Nicholas. "Attuning to the Chemosphere: Domestic Formaldehyde, Bodily Reasoning, and the Chemical Sublime." *Cultural Anthropology* 30, no. 3 (2015): 368–93.

Shaw, Ian G. R. "Scorched Atmospheres: The Violent Geographies of the Vietnam War and the Rise of Drone Warfare." *Annals of the American Association of Geographers* 106, no. 3 (2016): 688–704.

Smith, Mark M. "Transcending, Othering, Detecting: Smell, Premodernity, Modernity." *Postmedieval: A Journal of Medieval Cultural Studies* 3, no. 4 (2012): 380–90.

Spackman, Christy. "Ordering Volatile Openings: Instrumentation and the Rationalization of Bodily Odors." *Food, Culture and Society* 22, no. 5 (2019): 674–91.

———. "Perfumer, Chemist, Machine: Gas Chromatography and the Industrial Search to 'Improve' Flavor." *Senses and Society* 13, no. 1 (2018).

Spector, R. H. "Vietnam War." In *Encyclopedia Britannica*. Britannica. Article published July 20, 1998; last modified January 27, 2024. https://www.britannica.com/event/Vietnam-War.

Tucker, William H. *The Science and Politics of Racial Research*. Urbana: University of Illinois Press, 1994.

Vesovic, Jovana, Anja Zlatanovic, and Smilja Teodorovic. "How Do I Smell? The Potential of Body Odor in Human Personal Identification." *Archibald Reiss Days* 9, no. 2 (2019). https://eskup.kpu.edu.rs/dar/article/view/82.

CHAPTER 12

Heroes at the Hindu Kush

Seeing the Afghan War Through the Soviet Lens

Markus Mirschel
Translated from German by Adam Blauhut

On January 13, 1980, Soviet head of state Leonid Brezhnev made an official statement about Russian intervention in Afghanistan. The leading Soviet newspaper *Pravda* quoted him as saying that it was unacceptable for Russia's traditionally important, strategic southern flank to fall into imperialist hands. His comments formed the core of the Soviet justification for military action in Afghanistan. It was essential, Brezhnev explained, that the Democratic Republic of Afghanistan remain within the Soviet sphere of influence. The now reestablished 40th Army, which had been dissolved after the Second World War, was to oversee the construction of important infrastructure without an official combat mission. According to Brezhnev, the Soviet Union needed to deploy a Limited Contingent of Soviet Troops in Afghanistan (OKSVA) to assist the Afghan army in its struggle against the domestic Afghan opposition, which was growing in strength, and the mujahideen operating out of Pakistan. Officially, this assistance was to take the form of logistic support and military training.[1]

This article was written as part of the research network "Landschaften der Verfolgung" and was funded by the German Federal Ministry of Education and Research.

The Soviet invasion of Afghanistan led to one of the late "hot" conflicts of the Cold War. Contemporary commentators—having experienced a phase of relative détente between the blocs in the 1970s—even referred to it as the start of a "Second Cold War."[2] The crossing of the Afghan-Soviet border on December 25, 1979, by 40th Army troops is generally considered the start of the Soviet war in Afghanistan. Two days later, elite Soviet forces stormed the presidential palace in Kabul, killing the sitting president Hafizullah Amin. Soviet-friendly Babrak Karmal was installed as the Afghan head of state, and there followed a more than ten-year war in which the Soviet and Afghan armies fought the Afghan resistance movement and the mujahideen. During its course, the troops sent by the leadership of the Communist Party and the military engaged in a grueling fight in the mountains, the rural settlements (*kishlaks*), and the oases (so-called green zones) of Afghanistan. Pakistan, the United States, Great Britain, and the People's Republic of China intervened in the war on the side of the mujahideen, providing weapons, intelligence, and logistics support. By the time Soviet troops officially withdrew on February 15, 1989, around fifteen thousand Soviet military personnel had lost their lives and tens of thousands had returned home with psychological and physical injuries. The intervention was equally devastating for the Afghan population. Although it is impossible to say exactly how many were killed in the war, estimates run between one hundred thousand and one million. Five million Afghans fled to the neighboring states of Pakistan and Iran, and an additional two million became internally displaced persons.[3]

At the same time, a protracted strategic "war of images" began. This chapter will use Soviet press and military photographs to shed light on how the war in Afghanistan shaped seeing and how seeing in turn shaped the Afghanistan war. It will illustrate which militarily charged subjects the conflict produced and which specific Soviet traditions these subjects came from.[4] Visual studies and sensory history have emphasized that seeing is not a timeless biological constant but a culturally specific and historically variable practice. From an anthropological perspective, what is seen, how it is seen, and what is ignored is always linked to the recognition of entirely different historical risks and chances of survival.[5] The history of seeing has been determined not only by natural dangers but also by conflicts and numerous technical inventions, including observation from elevated "bird's-eye" views (e.g., balloons and drones), optical reconnaissance and targeting systems, and modern imaging techniques such as night vision, thermography, and sonar. According to sensory historian Robert Jütte, these innovations transform the eye into "a weapon."[6] However, the front is not the only place where seeing is shaped. During military and nonmilitary conflicts, political propaganda also attempts to condition the gaze of civilian society. The Soviet Union was particularly influential in the field of photographic modes of seeing. With its photo art, the Soviet avant-garde exerted a significant influence on international photography, and early on, the Soviet state used photographs to visually stage politics. This is shown by numerous well-known examples from the first half of the twentieth century: in some cases, official state photographs of the nomenklatura were retouched to erase from view disgraced figures including Leon Trotsky, Lev Kamenev, and Grigory Zinoviev;[7] in others, historical events were restaged, idealized, and iconized—for example, the raising of the Red Flag over the German Reichstag in Berlin by Soviet troops in 1945.[8]

During the Cold War, too, the imagery of Soviet photos was complex in terms of its genesis and the way it was perceived. The visual discourse, however, was determined by the officially sanctioned photos disseminated by press agencies and daily newspapers. Their imagery was devoted to enforcing and securing the ruling doctrine. In the young Soviet Union, photos served mainly as a means of communication—typical of largely illiterate societies. The Soviet leadership wanted utopias to be presented as both feasible and desirable through such images.

Views from a Distance: The War that Was Not Supposed to Look Like a War

Following the guidelines for depictions of "internationalist brotherly aid," photographers in Afghanistan produced images that served mainly to show the peaceful reconstruction of the country after the April Revolution of 1978. By contrast, the military-related photos focused on the successes of the Afghan army and depicted the contingent of Soviet troops as far removed from the actual conflict. The war photos documenting the troops' mission were taken mainly by military personnel, and most were published in one of the Soviet Union's fifteen military newspapers—primarily in *Krasnaja Zvezda*, which was increasingly targeting a civilian readership and, due to its large circulation, had a far-ranging impact on Soviet society.[9] Traditional images of a political transformation process that included the development of key industries and education campaigns were reserved mainly for the civilian press.

In both the military and civilian press, photos from Afghanistan were subject to extensive censorship by the USSR Council of Ministers, the military authorities, and the Soviet secret service, the KGB.[10] As a result, Soviet society only got to see a select, closely curated corpus of images, which governed the view of the Soviet-Afghan war from the outset. Neither the bloody storming of the presidential palace in Kabul on December 27, 1979, nor the roughly thirteen hundred Soviet soldiers killed in 1980 were covered by the media. The images of the war that still exist today are propagandistic in nature. Despite all the regulations, though, private shots were also taken. These circulated among the contingent soldiers and were only made accessible to a broader public through efforts to come to grips with the past and to promote a culture of remembrance. Their reception took place later on in the form of commemorative books and meaningful exhibitions organized by newly constituted veterans' associations or the military.[11]

A scene captured in spring 1980 by the photographer Georgy Naděždin, who worked for the Soviet news agency TASS, shows how the deployment of contingent soldiers was visually reinterpreted as an aid mission and how the soldiers' military role was initially negated. In fall 1980, the untitled image ran in slightly cropped form in *Krasnaja Zvezda*. The numerical proportions of the two groups shown highlights the efficiency of the regular Afghan army:[12] in the image, a single Afghan soldier escorts six "counterrevolutionaries."[13] The visual representation of the Afghans reveals both a positively and negatively charged construction of the "other." The young male guard is armed with a modern Soviet-made assault rifle. His face is shaven in a modern style, and he wears the regular field uniform of the Afghan army. His mostly older prisoners have long beards, turbans, and everyday clothes, giving them a traditional appearance. Unarmed and with their hands tied behind their backs, they symbolize an eliminated and thus controllable danger. This is also emphasized by the protagonists' line of sight: except for one prisoner who wears a furtive glance, they are all looking at the ground or at a point outside the frame. The young soldier gazes directly and confidently at the camera (see fig. 12.1).

The photo conveys the idea that the progressive government in Kabul is successfully opposing conservative Afghanistan. In Soviet society, attributes such as beards and turbans stood for backwardness, religiosity, and tradition. The young soldier, by contrast, embodied the country's future. The visual language suggests that "while the young soldier is the future, the elderly outlaws are a phenomenon of the past."[14] The caption itself is normative; in place of the usual factual formulations that soberly describe what viewers can see with their own eyes anyway, it offers an evaluative interpretation

Fig. 12.1 Staging superiority: a single Afghan soldier escorts six "counterrevolutionaries" in 1980. Photo: picture alliance / TASS / George Nadežhdin.

in the sense of instructions or even a subliminal training of the eye: "Thus continued the successful operations to liquidate the mercenary counterrevolutionary groups that were sent into the country from abroad. . . . They cannot escape retribution."[15] Such images suggested that structures existed in Afghan that would continue to function in the future even without Soviet support. They held out the prospect of a successful end to the Soviet mission and a return to normalcy. In addition, they provided evidence of foreign interference in the affairs of the Democratic Republic of Afghanistan, which the Soviet government officially cited to legitimize its intervention. The captions focused the gaze and simultaneously conditioned the way Soviet citizens saw the new subjects. In these visualizations of the "other," representations of the negatively charged mujahideen remained more or less the same until the end of the Soviet engagement. For the Soviet Union, it became increasingly important to portray the mujahideen as adversaries. By contrast, the group of Soviet allies grew increasingly diverse, always in line with the current political situation. Over the years, even the tribal leaders and warlords who initially were exoticized were presented as heroes.[16] This mostly occurred when they were shown fighting side by side with the troops of the Afghan government against the common enemy, the mujahideen. Soviet soldiers, for their part, were depicted far from the actual conflict, securing Afghan airspace or remaining in their camps.[17]

Initially, the Soviet Union was able to maintain its self-image as a peacekeeping force. Photos of the early years of the war show joint work assignments (dubbed *subbotniks*) and friendly meetings between the Afghan population and members of the Soviet army. Three groups of motifs can be identified: (1) shots of the Afghan army, captured mostly during field exercises or with captured enemies (used to show "Afghan efficiency");[18] (2) visualizations of enemy activities, mostly in images of confiscated weaponry or enemy propaganda (used to show "legitimization of intervention");[19] and (3) photos of the Soviet presence focusing on patrols, maintenance work, and everyday scenes in the troops' living quarters (used to show "support far from the conflict").

Black Tulips at the Hindu Kush: Changing Visual Symbols

Coverage of military conflict plays a special role in the history of Soviet photography. This is especially true of the key military event of the twentieth century, the Second World War (known as the "Great Patriotic War" in the Soviet Union). In contrast to the Western Allies and Nazi Germany, whose image policies sought to conceal the atrocities of war, the Soviet press made extensive use of photographs to present evidence of fascist atrocities. These images often served as "hooks" on the front pages of the daily press.[20] However, during the Soviet Union's later military conflicts, especially its military intervention in Afghanistan, such visual language was rarely repeated. In the 1980s, the Soviet press published only a few images whose subjects came close to showing the cruelty of war. In the coverage of Afghanistan, images provided evidence of the actions of the revolution's opponents. Dead Afghans were the only victims of war that Soviet society got to see. The humanitarian actions of the Soviet army were emphasized, while those of the enemy were portrayed as violent and brutal.[21]

A crucial difference between the Great Patriotic War and the Soviet-Afghan war lay in the accessibility of the frontline experience in the former conflict, which enabled the Soviet photographers of the 1940s to show people at the front—soldiers and their commanders—during tactical combat operations. By contrast, the war at the Hindu Kush was a clandestine one for a long time, as Vladimir Vyatkin, one of the first on-the-ground photographers in Afghanistan, made clear. "Not only were we forbidden to take photos of our troops and military actions, it was also impossible even to talk about them," he reported. "In other words, [for the first two years] we were not even allowed to use the word 'war.'"[22] The Soviet photographers of the Second World War had been active soldiers and officers of the Red Army, who saw action at the front. This is how many of their dynamic images emerged, including *Kombat* by Max Alpert, which shows an officer giving his soldiers the signal to attack, and *Ataka* by Dmitri Baltermants, a blurred photo of an infantry assault. Situationally, these two exemplary images were taken from below and thus borrow from Alexander Rodchenko's ideas on the use of perspective. By contrast, in Afghanistan, journalists and photographers did not have direct access to the theater of war: "They were deprived of the freedom to publish information about the real fighting."[23] Furthermore, it was difficult to create photos of a traditional maneuver war due to the asymmetrical nature of combat in the rugged valleys of the Hindu Kush. Soviet soldiers in Afghanistan were shown standing guard, securing exposed ridges, or transporting matériel, water, and supplies from the Soviet Union through the narrow mountain passes to their own troops and allies.

Depictions of the use of technology to control geographical space were part of the visual canon of both wars. This is true of both airborne and land forces. In terms of perspective, photos of both wars were optically similar and differed only in terms of the state and type of technology portrayed. In the Great Patriotic War, it was the Ilyushin Il-2 fighter plane, the Sturmovik, which took on symbolic value for the air force. Once the Soviet Union had gained air superiority, frontline photographers such as Mark Redkin and Boris Vdovenko (who also served as a gunner on twenty-nine missions)[24] began working directly from the cockpit. In the Soviet-Afghan war, it was the heavy attack helicopters, the Mil Mi-24 gunships, that assumed this visual role. Appearing in staggered formation across the depth of photographed space, they formed the focal point of the images. The horizon in the distance, as well as the prominent ridges of the Hindu Kush, functioned as boundaries to the landscape they flew over. OKSVA helicopter forces shouldered much of the burden of the war, protecting supply convoys, conducting operations in the mountainous hinterlands, and transporting troops—an unusual task for combat helicopters at the time. Due to its omnipresence, the Mil Mi-24 took on the symbolic propagandistic value of the Ilyushin Il-2 or the Soviet T-34 tank in the Great Patriotic War. Because of the large number of missions flown, as well as their versatility and ubiquity (which distinguished them from fast, high-flying fighters and combat planes), the Mil Mi-24s were predestined to serve as visual motifs. The airborne units were often photographed diagonally across the frame—once again, borrowing from Rodchenko—or in tiered formations. Finally, the aircraft also became the focus of attention because artillery battles were ineffective for Soviet forces: the mujahideen operated out of the mountains to evade Soviet fire, or they shifted their activities to the night. In other words, the enemy's war strategies also influenced the images of the conflict.

Omnipresent in the media, the pilots acquired the prestige of the veterans of the war against Nazi Germany. Of the eighty-six OKSVA members to be presented with the title "Hero of the Soviet Union," one-quarter came from the air force. In a letter to the editor of *Kraznaja Zvezda*, one former airman compared the deeds of the aviation heroes Sergej Filipčenkov and Vladimir Kučerenko in Afghanistan to those of aviators in the Great Patriotic War. Soviet photographers frequently used the Mil Mi-8's rounded porthole window to frame their helicopter subjects, which were shown in mixed formations of Mil Mi-8 multipurpose helicopters and combat choppers. The circular frame guided the eye and enhanced the effect of the subjects. Attention was focused on the essentials, as through a telescope. Photos of the flying formations had their heyday in the early years of the Afghan war, but they grew less important toward the end, as more helicopters were shot down due to the increased use of mobile surface-to-air missiles, primarily American Stingers and British Blowpipes.[25] Of the 301 Mil Mi-8s and Mil Mi-24s lost, 145 downings dated to the period 1985–87.[26] As a result, it was no longer possible to present the aircraft as a successful long-distance weapon in the war.

In many of the photos, the subjects are framed by the high ridges of the Hindu Kush. The mountains were the very epitome of a scenic backdrop and could be used for a variety of subjects. To understand the effect of this mountain range, we can draw on Roland Barthes's theory of myths, according to which any material can be endowed with a subjective meaning. As Barthes explains, images reveal their meanings all at once, transforming photos into statements.[27] The fact that these messages cannot be planned makes it difficult to use them strategically. Their interpretation remains subjective and dependent on personal socialization and collective experience, as the sensory history of seeing has shown.[28] How "things" are viewed changes with the historical context. Because of its visual ubiquity, the Hindu Kush, for example, established itself early on as the site of the Afghan conflict—a non-European space of hostilities that was clearly definable for all. The mountain range emerged as a symbol of both an implicit exoticism and the challenges facing the soldiers, and it transformed their ever-smiling faces into a tableau of soldierly romanticism. The barrenness of the mountains conveyed a sense of deprivation; at the same time, the landscape evoked a pioneering, adventuresome spirit. In this way, the conflict provided the soldiers with a meaningful objective for their deployment in Afghanistan: emulation of the heroic deeds of their grandfathers. As one artillery captain wrote in an exemplary passage in his memoirs, "You regretted being born too late and not being around for 1941."[29] Such statements reflected the spirit of sacrifice that stood in continuity with the Great Patriotic War; they also highlighted the internationalist idea. As such, they placed the romanticized soldierly ideals on a historical continuum. However, in the lived experience of the contingent soldiers, the mountain formations were less a romantic backdrop than an unforgiving place where they had to contend with freezing temperatures, danger, and death, as the recollections of one Soviet soldier drastically illustrate: "Three of us had frozen to death. It had happened as usual—a guy fell asleep, and in the morning, he was dead. We dragged those three bodies like enormous icicles."[30]

Turning our attention to the Soviet air force, we find a second piece of evidence for a shift in the connotation of images from positive to negative. The Antonov An-12 and An-26 were frequently used military cargo planes. They were reliable and robust and mainly deployed to transport troops and materials. The visual staging of the An-12 reflected this assessment. Photos of the plane symbolically linked the militarily charged experiential space of Afghanistan to the civilian experiential space of the Soviet Union. After a maximum of two years of service, young men alighted from the planes having graduated from the school of life, the so-called Škola Afganistana, in the Democratic Republic of Afghanistan, as the official interpretation went. Photos showed members of a determined "roll-up-your-sleeves" generation ready to face the adverse conditions of late socialism in the Soviet Union and to meet the demands placed on them by the party leadership. Such images were influenced by a visual tradition focused on camaraderie and confidence.[31] A shift in perception took place in environments where curated visual templates collided with the experienced violent space of Afghanistan.[32] During the Soviet intervention, images, as well as texts, were closely monitored not only by the censors at home who were responsible for the official visual canon but also by regulations in the field. Soviet soldiers were strictly forbidden to take photos or even to have cameras with them. Unlike in the Great Patriot War, in this war the Soviet leadership did not want the soldiers' personal view of events to seep into the closely monitored official imagery. The flow of visual and narrative information from the troops was blocked by strict regulations. In addition, throughout the war, OKSVA's political officers issued rules of their own: "Don't [talk] about fallen comrades because we're a large, strong army. Don't talk about relationships in violation of service regulations because we're a large, strong, and morally sound army. Tear up photos, destroy films."[33] Nonetheless, regulating information flows proved difficult. More than six hundred thousand people, both military and civilian personnel, came into contact with the realities of war during the intervention. It was inevitable that the returnees' impressions and experiences gradually penetrated the protected civilian space of the Soviet Union, calling into question the official Soviet imagery.

Under the code name "Gruz 200" ("Cargo 200"), the bodies of the fallen were placed in sealed coffins and transported home on An-12 aircraft. However, such transports could not be kept secret for long. For the Russian war veterans, or *afgancy*, the frequently photographed An-12 cargo plane became a symbol of military casualties and was colloquially referred to as "Chernyy tyulpan" (Black Tulip). Photographer Vladimir Vyatkin described his first contact with the top-secret mission: "The crates lay there, covered in a kind of camouflage netting. . . . I asked the guard jokingly, 'What's that? Spare parts?' He replied with a sad irony, 'No, that's meat nobody wants anymore.' The crates contained dead soldiers, so-called Cargo 200."[34]

Black Tulips eventually became part of Soviet/Russian memory culture as a symbol of human sacrifice. Stylistically diverse representations of Black Tulips can be found throughout the former Soviet Union in the architecture of the monuments erected to the fallen soldiers.[35] Leningrad singer-songwriter Aleksandr Rozenbaum memorialized the An-12 and the *afgancy* in his song "Monolog pilota 'Chyornogo tulpana'" (Monologue of the pilot of a Black Tulip). The power of photography to steer public opinion eroded under the conditions and experiences of the conflict.

Heroes in Three-Quarter Profile: Camouflage and White Gowns

In Soviet society—populated by "heroes at the ready"[36]—the hero narrative was a universal phenomenon that spanned the civilian sphere (narrative of the "Hero of Socialist Labor") and the military realm (narrative of the

"Hero of the Soviet Union"). The idea of a Soviet army that stood in defense of communism was deeply rooted in the master narrative of a "historical salvation mission" that originated in the experience of the Great Patriotic War.[37] Numerous courageous acts by individuals were reimagined as a mass heroic phenomenon. Under Leonid Brezhnev (1964–1982), this perspective became ever more important because of the general loss of legitimacy of socialist ideals. However, as a result of the merry-go-round of general secretaries that culminated in the appointment of Mikhail Gorbachev (1985–1991), a situation arose in which the reputation of the Soviet army was at risk of being harmed by an inconsistent Afghanistan strategy. Furthermore, just a few months after the start of the Afghanistan intervention, it became clear that the conflict could not be concluded in the envisioned timeframe. The responsible parties recognized that they would have to prepare for the return of the contingent soldiers to Soviet civilian society. These soldiers could not be defined exclusively as a "troop of gardeners" who were planting "avenues of friendship" in Afghanistan—or so was the insight gleaned from the previous coverage of the war.[38] Increasingly, the military demanded the respect it believed it deserved, and from its perspective, the time was ripe for a media strategy of its own. This is why the armed forces attempted to construct a visible media utopia with which to influence civilian society and the post-conflict phase of the intervention. The military continued to assign photos an important role. A 1989 survey by the Russian Public Opinion Research Center (Vserossijskij centr izučenija obščestvennogo mnenija, VCIOM) shows that this policy was correct: 50 percent of respondents said that between 1984 and 1987, their main source of information about events in Afghanistan had been daily papers.[39]

In practice, the awarding of the title of "Hero" was based mainly on military deeds. However, showing these deeds in photos meant admitting that combat operations were underway in Afghan territory. As discussed above, such operations were deliberately suppressed in the Soviet Union's early image strategy. At the start of the war, the visual discourse was considered less important than communication through text with its more clearly recognizable ideological messages. Soviet newspaper publishers continued to follow the decades-old dictum that images were subordinate to words, even reducing photos in size when more space was needed for text.[40] Early on, attentive readers were left wondering what type of "brotherly aid" would qualify soldiers for military medals in Afghanistan.[41] As the war progressed, military newspapers in particular adapted their policies and increasingly filled their pages not only with text but also with images that were linked thematically to Afghanistan.

The first tentative admission of the soldiers' participation in combat operations appeared in the Soviet print media in 1981–82. At that time, there was a clear shift in the hero narrative, followed by new visual strategies that focused on images of "model heroes." One example was Ruslan Aushev, an Ingush native who was celebrated in the media until the end of the intervention and whose story can thus be taken as a useful example of a staged hero narrative. In addition, in the various phases of the conflict, the media temporarily promoted other "Heroes of the Soviet Union," the most notable of whom were Valerij Očirov, an air force officer of Kalmyk descent, and Nabi Akramov, a member of the Tajik ethnic group. They underscored the multiethnic character of the 40th Army and provided a counterpoint to the otherwise Slavic-dominated pantheon of heroes. The visual canon remained committed to traditional imagery from the years of the Russian Revolution, the Civil War, and above all—once again—the Great Patriotic War. The goal was to use photo essays and the skillful combination of historical and contemporary imagery to create a causal link between the Soviet army's finest hours and the events of the 1980s. In 1987, to celebrate the seventieth anniversary of the "Great Socialist October Revolution," Soviet photographers even took things one step further by dressing a group of (Afghanistan) heroes in historical Red Guard uniforms. The banner the soldiers hold is inscribed with the slogan of the communist movement: "Workers of the world unite!" The sunlight breaking through the clouds in the background (an effect probably created in a post-exposure process) conveyed the idea of a "fateful dawn."[42]

The use of the military hero narrative reached a peak in 1984. The newspaper *Kraznaja Zvezda*, for instance, ran the front-page articles "Geroi v našem stroju" (Heroes in our ranks),[43] "Čest' oficera" (Honor of the officer),[44] and "Geroi našich dnej" (Heroes of our time).[45] These pieces were illustrated with group photos or portraits of individuals presented in modern, heroic, three-quarter profile. The latter style, which showed subjects with their heads turned slightly to the side, focused attention on the Golden Star worn on the left side of the uniform to signal recognition as a hero. The facial expression and head position were part of the traditional "visionary gaze," which was meant to express determination and confidence.[46] Newspapers also used a growing number of one-in-the-middle compositions that showed inquisitive (or so it seemed) young officers filling open notebooks with firsthand information from an Afghanistan hero.[47]

The final years of the conflict at the Hindu Kush saw an "Afghanization" of the war, and the gradual withdrawal of the 40th Army influenced the selection of photographic subjects. Adhering to traditional visual templates, the civilian press emphasized the seeming successes of state consolidation in Afghanistan. By contrast, *Krasnaja Zvezda* employed reintegration themes. Visually speaking, the path led back to the Soviet Union. The communicated achievements of military intervention—a stable state structure—stood in contrast to the real experiences of the war. An additional goal of the military press was to make the returnees less afraid of civilian society by concentrating visually on how they would be received by their wives, former coworkers, and state institutions.

By the time the Soviet withdrawal began in May 1988, thousands of Soviet soldiers and officers had lost their lives in Afghanistan. The heavy price Soviet society paid for the war also included thousands of war invalids and wounded fighters. Due to the lack of images of fallen soldiers, the invalids came to play a dominant role in Soviet imagery, and doctors and nurses became the new heroes of the age. Their photos can be understood as a tentative and at least indirect allusion to the victims of the conflict, who were gradually shedding their taboo status. In one picture essay, the photographer Vladimir Solov'ev, assuming the role of silent observer, presented the physicians' everyday routines. One of his pictures, shot slightly from below, shows a surgeon rubbing his eyes during a break, his glasses pushed up onto his forehead. Photos of medical treatment indirectly addressed the causes of the wounds—the numerous setbacks—and illustrated the doctors' tireless efforts, even if they left much to the imagination. In Afghanistan itself, the white gowns of medical personnel had stood out against the gray mountainous backdrop of the rural operational area and contrasted with the traditionally dressed population and the camouflage of the combat uniforms. In the Russian homeland, the medical work was staged in images that transformed the fight against a military enemy in the Afghan mountains into a struggle for physical recovery. The postwar phase of the conflict had begun.

When Lieutenant General Boris Gromov, commander of the 40th Army, symbolically crossed the Friendship Bridge as the last soldier to leave Afghanistan, he emerged from the experiential space of Afghanistan as the representative of numerous participants in the intervention in an act planned long in advance. The event was carefully staged for the media. While, for reasons of secrecy, no official photos had been disseminated at the start of the intervention, images of the binding withdrawal on February 15, 1989, went around the world as evidence of its end.

The photos published before this event concentrated on the military's efforts to return people and matériel to the Soviet Union. Its goal was to create the impression of a continuous, united movement of the 40th Army to the Soviet homeland. One example is the image of a BTR (Bronetransportër) armored personnel carrier titled "Na rodnoj zemle" (On home soil). This is one of the rare cases in which the portrayal of a clearly identifiable geographical location was not only permitted by military censors but also emphasized by the photo editors. Very little of the original photo remained in the printed version. Two-thirds of its visual content—the border to Afghanistan and additional troop carriers—was cropped out. The message was reduced to the returning soldiers: once the troop transporter had crossed the border, it had made it home. Distracting onlookers such as journalists and military personnel were eliminated, which calmed the photo visually and aligned it with the vertical stone marking the border. The Friendship Bridge, a symbol of the crossing from Afghanistan to the Soviet Union, was also cropped out, and the opposite Afghan bank of the Amu Darya River, which formed the actual border, is just a blur in the indistinct background. Through the compression of pictorial content, the experiential space of the Soviet Union was separated from the violent space of Afghanistan. The troops on top of the personnel carriers and their raised standard emphasize the symbolic message of a safe return, as attacks were now no longer expected. In the course of the previous media coverage of the war and its heavy losses, Afghanistan had become a negatively charged (pictorial) sign that was now erased from images. Symbolically speaking, there was no turning back—the staged imagery had left Afghanistan behind (see fig. 12.2).[48]

From the Soviet perspective, increasingly, the chapter of the Afghanistan war was closed visually. Interestingly enough, in terms of images, it was destined to end precisely where it had begun. After the withdrawal of the Soviet army, photos showed only deliveries of aid via an airlift set up between the Soviet Union and Kabul. As a result, distant brotherly aid once again emerged as a visual theme. In place of Soviet troops, Afghan forces reconquered visual space (used to show "Afghan efficiency"), and the Soviet Mil Mi-24 gunships were supplanted by Afghan air force helicopters. Painted in the recognizable camouflage patterns of the Afghan army and bearing the insignia of the Republic of Afghanistan, they flew over the country in the same staggered formations as the Soviet helicopters from the previous years.

Fig. 12.2   Avoiding images of defeat by cropping the view: a Soviet battalion crosses the "Bridge of Friendship" spanning the Amu-Daya River in 1988. Photo: picture alliance / TASS / Viktor Budan.

Conclusion

Once it became clear that the Soviet-Afghan war could not be won in the planned timeframe, pressure mounted to adequately respond to the rising casualty numbers and the realities of the military situation. Nevertheless, although permanent barracks gradually replaced tents in photos of Soviet army camps, images showing the realities of war were slow in coming.[49] Consistent with the photovisual templates of the Great Patriotic War, the military hero narrative was reactivated and assigned growing importance. In addition, the Soviet leadership never tired of staging the successes of reconstruction efforts in photos. Although the subjects reflected modern developments,[50] the image composition hardly changed. Traditional variations of the "visionary gaze" and the universally used "one-in-the-middle" composition were the means of choice throughout the war. They paid tribute to the audiences' viewing habits and were an expression of long-standing visual influences on photographers and photo editors. However, the military's strategy of using visual traditions to transform its own image revealed an inability to respond to the changing issues confronting late socialism.

The photographs drew on older Soviet principles that had been developed and consolidated partly in artistic avant-garde circles and partly in the propaganda photography of previous wars. The conflict at the Hindu Kush was documented not as a military confrontation but primarily as a political event. Nevertheless, on the home front, this visual propaganda was unable to achieve its intended goal. On the contrary, the defeats and losses of an unwinnable war, which could not be kept secret, gave birth to a Soviet civil society that opposed both the military and political leadership.

It is impossible to answer the counterfactual question whether traditional image templates could have achieved the intended effects if the war had been won in a shorter time, as originally planned. What we can say for sure is that the imagery of the Soviet Union eroded due to the real experiences of war in Afghanistan. The glorious idea of an invincible Soviet army broke down in the face of flawed tactical decisions, inadequate equipment and supplies, and a brutal war waged not only against soldiers but also against citizens. Tens of thousands of war casualties posed an additional visual challenge to the Soviet army's humanitarian mission. The war developed a dynamic of its own, and the experiential space of Afghanistan increasingly intermingled with the previously separate experiential space of the Soviet Union. Glimpses of the Soviet-Afghan war provided a political catalyst in that they uncovered the systemic failings of the Soviet social model. It is no coincidence that the visually charged term *glasnost* ("transparency") became the new political paradigm.

Notes

1. See "Otvety L. I. Brežneva na voprosy korrespondenta gazety 'Pravda,'" *Pravda*, January 13, 1980, 1.
2. See Bresselau von Bressensdorf, "Islam as an Underestimated Challenge," 173.
3. See "Sowjetische Verluste in Afghanistan, 1979–1989," *Russlandanalysen* 203 (2010): 19, https://www.laender-analysen.de/russland/pdf/Russlandanalysen203.pdf.
4. See Mirschel, *Bilderfronten*.
5. See Le Breton, *Sensing the World*, 31–61.
6. See Jütte, *History of the Senses*, 325–26.
7. See Waschik, "Virtual Reality."
8. For example, Glasenapp, "Die Sowjetflagge auf dem Reichstag."
9. See Momzikoff, "Military Journal *Zarubezhnoe Voennoe Obozrenie*."
10. Significant influence was exerted by GLAVLIT (Glavnoe upravlenie po ochrane gosudarstvennych tajn v pečati pri SM SSSR [Main Directorate for the Protection of State Secrets in the Press under the Council of Ministers of the USSR]). The highest authority for censorship in the Soviet Union operated under different names and jurisdictions until 1989.
11. See Roždestvenskaja, "Afghanistan."
12. See *Krasnaja Zvezda*, September 16, 1980, 3; "Fotofakt," *Pravda*, August 25, 1980, 5.

13. The word used for "opponent" varied throughout the conflict. In addition to "counterrevolutionary," the terms "diversant" (saboteur), "bandit," and "terrorist" were common. "Dushman"—a Persian term for enemy or ghost—was adopted by Soviet soldiers and used throughout the war.
14. Casula, "Between 'Ethnocide' and 'Genocide,'" 708.
15. *Krasnaja Zvezda*, September 16, 1980, 3.
16. See Dorronsoro, *Revolution Unending*, 184–87; "Na zaščitu stolicy," *Krasnaja Zvezda*, May 25, 1989, 3; "Afganskie perevaly," *Krasnaja Zvezda*, July 2, 1989, 3.
17. See "Geroi ratnyh del," *Krasnaja Zvezda*, May 13, 1980, 1.
18. See "Vozmezdie," *Krasnaja Zvezda*, September 14, 1980, 3; "Zloveščie sledy CRU," *Krasnaja Zvezda*, June 27, 1980, 3.
19. See "Vozmezdie," *Krasnaja Zvezda*, September 14, 1980, 3; "Zloveščie sledy CRU," *Krasnaja Zvezda*, June 27, 1980, 3.
20. See Shneer, "Picturing Grief," 30.
21. See *Krasnaja Zvezda*, August 13, 1985, 3. Photographs of the conflict's victims were consistently found in the analog collections of the Soviet photo agencies RIA Novosti and Fotochronika TASS. These are now available digitally. However, they were not published at the time and vanished into the classified image sections of archives. For an example at RIA Novosti, see Anatoli Solomonov, Фото #660569; Фото #12118, 1988.
22. *Soldatskij trud Vladimira Vyatkina*, "Kul'turnyj proekt RUSS PRESS FOTO," February 2, 2019, http://sovietfoto.ru/artikle_vyatkin.
23. "Pro vojnu," *Komsomol'skaja pravda*, February 9, 1989, 7.
24. See "Boris Evgen'evič Vdovenko," Museum of Russian Photography, https://mrf.museumart.ru/collection/boris-vdovenko.
25. See Krshiwoblozkis, *Asymmetrische Kriege*, 228–30.
26. See "Raspredelenie poter' po tipam aviacionnoj techniki VVS 40-j Armii v Afganistane za period s 1985 po 1989 gody," *Aviacija v lokal'nych konfliktach*, http://www.skywar.ru/afghstatloss.html.
27. See Barthes, *Mythen des Alltags*, 87.
28. See Le Breton, *Sensing*, 40; Rösl, "Visuelle Evidenz," 19.
29. Alexijewitsch, *Zinkjungen*, 82.
30. Heinamaa, Leppanen, and Yurchenko, *Soldiers' Story*, 52–3.
31. See "Vozvraščenie," *Krasnaja Zvezda*, April 25, 1986, 4.
32. See Behrends, "Afghanistan als Gewaltraum," 141–59.
33. Alexijewitsch, *Zinkjungen*, 74.
34. *Soldatskij trud*.
35. See Danilova, "Kontinuität und Wandel," 375.
36. See Satjukow and Gries, *Sozialistische Helden*, 16.
37. See Gasimov, *Militär schreibt Geschichte*, 80.
38. See *Krasnaja Zvezda*, June 3, 1980, 4; "Imeni afgano-sovetskoj družby," *Krasnaja Zvezda*, April 17, 1980, 3.
39. See Sapper, *Die Auswirkungen*, 197–98; Levada, *Die Sowjetmenschen*, 286.
40. Author's interview with Ivanko.
41. "Rota bogdanova," *Pravda*, December 12, 1981, 6, and "Voevaja učeva armii i flota," *Krasnaja Zvezda*, October 10, 1981, 1.
42. See "Zavtra, na krasnoj ploščadi," *Krasnaja Zvezda*, November 6, 1987, 6.
43. See "Geroj v našem stroju," *Krasnaja Zvezda*, April 15, 1984, 1.
44. See "Čest' oficera," *Krasnaja Zvezda*, August 26, 1984, 1.
45. See "Geroj našix dnej," *Krasnaja Zvezda*, January 15, 1984, 1.
46. See Gestwa, *Die Stalinschen Großbauten*, 351.
47. *Krasnaja Zvezda*, May 31, 1984, 2.
48. See "Na rodnoj zemle," *Pravda*, May 19, 1988, 1.
49. "Imeni afgano-sovetskoj družby," *Krasnaja Zvezda*, April 17, 1980, 3; "Parol'—družba," *Krasnaja Zvezda*, December 20, 1986, 6.
50. Thus, in 1984, the military censorship decided that one dead and one wounded person per month could be mentioned in texts. In July 1985, a Glavlit list followed: it was possible to report on "individual cases of the heroic demise of Soviet soldiers in the performance of their combat duties." See Sapper, *Die Auswirkungen*, 203; Allan and Bucherer, *Sowjetische Geheimdokumente*, 421.

Bibliography

Media Sources
Fotochronika TASS: Afghanistan, 1979–81, 1988–89.
Komsomol'skaja Pravda: 1979–81, 1989.
Krasnaja Zvezda: 1979–89.
Pravda: 1979–89.

Interview
Alexander Ivanko, journalist in Afghanistan, Izvestija, 2015.

Published Sources
Alexijewitsch, Swetlana. *Zinkjungen: Afghanistan und die Folgen*. Berlin: Hanser, 2014.
Allan, Pierre, and Paul Bucherer, eds. *Sowjetische Geheimdokumente zum Afghanistankrieg (1978–1991)*. Zurich: vdf Hochschulverlag, 1995.
Barthes, Roland. *Mythen des Alltags*. Frankfurt am Main: Suhrkamp, 1964.
Behrends, Jan C. "Afghanistan als Gewalttraum: Sowjetische Soldaten erzählen vom Partisanenkrieg." In Meier and Penter, *Sovietnam: Die UdSSR in Afghanistan, 1979–1989*, 141–59. Paderborn: Schöningh, 2019.
Bresselau von Bressensdorf, Agnes. "Islam as an Underestimated Challenge: NATO States and the Afghan Crisis of 1979." In *German Yearbook of Contemporary History*, edited by Agnes Bresselau von Bressensdorf, Elke Seefried, and Christian F. Ostmann, 2:173–210. Berlin: De Gruyter Oldenbourg, 2017.
Casula, Philipp. "Between 'Ethnocide' and 'Genocide': Violence and Otherness in the Coverage of the Afghanistan and Chechnya Wars." *Journal of Nationalism and Ethnicity* 43, no. 5 (2015): 700–18.
Danilova, Natalija. "Kontinuität und Wandel: Denkmäler des Afghanistankrieges." *Osteuropa* 55, no. 4–6 (2005): 367–86.
Dorronsoro, Gilles. *Revolution Unending: Afghanistan, 1979 to Present*. New York: Columbia University Press, 2005.
Gasimov, Zaur T. *Militär schreibt Geschichte: Instrumentalisierung der Geschichte durch das Militär in der Volksrepublik Polen und in der Sowjetunion, 1981–1991*. Münster: LIT, 2009.
Gestwa, Klaus. *Die Stalinschen Großbauten des Kommunismus: Sowjetische Technik und Umweltgeschichte, 1948–1967*. Munich: Oldenbourg, 2010.
Glasenapp, Jörn. "Die Sowjetflagge auf dem Reichstag—Ikone des Sieges." In *Bilder im Kopf: Ikonen der Zeitgeschichte*, 50–57. Cologne: DuMont, 2011.
Heinamaa, Anna, Maija Leppanen, and Yuri Yurchenko. *The Soldiers' Story: Soviet Veterans Remember the Afghan War*. Berkeley: University of California, 1994.
Jütte, Robert. *A History of the Senses: From Antiquity to Cyberspace*. Oxford: Blackwell, 2004.
Krshiwoblozkis, Lukas von. *Asymmetrische Kriege: Die Herausforderung für die deutsche Sicherheitspolitik im 21. Jahrhundert*. Marburg: Tectum, 2015.
Le Breton, David. *Sensing the World: An Anthropology of the Senses*. London: Routledge, 2017.
Levada, Jurij A. *Die Sowjetmenschen, 1989–1991: Soziogramm eines Verfalls*. Munich: dtv, 1993.
Maier, Esther, and Tanja Penter, eds. *Sovietnam: Die UdSSR in Afghanistan, 1979–1989*. Paderborn: Schöningh, 2019.
Mirschel, Markus. *Bilderfronten: Die Visualisierung der sowjetischen Intervention in Afghanistan, 1979–1989*. Cologne: Böhlau, 2019.
Momzikoff, Sophie. "The Military Journal *Zarubezhnoe Voennoe Obozrenie* under Perestroika (1985–1991): In the Vanguard of Change or a Bastion of Traditional Soviet Military Journalism?" *Journal of Power Institutions in Post-Soviet Societies* 16 (2014). http://pipss.revues.org/4092.
Rösl, Frank. "Visuelle Evidenz in der Biomedizin." *Gegenworte Hefte für den Disput über Wissen* 20 (2008): 16–19.
Roždestvenskaja, Elena. "Afghanistan im virtuellen Gedächtnis des heutigen

Russland." In Meier and Penter, *Sovietnam*, 253–69.

Sapper, Manfred. *Die Auswirkungen des Afghanistan-Krieges auf die Sowjetgesellschaft: Eine Studie zum Legitimationsverlust des Militärischen in der Perestrojka*. Münster: LIT, 1994.

Satjukow, Silke, and Rainer Gries, eds. *Sozialistische Helden: Eine Kulturgeschichte von Propagandafiguren in Osteuropa und der DDR*. Berlin: Ch. Links, 2002.

Shneer, David. "Picturing Grief: Soviet Holocaust Photography at the Intersection of History and Memory." *American History Review* 115, no. 1 (2010): 28–52.

Waschik, Klaus. "Virtual Reality: Sowjetische Bild- und Zensurpolitik als Erinnerungskontrolle in den 1930er-Jahren." *Zeithistorische Forschung / Studies in Contemporary History* 7 (2010). https://zeitges chichte-digital.de/doks/frontdoor /deliver/index/docId/1795/file/ZF_1 _2010_30_54_Waschik.pdf.

Contributors

CYRIL CORDOBA is a Postdoctoral Researcher at the Department of Contemporary History of the University of Fribourg and at UniDistance (Switzerland). He is the author of *China-Swiss Relations During the Cold War*. He has contributed essays to volumes such as *Europe and China in the Cold War* and *Transnational History of Switzerland* and coedited a special issue of the historical journal *Traverse* about Switzerland and East Asia. He is currently writing a political history of the Locarno International Film Festival (1946–81), a hub for "emerging cinema" during the Cold War.

MARK FENEMORE is a Senior Lecturer in modern European history at Manchester Metropolitan University. He is the author of *Sex, Thugs and Rock 'n' Roll: Teenage Rebels in Cold-War East Germany* and *Fighting the Cold War in Post-Blockade, Pre-Wall Berlin: Behind Enemy Lines*. In addition to studying subcultures, gangs, gender history, and German Democratic Republic education, he is interested in policing during the Cold War. He recently completed a book entitled *Dismembered Policing in Postwar Berlin: The Limits of Four-Power Government*, looking at the period between 1945 and 1950.

WALTER E. GRUNDEN is a Professor of History at Bowling Green State University in Ohio and a former member of the Cold War Advisory Committee for historical preservation under the US Department of the Interior. He is the author of *Secret Weapons and World War II: Japan in the Shadow of Big Science* and numerous articles and book chapters on the history of nuclear, chemical, and biological warfare. His research interests include comparative policy history from a transnational perspective, with a focus on the intersection of science and the state and the role of the scientist in wartime. He is currently researching Central Intelligence Agency biological and chemical warfare programs in Asia in the early Cold War era.

DAYTON LEKNER is Marie Curie Fellow at the Department of Asian and North African Studies, Ca' Foscari University of Venice. A historian of modern Chinese culture and society, he has published articles in major journals such as the *Journal of Asian Studies, Modern China, Twentieth-Century China,* and the *Journal of Chinese Cinemas.* His forthcoming book, *Flower–Power: The Writing of a Maoist Campaign,* explores the connections between literary practice and mass campaigns in the era of Mao Zedong. Lekner is also a translator of key works of intellectual and social history by Chinese authors. His translations have appeared in *Contemporary Chinese Thought, Voices from the Chinese Century* and *The Rise of Modern Chinese Thought.* He edits the online translation journal Revisiting the Revolution (http://prc history.org/revisiting-the-revolution-landing-page/).

JOSÉ MANUEL LÓPEZ TORÁN is an Associate Professor at the University of Castilla-La Mancha, Spain. He specializes in the study of modern wars with a focus on visual propaganda and emotions and has conducted research in France, Germany, and Belgium. He has contributed to international journals such as *Vínculos de Historia, Historia & Guerra,* and *Fotocinema* and has written several essays for collections such as *Hasta pronto, amigos de España: Las Brigadas Internacionales en el 80 aniversario de su despedida de la Guerra Civil* and *Hablar a los ojos: Caricatura y vida política en España (1830–1918).*

MARKUS MIRSCHEL is a Research Associate at the Chair of Eastern European History at Humboldt University of Berlin. He is the author of *Bilderfronten: Die Visualisierung der sowjetischen Intervention in Afghanistan, 1979–1989.* His research interests include the history of emotions under communism, Soviet-Afghan cultural history, and visual history. He is currently working on a book about emotional self-assurance in letters from prisoners in the German Democratic Republic.

BODO MROZEK is a Senior Research Associate at the Berlin Center for Cold War Studies of the Leibniz Institute for Contemporary History. He is the author of the award-winning transnational history of youth and popular culture *Jugend—Pop—Kultur: Eine transnationale Geschichte,* which appeared in French translation under the title *Histoire de la pop. Quand la culture jeune dépasse les frontières.* He is coeditor of *Popgeschichte,* a two-volume work on the contemporary history of popular culture, and has conducted research on sound history, transnational history, and the Cold War. He is currently writing an olfactory history of the twentieth century.

VICTORIA PHILLIPS is a Global Fellow at the Wilson International Center for Scholars and a Visiting Fellow in the Department of International History at the London School of Economics and Political Science. She is the author of *Martha Graham's Cold War: The Dance of American Diplomacy*. She has curated exhibits in the United States and Europe and lectured internationally. She is the Co-director of the Cold War Archives Research Institute at the Wilson Center and the Global Biography Working Group and serves on the boards of the Gilder Lehrman Institute of American History and the European Institute at Columbia University. She is currently writing a biography of Eleanor Lansing Dulles.

CARSTEN RICHTER is a doctoral candidate in the Department of History at Humboldt University of Berlin and a reserve officer serving at the German Military Representative to NATO and the EU. His doctoral thesis deals with psychological warfare and liberal democracy in Cold War Germany with a focus on West Germany. His research interests include the history of violence and military history, especially civil-military relations. He holds a master's degree from Goethe University in Frankfurt and an MLitt from the University of Saint Andrews. He is an alumnus of the German National Academic Foundation.

ANDREEA DECIU RITIVOI is William S. Dietrich Professor of English at Carnegie Mellon University. She is the author of *Yesterday's Self: Nostalgia and the Immigrant Identity*, *Paul Ricoeur: Tradition and Innovation in Rhetorical Theory*, and *Intimate Strangers: Hannah Arendt, Herbert Marcuse, Alexander Solzhenitsyn, and Edward Said in American Political Discourse* and the coeditor of the narrative studies journal *Storyworlds* and of several volumes. Her research interests include political rhetoric, interpretation theory, narrative studies, and exile.

CHRISTY SPACKMAN is Assistant Professor at Arizona State University with a joint appointment between the School for the Future of Innovation in Society and the School of Arts, Media, and Engineering. Trained in chemistry, molecular biology, and food studies, her research and creative practices examine how the scientific and technological management of sensory experiences shapes perceptions of the environment. She is author of *The Taste of Water*.

STEPHANIE WEISMANN is affiliated with the University of Warsaw and guest fellow at the Faculty Center for Transdisciplinary Historical and Cultural Studies at the University of Vienna. She is working on her second book, *The Smellscapes of Lublin,* an olfactory urban history of twentieth-century Poland, and conducted the Citizen Science project "Wien der Nase nach" (#wienriecht 2023). Her research interests include the study of urban sensescapes and emotional geographies, with a focus on Eastern Europe in the nineteenth and twentieth centuries.

Index

2,3,7,8-Tetrachlorodibenzo-p-dioxin, 158
38th parallel, 14

actants, 148, 160
actor-network-theory (ANT), 12, 148
Adler, Judith, 58
affect, 149
Afghanistan, 6, 9, 10, 220–35
    army of, 220, 222–23, 225, 233
    Democratic Republic of, 220, 224, 228
    resistance movement of, 221
    Soviet Border with, 221–23
    war (*see under* war)
Africa, 124, 239
aggression, 2, 14, 142, 186
Akramov, Nabi, 231
Albania, 10, 34
Alexanderplatz, 83
Allen Memorial Institute, 175–76
Allen, Morse, 171, 178
Alpert, Max, 226
America
    Civil War, 3, 5
    culture, 172
    democracy, 127
    kitchen, 35
    Latin, 144
    Psychiatric Association, 175
    sector, Berlin, 22
    Sino-rapprochement, 63
    United States of, 10, 22, 32–35, 79–117, 122–42, 169–75, 180, 203–15, 221
Amin, Hafizullah, 221
Anderson, Benedict, 7
Angel Dust, 177
animals, 12, 114, 148–49, 151, 155–61, 206
ANT (actor-network-theory), 12, 148
Antonioni, Michelangelo, 65
Arab World, 14
arms, 187
    nuclear, 204
    race, 5, 95
    sonic, 95
ARTICHOKE project, 171–72, 178–79
Asia, 11, 14, 144
    East, 12, 136, 141

assassination, 167–83
audio, 119
    communication, 78
    paper, 2
    signal, 4–5
    tapes, 59, 65
    technology, 95, 147
    visual, 2, 131–34, 138–39
Aushev, Ruslan, 231
Austria, 10, 25, 28, 160
Axis Powers, 133

Baishi Paotai, 95
balance of power, 8
balloons, 14, 33–35, 195, 221
Baltermants, Dmitri, 226
Bamboo Curtain, 58
Barthes, Roland, 227
Bavaria, 155, 191
Bay of Pigs Invasion, 140
Beatles, The, 121
Beaux, Ernest, 44–45
Beijing, 60, 62–64, 66–65, 101, 107
    Foreign Language Press, 59, 63, 67
Belarus, 14
Belcher, Oliver, 206
Bell, David F., 122
Benoît-Barné, Chantal, 127
Bentham, Jeremy, 77
Berlin, 6, 24–35, 73–88, 147–61, 186, 197
    American Sector of, 22
    British sector of, 80
    Cold War, 11, 73, 76, 87–88
    East, 8, 21–24, 32–33, 74–79, 83, 140, 148–55, 192
    Eastern sector of, 83
    Four Powers Agreement on, 154
    French sector of, 83, 86
    Soviet Sector of, 150
    wall of, 147–161, 186, 197
    West, 22, 26, 31–32, 77, 80, 86, 148–55, 158–59, 193
    Western Sector of, 85–86, 147
Bernoulli, Fernand, 61
Beyer, Gisela, 74
Biddle, Francis, 115

INDEX

Black Saturday, 141
Black Tulip, 13, 225, 229
Blauer, Harold, 177
Bloch, Marc, 5
BLUEBIRD project, 169–71, 178–79
BND (Bundesnachrichtendienst), 156
bombs, 26, 136–37, 140, 205
Bonaparte, Napoleon, 5, 47, 186
Bond, James, 80
Bonn, 77, 154
border, 6, 14, 28, 31
    Afghan-Soviet, 221–23
    aquatic, 8, 11, 93–108
    dogs, 155–57
    "of friendship," 45–46
    green, 156
    guards, 150, 185, 189, 195, 198
    Hungarian, 160
    inner-German, 12, 32, 77–78, 81, 147–48, 151, 155–56, 159, 184, 190
    Iron Curtain, 14, 42, 80, 112, 116, 118, 122, 124
    -lands, 12, 148, 157
    management, 147–61
    regimes, 161
    zones, 148, 160
border(land) studies, 148, 158–59
Bourdieu, Pierre, 23
Bourke, Joanna, 114
Brandenburg Gate, 21
Brandt, Willy, 77
Brecht, Bertolt, 62
Brelsford, Elinor, 65
Brezhnev, Leonid, 220, 230
British sector, 80
Bryn Mawr College, 24
Bulgaria, 27, 51
Bull, Michael, 4
Bundesnachrichtendienst, 156
Bundeswehr. *See* military

California, 121
Cameron, Donald Ewen, 175
Camp David, 141
Canada, 175
canine corps, 156
capitalism, 25, 30, 50–51, 61, 85
CARE (Cooperative for Assistance and Relief Everywhere), 25–26, 28, 31, 33–34
Caribbean, 140–42
"Carlos" (Ramírez Sánchez, Ilich), 126
Castillo, Luis Angel, 180
Castro, Fidel, 140, 179

Cavarero, Adriana, 113
CCP. *See under* China
chemistry
    chemicals, 32, 158, 171, 173, 177, 213
    Corps, 177, 180
    plants, 32, 152, 158, 159, 160
Ceaușescu, Nicolae, 124, 126
Central Intelligence Agency, 12–13, 24, 26, 32–34, 85, 115, 117, 167–81
Chanel, Coco, 45
CHATTER project, 170
Chicago, 35, 210
China, 9–11, 14, 58–70, 63–68, 93–108, 171–73
    Communist Party of (CCP), 93–94, 97, 99–101, 103, 105, 107
    People's Association for Friendship with Foreign Countries, 59, 63, 65
    Peoples Republic of 58–68, 95, 98–99, 102
    Republic of, 58, 95, 103, 221
Chiriac, Cornel, 121, 124
Church, Frank, 181
CIA. *See* Central Intelligence Agency
cinema, 12, 118, 131–32, 135–36, 139, 143
class, 4, 8, 42, 44, 76, 197
Classen, Constance, 185
Clay, Lucius D., 26, 115
Cold War Studies, 6
Cold Warriors, 1, 9, 14, 127
Columbia Broadcasting Service (CBS), 212–13
Committee for State Security (KGB), 2, 85, 223
communism, 61, 113, 116–22, 127–33, 136, 138–44, 177, 181–214, 230
    bloc, 32, 169
    party, 27, 41–43, 117, 221
communities, imagined, 7
communities, sensed, 7
Condon, Richard, 178
conflict, 5, 10–11, 13–14, 114, 133–34, 147, 225, 231–32
    Cuban, 140–41
    East-West, 10, 14, 195
    Korean, 173
    smell of (*see* smell)
    sound of (*see* sound)
    Soviet-Afghan, 10, 227
    studies, 3
    US-Vietnam, 203
Conrad, Sebastian, 9
containment, 6, 115

Cooperative for Assistance and Relief
    Everywhere (CARE), 25–26, 28, 31,
    33–34
Corbin, Alain, 114
Cornish, Paul, 5
Cottbus, 32
Council of Ministers, 222
Courmont, Juliette, 4
SSR. *See* Czechoslovakia
Cuba, 1–2, 10, 12, 131–32, 137, 140–44
    Missile Crisis, 12, 132, 140, 143
Cull, Nicholas, J., 6
cultural studies, 6, 149
Culture, 5, 41, 44, 46, 48, 81, 94, 117, 149, 213
    alien, 81
    American, 172
    Chinese, 98
    consumer, 48
    counter, 173
    Hokkien, 103
    institutional, 98
    memory, 229
    popular, 179
    youth, 191
Czechoslovakia, 10, 32, 34, 119, 155

Dadan Island, 95, 101, 104
Dadeji Beach, 104
Dallas, 179f.
Danube, 34
Daughtry, Martin J., 101
Davis, Natalie Zemon, 76
Dazhai, 64, 66
Deacon, John, 121
DeMille, Cecil B., 115
democracy, 25, 112–13, 115–14, 122, 127, 186, 194
Democratic Republic of Afghanistan. *See* Afghanistan
Derrida, Jacques, 23
detection, 156
    chemical 203–15
    dogs, 156
    olfactory, 8, 203–15
détente, 5, 6, 8, 10, 159, 221
deterrence, 8
Deutscher Soldatensender 935 (DSS). *See under* media
Diedrich, Torsten, 185
diplomacy, 24
    conflict, 8
    gastro, 10
    German-German, 12

    public, 8, 11
    secret, 11
disarmament process, 142
disgust, 149, 160
Disney World, 25
distrust, 188–89
division 95, 148, 158, 159
    1st Cavalry, 203
    1st Infantry, 212
    101st Airborne, 211
    Berlin, 78, 85
    Chinese, 93
    city, 25, 74, 85, 154
    Cold War, 94
    East-West, 26
    of families, 104
    Germany, 80, 159
    ideological, 95
    mortal, 104
    nations, 25
    political, 11
    Vienna, 25
    zones, 25
Dolar, Mladen, 103
Doorbell, Evan, 74, 88n2
DPRK. *See* Korea: Democratic People's
    Republic of
Dravnieks, Andrew, 210–12, 216n28, 29, 32
drones, 221
drugs, 13, 167–81, 182n18
DSS. *See* media: Deutscher Soldatensender
    935
Dulles, Allen Welsh, 24, 32, 34, 115, 169–73,
    179, 181
Dulles, Eleanor Lansing, 8, 22, 24–29, 31–34
Dulles, John Foster, 24, 27, 29
Durden, Tyler, 83

E63 manpack. *See* people sniffer
ear, 1, 3–5, 21, 62, 102, 187
    "state," 101
    witness, 9
Eastern Bloc, 31, 35, 41–42, 45, 47–52
East-West Divide, 26
Ebern, 191
Edwards, Sheffield, 169
Eisenhower, Dwight D., 22–24, 27, 32–34,
    115, 137, 141
    packages, 21–23, 25, 27, 29, 33
EK-Bewegung, 190
electroshock therapie, 175–79
Emission Control Act, Federal, 154

emotion, 8–11, 23, 42–43, 67, 80–83, 98, 105–8, 122–35, 138–49, 172
Enescu, George, 112, 121
Entlassungskandidaten-Bewegung, 190
equilibrium, 7
"Erika," 8, 80–87
espionage, 7, 14, 74, 77, 85, 87
  spies, 24, 33, 86–87, 128, 169–70, 176
  plane, 141
Europe, 21–25, 27, 41–43, 47–50, 52–53, 94, 133, 148
  Central Eastern, 12, 160
  Eastern, 12, 14, 21, 42, 76, 113–27, 160
  Western, 50, 133
Ewell, Julian J., 204
exiles, 112–28, 141
explosives, 126, 205

Fairhead, Edward, 214
famine, 10
Fang, Coco, 106
Fascist Spain, 10, 12
fathometer, 5
FBI. *See* Federal Bureau of Investigation
fear, 5–14, 50, 63, 76–79, 103, 107, 114, 127, 141, 149, 160, 167–71
Fechter, Peter, 151
Federal Bureau of Investigation, 116, 180
Federal Republic of Germany (FRG). *See under* Germany
Feifei, Chen, 8, 98, 100–101, 107
Feinberg, Melissa, 118
femininity, 48, 103
feminism, 89n47
Filipčenkov, Sergej, 227
film, 8–12, 59–65, 74–75, 107, 115, 118, 135–44, 168, 172–79, 229
food, 5, 8, 10–11, 21–35, 45, 67–68, 188, 204
  Berlin program, 24, 27
  chemists, 207
  Chinese, 68
  gifts, 35
  industry, 23
  operation, 27
  packages, 28–35
  preferences, 117
  prices, 45
  shortages, 34
  studies, 23
foreign policy, 133, 154
Foucault, Michel, 22, 77
Four Powers Agreement on Berlin, 154
fragrance, 10, 41–53

France, 24, 45, 50–51
Franco, Francisco, 132–33, 138, 143
freedom, 22–26, 35, 47, 80, 98, 104, 116–27, 197, 226
Freedom Bell, 26
French Security Service, 80, 85
FRG (Federal Republic of Germany). *See under* Germany
Friedrichshain, 83
Friendship Bridge, 132–33
Frohnau, 81
Fujian, 93, 99
Fulbright, William, 118

Gabrys, Jennifer, 206
Gardener, Paul, 212
Gastrodiplomacy, 10
Gaus, Günter, 153
GDR. *See under* Germany
gender, 8, 11, 22–42, 73–79, 86–87, 89n45, 102–3, 108n5, 109n47, 215
  studies, 11, 76, 87
  voice, 76, 87, 102–4
geopolitics 7–8, 41, 53, 84, 154
  ideology, 8
Georgescu, Vlad, 118, 124
German Democratic Republic *See under* Germany
Germany, 5–6, 10, 23–25, 78, 112, 126, 147, 159
  Democratic Republic, 32, 74, 84, 150, 152–60, 184–86, 188–98, 200n32, 200n45
  East, 25, 27, 29, 32, 33, 45–46, 77, 79, 86, 121, 153–54, 184, 191
  Federal Republic of, 153–55, 160, 184, 186, 190, 194, 196, 198
  Nazi, 5, 225, 227
  West, 46, 115, 153–55, 158, 184, 186, 191–92, 195, 197
Gierek, Edward, 45–46, 48
Giese, Fritz, 79
glasnost, 235
Goethe, Johann Wolfgang von, 23
Golay, Bernard, 59–60, 62
Goodman, Steve, 2, 77, 176, 185
Gorbachev, Mikhail, 230
Gottlieb, Sidney, 169, 172
Grenztruppen. *See* border: guards
Grew, Joseph, 115
Grieshaber, Jean, 59–60, 62
Gromov, Boris, 232
GRU, 2

Grunewald, 158
Guangzhou, 1, 66
Guernica, 138
Guillaume, Günter, 77
gulag, 51
Gulangyu Island, 104
Guningtou, 94–96, 99
    battle of, 94, 99

Hacker, Barton, 204
Halle, 32
Hallstein Doctrine, 153
Hanoi, 1
haptics. *See* touch
Harris, Robert, 177
Hartono, Paulina, 98
Harvard University, 24, 173
Hauser, Gerard, 127
Havana, 1, 142
Havana Syndrome, 1–2
hearing, 2, 11–12, 59–74, 82, 93–95, 100–125, 131–42, 181, 187, 205
Hillenkoetter, Roscoe, 169
Hindu Kush, 220f., 225–27, 235
Hinkle, Lawrence, 173
Hisano, Ai, 23
history, 7, 14–15, 42, 74, 87, 108, 131, 155, 192, 205–27
    agrarian, 5
    cultural, 3, 5–6, 76
    of emotions, 67, 83
    European, 6
    gender, 76
    global, 9
    media, 6, 144
    micro, 9, 76, 87
    nano, 9
    oral, 59
    political, 6
    sensory, 3, 9, 23, 74, 149, 168, 221
    of warfare 3, 148, 168, 204
    world, 9
Hobsbawm, Eric, 14
Hofmann, Albert, 173
Honecker, Erich, 155
Hong Kong, 14
Hongyan, Dai, 100–101, 104
Honolulu, 137
Hoover, J. Edgar, 116
Hot Springs, 171
Houbian, 106
Howes, David, 6, 185
Hujingtou, 95

Hulishan, 95
Hunan, 97, 104
hunger, 3, 31, 114, 149, 187
    "cards," 21
Hungary, 10, 14, 27, 30, 32–34, 157, 160
    People's Republic, 169
Hunt Jr., Ira A., 204
Hyde, Robert, 173
hypnosis, 167–70, 174, 178–80

Ierunca, Virgil, 118, 124
Illinois Institute of Technology, 210
images, 7, 44, 79, 131–46
India, 210
Indochina, 80, 203
Innsbruck, 81
intelligence, 8, 12, 31, 83–85, 97, 100, 156–57, 168–74, 184–202, 221
    Committee, 172
    community, 168, 172, 181
    electronic, 203–4, 214
    military, 184–202
    scientific, 173
    US Agencies, 2
    West German, 156
intersensoriality, 1, 7
Ionescu, Gelu, 124
Iran, 221
Iron Curtain, 14, 42, 80, 112, 116, 118, 122, 124
    See also border

Jaccard, Victor, 60, 68
Jackson, Charles D., 32–33
Jackson, William H., 117
Japan, 170
Jeanneret, Paul-Henri, 60
Jiaoyu Island, 95
Jinjian, Cai, 105
Jinlang, Chen, 106
Jinmen, 11, 93–111
Johnson, Lyndon B., 214
Jütte, Robert, 14, 221
Jung, Carl, 24

Kabul, 221, 223, 233
Kafka, Franz, 77
Kai-shek, Chiang, 97
Kamenev, Lev, 222
Karmal, Babrak, 221
Kennan, George, 115–16
Kennedy, John F., 141–42, 179–80
Kettler, Andrew, 211

KGB (Committee for State Security), 2, 85, 223
Khrushchev, Nikita, 141
Kinmen, 99
Kitchen Debate, 24, 35
Kittler, Friedrich A., 5, 107
KMT *See* Kuomintang
kode9. *See* Goodman, Steve
Koselleck, Reinhart, 15n22
Korea, 14, 94, 131–33, 136–45, 173
  Democratic People's Republic of, 168, 172
  North, 6, 10, 14, 96, 102, 131–45, 168, 172–73
  pop music, 14
  South, 14, 139
  war (*see* war)
Krakow, 51
Krause, Frank, 149
Kremlin, 21
Kreuzberg, 158
Kučerenko, Vladimir, 227
Kunren, Guo, 104
Kuomintang, 94, 95, 97–103, 105, 107
Kwon, Heonik, 108

Latin America, 144
Le Breton, David, 152
Leary, Timothy, 173
Lefebvre, Henri, 78
Lekner, Dayton, 11, 84, 93, 96
Lemercier, Alexandre, 45
Leuna, 154
Lichtenberg, 83
Lieyu Island, 95, 97, 102, 105
Limei, Tong, 99
Limited Contingent of Soviet Troops in Afghanistan, 220, 226–27, 229
Lingfeng, Gao, 106
listening, 5, 11f, 66, 76, 105–6, 108, 112–30, 137, 191–92, 194
  covert, 120
  practices, 100, 113–14, 126–28
  surreptitious, 8
  tactical, 8
Lizhu, Tang, 104
love, 23, 47–48, 82, 85, 87
Lovinescu, Monica, 118, 124
Lower Saxony, 156
LSD, 167, 173–81
Luce, Henry, 115
Lüxingshe, 58
Lysergic acid diethylamide, 167, 173–81

Macrea-Toma, Ioana, 125
Madison Avenue, 23
Madrid, 132
Măgură, Ioana, 123
Main Directorate of the General Staff of the Armed Forces of the Russian Federation, 2
Major, Patrick, 78
Manchuria, 173
  Candidate, 167–68, 178–79
Manila, 180
manipulation, 14, 23, 82, 114–17, 131, 144–45, 167, 180
Mannheim, Karl, 5
Mao Zedong, 62, 66–67, 97, 240
Marcos, Ferdinand, 180
Mariendorf, 151
Marienfelde, 158
Marks, John, 168
Marks, Laura, 135
Marshall Plan, 25
Marxism, 21
masculinity, 192
Mashan, 95, 105–6
Matthes, Günter, 154
Maurer, Jochen, 185
Mazumdar, B. Theo, 6
Méchoulan, Éric, 122
media, 59, 134, 144, 198, 227
  Columbia Broadcasting Service (CBS), 212–13
  Deutscher Soldatensender 935, 190–94, 199n22, 200n27, 200n35
  fake news, 2, 14, 195
  internet, 13, 44
  Krasnaja Zvezda, 223, 227, 231–32
  magazines, 187, 193
  magazine, science, 210
  magazines, women's, 42–52
  Mainpost, 131
  news agencies, 222–23
  newspaper, 13, 27, 30–32, 61–65, 144, 154, 191–97, 213, 220–22, 230–32
  news reports, 22, 99, 112, 213–15
  New York Times, The, 208, 213
  Pravda, 220
  radio, 8–14, 22, 34, 62–66, 99–100, 112–28, 133, 147, 171, 179, 190–95
  Radio Free Asia, 99
  Radio Free Europe, 8, 12, 14, 34, 99, 112–28
  Radio In The American Sector, 22, 28, 31
  Rührt Euch, 193fig.10.1

Tagesspiegel, Der 154
TASS, 223
television, 12, 132, 144, 179, 212, 214
Voice of America, 60, 116
Volksarmee, 196fig.10.2
Welt, Die 155
Menuhin, Yehudi, 121
Miami, 141
Miard-Delacroix, Hélène, 9
military, 177, 184, 184–99, 203–15, 220–35
  actions, 142, 220
  advisers, 206
  campaigns, 3
  Chinese, 168
  confrontation, 235
  communication systems, 7
  encounters, 12
  draft, 13, 184–99
  East-German, 155, 190, 193
  entertainment complex, 107
  German, 4
  intelligence, 184–202
  interventions, 136, 142
  inventions, 5
  Korean, 168
  methods, 7
  National Peoples Army, 185–66, 186, 189–90, 194–96, 198
  operations, 136
  para-, 172, 186
  photography, 221
  planes, 26
  propaganda (*see under* propaganda)
  research, 168, 203–15
  secrets, 154
  service, 93, 105, 168, 173, 184, 188
  Soviet, 220–35
  Soviet doctrine, 189
  standoff, 6
  strikes, 14
  technologies, 5, 13
  training, 98, 220
  US, 170, 203–15
  West German, 186, 190–94
Michel, Auguste, 45
microwaves, 1, 179
Mielke, Peggy, 176
Mihăilescu, Călin-Andrei, 121
mind control, 167–81
Mindszenty, József, 168–70
Ministry for State Security. *See* Stasi
Ministry of Foreign Affairs, 154
missiles, 142, 227

mistrust, 44, 127
Mitter, Rana, 78
Mitty, Walter, 80
MKULTRA project, 167–68, 171–72, 175, 179, 181n3
Montreal, 175
Moscow, 1, 22, 25, 27, 33, 35, 44, 118, 168
Mrozek, Bodo, 199
Mujahideen, 220–21, 224–25, 227
multisensoriality, 4, 134, 144
Munich, 12, 126–27
Munteanu, Neculai Constantin 127
music, 11, 93, 100–106, 119, 135, 137–44, 176, 193, 200n36
  bourgeois, 8
  Chinese, 61–62, 64, 67
  classical, 112, 121
  composer, 141
  contemporary, 121
  K-Pop, 14
  melodies, 22, 95, 135
  popular, 107, 121–22, 190–91
  Romanian country, 121
  songs, 62, 66, 95–97, 102–7, 117
  Western, 191

Nadeždin, Georgy, 223
Nancy, Jean-Luc, 122, 124
Nanjing, 66
Nation of Islam, 210
National Bureau of Investigation (NBI), 180
National Committee for Free Europe, 115
Nationale Volksarmee (National Peoples Army). *See under* military
Navalny, Alexei, 2
NBI (National Bureau of Investigation), 180
Neukölln, 150
New York City, 35, 121, 175
New York State Psychiatric Institute, 177
New York Times, The, 208, 213
Nickels, Horace, 117
NO-DO (Noticiario y Documentales), 12, 131–45
Nöel, Bernard 118, 121, 124
nose, 3, 10, 41–51, 151, 156, 160, 178, 211, 214
  dog's, 155
  electronic, 204
  French, 45
  witness, 9, 148
Noticiario y Documentales (NO-DO), 12, 131–45
Nuremberg Code, 181

Očirov, Valerij, 231
Office for Policy Coordination, 115
Office of Scientific Intelligence, 173
olfaction, 4, 13, 41–42, 50, 148, 151–52, 203, 205
  conflict (*see* conflict)
  events, 159
  forensics, 160, 210–11, 215
  gas chromatograph-, 208
  history (*see* history)
  investigation, 149
  landscape (*see* smell: scape)
  map, 152–54
  particles, 152, 215
  receptors, 155
  signals, 211
  warfare (*see* warfare)
Olson, Frank, 175
operation, 10, 32, 116, 141, 170, 175, 224, 230
  air, 8, 10, 140
  CARE, 28
  Christmas East, 32–33
  combat, 230–31
  covert, 6, 12–13, 115; 171, 226
  food, 27, 35
  Gold, 74
  leaflet, 34
  military, 136
  oversee, 97
  Polish–Soviet, 51
  psychological, 8, 167–81, 194
  Reindeer, 33
  special, 173
  tactical combat, 225
  Vittles, 26
Orlikov, Velma, 176
Orwell, George (i.e. Blair, Eric Arthur), 77
Oswald, Lee Harvey, 179–80
othering, 6–7, 211

Pacific, 98
pain, 1, 7, 135, 138, 177, 187
Pakistan, 220–21
Parada, Manuel, 141
Paxman, Jeremy, 177
peace, 4, 23, 98, 115, 140–41, 159, 185, 222, 225
people sniffer, 13, 204, 208–9, 207–15
People's Liberation Army, 97, 99
perception, 41, 52, 95, 135, 172, 199, 228
  contemporary, 3–6
  human systems of, 7
  olfactory, 160, 207

practices of, 212
sensory, 84, 145
soldiers', 194
visual, 67
Western, 59
perfume, 8, 11, 41–53
perfumery, 8, 11, 41–53
Pewex, 46
Phillips, Victoria, 85
photoelectricity, 208
photography, 13, 74, 220–38
  military, 221
  photo, 67
  satellite, 5
photos, 9, 21, 59, 60, 63–64, 141–50, 158–59, 220–38
  aerial, 5
  exhibition, 67
  manipulated, 14
Plovdiv, 27
Pogany, Dennis S., 203–4
Poland, 10, 14, 32–34, 41–53
  French relations with, 48
  Peoples Republic of, 41–53
poison, 2, 126, 149, 159
police, 14, 32, 74, 119, 148–49, 186
  dogs, 155–60
  people's, 78–88
  policing, 86–87, 155–61, 204
  Romanian secret, 123
  secret, 7, 123
policy, 230
  central, 95, 98
  energy, 154
  foreign, 133, 154
  national, 99
  Office for Coordination, 115
  public, 128n9, 128nn12–13, 128n17
  social, 46
politics, 5–6, 8, 78, 203, 213, 222
  bio-, 181n3
  geo-, 8
  international, 142
  micro-, 6, 10–11, 148
  office, 84
Poole, DeWitt, 115
Porteous, J. Douglas, 159
Potsdam, 32
Poznań, 34
Prague Spring of 1968, 126
Pravda, 221
PRC. *See* China
Prenzlauer Berg, 83

Pretzsch, 155
Pritchard, Helen, 206
projects
   ARTICHOKE, 171–72, 178–79
   BLUEBIRD, 169–71, 178–79
   CHATTER, 170
   Cold War International History, 128
   infrastructure, 64
   MKULTRA, 167–68, 171–72, 175, 179, 181n3
   propaganda, 2, 4, 15–35, 58–67, 80, 97–107, 113–19, 125–26, 172, 222–25
   military, 13, 184–86, 193, 196–98
   sonic, 94, 140
   songs, 66
   strategies, 8
   visual, 32, 131–47, 235
   war (*see* war)
psychology
   chemical program, 177
   Kampfführung (*see* warfare)
   operations, 8, 167–81, 194
   PSYOP (*see under* operations)
   psywar (*see* warfare)
   Strategy Board, 10, 25, 27–29, 33–34
   Warfare Division, 194

Qing, Jiang, 66
Qiwu, Zheng, 104
Queen, 122
Queshan, 105

race, 8, 42, 206, 208, 210–11, 215
racism, 3, 8, 211
radiation, 172, 179
radio *See* media
Ramírez Sánchez, Ilich ("Carlos"), 126
rearmament, 186
reconnaissance, 208, 211, 221
   aerial, 5, 142
   optical, 221
Red Army, 226
Red Cross, 24, 28–29
Red Guards, 60–61
Reddy, William M., 9
Redkin, Mark, 226
refugees, 25, 34, 115–16
   Reichsbahn, 150–51, 158
Reichstag building, 222
Reinickendorf, 155
relations, 52, 63, 67, 104, 198
   bilateral, 133
   entangled, 50–52, 85, 203

FRG-ČSSR-GDR, 155
German-German, 150, 154
international, 133, 142
Polish-French, 48
power, 23
revolution, 65–66, 98, 119, 134, 159, 204, 223, 225
   of April 1978, 222
   color, 14
   Cultural Chinese, 11, 58–68
   Hungarian, 126
   Orange, 14
   Russian, 3, 45, 231
Radio Free Asia (RFA), 99
Radio Free Europe (RFE), 8, 12, 14, 34, 99, 112–28
Radio In The American Sector (RIAS), 22, 28, 31
resistance, 26, 78, 87, 115, 221
Riga, 210
Rinkel, Max, 173
ROC. *See* China: Republic of
Rockefeller, Nelson A., 22, 181
Rolling Stones, The, 121
Romania, 8–10, 12, 112–28
"Romeos," 77
Roosevelt, Franklin D., 24
Rowan, Steve, 212–13
Rozenbaum, Aleksandr, 229
Ruby, Jack, 179
Russia, 2, 5, 14, 35, 44–45, 115, 220
   Public Opinion Research Center, 230

sabotage, 25
sadness, 11
satellite nations, 27, 33–34
Saunders, Nicholas J., 5
Sava, Iosif, 121
scent, 9, 41–53, 152–53, 157, 206, 212
Schafer, R. Murray, 5, 134
Schlögel, Karl, 44
Schmidt, Helmut, 155
Schütz, Klaus, 153
Secret Intelligence Service, 85
Securitate, 123, 126
SED (Sozialistische Einheitspartei Deutschlands), 189, 197–98
seduction, 35, 67, 74–77, 83–84
seeing. *See* sight
self, 6, 135, 206
   conception, 47, 49, 52
   image, 225
   interest, 23, 116

self (*continued*)
  national, 107
  sense of, 3
Seligman, Adam, 127
sensations, 23, 41–42, 53, 135, 151, 155, 167, 169, 187
  phantom, 148–51
senses, 2–29, 35, 67, 74, 105–22, 131–39, 143–44, 167–68, 176–77, 180–90
  collectives, 185
  deprivation of, 13, 167, 174–76
  history of (*see under* history)
  landscape, 214
  overstimulation of, 184, 186
  signals, 5, 9
  studies of, 7, 59, 135, 148, 151, 159
sensing, 6, 58–59
  practices, 205–8, 211–15
sensorium, 4, 6–8, 35, 148, 190, 205–8, 212–15
  animal, 114, 155, 206
  overstimulation, 184, 186
Schütz, Klaus, 153
sensuality, 74, 77
Seveso, 158
sex, 77, 193
sexualization, 13, 76, 79, 87
Shanghai, 66
Shaoshan, 66
Shenghe, Hang, 100
Shimaotou, 95
Shize, Wu, 97, 99–100, 104
sight, 3, 11, 30–33, 58–61, 67, 133–42, 187, 196, 208, 115–23
Sino-American rapprochement, 19, 71–72, 63
sirens, 5, 74, 79, 86, 98
SIS. *See* intelligence
smell, 7–13, 23, 26, 41–53, 67, 114–17, 134–35, 147–61, 188, 205–15
  barriers, 12, 155, 157
  of cat dung affaire, 155
  of death, 12, 148–51
  scape, 44, 159
  stench, 3–4, 42, 44, 148, 150–51
  studies, 158
Smith, Mark M., 3, 5, 9, 211
Smuts Barracks, 80–81
sniffing, 41, 52, 156, 203–16
society, 44, 64, 82, 117, 127, 135, 185, 190, 215
  civil, 104, 127, 199n1, 222, 232
  capitalist 43
  mass, 131

secret, 84
sonic, 84
Soviet, 222–35
Spanish, 138
Western, 211
Solov'ev, Vladimir, 232
sonic environment, 59, 62, 66–68
sonic studies, 95
Soszy'nski, Ignacy, 50–53
sound, 1–9, 61–62, 74–78, 112–28, 132–38, 140–42, 144–48, 176, 187, 213
  aquatic barrier, 8, 11, 93–108
  background, 123
  barrier, 11
  of battle, 134, 137
  conflicts, 2
  distant, 126
  distorted, 123
  environment, 127
  high volume, 105
  infra-, 1
  scape, 5, 55, 59, 66, 97
  signal, 5
  souvenirs, 65
  Soviet, 118
  speaker, 101
  studies, 2
  track, 123
  ultra-, 1
  of war, 134
  warfare, 87
  waves, 9
Soviet Sector of Berlin, 150
Soviet Union, 13, 26, 43–51, 94–115, 127, 133, 140, 169–74, 210, 222–35
  Afghan War (*see* war)
  occupied countries, 10
  Sovietization, 11
Sozialistische Einheitspartei Deutschlands, 189, 197–98
Spain, 5, 10, 12, 131–45, 197
  Civil War, 12, 138
  Fascist, 10, 12
Spandau Prison, 81
Spandau, 80–81
St. Petersburg, 44, 210
Staaken, 81
Stalin, Joseph, 22, 24–26, 168, 172
Stalingrad, 85
Stanislavski, Konstantin, 98
Stasi, 77, 79, 81–82, 86–87, 185, 189, 191, 195, 198
State Department, 24–25, 29, 116–17, 168

State Security, Ministry for. *See* Stasi
stench. *See* smell
Stettiner Station, 149
strategy, 35, 86, 98, 113, 133, 138, 140, 144
   covert, 77
   geopolitical, 7
   media, 230
   military, 5, 8
   multisensory, 4
   overt, 77
   political, 115
   propaganda (*see* propaganda)
   psychological, 28
   visual, 12, 231
Strauß, Franz Josef, 155
SU. *See* Soviet Union
surveillance, 11, 74, 76–80, 85–88, 123, 227, 204, 207
   studies, 74, 77
Suyin, Han, 63
Swiss Agent. *See* Jung, Carl
Switzerland, 10, 24, 63
Synnott, Anthony, 44
Szonyi, Michael, 107

tactics, 8, 11, 131
tactility. *See* touch
Tagesspiegel, Der, 154
Taipei, 98–101, 107
Taiwan, 10–11, 14, 93–108
   Strait, 11, 93–108
   Strait Crisis, 94–95, 99–100
TASS, 233
taste, 3–11, 21–30, 34, 52–53, 84, 117, 152, 174, 193
   buds, 9–10, 160
   tastelessness, 44
Taylor, Roger, 121
TCDD, 158
television. *See under* media
thermos reception, 7
thirst, 187
Tegel Airport, 155
Teltow, 152
Teresi, Denny, 84
Teufelsberg, 76
Texas, 179–80
Third World, 6–7
Tianjin, 66
Tilh, Arnaud du, 82
tongue, 3, 26, 160
   "honey," 73
touch, 7, 10, 135, 196, 205

torture, 137, 175
treaty, 154, 194
   of Versailles, 24
Trotsky, Leon, 222
Trump, Donald J., 2
trust, 8, 44, 58, 114–19, 123–27, 188–89, 195, 198
Tsarist Empire, 44
tunnels 29, 99, 105, 149–51
   British-American, 74
   escape, 150–51
   "senior citicens'," 150
Turkey, 141

UGO Putsch, 86
Ukraine, 2, 14
underground movements, 7, 33, 115, 119
Unit 29155, 2
United States of America. *See* America
University of Latvia, 210
Urry, John, 58
USA. *See* America
US Air Force, 136, 168
US Army, 8, 13, 167, 177–78, 180–81, 203, 207, 210–11, 213
US Intelligence Agencies. *See* intelligence
US Navy, 170
US studies, 59

VCIOM. *See* Russian Public Opinion Research Center, 230
Vdovenko, Boris, 226
Vienna, 25–26, 29
Viet Cong, 204, 208, 212–13
Vietnam, 6, 8, 10, 94, 182n43, 203–15
vision, 7, 58–59, 76, 221, 231, 234
visual studies, 221
voice, 73–88, 93–108
   acousmatic, 11, 22
   gendered, 76, 87, 102–4
   siren's, 74, 103
Voice of America, 60, 116
Vrancea, 124
Vyatkin, Vladimir, 225, 229

wall, Berlin, 147–161, 186, 197
Walewska, Maria, 57
"Waltraud," 80, 82, 87
Wangong, Tian, 99
war, 2–14, 21, 114–15, 126/5, 172, 185–95, 203–15
   Afghan, 9, 13, 220–21, 223, 225–27, 233–35

war (continued)
    of aggression, 2, 14
    American Civil, 3, 5
    civil, 59, 60, 66, 78, 94, 104
    Crimean, 3
    crimes, 174
    Franco-Prussian, 4
    "Great Patriotic" (see war: World War II)
    of images, 147
    Indochina, 203
    Korean, 6, 12, 132–33, 136–45, 140–41, 143, 168, 173, 181n4
    propaganda, 78
    proxy, 12
    Second Cold, 221
    Soviet-Afghan, 10, 13, 220–35
    Spanish Civil, 12, 138
    total, 3, 22
    against Ukraine, 2, 14
    Vietnam, 8, 13, 203–15
    World War I, 4, 137
    World War II, 5–13, 23–25, 43, 94–133, 149, 169–21, 225–26, 228, 230–31
warfare, 1–15, 131, 167–68, 177, 186, 204–6, 214
    biological, 168, 239
    brain, 171
    chemical, 239
    covert, 14
    "heart," 84, 94, 98–99, 103
    modern, 3, 131
    nuclear, 239
    olfactory, 160
    overt, 12
    psychological, 13, 22, 24, 28, 33, 115, 171, 194
    sensory, 7–9, 11–12, 13–14, 84–85, 185
    sonic, 2, 8, 148, 185
    sound, 87
    urban, 149

Washington, District of Columbia, 22–29, 33, 35
weapons, 2–14, 30, 62, 94, 108, 134–47, 171, 187, 206, 221
    chemical, 173, 177, 180
    conventional, 184
    nuclear, 184
Wedding, 148
Weissensee, 83
Wenzke, Rüdiger, 185
Werra, 159
Westad, Odd Arne, 7
Western Front, 4
Wirsching, Andreas, 9
Wisner, Frank, 116–17
Wolf, Markus, 77
Wolff, Frank, 157
Wolff, Harold, 173, 179
"Wolfgang," 23, 80–87
Würzburg, 191

Xiamen, 11, 94, 97–108
Xiangshan, 95
Xiaoping, Deng, 104
Xinmei, Chen, 8, 97–98
XM-2 personnel detector. See people sniffer

Yangtze River, 64
Yilin, Fan, 101
Yiwen, Wang, 93, 106
Yuanhan, Tan, 105
Yugoslavia, 10, 34

Zaugg, Michel, 65–66
Zhengxiong, Li, 106
Zhiping, Chen, 102
Zinoviev, Grigory, 222

Printed in the USA
CPSIA information can be obtained
at www.ICGtesting.com
CBHW072045050824
12567CB00001B/1